# TRACKLESS TO TROLLEYBUS

Trolleybuses in Britain

by Stephen Lockwood

Incorporating
The Atlas of British Trolleybus Systems
with maps by Roger Smith

## Introduction by Stanley King
Hon. President of the Trolleybus Museum, Sandtoft

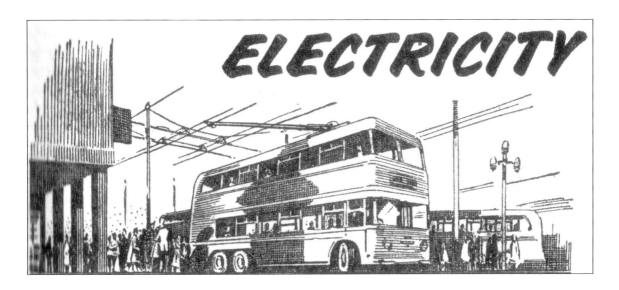

ELECTRICITY

Published by Adam Gordon

## COLOUR PHOTOGRAPHS

### Front Cover

In August 1966, newly repainted Bournemouth Sunbeam MF2B no 281, with Weymann body, and new in August 1959, was captured by the photographer descending the very steep Richmond Hill. The attractive Art Deco Bournemouth Daily Echo building is in the background. (C.F.Isgar)

### Back Cover

Top — The trackless era. Keighley Cedes-Stoll cars 4 and 6 exchange trolleys at Hawcliffe Woods on the Sutton route in 1915. The conductor shows a flag (not, apparently, a red one) to warn other traffic. (Transport World, colour added by Malcolm Fraser)

Centre left — The Sunbeam Trolleybus Company triangle badge, as affixed to the front of many of its products.

Bottom left — The circular BUT badge, as applied to the wheel hubs of their products.

Bottom right — The last appearance of the British trolleybus on the streets. Bradford Sunbeam no. 844 commences the last ever trolleybus journey on Sunday 26 March 1972. Bradford City Hall is in the background. (Travel Lens Photographic)

### Page 1

An artist's impression of a trolleybus, as shown in a 1950s Electricity Board advertisement.

### Page 377 Colour Photographs

Top left: — Tees-side no. 1, a 1950 Sunbeam rebodied by Roe in 1964, is seen operating in the turquoise livery of the final owners of the system, Teeside Municipal Transport. It is descending from the railway bridge near the depot at Cargo Fleet. The 1966 diversionary route mentioned in the text can be seen on the extreme right of this view.

Top right — A busy scene in Broad Street Reading on 28 June 1967. Both six- and four-wheel trolleybuses are seen in operation, the example on the left being one of the front-entrance batch new in 1961. (R.T.E. Box)

Centre left — London L3 type trolleybus 1521 turns at Twickenham on a Sunday working of route 605. This vehicle subsequently became the last trolleybus to operate in the capital. (P. Moore)

Centre right — Portsmouth AEC trolleybus no. 17 is seen when new in 1935. Note the combined tram and trolleybus overhead wiring, and the driver in white coat and hat (AEC, colour added by Malcolm Fraser)

Bottom — State of the art trolleybuses in 1929 were these English Electric examples from Bradford. They are seen posed when new in Rooley Lane, between Dudley Hill and Bankfoot. (Colour added by Malcolm Fraser)

### Page 378 Colour Photographs

Top left — Cardiff BUT trolleybus no. 216 is seen at the Gabalfa terminus on 24 September 1967. The sign on the pole to the right of the vehicle indicates that the road is private for trolleybuses only. (R.T.E. Box)

Top right — This South Shields vehicle is an example of the wartime Sunbeam / Karrier W type trolleybus. It has a Park Royal body, and was built in 1945 for Pontypridd UDC. Sold in 1957, it ran in South Shields until 1963, retaining its wooden slatted seats. Note the ragged state of the trolley booms.

Centre left — Nottingham BUT trolleybuses gather at the Colwick Road terminus on 3 April 1965. (R.T.E. Box)

Centre right — The last trolleybuses to enter service in Glasgow were ten single-deck BUT's with 34ft long Burlingham bodies. The final one of the batch, TBS21, is seen at the Mount Florida terminus of service 108 in Glasgow's distinctive green and orange colours.

Bottom. — Huddersfield dressed up this pre-war Karrier trolleybus for the Queen's Coronation in June 1953. It ran in service on all routes in turn, and is seen here at the Riddings terminus. Following its royal duties, the body of no. 535 was scrapped and the chassis re-appeared later that year with a new Roe body, running for almost another ten years.(B.G. Tweed, colour added by Malcolm Fraser)

---

This work is dedicated to my wife Eileen, who has endured my obsession with the trolleybus for very many years. She has, as ever, supported me throughout this project, keeping a close and unbiased eye on the text and my use of grammar.

---

ISBN 978-1-874422-86-0
Publication no. 90
Published in 2011 by Adam Gordon, Kintradwell Farm, Brora, Sutherland KW9 6LU
Tel: 01408 622660
E-mail: adam@ahg-books.com

First printing limited to 400 copies

Printed by: 4Edge, 7a Eldon Way, Hockley, Essex SS5 4AD
Production by: Trevor Preece, 2 Sella Bank, The Banks, Seascale, Cumbria CA20 1QU
E-mail: trevor@epic-gb.com

# CONTENTS

The last trolleybus body built for a six-wheel chassis for use in Britain was built by East Lancashire Coachbuilders in 1962. It was placed on a Huddersfield Corporation 1949 Sunbeam MS2 chassis replacing the original Park Royal bodywork. No. 585 had only a short life in this form, running until 1967. The vehicle is seen here at the hillside terminus of the Lockwood route, to which trolleybuses ran until July 1966. (J.S. King)

# AUTHOR'S NOTE

A little while ago, whilst attending an event at the Trolleybus Museum, Sandtoft, I was browsing at the stall of a well-known transport book seller and publisher. The person standing next to me enquired of the stall holder whether there was a book available that described all British trolleybus systems. An expert reply was forthcoming, listing all the relevant standard works (beginning with 'Trolleybus Trails'), but with the qualification that unfortunately, the most recent of these had been published twenty-five years ago, and all were long out of print.

Although this incident was not the spark that set me on course with this project, for I had already done considerable work on it at the time, it neatly explains the reasoning behind this book – a one-volume historical survey of the British trolleybus, with an emphasis on the towns and areas where they operated. The centenary of the opening of the country's trolleybus systems gives a further reason why such a book should be produced now.

It is also true, of course, that first-hand knowledge of trolleybuses on British streets is steadily diminishing. Anyone under 50 years old is not likely to have any such memories, and those who worked on them, or managed them, will now be aged over 60. There cannot be many people still employed in the passenger transport industry whose working experience has included trolleybus operation. I am lucky enough to be one of these, and another that I am aware of is the UK Bus Division Managing Director of one of the country's largest transport groups, who started his career in the late 1960s as a Bradford trolleybus driver.

My fascination for the subject started at a very young age. In my early childhood during the 1950s, I was lucky enough to live adjacent to the terminal loop of one of the busiest trolleybus routes in Huddersfield, and soon became familiar with all the varied types of vehicles, as well as the most interesting aspects of trolleybus operation; the overhead wiring that mapped out the routes in the sky; the operation of hand-operated frogs by the conductor, and the procedure following (occasional) dewirements. From 1960 I travelled across town every school day by trolleybus to grammar school. At this time my knowledge of trolleybuses in general was widened through contact with others having similar interests at the local monthly meetings of tram and trolleybus enthusiasts organised by Roy Brook, many of whose superb photographs appear in this book. This interest led to a life long career in public transport, starting as a clerk at Bradford City Transport, where I worked for nine years, including the period of the final trolleybus closure. My career subsequently took me to Darlington, another trolleybus operator, but sadly these vehicles had long gone before my arrival.

I have endeavoured to include as much information as possible, though in a non-technical way, about the sixty years that trolleybuses ran on the streets. Major sections of the book are the concise descriptions of each system, and the Atlas of British Trolleybus Systems, which consists of individual detailed route diagrams. The photographs are from several varied sources, and I have used many from my own collection which has its origins in the visits to the aforementioned meetings in the 1960s. More recently I have built up a collection of commercial postcards showing trolleybuses, and many of these are included. Any uncredited views, where the originator cannot be identified, are from my collection.

Grateful thanks are given to the following, without whose assistance this project would have been impossible to bring to fruition. Roger Smith, tramway and trolleybus cartographer, readily agreed to tackle the mammoth task of producing detailed route diagrams of every British system, and the resulting 'atlas' is a superb record of where trolleybuses ran. Stanley King, one of the best known figures in the British trolleybus scene, both as an enthusiast and as a local politician, has written the thought-provoking introduction to the book, and also, at my suggestion, has selected ten of his own favourite trolleybus photographs for inclusion. He has also read through my text and suggested several improvements and clarifications. Fellow trolleybus aficionados Colin Barker, Hugh Taylor and Carl Isgar (editor of 'Trolleybus Magazine') have also read through the text and made useful suggestions. Malcolm Fraser has applied his skillful colouring technique to several photographs.

Thanks are also due to those who have so willingly responded to my request for specific photographs and allowed me access to their collections. These are: Philip Battersby, John Banks, Roland Box, John Fozard, Adam Gordon, Carl Isgar, Don Jones, Stanley King, John Meredith, Eric Old, Colin Routh, David Smithies, Hugh Taylor, John Watson, Paul Watson and Tony Wilson. Finally, my gratitude goes to Trevor Preece, who has patiently created this book from the great mass of text and photographic material that was supplied to him.

It should be understood that any errors and omissions within this book are entirely my responsibility, and not those of any other contributor.

*Stephen Lockwood, Darlington, July 2011*

## ABBREVIATIONS USED IN THE TEXT

| | |
|---|---|
| ADC | **Associated Daimler Company.** The organisation used by AEC (qv) and Daimler to jointly market their products in the 1920s. |
| AEC | **Associated Equipment Company.** Bus and trolleybus manufacturer based at Southall, London. |
| BICC | **British Insulated Callender's Cables.** Trolleybus wiring equipment manufacturer based at St Helens Lancashire. |
| BUT | **British United Traction.** The company used by AEC and Leyland to jointly market their trolleybus products after the second world war. |
| LUT | **London United Tramways.** Tram operator based in west and south-west London who opened London's first trolleybus operation. |
| Notts and Derby | **Nottinghamshire and Derbyshire Traction Company.** Trolleybus operator. |
| SHMD | **Stalybridge, Hyde, Mossley and Dukinfield Joint Transport Board.** Municipal bus operator in north-east Cheshire who owned and maintained trolleybus overhead in its area used by Ashton and Manchester vehicles. |

I was privileged to be able to be present, as an observer, during the last ever Ministry of Transport trolleybus driving test, which took place on Friday 30 July 1971, just eight months before the closure of the Bradford system. The participants are seen in Tyrrel Street immediately before the test started. Standing in front of BUT training trolleybus 063, (formerly no. 746) are (from the left): the driving instructor, the final trainee (Mr G.S. Watson), the chief driving examiner, the chief driver training inspector, and myself, then a 22-year-old schedules clerk with Bradford City Transport. (R.S.Ledgard)

A Darlington single-deck wartime utility trolleybus turns at the Neasham Road terminus on 14 July 1957, just two weeks before the system closed. Apart from the trolleybus and wiring, this scene is very much the same today. (J. Copland / A.D. Packer)

# FOREWORD

The date of publication of this book is timed to co-incide with the centenary of Britain's first trolleybus operations. Sadly, these vehicles only survived in public use for just over 60 of these years, and at various dates during this period there were 50 systems established. The peak year for trolleybus operation was 1950, when there were 37 systems in operation, varying in size from London, with over 1800 vehicles, to Pontypridd with a fleet of just 8.

As the title of this book suggests, the vehicle evolved from a trackless tram, running low-cost feeder routes to tram termini, to a public transport system in its own right, which in most cases replaced whole tram systems. It was very much a municipal (or publicly-owned) style of operation, only six of the post-war systems being company operated, and of those only two (Hastings and Llanelly) were entirely self contained systems with no operational involvement with a municipal system.

It is unfortunate that, not long after the demise of the British trolleybus, environmental issues began to come much more to the fore. Had they done so earlier, attributes of the vehicle such as its low noise level combined with hill-climbing ability and smooth acceleration may well have been taken more into account than adverse short-term considerations. Climbing at full speed up the long hill out of Elland towards Huddersfield, easily passing a motorbus crawling up in bottom gear, or ascending Sunbridge Road, Bradford from a standing start with superb acceleration, are both examples which showed the trolleybus at its best, and they linger in the memory of those that experienced them.

The environment that trolleybuses worked in reflected the changing and challenging times of the mid-twentieth century. Typically their routes ran through central streets, flanked by soot-blackened buildings and paved with stone setts, then out to the suburbs on roads lined with pre-war semis to a terminus at a post-war housing scheme. Unlike trams, which could simply change direction in the road, trolleybuses needed special arrangements to turn round. These included reversing into a side road, for which special overhead wiring provision was required. A safer arrangement was a neat roadside turning area, or a one-way circuit around side streets.

Today, 100 years on, the trolleybus experience is only available at the three operating museums in the country. Whilst these excellent establishments allow visitors to ride and watch the many and varied vehicles that have been preserved in working order, it is difficult to replicate the sights and sounds of the trolleybus in its natural habitat, providing mass public transport in towns and cities.

## SOUNDS

Often described as 'the silent service', or more morbidly, 'the silent death', the trolleybus was not entirely a silent vehicle. Its sound came from the motor, transmission, tyres and the overhead. The motor noise was not as harsh as that on a tram, owing to the lack of reverberation caused by tram track, but nevertheless it was distinctly audible. The Metro-Vick motors on Sunbeam/Karrier chassis made a gentle whine, whereas the English Electric type on BUT chassis had a deeper and slightly noisier tone, accentuated when starting from rest. Tyre noise was greatest on six-wheel vehicles especially on bends in the road. Overhead, the passage of trolley skids along the wires was almost silent (unlike the continual 'singing' noise when trolley wheels were used), except at crossings and frogs, where the passage of the heads through these items sounded like a dull clatter.

This is the 'avant-garde' AEC 'Q' type trolleybus that became Bradford no. 633 and which fired Stanley King's enthusiasm for trolleybuses (see page 11). It is seen in its original demonstration livery at Five Lane Ends, Bradford in early 1934. More details of this vehicle are given later in the book.

Joint first to run public trolleybus services in Britain was Bradford. The original railless, no. 240, is seen in Sticker Lane a few days after entering service in June 1911.

Fifty years later, two trolleybuses pass in Sticker Lane at almost the exact spot as the previous view. Both are second-hand vehicles, that on the left, (operating an enthusiasts' tour), is a Sunbeam from Hastings, whilst that on the right, (operating on service 34, a lengthened version of the original route), is a BUT from St Helens. (J. Fozard)

Britain's largest trolleybus system was at London, running over 1800 vehicles at its peak. This is a scene at the Shepherd's Bush terminus of the 607 service to Uxbridge, demonstrating how frequent the services were. One of the 127 post-war Q1 vehicles, no. 1851, has just departed. This vehicle, new in 1952, was sold to Spain in 1961 where it ran in Bilbao. (Jack Gready / London Trolleybus Preservation Society)

The smallest post-war trolleybus operation was at Pontypridd, where a fleet of just eight vehicles was operated by the Urban District Council. The only overhead wiring junction along the three-mile route was at the junction of Fothergill Street and The Broadway, seen here in this early 1950s view. Wartime 'utility' Karrier W no. 9 emerges from Fothergill Street on a journey from Treforest to Cilfynydd. The wires giving access to and from the depot are in the foreground. (W.A. Camwell / National Tramway Museum)

A British trolleybus streetscape. This is Effingham Street Rotherham in the early 1950s showing a single-deck trolleybus about to negotiate a major wiring junction. The setted roadway shows the signs of recently removed tram tracks. In the right centre, beside the clock, the Salvation Army band is playing. The vehicle, no. 16, is one of the 44 Daimler 6-wheelers with East Lancashire bodywork which entered service between 1949 and 1950. In 1957, it was one of 20 vehicles which were rebuilt with Roe double-deck bodywork, being renumbered 43 at the same time. (Roy Brook / Paul Watson)

A photograph which demonstrates the superb hill-climbing ability of the trolleybus. This Bradford trolleybus is beginning the ascent of St Enoch's Road on the Buttershaw route, and it is easily and silently overtaking the AEC motorbus which is grinding along in bottom gear. The trolleybus (fleet no. 833) is a 1949 BUT which originated with Darlington, sold to Doncaster then to Bradford, where, in 1962 its original East Lancashire rear entrance bodywork was replaced by a front-entrance body from the same bodybuilder. The date of this scene is 20 July 1968, and the trolleybus ran until mid-1971. (J. Copland / A.D. Packer)

# INTRODUCTION

## A personal introduction to trolleybuses by Stanley King

Bradford City Councillor 1970-2008
Member of Bradford Corporation Transport Executive Group 1970-1974
Lord Mayor of Bradford 2000-2001
Member of West Yorkshire Passenger Transport Authority 1985-2000, 2001-2008
Chairman and alternate Deputy Chairman of West Yorks PTA 2004-2008
Appointed Hon. President of the Trolleybus Museum at Sandtoft 2008

Why trolleybuses? What is their attraction, and why have I consistently (and perhaps persistently) championed them in the course of my public life? These are pertinent questions for me to answer in the year of this Centenary, thirty-nine years after the last United Kingdom service trolleybus retired in a blaze of glory, and in an age which seems increasingly unable to afford major improvements to public transport provision.

I was born on a Bradford tram route, travelled to school by motor-bus and was conveyed to my place of employment by trolleybus. In that way I was able to assess and appreciate at first hand the merits and shortcomings of each transport mode:

| | |
|---|---|
| **Trams:** | punctual, reliable and predictable but hampered by obsolete legislation. |
| **Motor-buses:** | supremely flexible, mechanically complex and wholly dependent upon imported fossil fuel oils. |
| **Trolleybuses:** | quick, quiet and clean, and – if their chosen routes are carefully designed and their drivers appropriately trained – as flexible as they need to be. |

By a stroke of good luck or providence, the first trolleybus I ever encountered in far-off 1934 was the avant-garde and ultra-modern AEC 'Q' type, which not surprisingly aroused in me an enthusiasm for progressive development, evolution and improvement. When I became a city councillor I had the privilege of meeting and exchanging ideas with many of the senior professionals whose dedication, innovation, ingenuity and advocacy had done so much to promote electric transport even when the tide had turned against it.

It therefore seemed perverse, illogical and surprisingly short-sighted that at the moment when British trolleybuses had achieved a state of excellence and popularity, electricity as a mode of traction began to fall out of favour, and its virtues were brushed aside as the 'age of affluence' took its toll on the traditional belief in economy, durability, value for money and the nurturing of home industries.

Many people, professionals as well as laymen, have always shared my belief that like our neighbours on the Continent and in North America, we should have continued to develop and expand our urban trolleybus services, especially in the context of our increasing concerns about 'global warming' and the finite nature of oil supplies.

If governments and transport providers are serious in their support for 'green issues', they would be well advised to consider the adoption of trolleybuses where circumstances and finances permit. The process might be costly in the outset, but it should be seen as the long-term investment which it undoubtedly is.

So I remain an optimist; in public life you have to be!

*Stanley King*

Councillor J.S. King, Member of Bradford Transport Executive Group with Bradford City Transport motorbus no. 279 at Bradford Moor shortly before the end of municipal transport in the city on 31 March 1974.

## Stanley King's ten favourite trolleybus photographs

Stanley King took many trolleybus photographs, recording the systems that he visited. He has selected and captioned his ten favourite views, and, as can be seen from hereon, he often ensured that overhead wiring detail was prominent.

Photographed on its first morning of service in Bradford, no. 832 was the first of five trolleybuses (831 – 5) which were basically third-hand, i.e. their chassis frames, rear axles, motors and prop-shafts had already seen service in Darlington and Doncaster, but after a thorough refurbishment and modernisation, had acquired new East Lancs forward entrance bodies with air-operated doors, automatic acceleration, fluorescent lighting and saloon heating. Also they were BUTs – what more could one have asked?

A hot summer day in Bournemouth Square on 7 August 1959, with an elegant Sunbeam MF2B enhancing the scenery – a good beginning for a happy holiday.

As seen here in West Auckland Road on June 7 1957, Darlington's overhead wires varied casually from 1' 6" to 2' 0" separation and single-deck Karrier W no. 7 was not exactly modern – but it had considerable potential, as two years later it was transformed into Bradford's modern 71-seat double-decker no. 788.

Doncaster had a neat, compact trolleybus system served by apparently identical trolleybuses, many of which had been acquired from systems as distant as Southend. Here, 'native' Karrier W 370, rebodied by Roe, was photographed heading for Hexthorpe on 22 August 1959.

An elegant vehicle in an elegant setting – Portsmouth's Guildhall provided the background for pre-war Cravens-bodied AEC/EE no. 252 with its gold-lined plum and ivory livery, on 6 August 1959.

Modern, fast and hardworking: St Helens Sunbeams 375 and 376 pause at the Nutgrove turning circle on 28 June 1958, a few weeks before starting a new life 'beside the seaside', at South Shields.

South Shields' trolleybuses were as long-lived as the routes on which they ran were varied. Karrier E4 no. 204, one of the town's original trolleybuses, was photographed on 26 September 1959 at the pleasant surroundings of Pier Head before venturing into the workaday area of Tyne Dock. Half a century later, no. 204 is still working hard at the Sandtoft Museum.

Made it at last! The Tees-side Railless Traction Board had to wait more than forty years to achieve its ambition of reaching the village of Eston. On 6 April 1968, a week after passing into the ownership of Teesside Municipal Transport, Sunbeam no. 12 was seen resting temporarily in Eston Square.

In normal circumstances, Walsalll's famous 30 feet long 'Goldfish Bowls' were not allowed to run under Wolverhampton's wires, but on 11 June 1961, Walsall no. 870 was permitted to venture into the unknown, being seen here in Bilston with its designer, Mr R. Edgley Cox, watching on the pavement.

Merry Hill – an attractive destination indeed, although when I visited it on board Wolverhampton no. 446 on 1 August 1963, I failed to find any trace of a hill, although the 'Butlers Ales' available in the Merry Hill pub (right) may have supplied all the merriment that was expected.

# THE STORY OF
# THE BRITISH TROLLEYBUS

## Pre-history – early trolleybuses outside Britain 1882 to 1910

Unlike other significant transport innovations, such as the mass transportation railway or the jet engine, the trolleybus is not a British invention. It has its origins in late 19th century Germany, and was developed as a transport mode in Europe in the early years of the 20th century.

It is well known that the first vehicle to run on the trolleybus principle was demonstrated by Werner von Siemens at Berlin in September 1882, three years before Britain saw its first electric street tramway (Blackpool, September 1885).

Siemens' vehicle was no more than a dog-cart, taking motive power from a flexible cable connected to two parallel overhead wires, one positive and one negative, by means of a wheeled 'troller', or trolley, which ran along the top of these wires.

Immediate subsequent development of current-collection was concentrated on tramways, some early American systems using a method similar to Siemens. By 1891, Leeds opened its Roundhay Park electric tramway with a rigid trolley boom with trolley wheel, using American designs.

Workable railless trolleybuses used as public transport came into existence in the very early years of the twentieth century, in France, Germany, the Austro-Hungarian Empire, and Italy. These were often short-lived operations, using small single-deck vehicles (sometimes towing a trailer). They tended to be run as feeder services to tramway systems, or as a cheaper alternative to trams in small towns, connecting to the main railway station. Before 1911, there had been 39 such trolleybus systems instituted. Apart from two of these, all were located in the

regions mentioned above. The exceptions were at Drammen in Norway, started in 1908 (and lasting until 1967, using a single pole arrangement forked at the top), and a rural trolleybus line in the USA. This was at Hollywood, Los Angeles, where, commencing in 1910, the Laurel Canyon trackless route connected with the Pacific Electric Tramway at Sunset Boulevard. It took tourists through a largely undeveloped and steeply graded area using primitive 16 seat vehicles with rigid trolley booms.

By 1910, three principal methods of current collection had been established for trolleybus operation. These were:

**The Schiemann system.** Rigid twin trolley booms, using springs to press these against the underside of the power wires.

**The Cedes-Stoll system.** A flexible cable system, connecting to power wires via a four wheel 'trolley' running along the top of these wires. A variation to this was the *Lloyd-Kohler or Bremen system,* where the power wires were strung vertically, and a two-wheeled trolley ran on the upper wire, with a springed bow pressing against the lower wire.

**The Filovia system.** This originated in Italy (filo via – literally 'wired way' in Italian). It comprised one rigid trolley boom with a wheeled trolley at its end, running along the underside of the power wires. This was never used in Britain, although C.J. Spencer, the Bradford tramways manager very nearly chose this method rather than the Schiemann system.

The first trolley vehicle. This is Werner Von Siemen's 'Elektromote' on demonstration in Berlin in 1882. The wheeled trolley running along the conductor wires can be plainly seen. (Transport for London / London Transport Museum)

One of the early public trolleybus operations, using the Scheimann rigid pole
collector system, was at the Rhineland twin-spa towns of Ahrweiler-Neuenahr
in Germany. The design of the vehicle and trailer is obviously based on a
horse drawn carriage design. The system opened in 1906 and closed in 1919.
(Transport for London / London Tranport Museum)

This early Italian trolleybus is using the Filovia method of current collection. The rigid pole
with four–wheel 'trolley' at the top is seen stretched out to the left of the vehicle, which
has the legend 'Societa per la Trazzione Electrica' on its side. This photograph was taken
by C.J. Spencer, the Bradford Tramways manager, during his inspection tour of Italian
trolleybus operations, prior to introducing trolleybuses in Bradford (J.S. King collection)

# The first demonstration in Britain – 1909

The first trolleybus to run in Britain was the Railless vehicle demonstrated by the Metropolitan Electric Tramways at its depot at Hendon. It had two BTH 25hp motors, with chain drive transmission. The body was built by GC Milnes-Voss and Co, prominent tramcar builders based in Birkenhead. (Transport for London / London Tranport Museum)

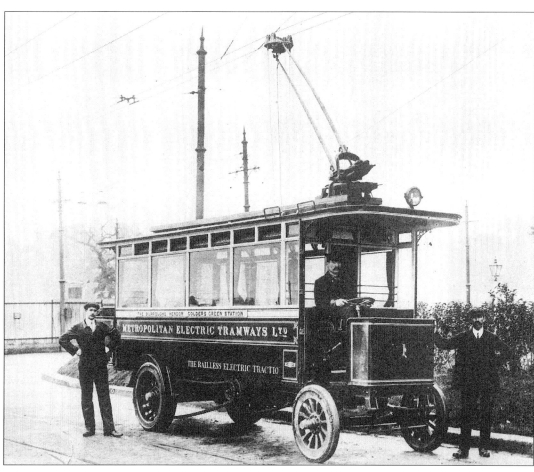

Trolleybus activity on the Continent in the first years of the twentieth century prompted interest from Britain. Transport managers and municipal tramway committees visited these trolleybus installations to assess their value in providing transport links where the high cost of tramways was not justified. A significant development was the formation of a British company to market and supply trolleybus equipment. This was the Railless Electric Traction Company (RET), which held the UK licence for the Schiemann fixed trolley system. Amongst several operators actively interested in introducing the trolleybus was the Metropolitan Electric Tramways (MET), the large tram operator in north and west London. In 1909, it prepared a roadway, equipped with two-way trolleybus overhead and turning circles at each end within the grounds of its Hendon depot and works at Edgware Road. RET provided a vehicle, with a Milnes Voss rear entrance body with accommodation for 24 passengers. Britain's first trolleybus operation, albeit not a public service, started on 25 September 1909, and delegates to the Municipal Tramways Association Conference were invited to the demonstration over the next few days. Further demonstrations were held in October, these being for local authority representatives. The red and cream trolleybus, bearing the fleet number 1, had a unique variation of the Schiemann rigid twin trolley pole layout, the poles being mounted close to each other and both supported a single large circular four-wheeled trolley head. This arrangement was possibly copied from the Filovia current collector. Lettering on the side of the vehicle indicated a route between Golders Green and Hendon. This was no conjecture, and MET actively pursued its intention to introduce such a service, negotiations with the local authority reaching an advanced stage. However, formal powers were never obtained and the idea lapsed. Powers were later obtained by MET (The Metropolitan Electric Tramways (Railless Traction) Act 1913) for a railless route in Tottenham, but despite several extensions of time being granted, the MET never became a trolleybus operator. The Hendon demonstration wiring was dismantled in 1911 but the fate of Britain's first trolleybus is not known.

# The real beginning – Bradford and Leeds 1911

The rising tide of British interest in the trolleybus culminated in 1911 when the West Yorkshire near-neighbour cities of Bradford and Leeds each introduced public trolleybus services. Both authorities co-ordinated the formal civic openings of their respective routes, these occurring on 20 June 1911, although neither commenced public services until 24 June. Bradford's route was a mile long, and connected to tram services at each end. That at Leeds was much different, being four miles long and starting in the city centre, running for some distance alongside trams, then taking its own increasingly rural course to the outer terminus. Both cities used Railless vehicles with Schiemann type twin trolley poles.
*The term 'railless car' or 'trackless tram' was a literal translation of the German 'Gleislose Spurwagen'*

Bradford's first trolleybus, Railless no. 240, is seen posed at Laisterdyke terminus, with the conductor holding the trolley ropes. The vehicle is about to turn into Latimer Street, from where it will reverse out into Sticker Lane. This view is dated 28 June 1911, four days after the service started, and during the period when no. 240 ran alone, before being joined by no. 241.

Sunbeam of Wolverhampton entered the trolleybus chassis market in 1931. It soon gained substantial orders, including the Wolverhampton and Bournemouth municipal fleets. 102 of the MS2 type six-wheelers entered service in Bournemouth between 1934 and 1936, these having Park Royal bodywork with rear entrance and front exit. No. 171, of the final batch to enter service is seen when new outside the Moordown depot. Note the route board fixed below the lower deck windows and the Park Royal transfer on the extreme lower front corner, just ahead of the offside wheel. (A.D. Packer collection)

Another trolleybus manufacturer in Wolverhampton was Karrier, which since 1935, following the takeover of the Huddersfield-based firm by the Rootes Group, was in common ownership with Sunbeam. Their six-wheel chassis was the E6 type, and their principal customers were Nottingham and Huddersfield. Between 1937 and 1940, 108 of these trolleybuses, with distinctively styled streamlined bodies built by Park Royal or Weymann, entered service. Three of the batch of eight delivered in May 1937 to replace trams on the Newsome route, are seen posed in the town's St Georges Square prior to entering service. (Paul Watson collection)

London's bulk trolleybus orders for trolleybuses were split between AEC and Leyland, with both types of chassis having bodywork to a standard design. AEC's chassis was the 664T type, a development of the previous 663T type with underfloor mounted motor. Leyland's version was the LTPB70 type, with Leyland built bodywork. This view shows the rear of one of the hundreds of these vehicles built during the 1930s undergoing a tilt test at Leyland's works.

This early 1938 scene is at North Finchley, London, and shows modern trams and trolleybuses in operation, part-way through the tram to trolleybus route conversion programme. The route being worked by the Feltham tram, built in 1931, would be replaced by trolleybuses later in the year. No. 2079 was then transferred to work on the south London tram routes until 1951, after which it ran in Leeds as no. 550 until 1957. The C2 class trolleybus no. 209, new in 1936, would not last as long as the tram, and would be withdrawn from service in 1955. The 645 route to Edgware was extended to Canons Park in June 1938. (London Trolleybus Preservation Society)

## ENGLISH ELECTRIC BODIED FOUR-WHEEL DOUBLE-DECKERS

English Electric bodied trolleybuses, usually on the AEC four-wheel chassis (type 661T), appeared in several British systems in the 1930s. Some examples are depicted here, showing their similar appearance.

London's only 4-wheeler was of this type, and it entered service in 1934. Despite being unique in the fleet, it had a full life, not being withdrawn until the early 1950s. Seen when new before entering service, it is standing in the yard at Fulwell depot. (Transport for London / London Transport Museum)

In 1935, Portsmouth took delivery of nine English Electric AEC trolleybuses, numbered 16 to 24 in the fleet. Three of them are seen running on the trolleybus test circuit within the AEC factory grounds at Southall.

Bradford's first 'modern' looking trolleybuses were 36 of this type of trolleybus, numbered between 597 and 632 and delivered in 1934/5. A further example, no. 634, which had been exhibited by the maker at the Commercial Motor Show, was acquired in 1937. All of these were rebodied between 1943 and 1956, and many lasted in service into the 1960s. This pre-war scene shows no. 630 at the city terminus of the Duckworth Lane route. It was given a new Northern Coachbuilders body in 1947, as seen later in the book. (G.H.F. Atkins / courtesy and copyright John Banks collection).

Not all of this style of English Electric body ran on AEC chassis. Ashton's first 'modern' trolleybuses were three Leyland TB4 type vehicles with English Electric bodies, new in 1937. These were numbered 48, 52, and 55. No. 48 is seen at Ashton Market Place in post-war days. (R. Marshall)

Belfast purchased its first trolleybuses in 1938, the initial batch of fourteen, all six-wheelers, being a selection of most chassis types then available. This is T10, a Karrier E6 with locally made Harkness body, seen on test before the opening of the system with the City Hall in the background. Also in view are an AEC motorbus and a McCreary type streamlined tram. Trams, buses and trolleybuses ran side by side in the city until the last tram ran in 1954.

Daimler entered the trolleybus chassis market in the late 1930s, their 4-wheel demonstrator vehicle, which was later sold to South Shields, visiting several systems at that time. The only order for 4-wheelers came in 1938 from Derby, who placed six in service. These are seen here lined up before entering service. Bodywork was by Brush, Derby's usual supplier.

At the end of the 1930s, several of the older trolleybus systems were still operating their original stock, which when new, ran on solid tyres. Amongst these was Ashton, whose Hathershaw route (the remaining part of the unsuccessful joint route to Oldham) survived until the equipment was worn out, closing in1939. In its twilight days the route was used to test new trolleybuses for the Manchester-Ashton-Stalybridge service. Manchester's Crossley 4-wheeler no. 1006 is seen on test on the Hathershaw route, being passed by Ashton 1926 vintage Railless no. 56.
(C. Isgar collection)

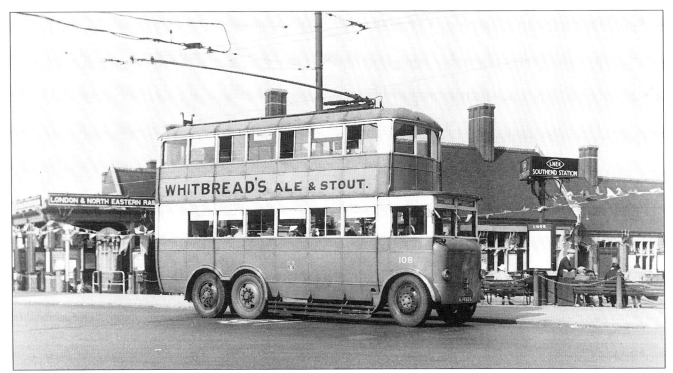

This double-deck Garratt trolleybus, Southend no. 108, was only nine years old in this 1938 view at Victoria Circus, but it would have compared very unfavourably with the 'modern' styling of trolleybuses entering service just before the war. The vehicle has been painted in the light blue livery introduced during the 1930s. (D.A. Thompson / London Trolleybus Preservation Society)

Brighton was the last pre-war operator to introduce trolleybuses when 44 of these AEC four-wheelers with Weymann bodywork entered service during 1939. Seen at the Lewes Road terminus (Barracks) of the first route shortly after opening is no. 15, which in 1942 was to spend a few weeks on hire to Newcastle.

# Loss of power – 1941 to 1950

Although trolleybus developments slowed during the Second World War, they did not cease altogether. In the early war years, systems such as Manchester Notts and Derby and Belfast received new vehicles built to peacetime standards. The only new system to open was at Cardiff in March 1942, where ten grey painted AEC six-wheelers replaced a tram route. This was another city whose decision to introduce trolleybuses was influenced by the desire to support the local mining industry. Brighton Hove and Distrct, whose vehicles had been in store since delivery in 1939, commenced operation in early 1945.

Some systems, such as Manchester, South Shields and Darlington expanded owing to the needs of war production, opening new routes or extensions, some of these being authorised under emergency powers. Many in industrial areas needed to boost their fleets quickly to cater for increased passenger loadings. Some purchased surplus vehicles from quieter areas – many of the Hastings single-deck Guy trolleybuses migrated north to Nottingham, Derby and Mexborough. Both Newcastle and South Shields bought out-dated English Electric six-wheelers from Bradford. Other systems desperate for extra capacity borrowed vehicles from trolleybus towns in the southern coastal areas. Brighton, Portsmouth, Southend and particularly Bournemouth, loaned out their vehicles in this way. The latter's yellow vehicles could be seen, at various times during the war, in such diverse places as Wolverhampton, Newcastle, South Shields, Walsall, Llanelly and London. New

| SYSTEMS OPENED 1941 TO 1950 | |
|---|---|
| **Opened** | **Location** |
| 1942 | Cardiff |
| 1945 | Brighton Hove and District |
| 1949 | Glasgow |

vehicles, especially after 1942, were very difficult to obtain. Batches of trolleybuses being built for South African operators were diverted to run in Britain, complete vehicles joining the London fleet, whilst those in chassis form were bodied to utility specifications and distributed to Nottingham, St Helens and Bradford. The Sunbeam company was authorised to mass produce a 'no frills' four-wheel trolleybus chassis, given the type designation 'W' and over 400 were built between 1943 and 1949, these being allocated to operators after being fitted with sparsely appointed steel panelled utility bodywork by various builders. Many were badged as 'Karrier', but were otherwise exactly the same product.

Enemy action caused particular problems for trolleybus operators. Even if bombing spared the vehicles, there was little an operator could do to protect trolleybus wiring. Following enemy raids, impromptu diversions and emergency repairs were the norm to keep services moving. As might be expected, the recently introduced trolleybus network in East London was particularly affected, several vehicles being totally destroyed and many more required new bodywork. The only other operator to have irrepairable damage to vehicle bodies was South Shields, where three trolleybuses had their bodies destroyed during a raid in 1941. Hull, one of the most bomb damaged of the provincial cities, was spared severe vehicle damage (probably due to its trolleybus depots being situated in outer areas), but did suffer from considerable destruction to its overhead wiring.

The change of government at the end of hostilities resulted in an action that was to have a great negative effect

New deliveries of trolleybuses, built to full peace-time standards, continued into the early war years. The Notts and Derby system received ten Weymann bodied AEC four-wheelers, the last of this type (661T) to be built, in 1941 and 1942. This post-war view shows no. 342 standing at the Nottingham city centre terminus of the Ripley route. Behind it is one of the four Park Royal bodied AEC trolleybuses purchased by Nottingham in 1940 from Cleethorpes Corporation. These were fairly new vehicles, dating from 1937 and 1938 and were deemed surplus to requirements owing to reduced passenger demand in this sea-side town. (R. Marshall)

The only new trolleybus system to open during the war was at Cardiff, where 10 AEC 664T six-wheelers commenced service on 1 March 1942. Originally running in a matt grey livery, these vehicles were given a flamboyant streamlined livery style after the war. No. 208 is seen in Wood Street in 1950. (A.B. Cross)

Nottingham needed urgent additions to its trolleybus fleet to keep up with wartime passenger demand. Six of these 1928 vintage single-deck Guys from Hastings joined the fleet in 1942. No. 305 was originally no. 24 in the Hastings fleet, and is seen here in the condition that it ran in Nottingham, at the Trent Bridge terminus. They were nick-named by the crews 'kiddie-cars'. They ran until 1946.

on the British trolleybus. This was the passing of the Electricity Act 1947, which allowed, in 1948, the formation of area Electricity Boards which effectively nationalised almost all municipally run local power stations. No longer could trolleybus operators benefit from advantageous rates for their source of power. From now, the attractiveness of the motorbus, mentioned in the 1930s section, would be even more compelling to austerity-hit transport operators.

London Transport and Glasgow did retain their own power generating ability and this was undoubtedly one factor which allowed Glasgow to start trolleybus operations, replacing a tiny part of its vast tram system, in 1949. London, however, had already decided, just after the war not to replace its tram network south of the Thames with trolleybuses.

Trolleybus manufacturing was somewhat rationalised after the war. AEC and Leyland, the greatest of rivals in motorbus circles, decided to combine their trolleybus interests and established a jointly owned company – British United Traction (BUT). Karrier and Sunbeam, which had the same owners and manufacturing base, were bought by Guy Motors in 1948. The Karrier name and range was dropped, although in 1947/8, immediately prior to the sale, 34 Sunbeam MS2 type six-wheelers were produced bearing

Karrier badges. These were supplied to South Lancashire Transport (6 chassis) and, very appropriately in view of the origins of the Karrier name, to Huddersfield (28 chassis). Guy itself did not produce trolleybus chassis under the Guy name after 1950, and Daimler's home trolleybus market dried up after supplying chassis to Rotherham and Glasgow between 1948 and 1950.

Operators took advantage of a relaxation of regulations at this time, to introduce 8 feet wide bodies in place of the previous maximum 7 feet 6 inches wide variety. Many of the larger systems introduced large batches of new vehicles at the end of this period to replace their pre-war fleets, including Nottingham and London, the latter purchasing 77 BUTs to replace the original 1931 London United 'Diddler' trolleybuses and others lost during wartime. Other systems, including Belfast, Newcastle, Cardiff and Glasgow were all still actively extending their trolleybus operations and ordering additional vehicles. However, it was perhaps significant that in 1950, both Ipswich and Darlington, whose municipal transport systems were hitherto the only ones to rely entirely on trolleybuses, introduced motorbuses on new routes into housing estates instead of extending their trolleybus wires. No trolleybus systems were closed during this period, but this fact was certainly not an indicator of future trends.

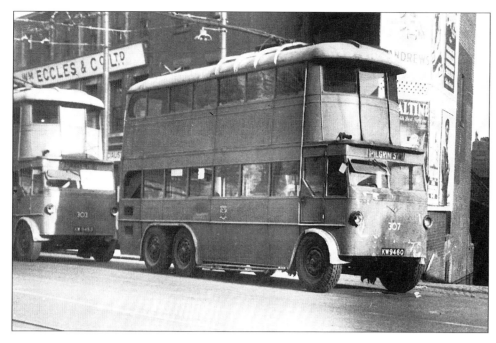

Newcastle sourced additional vehicles from Bradford, and obtained ten 1929-built English Electric six-wheelers. Only six actually entered service, and they were used at peak hours on routes serving the shipyards in the west of the city. Battered looking nos 307 and 303 are seen in New Bridge Street in grey livery. These vehicles were formerly Bradford nos 591 and 584 respectively. Note that 303 retains its English Electric badge on the front dash panel. (J. S. King collection)

The Pontypridd system borrowed trolleybuses from Hull, Portsmouth and Bournemouth. Portsmouth sent its quartet of high-capacity six-wheelers, including AEC no. 215, seen here at the Treforest terminus. The Metro-Cammell body resembled that on the Birmingham Leyland trolleybuses. (W.J. Haynes)

Bournemouth loaned 30 of its Sunbeam MS2 vehicles to various other operators during the war. Wolverhampton took twelve, where some, including no. 130 seen here, ran from 1940 to 1948.

25 Sunbeam MF2 chassis destined for Johannesburg were diverted to home systems in 1942. Ten of these went to St Helens, receiving Massey lowbridge utility bodies, and the remainder received Weymann 'utility' bodies, five going to Nottingham and ten to Bradford. Being 8 feet wide, six inches wider than the maximum permitted width in Britain, they needed special dispensation to operate from the Ministry of Transport. Bradford 698 is seen when new in wartime guise with headlight masks, and splinter proof netting on the windows. It has the newly introduced light blue livery which was adopted after Bradford borrowed some Southend AEC trolleybuses earlier in the war.
(A.D. Packer collection)

London Transport received 43 complete six-wheel trolleybuses that were also diverted from South African operators. These comprised 25 Leylands (type TTB) built for Durban, and 18 AECs built for Johannesburg. All carried Metro Cammell bodies which incorporated darkened window panes and a second doorway behind the front axle. This latter feature was not used in London. One of the Leylands, no. 1725 of class SA1 is seen at Barking terminus during the war, shortly after entering service. The front disused front doorway can be seen.
(C.F. Klapper)

# THE UTILITY TROLLEYBUSES

The Sunbeam Company produced 468 of the 'W' type chassis between 1943 and 1949, although 37 of these built after the war were exported to South Africa (Johannesburg and Pretoria).

The first type 'W' trolleybuses built were eight single-deckers for Darlington, delivered in February 1942. These were given Brush single-deck bodies with centre-entrances. Two of these are seen passing in Darlington town centre, the nearest being no. 24 (chassis number 50006). In the background is no. 19, which had the first 'W' chassis, no. 50001. These, and several other 'W' chassis, bore 'Karrier' badges rather than Sunbeam. (P. Battersby collection)

The first of many double-deck 'W' vehicles was Reading no. 132 (chassis no. 50009), one of six which entered service in April 1943. Bodywork was by Park Royal, one of several bodybuilders that supplied bodies for the W chassis. During the war, Reading re-named its trolleybus termini, using less obvious names which would be less helpful to the enemy. In this case the vehicle is showing the wartime destination for the Wokingham Road route. Reading's utility trolleybuses had a short life, being withdrawn by 1950. (W.J. Haynes)

Another early Sunbeam W was this example, one of four supplied to South Lancashire Transport in late 1943. No. 61 has chassis number 50035 and a Weymann body. Two further examples joined the fleet in mid-1944.

50

This sunny wartime scene in Walthamstow, London, shows E1 type trolleybus (AEC with Brush body) 554 in Forest Road, on a 623 journey to Woodford. However, this photograph is dated Saturday, 7 September 1940, a fateful day in London's history. In the late afternoon the East End and Docks were attacked by enemy bombers, marking the start of the Blitz. Note the third (centre) set of wires. This was used in either direction to allow access to the nearby Walthamstow depot. (A.B. Cross)

The Blitz of 1940-41, and the later V bombs campaign of 1944-5 caused considerable damage to London's trolleybus fleet. Fifteen vehicles were totally written off and 61 others were rebodied. Bexleyheath depot received direct hits in 1940 and again in 1944. This scene shows the remains of vehicles inside the depot after the bombing on 7 November 1940. The rear of H1 class trolleybus no. 795 is evident. This vehicle was later rebuilt with a new Weymann body, being numbered 795A. Note the vehicle in the left background, whose body has completely collapsed. (Transport for London / London Transport Museum)

Provincial trolleybus systems also suffered war damage. Hull city centre was very badly damaged during the Blitz, and this 1947 view shows trolleybuses on King Edward Street, in the heart of the central shopping area. All the main buildings have been destroyed. In view is Hull 90, a newly delivered Sunbeam W, with Roe body built to peacetime standards. Behind this is one of the pre-war Weymann bodied Leylands, with which Hull started trolleybus operations in 1937. (C. Carter)

## POST-WAR NORTHERN COACHBUILDERS BODIES ON FOUR-WHEEL CHASSIS

Having supplied new replacement bodies on some war-damaged London trolleybus chassis, Northern Coachbuilders of Newcastle provided similar looking trolleybus bodies for several fleets.

Bradford 630 had a 1934 AEC chassis, originally with an English Electric body. This was replaced in 1947 with this Northern Coachbuilders example. 23 vehicles were given this style of body, although six with a less pleasing appearance had appeared in 1946 (see Bradford section). No. 630 is seen on a dreary 28 April 1947 ascending Wakefield Road towards Dudley Hill (J. Copland / A.D. Packer)

Newcastle was a regular customer of Northern Coachbuilders products in the early post-war years. In 1950 it took delivery of fifty 4-wheel chassis with this type of body, split between Sunbeam F4 and BUT 9611T chassis types. No. 551 was one of the Sunbeams, and is seen at the Central Station terminus. (J. Fozard)

Maidstone's first post-war trolleybuses were twelve Sunbeam Ws delivered between 1946 and 1947. The first one, no. 62, is seen at Newcastle before delivery. The distinctive rear upper deck emergency window shape used on these bodies was derived from London Transport design, as specified on the bodies supplied to London. Note the ornate Maidstone livery style.

Newcastle's near neighbour, South Shields, was also a keen Northern Coachbuilders user. This example, the first of three Sunbeam Ws entering service in early 1947, seen approaching the Market Place, is about to pass under a section feeder. (R.F. Mack / Trolleybus Museum Company)

## THE Q1 TYPE TROLLEYBUS

One of the most famous and popular type of British trolleybus was the six-wheel BUT / Metro Cammell Q1 design, delivered to London in 1948/9 and 1952/3. Similar vehicles were supplied to Newcastle and Glasgow, the latter also having some identical bodies on Daimler chassis.

London had 127 Q1s, 77 coming in 1948/9, and a further 50 in 1952/3. No 1860, one of the 1950s batch, is seen at the Uxbridge terminus of route 607, one of the regular haunts of these vehicles. Like most of the others, it was sold to Spain in 1961, where it ran in San Sebastian. (A.B. Cross)

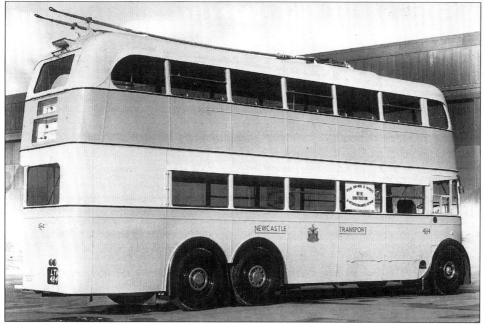

Newcastle also had two batches of Q1 type vehicles, the first twenty entering service in April 1948, just after the first of those in London. These had London features, including the style of destination apertures. A further 50 vehicles followed in 1950, these incorporating standard Newcastle destination arrangements. No. 484 of the 1948 batch is seen before delivery, showing the London type destination boxes.

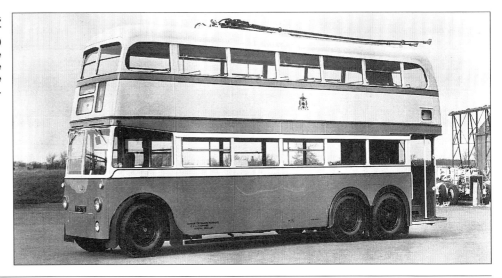

Glasgow started its trolleybus operations in 1949 with 35 BUT Q1 type vehicles, followed by 30 on Daimler chassis. One of the latter, TD17 is seen at the bodybuilders factory before delivery in 1950.

# Survival of the fittest – 1951 to 1960

Smaller trolleybus fleets that were faced with an urgent need to invest in vehicles and infrastructure made up the majority of the system closure list during this period. In the early 1950s demand for bus services was at its peak, and for many of these trolleybus systems, it was the motorbus that operators turned to when introducing new services.

Birmingham, not a small trolleybus system in terms of fleet numbers, but still only a minor part of the city's transport operation, included its trolleybus operation within its tramway replacement programme. The company systems of Llanelly, South Lancashire (SLT) and Notts and Derby were owned by organisations with considerable motorbus interests, and this sealed their fate, the SLT operation still running much of its original fleet of early 1930s Guy trolleybuses. London, the largest of them all, made a policy decision in 1954 to replace its trolleybus network, and began to prepare for this, but it was not until 1959 that the first routes under the conversion programme were switched to motorbus operation.

Two systems, Bradford and Walsall, were re-vitalised by the arrival of new General Managers, both of whom introduced pro-trolleybus policies. Throughout this period, both expanded their route network into new housing areas. Cardiff and Glasgow also continued the growth started in the 1940s, although the expansion of the Newcastle and Belfast operations had largely peaked in the early 1950s.

Those trolleybus operators who wished to continue their operations took advantage of opportunities to renew fleets in a cost-effective way. These were the re-bodying of existing

vehicles and the purchasing of second-hand vehicles from closing systems. Bradford had pursued a rebodying policy since the Second World War, and many of its pre-war vehicles were treated in this way. From 1956 onwards it improved on this method, introducing very modern vehicles with doors and heaters on older and second-hand chassis. Neighbouring Huddersfield also rebodied many of its pre-war and immediate post-war six-wheelers, prolonging the life of such chassis. Rotherham was able to increase the pay-load of its trolleybuses by replacing single-deck bodies with new double-deck versions on many of its post-war Daimler chassis.

Many of the systems that closed in the 1950s sold vehicles to other trolleybus operators. Darlington and Notts and Derby disposed of their entire serviceable fleets at the time of closure to Bradford. Mostly these second-hand bargains were the wartime Sunbeam / Karrier W type, or newer post-war four-wheel chassis. More systems benefiting in this way from the closure of others included Doncaster, Maidstone, Bournemouth and Walsall.

There were still significant deliveries of new vehicles in the 1950s. Crossley, taken over by AEC in 1948, continued to supply its own designs to Manchester and Cleethorpes until chassis production ceased in 1951, leaving just BUT and Sunbeam to supply the market. The change in maximum allowable passenger vehicle length in the mid-1950s, following an experimental batch of 30 feet long trolleybuses on Sunbeam chassis for Walsall, meant that four-wheel vehicles could now be 30 feet long. This took away the need for six-wheel vehicles, although conservative Huddersfield bought ten Sunbeam S7 type trolleybuses (with 7 feet 6 inches wide bodies) in 1959, the last new six-wheelers to enter service in Britain. Innovations in trolleybus vehicle design included Hull, which introduced two-entrance vehicles using a Sunbeam chassis with set-back front axle and trolley retrievers in 1953, and Glasgow where at the same time single-deck-standee trolleybuses were introduced, using BUT chassis, also with a set back front axle. Later, Glasgow's last trolleybuses were ten single-deck chassis lengthened to 34 feet, for which special dispensation was required from the Ministry of Transport, these being used on the last tram to trolleybus route conversion in Britain. In the meantime, Glasgow had also taken delivery of 90 more conventional double-deck BUT vehicles but built to the new 30 feet length. These, like many other BUT chassis built in the 1950s, were assembled at the former Crossley factory at Stockport.

| SYSTEMS CLOSED 1951 TO 1960 | |
|---|---|
| **Closed** | **Location** |
| 1951 | Birmingham |
| 1952 | Llanelly |
| 1953 | West Hartlepool |
| 1953 | Notts and Derby |
| 1954 | Southend |
| 1957 | Pontypridd |
| 1957 | Darlington |
| 1958 | St Helens |
| 1958 | South Lancashire |
| 1959 | Brighton Hove and District |
| 1959 | Hastings |
| 1960 | Grimsby-Cleethorpes |

The early 1950s were the peak years for the numbers of passengers carried by public transport. This is illustrated here by the queues waiting in John William Street, Huddersfield, to ride home by trolleybus. In view are two of the Sunbeam MS2 / Park Royal vehicles delivered in 1949. Both were subsequently rebodied, no. 578 by Roe in 1959, and no. 592, the last of the batch, was given a pre-used East Lancashire body in 1963. Both of these vehicles were withdrawn on the same date in July 1965. (J. Copland / P. Watson)

The Notts and Derby system, which closed all at once in April 1953, sold its entire fleet to Bradford. The fifteen BUTs with Weymann bodywork were only five years old, and some entered service in their new home without being repainted. The Notts and Derby blue livery was a darker blue than Bradford's shade, and no. 774 is seen in service at Thornbury terminus in this state, complete with 'Kimberley Ales' advertisement, a brew surely unobtainable in Yorkshire! (M. Peck)

One of the trolleybus systems that modernised its fleet by the rebodying of existing vehicles was Huddersfield. Typical of these rebuilt vehicles which entered service in the 1950s was no. 566, a Karrier MS2 which had entered service in 1948 with a Park Royal body. This was replaced in 1957 by a new East Lancashire body. Jim Copland captured this view of it standing at the outer terminus of the seven mile long Marsden route, on its first day in service, 1 June 1957. It ran until 1963. (J. Copland / P. Watson)

In the 1950s Bradford, as well as purchasing used vehicles, also followed a policy of rebodying older chassis, a process begun during the Second World War. The last completely new trolleybuses were a batch of eight Weymann bodied BUTs delivered in 1951, one of which, no. 755, is seen on the right of this view. On the left is a rebodied 1942 AEC trolleybus, new to Notts and Derby. It received this new East Lancashire body with platform doors, in 1958. The location is Holme Wood terminus, at the end of Bradford's last trolleybus route extension which was brought into use in 1960. The triangular reverser is just visible on the left of the photograph. (R.F. Mack)

## NOTABLE VEHICLE DEVELOPMENTS IN THE 1950S

In the early 1950s, Hull's general manager designed a trolleybus suitable for operation with one-man. This had a front-entrance and centre exit, and used trolley retriever equipment. The prototype, no. 101, was delivered in late 1952 and had a Sunbeam MF2B chassis and Roe bodywork. Fifteen production examples followed in 1954/5, and they were collectively known as 'Coronations'. The prototype is seen later in its life in King Edward Street. Note that by this time the city centre had been rebuilt following wartime devastation.

The first of Bournemouth's Sunbeam MF2B vehicles, new in 1958, is seen at Mallard Road depot in 'as delivered' condition. These vehicles had rear entrance and front exits, with two staircases. The initial batch was of 20 vehicles, and nineteen more followed in the next four years. (D. Conrad)

56

The ten 34 feet long Glasgow single-deckers delivered in 1958 replaced trams on a suburban route. This was the last tram to trolleybus conversion in Britain. The vehicles had BUT RETB1 (Leyland derived) chassis, with rather spartan Burlingham bodywork. TBS15 is seen at Paisley Road Toll terminus. (Roy Brook / Paul Watson)

The last six-wheel trolleybuses built for British service were ten Sunbeam S7s which entered service in Huddersfield in late 1959. By this time, wider 8 feet wide vehicles were the norm, but like all this town's trolleybuses, these vehicles were only 7ft 6in. wide. This is no. 634, with handsome East Lancashire bodywork, which is seen on football special duties in Northumberland Street. This inner urban area had recently been cleared of slum housing, the inhabitants being moved to estates on the fringes of the town, some served by extended trolleybus routes. This particular vehicle became the first of its type to be withdrawn, when it overturned after falling from the reverser platform at Longwood terminus in February 1967. (Roy Brook collection / P. Watson)

The revolutionary rear-engined Leyland Atlantean motorbus came into production in the late 1950s. The first trolleybus system to be usurped by this type of vehicle was at Hastings, where Atlanteans replaced the trolleybuses in May 1959. This scene in the Silverhill depot shows the brand new motorbuses, and the rear of 1946-built Sunbeam W no. 22, together with the open-top Guy trolleybus no. 3A. Both trolleybuses would have a life after Hastings, no. 22 becoming Bradford no. 807, whilst no. 3A was converted to a motorbus by the fitment of a Commer engine, and it still exists in preservation. (C.W. Routh)

Another system to collect second-hand vehicles was Walsall, where examples from Pontypridd and Hastings had joined the fleet in the late 1950s. More came in 1960 following the closure of the Grimsby-Cleethorpes system. Amongst these were the two Crossley trolleybuses which were delivered to Cleethorpes Corporation in 1951. These were the only post-war Crossley trolleybuses used outside the Manchester / Ashton area. The chassis was of the 'Empire' type, and bodywork was by Roe. No. 850 (formerly Grimsby-Cleethorpes no. 163) is seen approaching Walsall bus station, followed by one of the long Willowbrook bodied Sunbeam F4As. (A.B. Cross)

At the end of the 1950s, Maidstone opened a new route extension to the Parkwood housing estate, and had its five 'utility' bodied Sunbeam Ws rebodied by Roe. No. 58, newly into service with its new Roe bodywork, is seen at the terminus of the extended route at Brishing Lane. The route was further extended in 1963, resulting in Brishing Lane losing its trolleybus wiring. (D. Tate)

London started its trolleybus replacement programme in early 1959 and Routemaster buses were used from the end of that year. This is the scene at North Finchley terminus on Sunday 6 August 1961, during a period when, on Sundays, trolleybus replacement Routemasters from Highgate depot ran jointly with trolleybuses from Finchley depot on route 609 between Barnet and Moorgate. Routemaster RM 586 is crowded out by, from the left M1 class no. 1544, L3 class no. 1512, and N1 class no. 1624. (C.W. Routh)

# The trolleys come off – 1961 to 1970

At January 1961 there were 24 trolleybus systems in operation, but within ten years only two remained. During this period, the 'last trolleybus' scenario was being played out year-by-year. London was hastily converting its routes to Routemaster operation, its final trolleybuses running on 8 May 1962 in scenes reminiscent of the last tram ten years earlier. More and more systems took the decision to close – the economics of running motorbuses had become too attractive; the 'inflexible' trolleybus could not cope with impending major urban road building and redevelopment schemes; the support industry for parts and overhead equipment was rapidly disappearing – these were all reasons commonly quoted for such decisions.

It was not all entirely doom and gloom. In June 1961, Bradford celebrated 50 years as a trolleybus operator. Its system had been considerably modernised over the previous decade, an extension into a new housing estate being opened as late as 1960. Modern vehicles, consisting of new bodies on reconditioned second-hand chassis (and even third-hand) were still entering service, and continued to do so until 1963. Moreover, the operation was debt free and as yet no decisions had been taken to run down the system. However, adverse changes to policy began when a new General Manager took over just weeks after the celebrations.

Other systems were also continuing to develop during the early 1960s. New Sunbeam trolleybuses entered service at Reading in 1961 and at Bournemouth in 1962. The latter proved to be the last new trolleybuses to enter service in Britain. Older trolleybuses were still being re-bodied at Wolverhampton, Tees-side and also at Huddersfield, where the last new trolleybus body on a six-wheel chassis entered service in 1962. Route extensions into new housing areas occurred at Reading, Maidstone, Tees-side and Walsall.

However, two large city systems, those at Newcastle and Nottingham, closed in 1966, both having been rapidly reduced within about three years. Indeed, the Nottingham system had been virtually intact at the beginning of 1965, but by the end of that year it had been reduced to just one route. These frantic conversions to motorbuses should be compared with the case of Huddersfield, who paced out its route closures between 1961 and 1968, ordering a batch of new motorbuses every year to replace one route at a time. By the mid-1960s there were only three systems that had not declared their intention to close. These were Reading, Walsall and Tees-side. Bradford had started route closures in 1963, due to massive city centre redevelopment, and this continued sporadically until 1967, following which there was still a sizeable system in operation. It was determined to get the full benefit from earlier vehicle and infrastructure investment, rather than consign relatively new equipment to scrap. However, the decision by the major overhead wiring supplier, BICC, to cease specialist trolleybus component manufacture, prompted Reading to change its pro-trolleybus policy.

Apart from Bradford, the remaining trolleybus champions were Walsall and Tees-side. The fate of the Walsall system was sealed in 1969 when the undertaking was absorbed into the newly formed West Midland Passenger Transport Executive, and in just over a year the trolleybuses there were gone. Like Walsall, Tees-side had never wavered from its pro-trolleybus policies. Its entire 15-vehicle fleet had been rebodied between 1960 and 1965. During a period when its main route was severed due to bridge works in 1966, it wired up a diversionary route rather than suspend the trolleybus service, demonstrating that the trolleybus was not really such an 'inflexible' vehicle. It planned to open a new route extension, running through recently built housing, linking two of its termini to enable a circular service to operate. However, its future was uncertain because it was to be absorbed into other local municipal transport fleets in 1968. The new extension, Britain's last new trolleybus route development, opened on the day before the new undertaking came into being. Subsequently, some of the oldest vehicles were replaced by second-hand 1961 vintage trolleybuses from Reading, and the system celebrated its 50th anniversary in 1969, but the uncertainties of a long-term future were very real.

Near the end of this period Cardiff closed its trolleybus system, which had been steadily contracting throughout the 1960s. The significance of this was that Cardiff ran the last 6-wheel trolleybuses in Britain.

The 50th anniversary of Bradford's and Britain's trolleybuses was celebrated in June 1961. A commemorative tour of the system was operated, using the two vehicles painted in special liveries. Seen at the Eccelshill terminus of the route extension opened in 1959, is 1934 built AEC 603, with 1947 Northern Coachbuilders body (1911 livery), followed by 1938 built Karrier E4 with original Weymann body (1930s livery). (R.F. Mack)

Reading took delivery of twelve new trolleybuses in 1961. These had Sunbeam F4A chassis and Burlingham front-entrance bodies. They replaced the last of the pre-war AEC vehicles. The last of the delivery, no. 193 is seen on a special enthusiasts' tour near Tilehurst before entering service. (D.F. Parker)

| SYSTEMS CLOSED 1961 TO 1970 | |
|---|---|
| **Closed** | **Location** |
| 1961 | Mexborough and Swinton |
| 1961 | Brighton |
| 1962 | London |
| 1963 | Ipswich |
| 1963 | Portsmouth |
| 1963 | Doncaster |
| 1964 | South Shields |
| 1964 | Kingston upon Hull |
| 1965 | Rotherham |
| 1966 | Nottingham |
| 1966 | Newcastle |
| 1966 | Ashton |
| 1966 | Manchester |
| 1967 | Maidstone |
| 1967 | Wolverhampton |
| 1967 | Derby |
| 1968 | Belfast |
| 1968 | Huddersfield |
| 1968 | Reading |
| 1969 | Bournemouth |
| 1970 | Cardiff |
| 1970 | Walsall |

London's last trolleybus ran on 8 May 1962. L3 class no. 1521 is seen here operating the final journey from Wimbledon to Fulwell depot. Earlier in the day, the original 'Diddler' trolleybus no. 1 preserved in the London Transport Museum, ran on a short commemorative trip for invited guests. (Mirrorpix)

The last new British trolleybuses were the nine Sunbeam MF2Bs supplied to Bournemouth in 1962. A tenth chassis was destroyed by fire at the Weymann factory. They were also the only trolleybuses to carry 'reversed' registration numbers. The last one built, and therefore Britain's last new trolleybus (other than the 1984 experimental South Yorkshire vehicle) was no. 301, which is seen here late in its short public service life (less than seven years) at Pokesdown, on a service 20 journey from Christchurch to Bournemouth Square (D.F. Parker)

Nottingham closed its trolleybus system almost entirely during 1965. This view shows BUT 506, one of the batch with 8 feet wide bodies, in South Parade near the Old Market Square on 9 October 1965, the last day of operation of service 40. Only one main route, and the truncated section of another remained in operation after this date. No. 506, suitably lettered, became Nottingham's last trolleybus in the following year. It was saved for preservation, and is now restored in working order at the Trolleybus Museum, Sandtoft. It can be seen later in the book in a rather strange environment. (J. Copland)

Britain's last trolleybus route extension was opened at Teesside in March 1968, when wiring connecting the two termini at Grangetown and Normanby, running via the village of Eston, was brought into use. No. 2, a 1950 Sunbeam F4 with 1964 built Roe body is seen on this section, sweeping into Eston village from the Normanby direction. The vehicle is painted in the turquoise livery of Teesside Municipal Transport, who took over ownership of the system the day following the opening of the extension. (J. Fozard)

The rundown of British trolleybus systems during the 1960s resulted in many trolleybuses being purchased for preservation. Before operating museums were established, some systems allowed owners of such vehicles to operate them on enthusiasts' tours. In October 1968, shortly before the Reading system closed, two preserved trolleybuses operated simultaneously. These were Belfast Guy 168 and Huddersfield Sunbeam 631. The latter vehicle is seen on that occasion in King's Road, leaving the contra-flow bus lane which had been established as part of a one-way traffic scheme earlier that year (to avoid re-routing the trolleybuses). Trolleybuses operated against the flow of traffic, and this arrangement was the first such permanent provision in Britain. (R.F. Mack)

The last six-wheel trolleybuses to run in Britain were at Cardiff, where the system closed at the end of 1969. Closure ceremonies took place early in 1970, and the BUT vehicles used on the final tour are seen lined up in St Mary Street on a very wet Sunday, 11 January. Later that afternoon, the decorated no. 262 became the last trolleybus to run along Newport Road to the depot. This vehicle was already in private ownership. Behind it in this view are nos 215 and 276. (D.F. Parker)

# And then there were two – 1971 to 1972

Events moved swiftly to a close. Bradford's four-year inter-mission in route closures came to an end in early 1971, when one route was changed to motorbuses as part of a service reorganisation exercise. Sufficient new motorbuses were expected in the coming months to replace the rest of the trolleybus fleet. Three more routes were converted in mid-1971, leaving just two; to Duckworth Lane and the cross city Thornton to Thornbury service. Notwithstanding these closures, Bradford still managed to celebrate its 60th anniversary of operation in 1971.

Meanwhile, further north, Tees-side's new owners strug-gled with the maintenance of a trolleybus system that was only a tiny part of their overall operation, and called a halt to operations in April 1971.

Motorbuses partly replaced Bradford's remaining trolley-buses in November 1971, and a date for the complete conversion was set for March 1972. All that was left now was the final act, which in the event was played out in unex-pected fashion. A miners' strike and associated electricity cuts took trolleybuses off the streets in February 1972, but they were back for three final weeks of operation in March, allowing Bradford's, and Britain's, last trolleybus to run into Thornbury depot on the afternoon of Sunday 26 March 1972.

Despite the recent route extension and influx of more modern vehicles from Reading, the Tees-side system closed in April 1971. The decorated last vehicle, no. T291 (formerly Reading 186) is seen here reversing into the depot at Cargo Fleet after the closure celebrations, bringing an end over 50 years of operation. (D. Tate)

The only event to commemorate the 60th anniversary of Bradford's trolleybuses was an enthusiasts' tour held on Sunday 20 June 1971. This used the only remaining rear-entrance vehicle, BUT no. 758, which is seen here at Greengates terminus. Just over a week later this route would be converted to motorbuses, but no. 758 survived until the end of July, when its planned use as the last trolleybus to Clayton had to be aborted at the last minute after it suffered an electrical defect. (D.F. Parker)

It fell to Bradford to bring down the curtain on Britain's trolleybus operations. The last act is being played out here on 26 March 1972, as the final vehicle, no. 844, on its ceremonial run, climbs Leeds Road from the city centre on its way to Thornbury depot, where vast crowds awaited. It is passing Sticker Lane at Laisterdyke, where it all began in June 1911. (Travel Lens Photographic)

# Preservation

Like most types of transport in Britain, there is a well established preservation movement for trolleybuses. That for the trolleybus is, of course, unusual because, at the time of this book's publication, the preserved examples are the only ones of this form of transport in existence.

The pioneer in trolleybus preservation was London Transport, who had long pursued a policy of retaining significant historical vehicles for posterity. In 1948, it set aside trolleybus no. 1, an ex-London United 'Diddler', and by the close of the system in 1962 it had added Leyland K2 type 1253 and Q1 BUT 1768. In the 1950s, the British Transport Commission set up the Museum of British Transport in a former tram depot at Clapham, and no. 1 was displayed there, together with two trolleybuses acquired by the Science Museum – Ipswich single-decker no. 44 and Brighton Hove and District AEC no (6)340. The establishment of the National Railway Museum at York meant that the Clapham museum closed and 'Diddler' no. 1 returned to storage (following a very brief excursion under power on the last day of London's trolleybus operation). The Brighton and Ipswich vehicles returned to the care of the Science Museum.

Private preservation of trolleybuses began in the early 1960s. The Reading Transport Society purchased the last Reading pre-war AEC no. 113, and this was followed by a Cardiff AEC six-wheeler no. 203, and South Shields Karrier 204. A more broad-based society, the National Trolleybus Association also acquired vehicles, notably Huddersfield Karrier no. 541, which was donated by the Corporation.

A notable year was 1966, when in May the aforementioned Huddersfield vehicle became the first preserved trolleybus to operate, when it toured the remains of the Wolverhampton system. Then in December of that year, a privately preserved trolleybus, Manchester 1344, became the last ever trolleybus to run on the Manchester system.

Some, but by no means all, of the surviving systems in the late 1960s were quite happy to allow preserved trolleybuses to operate, resulting in rather bizarre scenes such as a Bournemouth open-topper appearing in Cardiff.

By the end of the 1960s, at least one vehicle had been saved from most of the systems that had closed in that decade, the only exceptions being Mexborough and Swinton (although rebodied examples from Bradford were later acquired), and Hull, where enthusiast groups faced insurmountable obstacles placed in their way by the municipal authority to all efforts to purchase one of the groundbreaking 'Coronation' trolleybuses. All went for scrap.

The longer-term aim for enthusiast societies was the establishment of an operating museum, similar to the tramway museum at Crich. The National Trolleybus Association made several attempts to do this, concentrating on sites in the south of England. However, a separate significant development came in 1969, when a consortium of preservation societies headed by the Reading Transport Society, came together to establish a working trolleybus museum on part of an ex-RAF aerodrome at Sandtoft near Doncaster.

There are now three museum sites in Britain that regularly operate trolleybuses under power, and one other that was very short-lived and is now defunct. Added to this there are museums that exhibit static vehicles. These include The London Transport Museum, Covent Garden (London 1253), the Manchester Museum of Transport (Ashton 80 and Manchester 1250), Bradford Industrial Museum (Bradford

London 'Diddler' no. 1, Britain's first preserved trolleybus, enjoys a brief outing carrying invited guests over the trolleybus routes in Kingston on the last day of the London system, 8 May 1962. (R.F. Mack)

737), and the Ipswich Transport Museum (Ipswich 2 and 126).

The largest operational museum is the **Trolleybus Museum at Sandtoft**. There are approximately 50 trolleybuses here, including a few from foreign systems. About half of these are in operating condition and able to carry passengers over the two way wiring circuit.

The **East Anglia Transport Museum at Carlton Colville**, eight miles south of Lowestoft, was developed from the 1960s, and in 1981 was able to operate trolleybuses on the museum site. The collection of the London Trolleybus Preservation Society is located here.

The **Black Country Museum**, on an open-air site in Dudley, West Midlands, incorporates a trolleybus circuit operated by the Black Country Museum Transport Group. The circular route of just under a mile in length is notable in that it includes a gradient, and also provides a genuine transport service, enabling visitors to travel from the museum entrance to various exhibits, including the village school. The two resident vehicles are Sunbeams from

Wolverhampton and Walsall, and these are regularly augmented by visiting vehicles normally based elsewhere.

The fourth museum operation was at **'Transperience'**, a transport-themed museum situated at Low Moor near Bradford. This was opened in 1995 and run by the West Yorkshire Transport Trust using regeneration funding. From the outset, trolleybus wiring was provided around the site, which was unfortunately bisected by a very low bridge, denying double-deck operation over the whole circuit. Sadly, visitor numbers fell very short of the forecasted numbers, and the site closed after two years. The former Bradford and Huddersfield trolleybuses used were either sold, or transferred to other museums.

The only other museum site able to operate trolleybuses is at **Beamish** in County Durham, where there is a length of overhead (without turning facilities) alongside the museum tramway between the depot and the visitor entrance. This allowed occasional operation of Newcastle Sunbeam no 501, owned by Tyne and Wear Museums, before this was transferred on loan to Sandtoft.

Former Huddersfied Karrier MS2 no. 541 is seen running at Wolverhampton in May 1966, the first occasion that a preserved trolleybus operated on a 'foreign' system.

The large number of vehicles available to operate at The Trolleybus Museum, Sandtoft allows scenes such as this to be commonplace on running days. London Q1 BUT no. 1812, was repatriated from Spain after it had been withdrawn from service on the Santander-Astillero interurban line in 1974. It was subsequently restored to London condition as seen here. Rotherham Daimler 37, seen on the right, is one of two of this type that has survived into preservation. In the background are four-wheel trolleybuses from Bradford and Reading.

One of the earliest trolleybuses to be privately preserved is Cardiff AEC no. 203. It is seen after painting in the original wartime grey livery running on the Black Country Museum trolleybus circuit, descending the hill after leaving the transport depot terminus. Subsequenly it has been given the early post-war streamlined livery and is based at the Sandtoft museum. (D.F. Parker)

# Renaissance?

It was perhaps fitting that the first serious proposals to re-introduce trolleybuses in Great Britain came from Yorkshire. Both the region's Passenger Transport Executives set up in 1974, absorbing the municipal bus operations, formulated plans to run trolleybuses. The West Yorkshire PTE intended to re-introduce them over routes in Bradford and Huddersfield, whilst the South Yorkshire PTE looked to do so in Doncaster.

It was Blackpool, of all places, that saw the first, but short-lived, trial of a trolleybus, when in 1983, a Renault articulated vehicle from Nancy was operated using specially erected overhead in Blundell Street, adjacent to the tram depot. The following year, South Yorkshire PTE progressed as far as obtaining an experimental vehicle, and equipping a test 'track' of wiring which was available for use in the following year. The vehicle was adapted from the operator's standard bus design, being based on a Dennis Dominator chassis and Alexander double-deck 80-seat body. An auxiliary diesel engine was included for running off the overhead wires. The mile-long test route led from the PTE bus depot at Leicester Avenue, crossed a public road (Leger Way) and then followed a private road (Sandal Beat Road) alongside the race course, terminating at a turning circle in a car park. Testing began in the autumn of 1985 and on one occasion paying passengers were allowed to travel.

However, circumstances at the time led to any development becoming stalled. The de-regulation of bus operations in 1986 meant that trolleybus installations would have no protection from predatory bus operations. The Doncaster experiment was not taken any further and the wiring was dismantled in the 1990s, the vehicle finding a home at the Sandtoft museum.

The more recent developments in electric street traction have concentrated on the introduction of light rail trams in several big cities, mostly combining central area street running with the use of former suburban railway formations. However trolleybuses have been proposed in London, for example on the Uxbridge corridor of the former 607 trolleybus route, and in Ilford and Barking.

Insurmountable difficulties with the establishment of a light rail system in Leeds resulted in the development of a less costly trolleybus scheme, and this has come closest to obtaining the necessary central government funding. Decisions on this are still awaited. The scheme comprises three radial routes to north, south and east Leeds, with a city centre loop, and linking park and ride sites as well as a major hospital. Total mileage proposed is 14km, although a smaller scheme comprising of just two routes is also under consideration.

The vehicles proposed for modern trolleybus schemes are single-deck multi-articulated, with capacity for 100+ passengers. Current is supplied at 750 volts, and to achieve a low floor throughout the vehicle, hub motors are proposed, a concept that goes back to the very beginnings of the trolleybus story.

**A mocked-up view of a proposed 1970s West Yorkshire PTE trolleybus, as used in PTE publicity at the time. The original photograph was of a standard contemporary motorbus.**

The South Yorkshire PTE Dennis trolleybus, numbered 2450 seen
using the trial wiring erected near Doncaster racecourse in 1985.

An artist's impression of how a bi-articulated trolleybus might look heading north into Leeds city
centre across the grade II listed Leeds Bridge over the River Aire. (Ashley Bruce / Electric Tbus Group)

# WORKINGS AND WIRINGS

## The Vehicle

The trolleybus was not a complicated vehicle, far less so than its oil-engined counterpart, or even the tramcar, which had to contend with the complexities of the steel rail / steel wheel interface. There were few moving parts, mainly the electric motor, propeller shaft and differential.

Power (at 550 volts DC) was collected from the overhead wires via the twin trolley booms. These were steel tubes, each containing a flexible power cable and covered overall by liberal amounts of insulation tape. This was to ensure that short circuits did not occur when the booms dewired, as well as protecting anyone coming in contact with them. At the end of each boom was a metal device known as the trolley head. This held a 'shoe' containing a carbon insert, which slid along the wire and it lubricated the wire as it proceeded. The carbon inserts could be replaced within minutes, and under normal circumstances could last up to 1,000 miles of running. In wet weather this was considerably less, and during periods of frost an insert would need replacing after only a very short period of operation. It was common practice on frosty mornings to fit vehicles with a metal insert to clear the wires of ice, a process accompanied by a spectacular display of flashes. The whole trolley head was attached to the trolley boom, complete with a safety rope (Bradford used chain), the purpose of this being that if the head became detached during a dewirement, it would not fall into the street. The carbon sliding shoe arrangement replaced the tramway type trolley wheel from the late 1930s onwards, although a small number of systems, notably Birmingham, Pontypridd and Notts and Derby, retained the trolley wheel method until the end of operations.

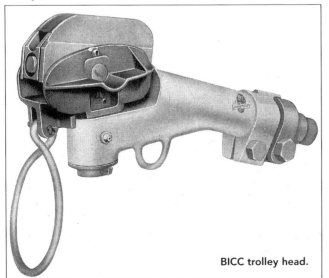

**BICC trolley head.**

At the other end of the trolley booms were powerful springs which by upward pressure, allowed the poles to maintain contact with the wires. The usual (and neatest) arrangement was that the springs lay along the bottom part of the boom, but in early days of the trolleybus other arrangements were applied. One of these was the Estler trolley base, where the booms were mounted on top of each other. This allowed very flexible movement of the booms, almost a full 360 degrees. This arrangement was common in the 1920s, but with the increased prevalence of double-deck trolleybuses (where the considerably higher Estler fitting caused problems), it fell out of favour. Darlington continued to specify the Estler base well into the 1930s for its all single-deck fleet, mainly due to the very restricted manoeuvring space within its depot.

From the trolley base, the power cable was routed through the bodywork into the driver's cab. It was common practice in some double-deck vehicle bodywork for the first upper deck window pillar on each side to be of extra thickness to accommodate the cables. Having reached the cab ceiling, the cables passed through circuit breakers that could be set 'on' or 'off' by hand. This device would automatically trip 'off' if the driver attempted to take power too quickly, and it would have to be re-set manually before the vehicle could proceed. Beyond the circuit breakers, the power reached the contactors, i.e. the switches which controlled the resistances. The contactors, usually sited in a fireproof cabinet on the nearside of the full width cab, were linked to the driver's pedal controls, left foot for power (acceleration), and right foot for braking. (Hastings had the pedals sited for the opposite feet, and these had to be altered at Bradford before several ex-Hastings trolleybuses entered service there). The power pedal was usually a substantial affair covering the whole of the driver's footprint. This allowed the driver to 'feel' the individual contactors (or 'notches') being switched in as the vehicle picked up speed. Later trolleybus design incorporated an 'automatic acceleration' facility, whereby the driver could push the power pedal down relatively quickly to the maximum required position, whilst the 'notches' would be selected automatically in gradual and proper sequence. Notably, apart from one experimental vehicle, London never used this system. The braking pedal incorporated rheostatic braking, again using resistances (now resistors), with the final stop being made by air brakes acting on the brake drums on each wheel. Rheostatic braking slowed the vehicle down to about 4mph, and, because it did not act on the road wheels, it could not induce wheel lock and skidding. Some trolleybuses in the earlier years were fitted with regenerative braking, which worked off the power pedal when the driver slowly 'notched back' to reduce speed. This turned the motor into a generator putting power back into the overhead. The disadvantage of this system was that the additional power generated could not always be used by other vehicles, thereby causing problems by overloading the electricity supply sub-stations. Without regenerative braking, it was not possible to 'notch back' on the power pedal, nor to take power and brake at the same time. The only way this could be done was by using the handbrake, a technique necessary when negotiating automatic frogs, to be discussed later.

# REGENERATIVE SYSTEM
## proves 30% saving
### *in* GUY
### TROLLEY BUSES

**Important advantages are:**

- Reduction of current costs.
- Considerable saving on brake linings.
- Saving in current consumption is equally effective on flat as on hills.
- Easier driving by stable position of power pedal at all running speeds.

GUY fleets of Trolley Buses are in service by the Wolverhampton Corporation, Hastings Tramway Co., The South Lancashire Transport Co., and the Corporations of Derby, Rotherham, Pontypridd, and Walsall, and also at Brussels, Milan, and Kyoto (Japan). Guy range of trolley buses includes 4- and 6-wheelers for single and double deckers.

*Write for illustrated booklet*

# GUY MOTORS LTD., WOLVERHAMPTON
### LONDON OFFICE, SHOWROOMS AND SERVICE—PORTEUS ROAD, PADDINGTON, W.2

The resistors, which generated considerable heat, were normally located low down on the underside of the vehicle where there was adequate ventilation. On single-deck trolleybuses it became common for this equipment to be placed on the roof for the same reason. The power, regulated by the resistances, reached the motor which rotated and turned the propeller shaft and differential(s) to produce traction at the rear road wheels. Trolleybuses in later years had only one motor, although these were of varying power outputs ranging from 60hp to 150hp. The latter type was fitted to Huddersfield's six-wheelers to enable them to cope with the steep gradients on that system.

It should be noted that the drive from the motor to the road wheels was always 'solid' on a trolleybus, and could not be disengaged in the same way as a motor vehicle using the clutch or fluid flywheel. This could cause difficulties when towing a trolleybus. Short distances were not a problem but on longer tows, such as on delivery runs from one town to another it was necessary to disconnect the transmission to avoid damage to the motor. This was achieved either by removal of the propeller shaft or half-shafts (which took the drive from the differential to the rear wheels).

Trolleybuses operating in hilly areas were usually required by the Ministry of Transport to have additional safety devices which could be deployed when ascending and descending steep hills. These were the coasting brake and the run-back brake. Both systems were designed to operate independently of the power supply, so therefore they would work if the trolley booms had dewired. The coasting brake allowed a controlled descent of steep hills, limiting the speed of the vehicle to 15mph or less. The brake

**COASTING BRAKE SECTIONS**
**Bournemouth**
Richmond Hill
**Brighton**
New England Road
Beaconsfield Villas
Ditchling Road
Elm Grove
Queens Park Road
Manor Hill
Braybon Avenue
**Hastings**
Harold Road
Elphinstone Road
**Huddersfield**
Newsome Road
Blackmoorfoot Road
Woodhouse Hill
Longwood Road
Thornhill Road
The Ainleys
**London**
Anerley Hill
Highgate Hill

*Source – J. P. Senior – Trolleybus Magazine no 187 National Trolleybus Association, 1993*

was switched in by the driver whilst the vehicle was stationary at the start of the descent, and from then speed during the descent was governed entirely by the brake. At the end

**The adverse effect on the height of a double-deck trolleybus fitted with the Estler trolleybase is demonstrated in this view of Southend no. 111, one of a pair of English Electric vehicles new in 1929. The large poster in the lower deck advertises a visiting circus, and it is possible that the full load being carried is connected with this. Both these vehicles were sold to Nottingham in 1940.**

of the section, the driver switched off the brake to resume normal control. Five systems had sections of route for which it was compulsory to use the coasting brake, these being Bournemouth, Brighton, Hastings, Huddersfield and London (see panel). The runback brake was generally automatic in operation, and was activated when there was a loss of power on an uphill gradient, and limited any running-back to 2mph.

The coasting brake control switch was part of the main control switch in the driver's cab, usually on the left of the driver's seat beside the contactor cabinet. This switch had forward, reverse, coasting brake and off positions. Other vital equipment in the cab included: the dewirement indicator, a visual neon light usually within the driver's sight above or below the windscreen, which, when lit, indicated that power was reaching the vehicle; and the air brake pressure indicator, which displayed a red 'stop' flag if the

air pressure was approaching levels inadequate to stop the vehicle.

One further mandatory safety procedure was the current leakage test. In certain conditions such as very damp days or in snow and ice, trolleybuses could become 'live', giving the unwary passenger a slight electric shock. Every trolleybus in service had to be tested daily for current leakage by plugging an ammeter into a special socket, usually placed in the driver's cab. Any vehicle detected as 'live' had to be withdrawn immediately for rectification. The instructions given to Huddersfield trolleybus drivers are given in the panel below. Here the test was performed as the vehicle arrived at the depot from service. Note that the test required all the major electrical components of the vehicle to be taking power.

---

**LEAKAGE TEST**

Stop at point indicated for leakage test.
Put all circuit breakers and lighting switches 'ON'.
Operate air brake pedal until compressor motor cuts in.
When told – but not before – move control pedal to first notch.

---

Trolleybus lighting could either be powered direct from the overhead, or by a low voltage system. Direct traction lighting meant that the interior lights, often bare light bulbs, were wired in series to share out the 550 volts, and it also had the effect of blinking off then on momentarily whenever the vehicle passed under a dead section in the overhead.

Several systems, notably London, Manchester and Notts and Derby, fitted their trolleybuses with traction batteries, which allowed the vehicle to have limited movement away from the overhead.

*See appendix v for a detailed account of how a 1930s trolleybus worked.*

**To assist drivers, these signs were provided by Huddersfield at either end of the coasting brake section on Newsome Road. The Newsome route closed in July 1966.**

Single-deck trolleybuses often had their resistances mounted on the roof for ventilation purposes. Rotherham Guy no. 49, with Cravens body and one of six new in 1937 shows its resistances fixed to the cab roof, forward of the trolleybase. The vehicles also has vertical trolley springs (just visible behind the resistances), a feature that was very rare at that time. (W.J. Haynes)

Huddersfield's Woodhouse Hill, on the Riddings route, was the steepest on the system at 1 in 8½. Trolleybuses were required to use the coasting brake for the entire length of the descent. This is a view of Fartown Green, at the bottom of the hill, which rises in the right of this view towards the church spire. The trolleybus on the right (Sunbeam MS2 no. 583) is at the compulsory stop where the brake was disengaged. On the left, Karrier MS2 no. 549 is about to tackle the ascent. In the left background is the Fartown Green turning loop, provided to enable trolleybuses to turn round whenever the hill was impassable due to snow and ice. Also of note is the string of lights suspended between the running wires. Known as 'fairy lights', these were switched on at times of poor visibility, especially fog, to guide trolleybus drivers through curves or, as here, wide road junctions. (Roy Brook / Paul Watson)

London made extensive use of the fleet's traction battery facility, allowing emergency running beyond the wiring for short distances. This allowed vehicles to turn in order to correct severe late running. K1 class Leyland no. 1134 is seen in this view operating 'off-wire' at Stamford Hill. (Jack Gready / London Trolleybus Preservation Society)

# The overhead wires

These, of course, were a vital part of any trolleybus system, and were also one of its most fascinating aspects.

## Trolley Wire

The actual wire carrying the traction current, in contact with the trolley booms, consisted of cadmium copper and was just under ½ inch diameter (in earlier years hard-drawn copper was used). In section, it was of 'cottage loaf' outline, with two grooves along the upper half. This groove allowed the suspension 'ear' to be secured by tightening screws against the contact wire without obstructing the path of the trolley head (this type of ear was known as a 'mechanical ear' (an earlier, and alternative method, deriving from tramway practice was to use round trolley wire, with clinch ears that were secured by being hammered on to the wire). The ear assembly was attached to a spacer bar, which connected to that of the second running wire. The entire unit, spacer bar, two ears and associated insulation was known as a 'twin line hanger'. This arrangement was pioneered in London and the USA – previously

## Overhead Line Suspension

The overhead wiring units (e.g. two x twin line hangers on a two-way trolleybus route) were usually suspended 21 feet above the road by two principal methods. Cross span wiring used galvanised wire strung across the road between traction poles or between 'rosettes' set into buildings at the roadside. Bracket arm suspension used a metal arm cantilevered out from the traction pole to support the wires, and was employed when trolleybuses traversed a road in one direction only, when the road was very wide (eg a dual carriageway), or when traction poles were only planted on one side of the street. In earlier days, eg in Reading, Huddersfield and Newcastle, there was a variation to the bracket arm suspension. This was tubular suspension, where the metal arm stretched across the whole of the road supporting both sets of wires, connecting with the traction pole on the other side. This method was used when former tram poles were retained and the additional tubular bar added strength to this equipment, which was originally designed to carry single tram wires.

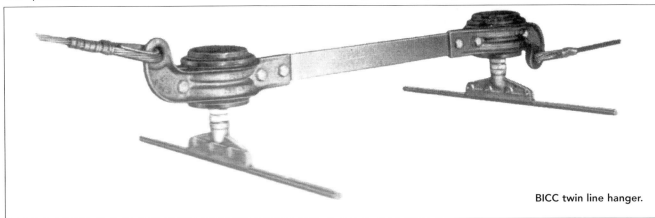

BICC twin line hanger.

adapted tramway hangers with porcelain insulators for spacers were used. It was normal practice for the wire nearest the kerb to be negative, and the wire nearest the centre of the road, positive, although the vehicle could operate equally well, and quite normally, whichever way round the positive / negative running wires were placed. The spacer bar ensured that the wires were kept safely apart to avoid short circuits. In later years the practice was for the positive and negative wires to be kept 24 inches apart, but the earlier standard had been 18 inches (and even 12 or 13 inches for the earliest systems). The 18-inch wiring was still in common use in the 1950s and 1960s on some systems, for example on parts of the Hastings and Rotherham wiring.

The actual running wires needed to be positioned along the centre line of the trolleybus in its normal road path. On curves, the wires were set so that the trolley booms were not travelling on a greater arc than that of the vehicle, otherwise a dewirement would ensue, because in this situation they would be having to travel faster than the vehicle. The suspension of wiring on curves was achieved by using additional wires ('pull-offs') connected to the traction poles to 'pull' the line hangers into the shape of the curve. In later years, systems that modernised their wiring provision used 'curve segments'. These pre-fabricated devices, very neat in appearance, held the wiring to the required radius and greatly reduced the need for 'pull off' wires, which for severe curves were seen as quite unsightly.

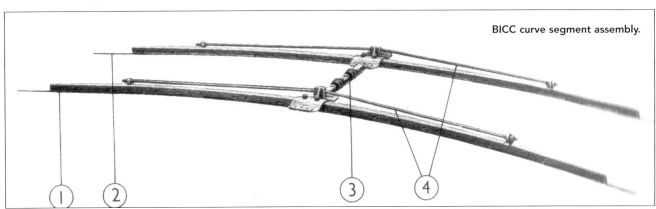

BICC curve segment assembly.

Apart from simple running wires, there were special units which needed to be incorporated into wiring layouts. These units were known as 'line assemblies' and comprised such items as section insulators, crossings, and frogs (turnouts). These items could be quite substantial, often comprising of solid metal castings. A 90-degree crossing assembly, for example, weighed 114 pounds, and for major wiring junctions this resulted in literally tons of equipment being suspended above the roadway, albeit very firmly secured!.

## Section Insulators
By law, the running wires were divided into electrically separate sections, a maximum of ½ mile apart. These sections were insulated electrically by 'section insulators', which consisted of a fitting incorporating a short piece of non-conductive material under which the trolley head passed. The driver needed to ensure that the vehicle was coasting at this point to avoid damage to the fittings by destructive arcing.

## Crossings
These units allowed one set of trolley wires to cross another set and they incorporated insulated units, similar to section insulators, at points where positive and negative wires intersected. The crossing units could be erected in such a way as to give power priority to one route (e.g. an uphill one), with the insulators, requiring the vehicle to shut off power, positioned on the downhill or level route.

## Frogs
Frogs, also known as turnouts, were necessary where routes diverged or converged. They fell into three main categories, these being hand pull, automatic, or spring loaded, the latter being used at reverser junctions which allowed the trolley booms to reverse through them into the reversing triangle, after which they would spring back to the normal position. Manually controlled facing frog junctions were set by the conductor using a hand pull attached to an adjacent traction pole. Normally the handle needed to be held down until the trolley heads had passed through the frog assembly, although London had some semi-automatic units which

were set by push button. This arrangement allowed the conductor to return immediately to the vehicle, the resetting of the frog being done automatically by a skate in the overhead. Fully automatic frogs dispensed with conductor involvement, and the frog setting was done remotely by the driver. The frogs were normally set for the through route, and the diverging route was selected when required by the vehicle taking power as the trolley heads passed through a skate sited in advance of the frog. The frog was reset by another skate on the diverging route some yards beyond the frog. The setting of the frog was shown by a signal on the nearest traction pole, usually a light indication.

As general road traffic and congestion increased, it became common practice at turnouts on busy roads for them to be set back, i.e. positioned several yards before the junction, with a piece of parallel dual wiring leading up to the actual route divergence itself. This allowed the vehicle to pass through the junction without slowing other traffic, and also allow the driver to concentrate solely on the turning manoeuvre at the junction rather than having to watch the trolley booms as well. A refinement of this practice, used in Bradford and Cardiff, was the interlaced turnout, where, at the set back turnout, the positive and negative wires only diverged by a couple of inches or so, each set being interlaced up to the road junction. This saved space and reduced the weight of the frog assembly and associated crossings.

This overhead wiring arrangement was necessary to allow trolleybuses to reverse by means of a three point turn. Although common, many trolleybus operators tried to avoid potential hazardous reversing manoeuvres by providing turning circles and 'round the houses' one-way turning loops.

**The Hastings system retained 18" spaced wiring throughout its existence. This is the wiring junction at Silverhill, showing 1946 built Sunbeam W no. 24 waiting to depart for the town centre. The wires leading off to the right give access to the depot at Beaufort Road. (D.A. Thompson)**

This 1930s view of Mansfield Road Nottingham shows, appropriately enough, the Nottingham catenary method of wiring suspension. Nottingham's early trolleybus wiring was of wide 30 inches separation between positive and negative wires and this is evident here. Tram wires are also included in this wiring display. The vehicle, no. 66, is a 1934 Karrier E6 with Brush bodywork. (R. Marshall collection)

Bracket arm suspension, in this case incorporating both directions of wiring, is evident in this commercial view of High Street, Doncaster. This was used by trolleybuses on the Racecourse route.

A variant of the bracket arm design was a 'bowstring' type, and examples of this were commonly found in London, as seen in this view of the Finsbury Square terminus at Moorgate. Class L1 (AEC chassisless) trolleybus 1364 is seen on the 611 route to Highgate Hill. The L1 vehicles were fitted with coasting and run-back brakes for use on this route. (C.Carter)

Examples of tubular suspension, common in pre-war years, could still be found on some systems in later times. This is Park Road Portsmouth, showing 1937 AEC no. 294 with Cravens body, heading towards the Dockyard on service 18. The dome of the Guildhall can be seen in the background. (Roy Brook / P. Watson)

This is the exit from Belfast's Glengormley terminus showing how the sharp curve from the main road is formed by multiple pull-off wires. The BUT trolleybus, no. 221, has just departed from the terminus. (V. Nutton / Travel Lens Photographic)

Two wiring features are evident in this view at the Stormont terminal loop at Belfast. AEC trolleybus 99 is passing under a curve segment, demonstrating how this device formed a curve in the wiring without the need for pull-off wires. On the wires in the left background are section insulators, incorporating power feeder cables. (R.F. Mack)

Four 90-degree crossing assemblies are used at this road junction in Portsmouth. The location is Albert Road, where the Eastney trolleybus services crossed those running from Lawrence Road into Waverley Road, to and from Southsea seafront. AEC trolleybus 294 is on Albert Road on a service 18 journey to the Dockyard, and the position of the crossing insulators indicates that it has power priority over the junction. (J. Copland / A.D. Packer)

This crossover arrangement allowed a connection between wires of different polarity. It was used on some systems for depot access wiring, or in this case, to allow trolleybuses to negotiate temporary road works. Major sewer replacement on Huddersfield's Newsome route in 1955 necessitated vehicles using the wires in the opposite direction for a short distance. Sunbeam MS2 trolleybus 590 is heading for Newsome on the 'right' wires in this view, the same wires being shared at this point by vehicles coming from Newsome. (Roy Brook / Paul Watson)

## Pull-frogs

At pull-frogs, set by the conductor, the pole-mounted handle was often accompanied by suitable signage. This example was situated at Leeds Road Huddersfield, where the Keldregate route branched off. In Huddersfield and Llanelly, the pull-handle was referred to as a 'trigger'. (Travel Lens Photographic)

The conductor of Hull Sunbeam F4 trolleybus no. 93 holds down the handle to enable the vehicle to turn at the East Park short working on Holderness Road. This wintry scene is dated 22 December 1962. (A.D. Packer)

After making sure that the trolley poles had negotiated the frog correctly, the conductor had then to return to the vehicle as quickly as possible. At Atherton (Punch Bowl) on the South Lancashire system, the conductor runs back to his vehicle, a 1931-built Guy BTX, no. 26 in the fleet. (H. Luff, Online Transport Archive)

The automatic frog arrangement at Westgate, Huddersfield, is evident in this commercial view. Vehicles on the West Vale route turning right here would take power as the positive trolley pole passed under the setting skate just visible at the line hanger in advance of the frog. The resetting skate is just beyond the frog itself.

Cardiff used this interlaced wiring arrangement at the junction of Cowbridge Road West and Grand Avenue on the Ely route. Beyond the frog the wires ran with only a very short gap between them until the actual road junction was reached. (J.C. Gillham)

Regarded as unsightly by many, but fascinating to some, trolleybus wiring junctions such as this were commonplace in trolleybus towns. This is the junction of Victoria Street and Cornmarket in Derby, showing trailing and facing frogs and a crossover. Thick brass runner was used to connect these assemblies rather than normal running wire, the latter tending to easily fracture due to the short length between rigid units.

Guard wires were often used to protect property from wayward trolley booms. They were also used to protect the running wires themselves from other hazards, such as telephone wires, and it was a statutory requirement to do this. Telephone wires at this railway overbridge at Parkgate near Rotherham were prevented from falling onto the live trolleybus wiring by this cat's cradle device. The single-deck Mexborough trolleybus is no. 25, the first of twelve Sunbeam F4s delivered in 1948. (J. Copland / A.D. Packer)

Power cuts were an occasional hazard of trolleybus operation. The majority of these were of short duration, and confined to a localised area. Systems with electrical infrastructure badly in need of replacement suffered more than most. This press photograph shows the result of a power failure in the Newcastle city centre area in the early 1960s, with trolleybuses lined up in Grainger Street, their crews enjoying an unscheduled break. The leading vehicle is no. 466, one of 36 Sunbeam F4s with Metro-Cammell bodywork which was new in March 1949. (Mirrorpix)

## TRIANGLES

This overhead wiring arrangement was necessary a allow trolleybuses to reverse by means of a three point turn. Although common, many trolleybus operators tried to avoid potential hazardous reversing manoeuvres by providing turning circles and 'round the houses' one-way turning loops.

*"...the overhead wiring is taken a little beyond the actual turning-point to enable the trolley bus to back into a blank turning; when this operation is completed the bus is facing the direction in which it is to proceed on the return journey, and when it has left the terminus the trolley poles have, in fact, effected a complete triangle under the overhead wiring. This is made electrically possible by insulating the negative crossings to form an open circuit.'*
*The Electric Trolleybus – R.A. Bishop 1931*

One of the most spectacular trolleybus reversing triangles was at Huddersfield's Longwood terminus, where the vehicles reversed from a narrow lane along a hillside, onto a substantial concrete platform built out from the roadside. The platform was built in 1939, and incorporated a turntable. This was used to turn trolleybuses until the early years of the war, when difficulties of using the apparatus in the blackout resulted in a more conventional triangular reverser being installed instead. The solid nature of the structure can be appreciated from this 1950s view, showing a Karrier/ Sunbeam MS2 vehicle on the platform. It is standing on the turntable plate, which was retained, albeit locked in position. (J. Fozard)

The last reverser to be brought into use in Britain was on the Tees-side system at North Ormesby. Major road construction forced the turning circle here to be abandoned, and a reverser provided instead, shortening the route by several yards. This arrangement came into use in March 1970. Tees-side Sunbeam F4 T281 (formerly no. 1) is seen in Smeaton Street about to reverse into Hampden Street. (Roy Brook / Paul Watson)

THE NEW BRIDGE, STOCKBRIDGE, KEIGHLEY.

A less common arrangement was for the trolleybus to drive into the side road and reverse out into the main road. This was more prevalent in pre-war years, but examples did exist, notably at Newcastle, into the 1960s. One such which existed briefly was at Keighley's Stockbridge terminus, where the construction of a new bridge in 1929 resulted in a reverser replacing the turning circle. The layout is depicted here in this commercial postcard view, showing that vehicles drove into the side road on the right (Cornwall Road) and reversed out on to the main Keighley to Bradford road. The original turning circle was in the left background, and a short stretch of wiring beyond the reverser has been retained. The reverser remained in use until the end of the system in 1932.

The South Lancashire trolleybus system included several reversing triangles. Trolleybuses turned at the Atherton terminus of the jointly operated service to St Helens using this reverser, which necessitated the vehicle reversing across the whole of the road. In the upper right foreground are the wires of the one-way-loop around Atherton town centre turning into Mealhouse Lane, which ran under the support wires of the triangle at this point. Guy BTX trolleybus no. 17, with rebuilt front-end, is seen unloading passengers before turning here. (Roy Brook / Paul Watson)

# AROUND BRITAIN BY TROLLEYBUS

## System index

Three trolleybus operators are relevant to this scene. A pair of Notts and Derby's BUT trolleybuses stand at the Nottingham terminus (under Nottingham Corporation wires) of the route to Ripley on the last night of trolleybus operation, 23 April 1952. The vehicle on the right is operating only as far as the depot at Langley Mill. Both vehicles have already been sold to Bradford, where they will run until the early 1960s. (G.H.F. Atkins / courtesy and copyright John Banks collection)

# Trolleybus Systems in the UNITED KINGDOM

Scotland

DUNDEE ○

○ GLASGOW

Northern Ireland

BELFAST ○

Eire

Wales

England

AL   ASHTON UNDER LYNE
B    BRADFORD
D    DONCASTER
HU   HUDDERSFIELD
HX   HALIFAX
MA   MANCHESTER
ME   MEXBOROUGH & SWINTON
O    OLDHAM
R    RAMSBOTTOM
SH   ST. HELENS
SL   SOUTH LANCS.
ST   STOCKPORT
W    WIGAN

NEWCASTLE UPON TYNE ○
SOUTH SHIELDS ○
HARTLEPOOL ○
DARLINGTON ○   ○ TEESSIDE

YORK ○○
KINGSTON UPON HULL ○
KEIGHLEY ○○
B ○
○ LEEDS
GRIMSBY
CLEETHORPES
R ○ HX ○ M̲
D ○   M̲ SANDTOFT
W ○   ○○ HU
SL ○○○
ME ○
SH ○ MA ○○○ AL   ○ ROTHERHAM
STOCKPORT   LOW MOOR
○ CHESTERFIELD

NOTTS. & DERBYS.
DERBY ○   ○○ NOTTINGHAM

CARLTON COLVILLE M̲

WOLVERHAMPTON ○   ○ WALSALL
BLACK COUNTRY M̲   ○ BIRMINGHAM

IPSWICH ○

ABERDARE
RHONDDA
PONTYPRIDD
LLANELLI ○   CARDIFF

SOUTHEND ○
LONDON ○
READING ○
MAIDSTONE ○
HASTINGS ○
PORTSMOUTH   BRIGHTON ○○
BOURNEMOUTH ○

0   50   100 km

○  trolleybus system
M̲  working museum - open
M̲  working museum - closed

A.G.Murray & R.A.Smith, 1/94.
Re-drawn 4/10. No.132, v2.0.

# THE TROLLEYBUSES OF NORTH EAST ENGLAND

## Newcastle upon Tyne

One of Britain's largest trolleybus systems, but which, by being confined to the north bank of the River Tyne, did not achieve its full potential.

The most northerly trolleybus system in England was at Newcastle upon Tyne, where distinctive cadmium yellow and cream vehicles ran on an extensive network on the north bank of the River Tyne. Trolleybuses came to Tyneside in October 1935, when a cross-city route was opened between Denton and Wallsend. Further conversion of tram routes occurred in 1937 and 1938, bringing trolleybuses to Byker and the northern suburb of Jesmond. By the outbreak of war, there were over one hundred vehicles in the fleet. Further expansion came during the war when the tram routes to Fenham and Delaval Road were converted to trolleybus operation in 1941 and 1944 respectively. Unlike some systems, Newcastle continued to replace trams with trolleybuses after the war. In 1948, trolleybuses took over the tram route along the Great North Road to Gosforth, followed in the following year by circular services in the Heaton and Jesmond areas. A short branch off the Gosforth route to Grange estate was brought into use during 1951. One unfulfilled ambition was to run trolleybus services across the Tyne into Gateshead, jointly with the Gateshead and District Transport Company, as had happened with each undertaking's trams. After several years of deliberation, the Gateshead Company decided to replace its trams with motorbuses, so the prospect of trolleybuses running over the Tyne Bridge never came to fruition.

The pre-war fleet consisted of AEC, Guy and Karrier six-wheelers, each with a front-exit door and two staircases as well as a conventional rear platform. During the war, eighteen two-axle utility trolleybuses entered the fleet, supplemented by six elderly second-hand vehicles from Bradford, as well as some loaned from Brighton and Bournemouth. These latter vehicles fitted in well at Newcastle, with similar entrance/exit arrangements and livery. After the war, 186 new vehicles were ordered for the projected new routes, resulting in the entire fleet being renewed by the end of 1950. The new fleet was a mix of six- and four-wheel Sunbeam and BUT chassis, many with bodies built locally by Northern Coachbuilders. The front exit arrangement was abandoned. Notable amongst the new arrivals were two batches of BUT trolleybuses almost identical to London's Q1 type, the first batch even having London's destination display arrangement.

In 1956 a new depot was opened at Slatyford near Fenham. This required some access wiring on roads not previously served by trolleybuses, allowing new circular services to be introduced. Despite this, there was no further significant development of

| FACTFILE – NEWCASTLE | |
| --- | --- |
| Opened | 2 October 1935 |
| Closed | 1 October 1966 |
| Route mileage | 37 |

| FLEET PROFILE ALL DOUBLE-DECK | |
| --- | --- |
| Maximum number vehicles in service | 204 |
| Rebodied vehicles | Nil |
| Second-hand vehicles | 6 |
| | |
| AEC 6-wheel | 27 |
| BUT 4-wheel | 25 |
| BUT 6-wheel | 70 |
| Daimler 6-wheel | 1 |
| English Electric 6-wheel | 6 |
| Guy 6-wheel | 35 |
| Karrier utility | 18 |
| Karrier 6-wheel | 50 |
| Sunbeam 4-wheel | 61 |
| Sunbeam 6-wheel | 30 |

| HOW THEY WENT – NEWCASTLE | |
| --- | --- |
| 2 June 1963 | Denton to Wallsend |
| 1 February 1963 | Gosforth, Benton Circular |
| 29 May 1965 | Fenham, Osborne Road, Heaton Circular, Wallsend Boundary |
| 1 October 1966 | Denton, Delaval Road, Brighton Grove, Walker |

the system, and massive city-centre redevelopment planned during the 1960s sealed the fate of the trolleybus in the city. The demise was swift. The pioneer Denton to Wallsend service closed in mid-1963, followed by the rest in three stages between 1964 and 1966. The last trolleybuses ran on Saturday 1 October 1966 on the routes between Denton and Delaval Road across the city to Walker.

Newcastle's first trolleybuses were of AEC, Karrier and Guy manufacture. This view of West Road Denton, shortly after services commenced, shows Brush bodied AEC no. 15 passing Metro-Cammell bodied Karrier no. 20.

In 1942, five of Brighton's AEC vehicles were loaned to the city, where they worked on the Osborne Road service. Brighton 15 is seen in Northumberland Street, being passed by a sister vehicle. (British Commercial Vehicle Museum)

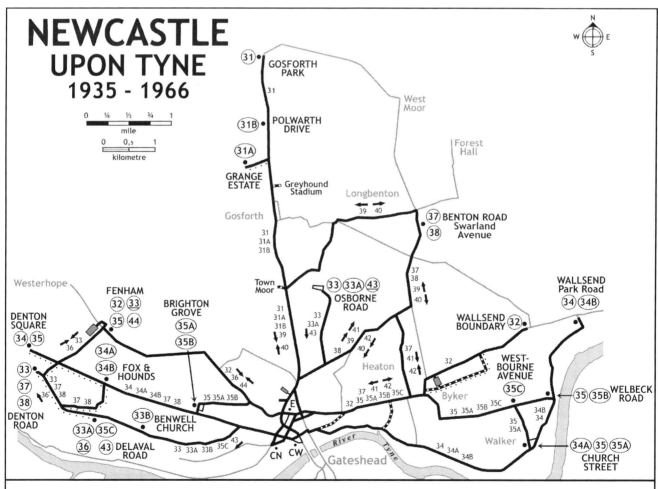

# NEWCASTLE
## UPON TYNE
### 1935 - 1966

GOSFORTH PARK

West Moor

POLWARTH DRIVE

Forest Hall

GRANGE ESTATE

Greyhound Stadium

Longbenton

Gosforth

BENTON ROAD
Swarland Avenue

WALLSEND Park Road

Westerhope

FENHAM

BRIGHTON GROVE

Town Moor

OSBORNE ROAD

WALLSEND BOUNDARY

DENTON SQUARE

Heaton

WEST-BOURNE AVENUE

FOX & HOUNDS

WELBECK ROAD

DENTON ROAD

Byker

BENWELL CHURCH

Walker

DELAVAL ROAD

River Tyne

CN  CW

Gateshead

CHURCH STREET

### Legend

— trolleybus route
····· trolleybus route extending beyond former tramway
▪▪▪▪ trolleybus route - no scheduled service
— electric tramway not replaced by trolleybuses
(33A)• terminus          ▨ depot
(36)• starting point of uni-directional service

### Notes

The following services terminated in the city centre :-
ELDON SQUARE (E)                                  33A,33B
CENTRAL STATION (Neville Street) (CN)   31,31A,31B,36,39,40,41,42,44
CENTRAL STATION (Westgate Road) (CW)   34B
All other services were "cross-city" services.
*Service numbers are those in use from 1948.*

S.Lockwood and R.A.Smith April 2010. No.944.

One of the 18 utility Karrier Ws is seen at the junction of Grainger Street and Westgate Road. This is no. 140, with Park Royal body which was new in mid-1945.

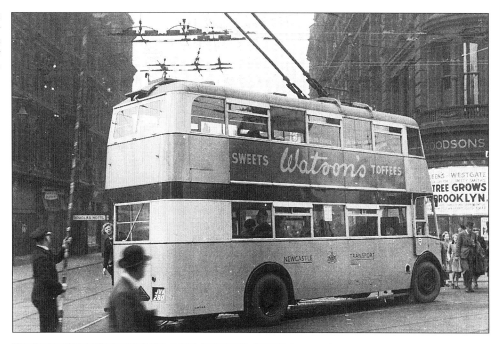

The main terminal for trolleybus services in Newcastle city centre was at the Central Station in Neville Street. Here, Roe bodied Karrier E6A no. 418, new in 1940 is seen in early post-war days. Originally numbered 118, like the rest of the fleet it had 300 added to its fleet number in 1946. It had a relatively short life, being withdrawn by 1950.

Trams and trolleybuses ran together in Newcastle until the late 1940s. This scene in Northumberland Street shows a trolleybus on the Osborne Road service using the same stop as the trams. Note the front exit in use. (A.D. Packer)

Although the 20 'Q1' type BUTs were normally found on the Gosforth services, their use elsewhere on the system was not unusual. No. 487 stands at the Welbeck Road terminus at Walker, with the shipyard cranes on the River Tyne in the background. (Roy Brook / Paul Watson)

The only BUT trolleybuses with this style of Northern Coachbuilders bodywork were the 25 four-wheelers delivered to Newcastle in 1950. No. 556 is seen in Pilgrim Street, outside the Odeon Cinema, having just completed a Heaton / Jesmond circular journey, the normal haunt for these smaller vehicles. The driver is changing the destination blind for the next journey before proceeding to Central Station. (J. Copland / Paul Watson)

This 1964 scene shows the wiring junction at the 'Fox and Hounds', West Road. On the left is the short working reversing triangle, where trolleybuses drove into the side road and reversed out into West Road. On the right, is the wiring to and from Ferguson's Lane. Note that this wiring junction is within the reversing triangle. Trolleybus 579, the first of the 50 strong second batch of BUT six-wheelers (unofficially referred to as the 'Q2' type), with normal Newcastle pattern destination display, is seen about to cross the junction on its way to Denton. (R.S. Ledgard)

A busy scene showing Sunbeam S7 no 528 making the turn out of Newgate Street into Grainger Street on a service 41 journey to Heaton Road. This wiring link was not provided until 1962, and it allowed vehicles on this service to turn in the city centre without going to Central Station. (P. Price / Travel Lens Photographic)

Another of Newcastle's reversers was the Delaval Road turning point on Whickham View. Here trolleybuses reversed into Delaval Road, which dropped away towards the river. BUT 628, Newcastle's highest numbered trolleybus, is seen reversing here in the 1960s. Upon withdrawal, this vehicle was saved for preservation and is kept at the East Anglia Transport Museum near Lowestoft. (A.B. Cross)

# South Shields

A compact system serving such contrasting locations as industrialised dock areas, as well as seaside beaches and cliffs.

Situated at the mouth of the River Tyne, seven miles downstream from Newcastle, is the town of South Shields, which in trolleybus days was in County Durham. The first trolleybus route, from the Market Place to Fremantle Road, opened in 1936. This service did not replace trams, but served an area beyond the tram routes. The success of this initial route resulted in extensions being made which reached the coast at Marsden and a coastal route between there and the Pier Head near the town centre. In addition most of the tram system serving the docks area was converted to trolleybuses. By the outbreak of war there were 35 blue and primrose trolleybuses in service, all four-wheelers. Apart from one Daimler, a former demonstrator, all these were of Karrier manufacture. Only one tram route remained, this being the reserved track service along King George Road, for which a modern centre-entrance tramcar was purchased in the same year that trolleybuses were inaugurated in the town.

The war years took its toll on the system. The bodies of three vehicles were destroyed by enemy bombing in 1941, although these subsequently returned to service carrying new bodywork. Greatly increased passenger traffic resulted in a route extension to Horsley Hill, and the acquisition of second-hand vehicles from Bradford (comprising an AEC 'Q' type trolleybus and three elderly six-wheelers) and Bournemouth (a single-decker), as well as double-deck vehicles loaned from the same source. Peacetime saw the end of the trams, when trolleybuses took over the King George Road route, this being extended at the town centre end to The Lawe, a promontory overlooking the Tyne estuary where trolleybuses used a reverser to turn. In 1948, the final extension to the system was opened, when a direct route to Horsley Hill came into use.

Post-war vehicles comprised 31 Karrier and Sunbeam four-wheelers, some with utility bodywork. The need to replace the pre-war fleet resulted in second-hand vehicles being purchased in the late 1950s, four utility Karriers (with wooden seats upstairs) coming from Pontypridd. Eight much more modern 8 feet wide Sunbeams came from St Helens.

By the end of the 1950s, there was great concern about

| FACTFILE – SOUTH SHIELDS | |
| --- | --- |
| Opened | 12 October 1936 |
| Closed | 29 April 1964 |
| Route mileage | 16 |

**FLEET PROFILE**
**All 4-wheel double-deck except where denoted**

| | |
| --- | --- |
| Maximum number vehicles in service | 67 |
| Rebodied vehicles | 3 |
| Second-hand vehicles | 17 |
| | |
| AEC | 1 |
| Daimler | 1 |
| English Electric 6-wheel | 3 |
| Karrier | 59 |
| Sunbeam | 18 |
| Thornycroft single-deck | 1 |

| HOW THEY WENT – SOUTH SHIELDS | |
| --- | --- |
| 7 February 1958 | Coast Road |
| 2 October 1961 | The Lawe to the Ridgeway |
| 1962 | Pier Head to The New Crown |
| 29 May 1963 | Horsley Hill, Marsden Inn and Marsden Grotto |
| 29 April 1964 | Tyne Dock and Stanhope Road |

the run-down state of the trolleybus system. The Coast Road route which had a low frequency service and was difficult to maintain because of its exposed location with salt-laden breezes, had already been converted to buses in early 1958. A section of the route along the seafront between the Pier Head and The New Crown was retained for use by extended journeys during the summer until 1962. In 1961 the King George Road (The Ridgeway) to The Lawe service was converted in the face of impending roadworks, and the western suburban routes to Horsley Hill and Marsden followed in 1963. This left the compact network of circular services serving Tyne Dock, where trolleybuses lingered on, their numbers diminishing as new motorbuses became available, until they finally faded away in April 1964.

The initial 1930s trolleybus fleet consisted of 34 of these Karrier E4 four-wheelers with Weymann bodywork. No. 202 was one of the first batch of four which started trolleybus operations in October 1936. It is seen here in post-war days at a mist-shrouded Market Place, which was the system's hub. It is waiting to depart on a journey to Marsden via Horsley Hill, a route opened in 1948. Note the location of the bamboo trolley stick above the lower deck windows – this was standard practice here. (R. Marshall)

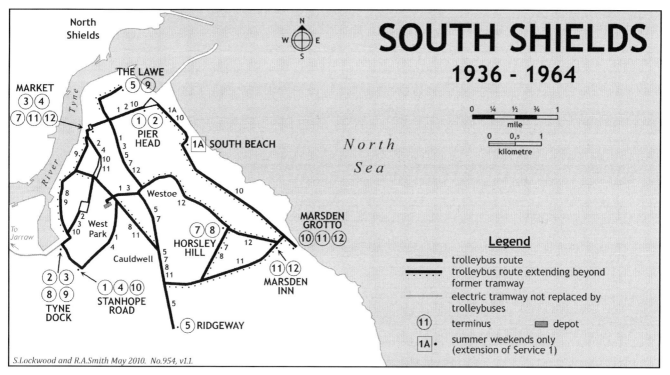

# SOUTH SHIELDS
## 1936 - 1964

**Legend**

▬▬▬ trolleybus route

••••••• trolleybus route extending beyond former tramway

——— electric tramway not replaced by trolleybuses

⑪ terminus ▭ depot

1A• summer weekends only (extension of Service 1)

*S.Lockwood and R.A.Smith May 2010. No.954, v1.1.*

In 1938, South Shields purchased the first Daimler four-wheel trolleybus, which had been visiting systems around the country as a demonstrator. In 1941, its Willowbrook body was destroyed in an enemy bombing raid, and the chassis reappeared in 1943 with a Roe utility body. It is seen here in post-war days standing in the Market Place just yards from where its original body was destroyed. Note the Coventry registration mark.

Although compact, South Shields trolleybus route network served a variety of locations. This 1959 scene shows Roe bodied Karrier 'W' trolleybus no. 241 climbing Redwell Lane, between Marsden Grotto and Marsden Inn, with the North Sea at Marsden Bay in the background. The railway overbridge in the background carried a private railway to a colliery. (J. Copland / A.D. Packer)

Contrasting with the scene in the previous photograph, this view shows the dank Tyne Dock area of the town. No. 263 is in Boldon Lane, between Tyne Dock and Stanhope Road, passing under the railway bridges at Tyne Dock Station on 26 September 1959. This vehicle was one of the last batch of trolleybuses for the town, being a Sunbeam F4 new in 1950. (J. Copland / A.D. Packer)

In the late 1950s, fleet renewals were badly needed to replace the pre-war vehicles. Four of these Karrier 'W's came from Pontypridd in 1957, this one being formerly Pontypridd no. 8. In April 1963, it is seen at the Marsden Grotto terminus, a cliff-top turning circle above the North Sea. (J. Copland / A.D. Packer)

Further fleet replacements came in 1958, these being eight Sunbeam F4s from St Helens. No. 205 is seen at the Pier Head terminus, waiting to depart for Tyne Dock on service 2. (R.F. Mack / Trolleybus Museum Company)

# West Hartlepool

**Although run by West Hartlepool, this was a jointly owned system with its neighbour Hartlepool.**

The first of the three trolleybus systems in County Durham to commence operations was at West Hartlepool, a coastal town situated north of Stockton on Tees. In February 1924, West Hartlepool Corporation commenced a trolleybus service along Stockton Road to the quaintly named terminus at Foggy Furze, replacing a temporary motorbus service which, in turn, had replaced the trams some months earlier. A further route along Grange Road to the Park, also replacing trams, was opened in February 1926. At this time, the adjoining town of Hartlepool to the north-east was administered by a separate Corporation, although West Hartlepool operated the through tram service between the towns. Trolleybus operation on this route commenced in February 1927, and the vehicles used were jointly owned, although operated by West Hartlepool.

The final tram service to be converted was the route along the coast south of the town to the seaside resort of Seaton Carew, where the trams ran along a roadside reservation. Trolleybus operation commenced in March 1927.

Apart from one unsuccessful Railless open-top double-decker, all the 31- strong fleet were single-deck, of Railless, Straker-Clough and Garrett manufacture. The 12 Straker-Cloughs were jointly-owned vehicles used on the Hartlepool service.

In the late 1930s, the fleet was replaced by 14 Daimler 4-wheel double-deckers, plus three very sleek looking Leyland

single-deckers. Eight of the Daimlers were jointly owned with Hartlepool, for use on the joint service between the two authorities. The Foggy Furze route was not included in this modernisation, and it was converted to motorbus operation in 1938.

After the war, it was decided to end trolleybus operation, and the exposed Seaton Carew route was converted to motorbuses at the end of 1949. The remaining routes to the Park and Hartlepool survived until March and April 1953 respectively.

| FACTFILE – WEST HARTLEPOOL | |
|---|---|
| Opened | 28 February 1924 |
| Closed | 2 April 1953 |
| Route mileage | 8 |

| FLEET PROFILE | |
|---|---|
| All 4-wheel, and single-deck unless denoted | |
| Maximum number vehicles in service | 31 |
| Rebodied vehicles | Nil |
| Second-hand vehicles | Nil |
| Daimler double-deck | 14 |
| Garrett | 12 |
| Leyland | 3 |
| Railless | 6 |
| Railless double-deck | 1 |
| Straker-Clough | 12 |

The quaintly named Foggy Furze route was Hartlepool's first trolleybus service. Seen near the terminus is Railless no. 3, accompanied by a tower wagon which was originally a London General B type bus (B2766). (West Hartlepool Corporation Transport)

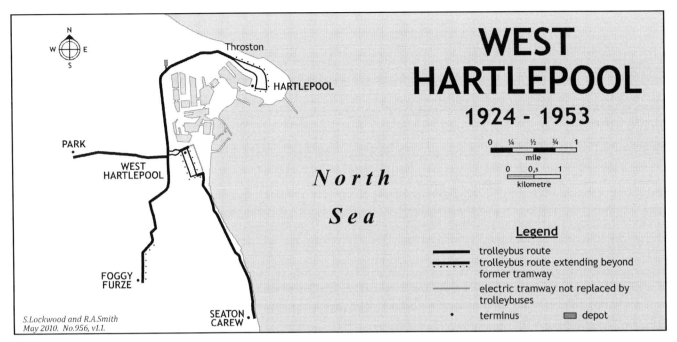

# WEST HARTLEPOOL
## 1924 - 1953

**Legend**

— trolleybus route
······ trolleybus route extending beyond former tramway
— electric tramway not replaced by trolleybuses
• terminus ▭ depot

*S.Lockwood and R.A.Smith*
*May 2010. No.956, v1.1.*

Railless no. 2 is seen in Church Street, West Hartlepool on its way to Foggy Furze in this commercial postcard scene dated 1925. Note that trams are still operating and also the skate hanging down from the rear of the trolleybus. On journeys to the depot (before the Hartlepool route was opened) this was trailed in the tram track to allow the vehicle to operate under its own power.

Straker-Clough no. 18, new in 1927, is seen at St Hilda's, on the terminal loop of the Hartlepool service. Note that it carries two civic emblems on its side. (A.E. Old)

94

Two of the late 1930s fleet are seen in 1947 at the Greenland depot, which was situated about half-way between West Hartlepool and Hartlepool. On the left is no. 7, one of the trio of centre-entrance single-deck Leyland TB7s with Roe bodies. The double-decker is Daimler CTM4 no. 38, again Roe bodied and one of the batch of eight that was jointly owned by the two towns. (A.E. Old)

Two of the 1938 Daimlers stand at the Park terminus in 1947. The leading vehicle, jointly owned no. 33, displays the Hartlepool borough seal on its front. These 'joint' vehicles rarely strayed from the Hartlepool route. Behind is no. 2, wholly owned by West Hartlepool. (A.E. Old)

# Darlington

**One of only two towns whose municipal transport was provided at one period entirely by trolleybuses.**

The railway town of Darlington replaced its entire narrow gauge 4-route municipal tramway system with single-deck trolleybuses within 3 months between January and April 1926. The Cockerton and Haughton Road routes were extended some distance beyond the former tram termini, the latter passing outside the existing borough boundary to reach Haughton le Skerne village. The through route between Harrowgate Hill and Yarm Road, (Eastbourne) was regarded as the 'main line', as it served both the LNER locomotive works in North Road, and the main railway station at Bank Top. It had two restrictive railway bridges en-route which is why single-deck trolleybuses were used. Extensions to the system followed in 1928 to Willow Road and Neasham Road, 1930 to Park Lane and in 1932 to Coniscliffe Road. The Haughton route was extended in 1933 to the northern end of the village, which by that time had been incorporated into the Darlington Borough.

The initial batch of 20 blue and cream Straker centre-entrance single-deckers was soon augmented by four more of the same type. Between 1928 and 1937, further vehicle deliveries were of Ransomes, English Electric, AEC and Leyland manufacture, all to the same basic design which by 1937 was decidedly old-fashioned. Additionally, four Strakers were purchased from Rotherham that year. A change of manager in 1937 resulted in the next fourteen trolleybuses being built to a very modern streamlined design. These were in three batches with Leyland and Karrier chassis and Brush or East Lancashire bodies. The pair of streamlined Karriers did not enter service until 1942.

The Eastbourne service was extended to Lingfield Lane for the benefit of war workers in 1942. In 1943 and 1944, 24 single-deck utility Karrier trolleybuses entered service, enabling scrapping most of the worn-out Straker vehicles.

After the war, the Eastbourne route was extended further to run along McMullen Road as far as the new Patons woollen yarn factory. Some of the cost of the wiring was paid for by the company, and a peak hour service commenced in March 1949. Two months later, six BUT double-deck trolleybuses entered service. These had been ordered in the expec-

## FACTFILE – DARLINGTON

| | |
|---|---|
| Opened | 17 January 1926 |
| Closed | 31 July 1957 |
| Route mileage | 12 |

## FLEET PROFILE
**All 4-wheel, and all single-deck unless denoted**

| | |
|---|---|
| Maximum number vehicles in service | 67 |
| Rebodied vehicles | Nil |
| Second-hand vehicles | 4 |
| | |
| AEC | 11 |
| BUT double-deck | 6 |
| English Electric | 6 |
| Karrier | 26 |
| Leyland | 20 |
| Ransomes | 2 |
| Straker-Clough | 28 |

tation that the roadway under the railway bridges on the busiest route would have been lowered to allow their use. This did not happen, and these high powered (120 hp) vehicles were confined to the only route that could accommodate them, the Willow Road to Park Lane service, on which there was only a relatively modest passenger demand.

Until 1950, Darlington's municipal transport had been provided entirely by trolleybuses, a distinction shared only with Ipswich. However, motorbuses were introduced that year on new routes into housing estates. This was a prelude to the end of trolleybuses in the town, and in November 1951 the through service from Haughton to Harrowgate Hill was converted to motorbus operation. At the same time the 'main line' service between Harrowgate Hill and Eastbourne was curtailed to terminate at Brougham Street, part way along North Road and reduced to peak hour operation. The six double-deckers were sold on to Doncaster in 1952. By the end of 1956 only the Neasham Road to Faverdale trolleybus route remained. As a consequence of the Suez oil crisis, it lingered on until the end of July 1957, when the last trolleybuses , all utility Karriers, ran without ceremony.

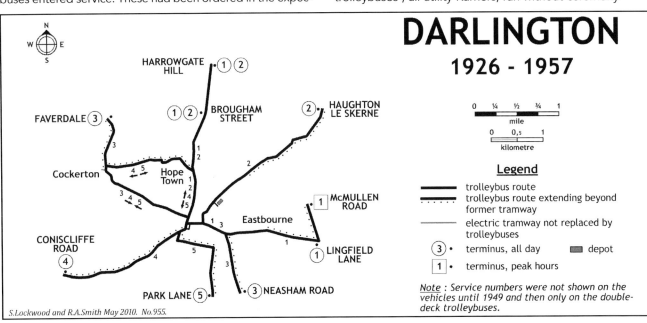

S.Lockwood and R.A.Smith May 2010. No.955.

Twenty centre-entrance Straker-Clough vehicles formed Darlington's first trolleybus fleet. No. 17 is seen at the turning circle on the Green at Haughton, shortly after services commenced. The route was extended to the north-east end of the village in 1933, and this turning circle was removed. The boxy style of the Roe bodywork is evident.

The hub of the system was the junction of Tubwell Row and High Row, where all services converged. This busy early post-war scene shows one of the eleven 1934/5 English Electric bodied AEC 662T vehicles turning from Tubwell Row into High Row. These were fitted with the Estler trolleybase. Darlington and Notts and Derby were the only British operators of this chassis type. Note the '5' (mph) speed restriction sign hanging from the span wire above the road. (W.A. Camwell / National Tramway Museum)

## HOW THEY WENT – DARLINGTON

29 November 1951
 Haughton and
 Harrowgate Hill
6 December 1953
 Park Lane and Willow
 Road
31 October 1954
 Coniscliffe Road
July 1956
 Eastbourne and
 Brougham Street (peak
 hours)
31 July 1957
 Neasham Road and
 Faverdale

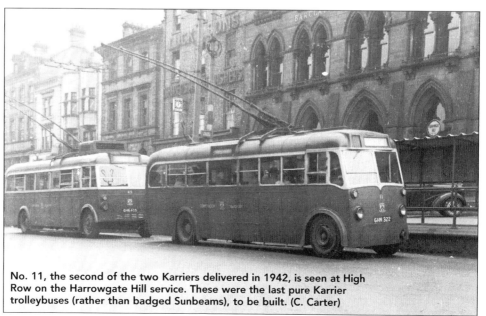

No. 11, the second of the two Karriers delivered in 1942, is seen at High Row on the Harrowgate Hill service. These were the last pure Karrier trolleybuses (rather than badged Sunbeams), to be built. (C. Carter)

# DARLINGTON'S NEW TROLLEY BUSES

**One of the new buses.—[N.D.]**

A number of Darlington's new trolley buses were put into service today. Five of the eight buses ordered have now arrived and the others are expected within a few days.

In addition to the ordinary destination indicator, the buses have a box arrangement for displaying the route number. They have been placed there with an eye to the future. The Borough transport manager (Mr. W. J. H. Penman) told the Northern Despatch today that it was ultimately intended that each route would have its own number, and members of the public would come to know their own particular route by that means.

"A single number," he said, "is more easily picked out, especially at night, than a word, the letters of which appear to run into each other when seen from a distance. It is not intended, however, to introduce the route number system for some time yet."

### COST £1,900 EACH

The new buses, which have cost about £1,900 each, are 32-seaters, like the buses already in use, but they show several improvements.

The most important change on the mechanical side is that they can be manœuvred independent of the overhead wires, having a battery for that purpose. Where at present the whole system may be interfered with when there is trouble with the overhead wires, all that will be necessary with the new buses is for the trolleys to be taken off the wires and the buses can then proceed under their own power. Similarly, at turning points the buses can turn under their own power, and it will be possible to manœuvre them easily in the depot.

The design of the buses is more in keeping with modern practice, having a stream-lined effect. They are painted in a lighter shade of blue than the old buses, and the interior colour scheme is in keeping, the upholstery being of blue hide.

In 1939, the previous conservative look of the vehicles was abandoned and this streamlined style was introduced for new trolleybuses. Fourteen of these were delivered up to 1942, twelve being Leyland TB5s with Brush or East Lancs bodies, and two on Karrier E4S chassis. This press article from July 1939 announces the entry into service of the first of these vehicles. The route number blinds were never used.

From 1943 onwards, 24 of these Brush bodied utility Karrier W vehicles entered service, and they allowed the withdrawal of most of the original 1926 fleet, each one taking the fleet number of the vehicle it replaced. No. 5 is seen turning from Parkgate into Neasham Road in the last year of the system. The partially dismantled wiring of the McMullen Road / Lingfield Lane wires can be seen in the upper foreground. In the background are the overbridges at Bank Top railway station – one reason why single-deck vehicles predominated in this town. All except one of these utility vehicles were sold to Bradford in the mid-1950s, and this one entered service there as no. 787 in 1959 with a new double-deck front-entrance East Lancashire bodywork. It ran in this form until 1971. (Roy Brook / Paul Watson)

This rear view of Karrier 'W' no. 21 in the Haughton Road depot shows the unusual method, due to the wiring layout and limited room, used to run the vehicles out into the depot yard – with reversed trolley poles. (G. Holt / P. Battersby collection)

The first double-deck Darlington trolleybuses were six East Lancashire bodied BUT 9611T vehicles delivered in 1949, numbered 68 to 73 in the fleet. Unable to be used on the busiest route due to low bridges, they spent their time on the Park Lane to Willow Road service. In 1952, when Darlington had started to abandon trolleybus operation, they were sold to Doncaster, and subsequently to Bradford in 1959. No. 69 is seen at High Row in 1949, waiting to depart for Willow Road. It became Doncaster 379, and at Bradford it was put into service with new East Lancashire front entrance bodywork in 1962 as no 831, running until 1971. (British Commercial Vehicle Museum)

This railway overbridge at New Malden carried the Southern Railway's main line to the west of England. Under the bridge ran the London United trolleybus route no 4 (later 604) between Hampton Court and Wimbledon. The narrow bridge caused problems, trolleybuses not being able to pass each other underneath the arch. In this 1934 view, work is underway to widen the roadway, and a 'Diddler' type AEC trolleybus bound for Wimbledon can be seen waiting to pass through. Overhead, the westbound passenger train is hauled by Southern Railway 'U' class 2-6-0 locomotive, one that had originally been a tank engine. As British Railways no 31797, it was scrapped in 1964. (Mirrorpix)

The demise of steam on British Railways roughly co-incided with that of the British trolleybus. In the 1960s, examples of both modes of transport were actively being saved for posterity. This rather bizarre 1967 scene records the face to face meeting of 'USA' 0-6-0 tank locomotive no 30072, and Nottingham's last trolleybus, BUT no 506. The location is the goods shed at Ingrow station, Keighley, on the heritage Keighley and Worth Valley Railway. The locomotive had been bought by the railway and delivered to Ingrow, where it was placed inside the shed, which was already occupied by the trolleybus that Nottingham had sold to enthusiasts in 1966. Whilst the trolleybus is now fully restored and running at the Sandtoft Trolleybus Museum, no 30072 has not been used by the railway for many years, other than as a static exhibit. Ingrow station is only yards from the former Ingrow terminus of Keighley's trolleybus operations. (Author)

Nearing the end of its journey on the joint trolleybus service between Walsall and Wolverhampton on 23rd May 1965, is Walsall Sunbeam trolleybus no 347, one of eight bought from Ipswich in 1962. It is seen in Horseley Fields, Wolverhampton, having just passed under the West Coast main line railway. Visible on the bridge is Stanier 2-6-0 type locomotive no 42957, which was locally based and scrapped in 1966. (J. Copland)

# THE TROLLEYBUSES OF YORKSHIRE

## Tees-side

**A small but long lived system that had three owners and four vehicle liveries throughout its life, and which constructed the last trolleybus route extension in Britain.**

The area served by the Tees-side trolleybus system was dominated by iron and steel works. It did not serve a particular town, but connected settlements on the south bank of the River Tees near Middlesbrough, then situated in Yorkshire's North Riding. Its formation was very protracted. A transport system, initially to be trams, was proposed by a syndicate of local businessmen in the early 1900s to link with the Middlesbrough trams at North Ormesby, and run to the areas of South Bank and Grangetown. The failure of this scheme led the syndicate to promote a trackless trolleybus system under the name of the North Ormesby, South Bank, Normanby and Grangetown Railless Traction Company. Construction of the overhead and depot was completed in 1916, but because of the First World War, the line could not be opened until 1919. By then the undertaking had passed to municipal interests in the form of a joint board – The Tees-side Railless Traction Board (TRTB), consisting of a 2/3rd share held by Eston UDC and the remainder by Middlesbrough Corporation. The route ran from near the Middlesbrough tram terminus at North Ormesby (separated by a level crossing), to Grangetown Square via Cargo Fleet and South Bank, with a branch from South Bank to Normanby. The electrical supply was taken from the adjoining Bolckow, Vaughan steelworks. Ten Railless single-deck trolleybuses in a grey-green livery and constructed by the Cleveland Car Company of Darlington started the operation, followed a year later by six Daimler vehicles bought from the long-closed Rhondda operation. Five Straker trolleybuses were delivered in 1920 and 1921, these being the first of this make built. An interesting vehicle entered the fleet in 1924, in the form of a Tilling Stevens dual-mode trolleybus/petrol electric vehicle. This was used to provide a service beyond the Normanby trolleybus terminus to Eston. It remained unique, and the Board replaced it by conventional motorbuses from 1926.

By 1930, the system was suffering from competition by motorbuses, which were providing a through service to Middlesbrough, something that the trolleybuses were destined never to achieve, but the newly appointed Traffic Commissioner agreed to impose protective fares provided that TRTB renewed its original fleet. Accordingly eight single-deck Ransomes vehicles with a new pale-blue livery entered service in 1932, and the last of the earlier fleet went in 1936 when five Leyland single-deckers were delivered. The final single-deck trolleybus, a unique Sunbeam MF2A, came in 1942, but wartime overcrowding meant that double-deck vehicles were essential, and following wiring alterations at a restrictive bridge in Grangetown, eight utility Sunbeam double-deckers were put into service in 1944 and 1945. By this time a livery of hedge green and cream had been adopted.

Apart from a minor shortening of the route at Grangetown Square terminus in the early years of operation, by 1950 the trolleybus route had not seen any change. The growth of housing beyond Grangetown terminus resulted in an extension being opened to Kingsley Road in April 1950.

| FACTFILE – TEES-SIDE | |
|---|---:|
| Opened | 8 November 1919 |
| Closed | 18 April 1971 |
| Route mileage | 8 |

| **FLEET PROFILE** | |
|---|---:|
| **All 4-wheel single-deck unless denoted** | |
| **Maximum number vehicles in service** | 21 |
| **Rebodied vehicles** | 15 |
| **Second-hand vehicles** | 11 |
| | |
| Daimler | 6 |
| Leyland | 5 |
| Railless | 10 |
| Ransomes | 8 |
| Straker-Clough | 5 |
| Sunbeam | 1 |
| Sunbeam double-deck | 20 |
| Tilling Stevens | 1 |

This was followed later that year by the delivery of seven Sunbeam double-deck trolleybuses, enabling the last of the single-deck fleet to be withdrawn from service. The 'utility' trolleybuses were extensively rebuilt in the late 1950s, but between 1960 and 1965 the entire fleet of fifteen vehicles was progressively rebodied with identical Roe bodies.

A further extension to the Grangetown route (to Fabian Road) opened in 1964, and plans were laid to extend the route as the housing area was developed, creating a circular service connecting with the Normanby route, running via Eston village. In the meantime, the rebuilding of the railway overbridge near the depot at Cargo Fleet resulted in wiring being erected over a temporary quarter-mile diversion during the summer of 1966 to enable the trolleybus service to continue.

By this time, the future of the TRTB undertaking was in doubt, and in 1968 the formation of the Teesside County Borough led to its merging with the municipal transport systems of Middlesbrough and Stockton to form Teesside Municipal Transport (TMT). The new circular route via Eston, the last trolleybus extension in Britain, opened on the final day of the Board's existence, 31 March 1968.

TMT, whose livery was a rather unsuitable turquoise and cream, resolved to retain trolleybus operation for some years, and to this end purchased five front-entrance Sunbeams from Reading Corporation to replace the oldest of the rebodied vehicles. The following year, road construction at North Ormesby resulted in the removal of the turning circle and the installation of a triangular reverser, the last time such a device was constructed in Britain.

However, the trolleybuses, which were a minor part of the new undertaking's operations, were becoming more and more difficult to maintain, and it was decided to close the system as soon as possible. Accordingly, the service came to an end on 4 April 1971, and a valedictory procession and celebration took place two weeks later on 18 April. So ended Britain's penultimate trolleybus system, one of only three to achieve 50 years of operation.

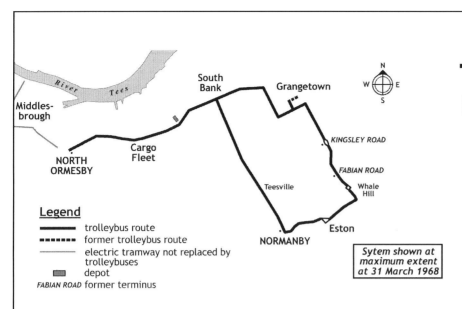

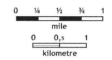

## TEES-SIDE
### Railless Traction Board
### 1919 - 1971

**Legend**

━━━━━ trolleybus route
▬ ▬ ▬ former trolleybus route
───── electric tramway not replaced by trolleybuses
▰ depot
*FABIAN ROAD* former terminus

*Sytem shown at maximum extent at 31 March 1968*

*S.Lockwood and R.A.Smith May 2010. No.957, v1.1.*

Middlesbrough · River Tees · South Bank · Grangetown · North Ormesby · Cargo Fleet · KINGSLEY ROAD · FABIAN ROAD · Teesville · Whale Hill · Eston · NORMANBY

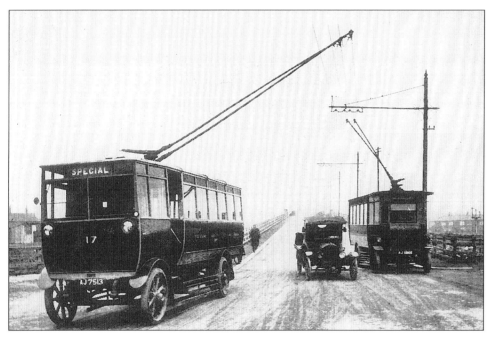

No. 17 was the first ever Straker-Clough trolleybus, built to the specification of the Tees-side manager in conjunction with Clough, Smith and Company, using a modified Straker motorbus chassis. It had a high capacity Roe 36-seat body. New in 1921, it is seen on the left, in company with no. 11, one of the six former Rhondda Daimler Brush vehicles. The scene is at the Cargo Fleet depot, and in the background is the railway bridge built to avoid negotiation of a level crossing. This was the bridge that was temporarily closed in 1966, resulting in a deviation to the trolleybus route over the aforementioned level crossing.

An unusual vehicle, unique in Britain, entered service at Tees-side in 1924. This was no. 22, a Tilling Stevens petrol-electric trolleybus, type PERC1 (Petrol-Electric Railless Chassis type 1). It was used to run a service to Eston, running with booms raised over the wires to Normanby, then in petrol mode for the rest of the journey. The concept was not developed, and the Tees-side undertaking purchased its first motorbuses in 1926 to operate routes beyond the trolleybus system. (R. Marshall collection)

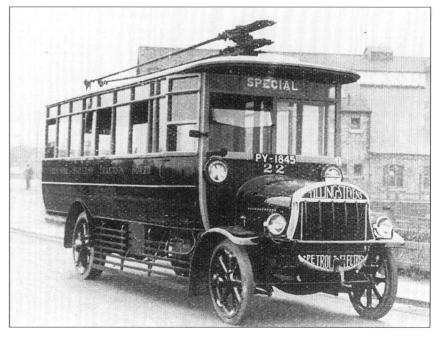

In the late 1920s, the vehicles received pneumatic tyres as seen here in this view of no. 51 (formerly no. 6) at Heworth terminus. The building in the background was originally used to store and recharge batteries for the battery buses that were operated on the service prior to trolleybuses being introduced.

The second York trolleybus fleet consisted of three Roe bodied Karrier E4 vehicles, the first of this four-wheel chassis type to be built. The trio were numbered 30 to 32. No. 30 is seen at East Parade, Heworth soon after entering service. Upon withdrawal in 1935, these vehicles were sold to Chesterfield for a further three years service.

# Kingston upon Hull

**A busy city system which was never as extensive as the former tram network and that latterly operated some of the most distinctive trolleybuses in Britain.**

The East Riding city of Kingston upon Hull, more commonly known as Hull, began trolleybus operations in July 1937, when three routes to Beverley Road, Chanterlands Avenue and Newlands Avenue, all in the north-east of the city, were converted from trams to trolleybuses.

It was not until after the outbreak of war that further trolleybus routes were converted, these being to Holderness Road in February 1940, Anlaby Road in June 1942 and finally to Hessle Road in July 1945, when the last tram ran. The Holderness Road route was unusual in that it crossed a lifting bridge over the River Hull, requiring special connections in the overhead wiring.

The early years of the war saw significant destruction of the city centre by enemy bombing, and although the overhead suffered much damage, there was no loss of vehicles, probably due to the trolleybus depots being located at the outer ends of the routes.

The initial trolleybus fleet consisted of Leyland and Crossley vehicles, painted in a flamboyant blue and white livery and initially proudly proclaiming 'Hull' in large letters on their sides. More Leylands arrived at the outbreak of war, followed in 1945 by 18 utility Sunbeams.

Apart from a short extension to the Anlaby Road route to Meadowbank Road in March 1947, there was never any development of the route network. This was partly due to an earlier co-ordination agreement with East Yorkshire Motor Services, which placed limitations on the sphere of trolley-

bus operations and was the reason why the trolleybus system was smaller than the former tram network.

In the early 1950s the General Manager designed a trolleybus with front entrance and centre exit, suitable for operation by the driver only (although at this time such a concept was not legal on a double deck vehicle). The prototype, with Sunbeam chassis and Roe body, was delivered in late 1952. 15 production vehicles followed in 1954/5, and the appropriately named 'Coronation' trolleybuses took over the routes from Cottingham Road depot, principally on the Beverley Road service. Sadly the potential of these vehicles was never realised, and early in 1960 the decision was taken to replace the trolleybuses with motorbuses. The last trolleybus journey was run without any ceremony by the prototype 'Coronation' class vehicle, at the end of October 1964.

FACTFILE – HULL

Opened 23 July 1937 (public service from 25 July 1937)

| | |
|---|---|
| Closed | 31 October 1964 |
| Route mileage | 17 |

FLEET PROFILE

All 4-wheel double-deck

| | |
|---|---|
| Maximum number vehicles in service | 100 |
| Rebodied vehicles | Nil |
| Second-hand vehicles | Nil |
| Crossley | 20 |
| Leyland | 46 |
| Sunbeam | 50 |

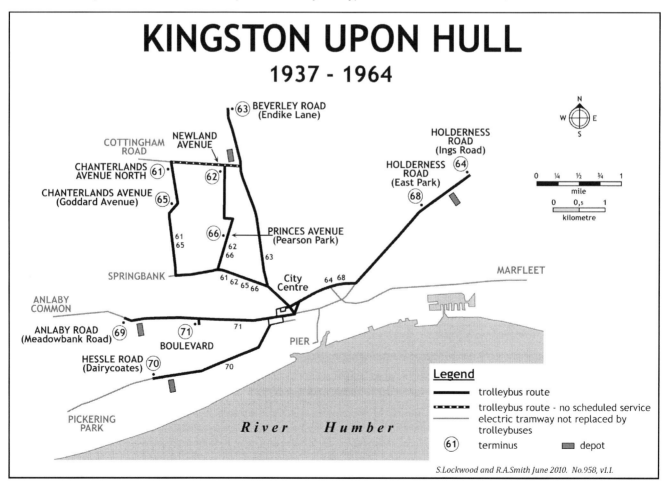

# KINGSTON UPON HULL
## 1937 - 1964

S.Lockwood and R.A.Smith June 2010. No.958, v1.1.

Hull's first trolleybuses were 26 Leyland TB4s with Weymann bodywork. This posed view of no. 1 shows the distinctive livery, and prominent 'Hull' legend on the vehicle's side. Note also the black on white destination blinds, a feature of the pre-war fleet. This vehicle ran in Pontypridd during the Second World War.

Following on from the Leylands were twenty Crossley TDD4s with Cravens bodies. The simplified, but still distinctive post-war livery is seen on Crossley no. 44, which, on 12 September 1958 is turning from Anlaby Road into the Boulevard, a spur of wiring that was used principally on Rugby match days. A reverser was situated a short distance along the street. Note that the destination display showed only the service number and a 'via' description. No. final destination was shown. Passing on the main Anlaby Road service is a post-war Sunbeam 'W' with Roe body, no. 90 in the fleet. (A.D. Packer)

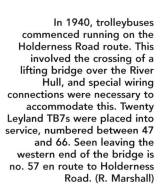

In 1940, trolleybuses commenced running on the Holderness Road route. This involved the crossing of a lifting bridge over the River Hull, and special wiring connections were necessary to accommodate this. Twenty Leyland TB7s were placed into service, numbered between 47 and 66. Seen leaving the western end of the bridge is no. 57 en route to Holderness Road. (R. Marshall)

Although only a modest sized system, Hull was served by four depots. It also had several level crossings on the routes, which caused delays to services. These features are represented in this view of utility Sunbeam 'W' no. 77, with much modernised Brush bodywork, negotiating the narrow exit road from Wheeler Street depot onto Anlaby Road. The Newington railway crossing and signal box are in the background. (J. Fozard)

HOW THEY WENT – HULL

| | |
|---|---|
| 28 January 1961 | Hessle Road |
| 3 February 1962 | Anlaby Road |
| 28 July 1962 | Chanterlands Avenue |
| 21 September 1963 | Holderness Road |
| 16 November 1963 | Newlands Avenue |
| 31 October 1964 | Beverley Road |

The sixteen 'Coronation' type Sunbeam MF2Bs were very distinctive vehicles. This is no 113, new in 1955, showing passengers alighting from the centre doorway.

The 'Coronation' trolleybuses spent their entire life based at the Cottingham Road depot in the north of the city. This is the terminus of the no. 63 Beverley Road service at Endike Lane, where the trolleybuses turned across the dual carriageway. On the left, no. 109 displays its trolley retriever ropes. Other than short-term experiments elsewhere, Hull was the only system to use this equipment. On the right, no. 104 waits to depart for the city centre. (Roy Brook / Paul Watson)

# Keighley

Two trolleybus systems operated here, the first using the Cedes Stoll system, and the second, which was the first to completely close a tram system, used more conventional equipment.

Keighley's municipal tram system was a small three-route undertaking. In 1909 and 1910, motor buses were introduced, linking the tram termini with outlying districts. These vehicles proved unreliable, and a better system was sourced, this being trackless vehicles using the Austrian Cedes-Stoll system of current collection, which used a flexible cable to connect the vehicle to the overhead, rather than rigid trolley poles. The Cedes-Stoll system has already been more fully described in the historical section of the book. The first route, commencing on 3 May 1913 from the Ingrow tram terminus, was to Cross Roads, Lees, a distance of under two miles. The fleet comprised a former Cedes-Stoll demonstrator and two new single-deckers. More routes were opened after the start of the First World War, from Keighley High Street to Oakworth in December 1914 and from the Utley tram terminus to Crosshills and Sutton in February 1915, a distance of over four miles. Further vehicles were delivered with more powerful motors. An extension of the Cross Roads route to Oxenhope was completed in 1916, but was not opened owing to the war. There were

## FACTFILE – KEIGHLEY

| | |
|---|---|
| Opened (Cedes-Stoll) | 3 May 1913 |
| Closed (Cedes-Stoll) | 3 May 1926 |
| Opened (Town routes) | 20 August 1924 |
| Closed (Town routes) | 31 August 1932 |
| Route mileage | 13 (Cedes-Stoll), 3.5 (ex-tram routes) |

## FLEET PROFILE

| | |
|---|---|
| Maximum number vehicles in service | 19 |
| Rebodied vehicles | Nil |
| Second-hand vehicles | Nil |

## HOW THEY WENT – KEIGHLEY

| | |
|---|---|
| 24 October 1921 | Oxenhope to Cross Roads |
| 2 December 1921 | Oakworth |
| 23 May 1924 | Sutton |
| 3 May 1926 | Cross Roads |
| 31 August 1932 | Ingrow, Stockbridge and Utley (ex-tram routes) |

(Story continues on page 113)

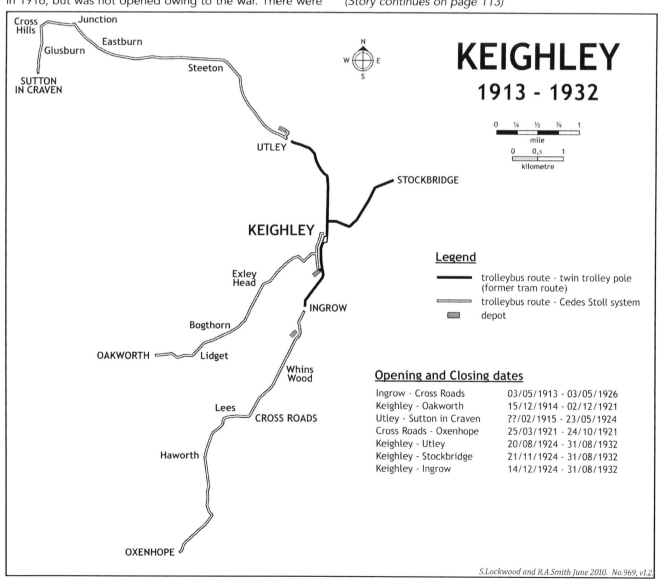

# KEIGHLEY
## 1913 - 1932

### Legend

— trolleybus route - twin trolley pole (former tram route)
═ trolleybus route - Cedes Stoll system
▬ depot

### Opening and Closing dates

| | |
|---|---|
| Ingrow - Cross Roads | 03/05/1913 - 03/05/1926 |
| Keighley - Oakworth | 15/12/1914 - 02/12/1921 |
| Utley - Sutton in Craven | ??/02/1915 - 23/05/1924 |
| Cross Roads - Oxenhope | 25/03/1921 - 24/10/1921 |
| Keighley - Utley | 20/08/1924 - 31/08/1932 |
| Keighley - Stockbridge | 21/11/1924 - 31/08/1932 |
| Keighley - Ingrow | 14/12/1924 - 31/08/1932 |

*S.Lockwood and R.A.Smith June 2010. No.969, v1.2.*

The Utley (Cedes) terminus is seen about 1922. Here, tramcar passengers from Keighley (see tram track in foreground) changed for the Sutton and Crosshills trackless. A newly painted (and un-numbered) Cedes-Stoll car unloads its passengers before crossing the road and reversing. In the distance can be seen the cumbersome overhead junction giving access to the Utley depot. (G. Crowther / J.S. King collection)

A Cedes car reverses at Ingrow Bridge terminus prior to setting off on another journey to Lees (Cross Roads) about 1920. On the right, passengers are queueing for the tram to Keighley town centre. The old horse tram passenger shelter with its clock remained in situ until about 1972. (G. Crowther / J.S. King collection)

Straker–Clough trackless no. 13 with Brush bodywork was new in 1924 and was part of the fleet which replaced Keighley's trams. It is seen at the Brush Company's works at Loughborough before delivery. (J.S. King collection)

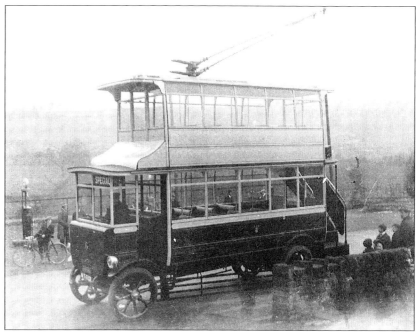

difficulties with the hub-mounted motors, and obtaining spares for Austrian designed equipment, not helped by the enforced winding-up of the Cedes Electric Traction Co. A double-deck car, formerly used on the demonstration route in Hove, was purchased, but the system was in difficulties by 1920 and operation on the routes varied from spasmodic (Cross Roads and Sutton), to non-existent (Oakworth). Efforts were made to revive the system, including a rebuilt car with front wheel steering for the Oakworth route, and the Oxenhope service finally opened in March 1921, only to be closed for good the following October, when the outer terminus reverted to Cross Roads. The Oakworth route closed two months later. One of the cars was given modern electrical equipment and later a new Straker chassis, and all the remaining vehicles (apart from the ex-Hove double-decker) were given front entrances and operated as 'one-man' cars. However the Sutton route closed in May 1924, and the remaining Cross Roads route soldiered on with the modernised car, assisted by one of the new tram replacement Straker vehicles fitted additionally with Cedes collection equipment. The end eventually came when operations were suspended as a result of the May 1926 General Strike, and did not resume.

Undeterred by its experience with trackless vehicles, the Tramways Department replaced its entire tram system with conventional trolleybuses, using eight single and ten double-deck Straker vehicles, between August and December, 1924. Four of the single-deckers had second-hand bodies from former Cedes-Stoll vehicles. This town system was never developed beyond the three routes to Utley, Stockbridge and Ingrow. Like York, the Corporation was obliged to hand over its municipal transport to the West Yorkshire Road Car Co, administered by a Joint Committee, and as a result Keighley's eventful trolleybus history came to an end on 31 August 1932 when crowds turned out to see the last trackless leave the town centre.

# Halifax

This one-route operation, which ran to Britain's highest trolleybus terminus, was opened three years after Halifax bought its trolleybuses.

As early as 1903, Halifax was interested in experimenting with trolleybus operation, but it was not until 1918 that it acquired the two redundant trolleybuses from the Dundee system, which had closed four years earlier. Wartime conditions prevented the equipping of a route, and these Railless vehicles were used as mobile engineering vans for the tramway system, being numbered 103 and 104 in the tram fleet.

In 1921, it was decided to use the trolleybuses to replace motorbuses on a two mile rural route linking the outlying areas of Wainstalls and Mount Tabor to the tram system at Pellon. The triangular reverser at Wainstalls was the highest trolleybus terminus in Britain, at 1027 feet above sea level. Operation began in July 1921. The body of one of the Dundee vehicles (no 104) was found to be beyond repair, and it was equipped with a new front-entrance body built in the Tramways Department workshops, the rebuilt vehicle being given the number 1.

The rough roads along the route proved troublesome, causing the pair of vehicles to spend periods off the road and a further trolleybus was purchased in 1922 to improve reliability. This was no 2, with a Tilling Stevens chassis and a single-deck body again built by the Tramways Department.

The operation lasted until 1926, when motorbuses, seen as more reliable, were introduced on the route and the last trolleybus ran on 24 October. Despite its very hilly terrain, Halifax was never again tempted to re-introduce trolleybuses.

FACTFILE – HALIFAX
| | |
|---|---|
| Opened | 20 July 1921 |
| Closed | 24 October 1926 |
| Route mileage | 2 |
| Maximum number vehicles in service | 3 |
| Rebodied vehicles | 1 |
| Second-hand vehicles | 2 |

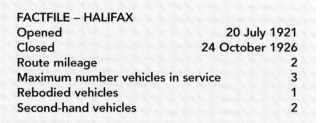

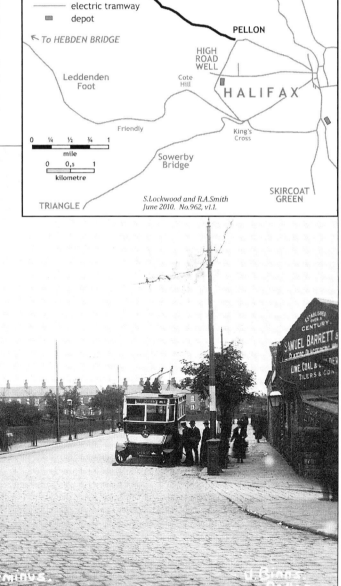

The trackless terminus at Pellon allowed passengers to connect with the tram service into Halifax. This commercial postcard view shows trackless no. 1, a former Dundee Railless vehicle given new bodywork by Halifax. It has its trolley poles anchored down, and it is not clear whether the people on the left are waiting for the trackless or the tram.

# Leeds

**Joint first to open, this trolleybus operation was never more than a very tiny part of the city's public transport provision and it closed after 17 years.**

Leeds and Bradford intentionally opened their respective trolleybuses systems on the same day, 20 June 1911. However, public services in both locations did not start until a few days later. The initial route ran from Aire Street, adjacent to City Square, then in a south westerly direction for almost four miles to New Farnley. Four Railless single-deckers, similar to those at Bradford but with front entrances, ran on the route.

During the First World War, two more routes were added, but these were far away from the New Farnley route, and indeed were outside the city itself. Commencing at the Guiseley White Cross terminus of the Leeds trams, these very rural routes ran to Burley in Wharfedale, near Ilkley, and Otley. For these routes, six additional vehicles were provided, the chassis of these being built by Bradford Tramways, and were similar to those entering service in that city at the same time.

Following vehicle developments in nearby Bradford, double-deck vehicles supplied by Trackless Cars were introduced from 1921, these incorporating a front-wheel-drive arrangement following an experiment on one of the single-deckers. The final double-decker, delivered in 1924 had very stylish low floor bodywork incorporating a centre-entrance. The final single-deckers bought were two box-like AEC vehicles, these coming in 1923.

In 1922, a turning circle was erected part way along the New Farnley route at the Cattle Market. From September, an additional trolleybus service was run to this point, replacing the Whitehall Road tram service and this was the first tram to trolleybus conversion in Britain.

There were no further developments to the system,

**FACTFILE – LEEDS**
Opened 20 June 1911 (Public service from 24 June 1911)

| | |
|---|---|
| Closed | 26 July 1928 |
| Route mileage | 9 |

**FLEET PROFILE**
**All 4-wheel, and single-deck unless denoted**

| | |
|---|---|
| Maximum number vehicles in service | 15 |
| Rebodied vehicles | Nil |
| Second-hand vehicles | Nil |
| | |
| AEC | 2 |
| Bradford Brown | 6 |
| Trackless Cars | 2 |
| Trackless Cars double-deck | 4 |
| Railless | 4 |

Leeds opting to expand and modernise its vast tramway system rather than consider its replacement with trolleybuses. The New Farnley service was cut back to the Cattle Market in March 1926, where the trolleybuses terminated at the turning loop that had been previously erected. However, this was only a temporary measure and this last part of the pioneer route was abandoned in the following July. Motorbus competition on the rural services sealed the fate of the trolleybuses on the Burley and Otley routes and both closed in July 1928.

*The New Farnley route was used by the Railless company, based locally, to test new vehicles. This scene at the rural outer end of the route shows the rear of a Railless demonstrator destined for South America, being passed by Leeds no. 502. (Travel Lens Photographic)*

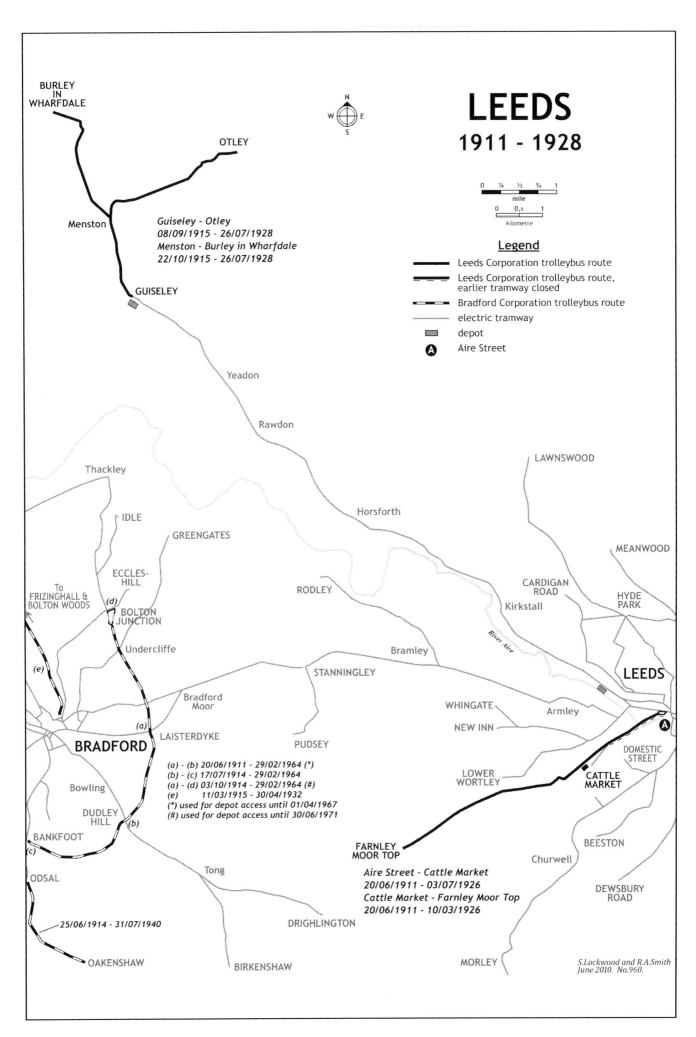

BURLEY
IN
WHARFDALE

OTLEY

Menston

**Guiseley - Otley**
*08/09/1915 - 26/07/1928*
*Menston - Burley in Wharfdale*
*22/10/1915 - 26/07/1928*

GUISELEY

# LEEDS
## 1911 - 1928

0  ¼  ½  ¾  1
mile

0     0,5     1
kilometre

### Legend

——— Leeds Corporation trolleybus route

———  Leeds Corporation trolleybus route,
earlier tramway closed

———  Bradford Corporation trolleybus route

——— electric tramway

▨  depot

Ⓐ  Aire Street

Yeadon

Rawdon

LAWNSWOOD

Thackley

IDLE

GREENGATES

Horsforth

MEANWOOD

ECCLES-
HILL

CARDIGAN
ROAD

HYDE
PARK

To
FRIZINGHALL &
BOLTON WOODS

*(d)*

BOLTON
JUNCTION

Undercliffe

RODLEY

Kirkstall

*River Aire*

*(e)*

Bramley

LEEDS

Bradford
Moor

STANNINGLEY

WHINGATE

Armley

*(a)*

LAISTERDYKE

NEW INN

DOMESTIC
STREET

**BRADFORD**

PUDSEY

Ⓐ

*(a) - (b) 20/06/1911 - 29/02/1964 (\*)*
*(b) - (c) 17/07/1914 - 29/02/1964*
*(a) - (d) 03/10/1914 - 29/02/1964 (#)*
*(e)      11/03/1915 - 30/04/1932*
*(\*) used for depot access until 01/04/1967*
*(#) used for depot access until 30/06/1971*

Bowling

LOWER
WORTLEY

CATTLE
MARKET

DUDLEY
HILL

*(b)*

BEESTON

BANKFOOT

*(c)*

Tong

FARNLEY
MOOR TOP

Churwell

ODSAL

**Aire Street - Cattle Market**
*20/06/1911 - 03/07/1926*
**Cattle Market - Farnley Moor Top**
*20/06/1911 - 10/03/1926*

DEWSBURY
ROAD

*25/06/1914 - 31/07/1940*

DRIGHLINGTON

OAKENSHAW

BIRKENSHAW

MORLEY

*S.Lockwood and R.A.Smith*
*June 2010. No.960.*

This view shows trackless car no. 505, the first of the Bradford / Brown type vehicles with Leeds Tramways front-entrance bodywork. These were used on the rural routes to Otley and Burley, but this one is seen at the New Farnley terminus. Note the primitive wheel guards. (Adam Gordon collection)

The first of the double-deck vehicles of the 1920s had very tram-like rear ends, as shown in this view of no. 510 at New Farnley terminus. Single-deck trackless no. 501 is also evident.

Photographs of vehicles on the Burley in Wharfedale route seem non-existent. However, this commercial postcard view does show the overhead wiring within the village.

# Bradford

**First and last. This was a comprehensive city system which attracted added interest due to the large number of second-hand and rebodied vehicles in the fleet.**

Like Leeds, Bradford's trolleybus service was inaugurated on 20 June 1911, although the public service did not commence until 24 June. This was a mile long route to the east of the city between Laisterdyke and Dudley Hill. It ran along Sticker Lane, linking to tram routes at each end of the route. At first, only one Railless Electric Traction car was used, but this was soon joined by another. In 1914 this route was extended at both ends, from Dudley Hill to Bankfoot in July and from Laisterdyke to Bolton Junction in October. Again, there were connections with the tramway system at both ends. Another route had opened in June 1914, from the Manchester Road tram route at Odsal to Oakenshaw. The following year, 1915, saw the introduction of a further service along Canal Road to Bolton Wood and Frizinghall. This ran from the city centre at Forster Square.

The 18 additional vehicles required for these routes were built by Bradford Tramways themselves, and were 29-seat front-entrance single-deckers. During the First World War, the two original trolleybuses were taken out of passenger service and converted into 'trolley lorries' carrying goods and parcels around the tram system using a skate in the tracks. For a period, one of these vehicles travelled once a day to Leeds, carrying cinema films. In late 1920 the first double-decker was placed in service, this being a 51-seater of ungainly appearance. Two years later a second version was built, in the form of a large 59-seater with twin-steer front axles. Six single-deckers, Bradford built but using AEC

| FACTFILE – BRADFORD | |
|---|---|
| Opened | 20 June 1911 |
| Closed | 26 March 1972 |
| Route mileage | 47 |

| FLEET PROFILE | |
|---|---|
| **All 4-wheel double-deck unless denoted** | |
| Maximum number vehicles in service | 188 |
| Rebodied vehicles | 134 |
| Second-hand vehicles | 85 |
| | |
| ADC single-deck | 7 |
| AEC | 97 |
| Bradford single-deck | 24 |
| Bradford | 1 |
| Bradford 6-wheel twin-steer | 1 |
| BUT | 50 |
| English Electric single-deck | 11 |
| English Electric 6-wheel | 25 |
| Garrett single-deck | 8 |
| Karrier | 56 |
| Leyland single-deck | 17 |
| Sunbeam | 29 |

parts, followed in 1923, these being usually operated by 'one-man'.

A service to the village of Clayton, to the south west of the city, was added to the trolleybus operation in 1926, this being notable because it ran into the city centre duplicating

Six of these Bradford-built trolleybuses, designed for operation with one-man, entered service in 1923. Numbered 523 to 528, they were later fitted with pneumatic tyres and lasted until 1931.

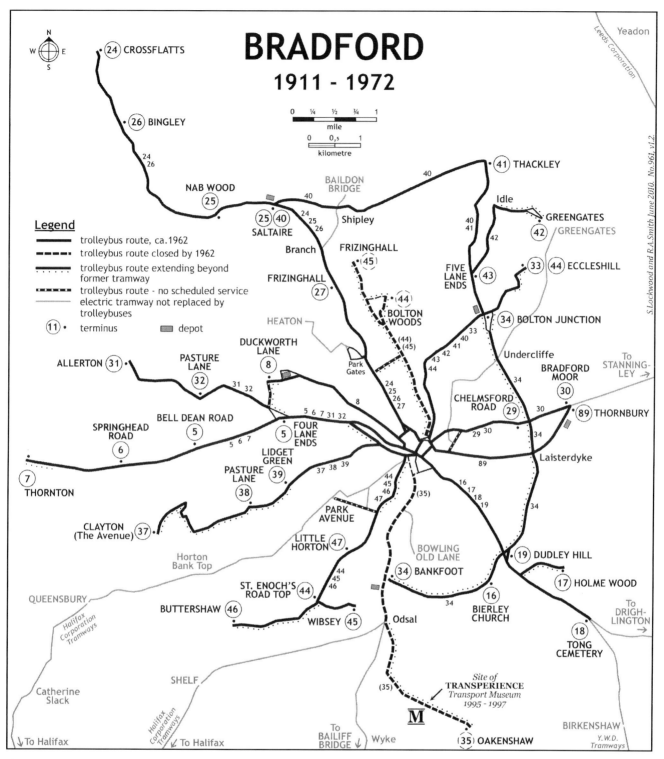

# BRADFORD
## 1911 - 1972

**Legend**

— trolleybus route, ca.1962
---- trolleybus route closed by 1962
····· trolleybus route extending beyond former tramway
-·-·-· trolleybus route - no scheduled service
— electric tramway not replaced by trolleybuses
(11)• terminus  ▭ depot

S.Lockwood and R.A.Smith June 2010. No.961, v1.2

the existing tram service from Lidget Green. In 1928 it was linked as a through service to the Oakenshaw route, which itself had been extended from its Odsal terminus along Manchester Road into the centre in 1927. For these developments, 32 single-deckers of Garrett, ADC and Leyland manufacture were acquired.

A momentous event in December 1929 was the conversion of the Allerton tram route to trolleybuses, quickly followed in March 1930 by the conversion of the Saltaire via Thackley tram service, and a year later by the branch to Greengates via Idle. 36 new English Electric trolleybuses, including 25 six-wheel double-deckers were thus added to the fleet. The 11 single-deckers were the last of this kind to be purchased new. Amongst this growth there was one contraction – the Canal Road service to Bolton Woods and Frizinghall, which was abandoned in 1932 as a result of an

agreement with a competing bus company (which also removed motorbus competition from the Clayton trolleybus route).

Further tram to trolleybus route conversions followed during the 1930s, bringing trolleybuses to Eccleshill and Thornton in 1934, Duckworth Lane in 1935, Tong Cemetery in 1938 and the long route to Crossflatts via Saltaire and Bingley, in 1939. For these routes, modern four-wheel double-deckers of AEC and Karrier makes were purchased.

The war halted further progress, and the lightly used City to Oakenshaw service, for which the electrical infrastructure was in need of renewal, was converted to motorbuses in 1940. Four AEC trolleybuses operated on loan from Southend in 1942 and this prompted the Corporation to introduce a lighter blue livery. Nine of the 1930s double-deckers were re-bodied with Brush utility bodywork, these being the very first examples of such rebuilding in the fleet. Added to this, ten Sunbeams ordered by Johannesburg joined the fleet in 1942. Their wartime utility bodies were 8 feet wide, and special dispensation had to be given for them to operate. 37 new Karriers with utility bodies came in 1945 and 1946, these becoming the backbone of the post-war trolleybus operations.

However, the general policy of replacing trams with trolleybuses ceased after the war because of the difficulty of obtaining new trolleybuses in the early post-war years, and the remaining tram routes became motorbus operated. The only exception to this was a cross-city extension of the Saltaire/Crossflatts service along Barkerend Road to Bradford Moor, restoring a link broken in 1939. 20 BUT trolleybuses with Roe or Weymann bodies entered service between 1949 and 1951, these being the last new trolleybuses purchased by Bradford. Some of them had been ordered to replace trams on the Undercliffe service, which was actually converted to motorbuses as a direct consequence of the nationalisation of the city's municipal electricity department.

At this point, Bradford's trolleybuses faced an uncertain future. However, a change of management, in the person of Chaceley Humpidge, resulted in a new policy of trolleybus development. The 1950s therefore saw a significant expansion to the system, beginning in 1952 when the City to Thornbury motorbus service became trolleybus operated using wiring already installed for depot workings. Trolleybuses began operation on the Little Horton Lane route in 1954, being extended to Wibsey in 1955, with a new branch to Buttershaw opening in 1956. There were also extensions to the routes to Clayton (1956), Eccleshill (1959) and finally a branch from the Tong Cemetery route to Holme Wood in 1960. In the city centre, a notable improvement was the construction of wiring along Broadway, giving a direct link between Forster Square and Town Hall Square, and allowing a through service to

be operated between Eccleshill and St Enoch's Road Top (on the Wibsey route). This expansion was achieved with minimum capital outlay through the purchase of second-hand trolleybuses being prematurely withdrawn in other towns. In two cases, namely Notts and Derby and Darlington, the whole serviceable fleet was acquired. Other bargains came from Llanelly, St Helens, Brighton, and Hastings. Some of these, together with many older native ones were rebodied to very modern standards, those being dealt with in the late 1950s having front entrances, saloon heaters and, experimentally, trolley retrievers.

By the time that the system celebrated its 50th anniversary in June 1961, the operation was at its peak, with 203 trolleybuses. The majority of the main roads out of the city were served by trolleybuses, and in the city centre, the overhead wiring was arranged, by means of duplicate wiring and passing loops, to allow maximum flexibility of operation.

In 1962, another change of management resulted in large orders being placed for motorbuses. Coupled with impending massive re-development of the city centre this

Fifteen single-deckers joined the fleet in 1926 and 1927, these being of Garratt and AEC manufacture. They were used on a new route to Clayton. The AECs were badged as ADC (Associated Daimler Company), this being the joint AEC and Daimler marketing organisation which operated in the 1920s. This is no. 529 (incorrectly numbered as 522), which was one of four with Strachan centre-entrance bodies.

Leyland supplied the chassis, based on the Lion motorbus design, for sixteen centre-entrance trolleybuses in 1928/9. Bodywork was also by Leyland, the first ten (544 to 553), being to the style shown here in this posed view of no. 549 outside the Town Hall. The later batch of six (554 to 559) had a slight 'V' shape to the front bodywork. All had been withdrawn by 1940.

meant the fortunes of the trolleybus would now be on the wane. A legacy of the previous regime ensured that the final twelve rebodied trolleybuses, mounted on third hand BUT chassis, and secondhand Sunbeam chassis from Doncaster and Mexborough respectively, entered service in 1962 and 1963. These vehicles were some of the best appointed public transport vehicles in the country, and were considered by the public to be superior to the mass-produced motorbuses coming into service at the same time.

The first route to close in this period was the Bradford Moor to City service near the end of 1962. Between then and 1967, several more services followed, as a result of major road works or route rationalisations. There followed a hiatus until 1970 and early 1971, when further reorganisations took place.

Even then, there was still a sizeable fleet of 51 vehicles, running on seven routes However, it was not now regarded as economic to maintain such an unco-ordinated network, and plans were laid to replace the remaining trolleybuses as soon as possible. Five routes were converted to motorbuses in the mid-summer of 1971, leaving just those operated from Duckworth Lane depot, which for some time was Britain's only wholly trolleybus depot. Motorbuses were introduced here in November 1971, partly replacing trolleybuses. In February 1972, trolleybus operation ceased suddenly owing to a miners' strike which rationed electricity supplies. However, trolleybuses returned to the streets in early March, to run for three weeks until the final public journeys on the evening of Friday 24 March 1972. Following the operation of pre-booked public tours, the final civic journey took place on the afternoon of Sunday 26 March, this marking the end, for the present, of the trolleybus on the streets of Britain.

| HOW THEY WENT – BRADFORD | |
|---|---|
| 30 April 1932 | Bolton Woods & Frizinghall via Canal Road |
| 1 August 1940 | Oakenshaw |
| 17 November 1962 | Bradford Moor to City |
| 17 November 1962 | Broadway link (city centre) |
| 31 October 1963 | Crossflatts via Saltaire |
| 29 February 1964 | Bolton to Bankfoot |
| 31 October 1964 | Eccleshill |
| 1 April 1967 | Tong Cemetery & Holme Wood |
| 30 May 1970 | Clayton (The Avenue) to Clayton (Black Bull) |
| 27 February 1971 | Allerton |
| 30 June 1971 | Saltaire via Thackley & Greengates via Idle |
| 31 July 1971 | Wibsey & Buttershaw |
| 31 July 1971 | Clayton |
| 24 March 1972 | Duckworth Lane |
| 24 March 1972 | Thornton to Thornbury |

English Electric supplied 24 of these 56 seat six-wheel double deckers between 1930 and 1931, to
replace trams on the Allerton and Saltaire via Thackley routes. They were numbered between 572 and
595, and an additional similar vehicle, previously a demonstrator, no 596 came in 1932. This is no 592,
seen in operation near Idle on the route from Saltaire to Bradford via Thackely, with a view across the
Aire valley in the background.  Eleven English Electric front entrance single deckers (nos 561 to 571) were
placed in service at the same time. Some of these double-deckers saw further service at Newcastle (no
592 became Newcastle no. 1) and South Shields during and towards the end of the war. (D.M. Bentley)

This pre-war commercial view of Town Hall Square shows, in the upper foreground, mixed tram and
trolleybus overhead. The trolleybus wiring on the left are the Oakenshaw route wires, connecting to
the terminal loop of the Thornton service. This allowed the cross-city Oakenshaw to Clayton service
to operate. The rear of one of the Leyland 'Lion' trolleybuses can be seen in the far background.

One of the larger batches of new trolleybuses delivered in the late 1930s were the 42 AEC 661Ts, with English Electric metal framed bodywork. Seen in Thornton Road near Town Hall Square in early post-war days is no. 655, in the light blue lined livery adopted during the war. These vehicles were numbered between 635 and 676, and sixteen of these were rebodied in the 1950s by Crossley or East Lancashire. Another (no. 639) was given the Northern Coachbuilders body from no. 620. 655 received a new East Lancashire body in 1956 and ran until 1967. (W.J. Haynes / Paul Watson)

The first of many Bradford trolleybuses to be re-bodied were nine of the 1934 batch of AEC661Ts in 1944. Their English Electric bodies were in dire need of renewal and they were given Brush utility bodies similar in styling to those entering service elsewhere on new Sunbeam / Karrier 'W' chassis. No. 601 is seen at the city centre terminus of the Duckworth Lane route in Sunbridge Road on 19 January 1952. (J. Copland / A.D. Packer)

Bradford took delivery of thirty-seven Karrier 'W's between 1945 and 1946. Nos 703 to 714 had Roe bodies, 715 to 733 Park Royal, and 734 to 739 Roe had a relaxed utility specification. All were rebodied in the late 1950s by East Lancashire with rear or front-entrance bodywork, and some survived to the very end of the system. This view dated 29 September 1951 shows Park Royal bodied no. 730 completing the turn at Bradford Moor terminus before departing on the cross city service to Saltaire. (J. Copland / A.D. Packer)

In 1946 and 1947, the remainder of the 1934 AECs were given new bodywork by Northern Coachbuilders. The first six of these were to a rather severe styling, as shown in this view of no. 621 at the Bolton terminus of the suburban service to Bankfoot. It was withdrawn in 1961. (W.J. Haynes / Paul Watson)

In the early 1950s, thirteen new Crossley bodies were placed on 1938 AEC chassis (seven vehicles) and 1938-1940 Karrier E4 chassis (six vehicles). One of the Karriers, no. 688, is seen in Thornbury depot yard in 1952 with its brand new body. Alongside is 1949 Roe bodied BUT 748. (J. Fozard)

Following the delivery of the 20 BUT vehicles in between 1949 and 1951, all trolleybuses new to Bradford were second-hand. Ten Karrier 'W's came from Llanelly in 1953 in chassis form only, and they entered service in 1956 with new East Lancashire bodywork These incorporated a sliding door at the rear entrance. The first one, no. 775, is seen in Thornton Road at Bell Dean Road on 23 February 1956, shortly after entering service. Note that, although the front axle was widened to suit the 8 feet wide body, the rear axle remained at 7 feet 6 inches wide, resulting in the body overhanging the rear wheels. (J. Copland / A.D. Packer)

After entering service in 1953 with their original Weymann bodies, the ten early 1940s AECs from the Notts and Derby system (nos 587 to 596) were given new East Lancashire bodies in late 1957 and early 1958. No. 588 is seen in Town Hall Square working on the cross-city service 44 between Eccleshill and St Enoch's Road Top, introduced in 1957. This vehicle, together with nos 589 and 592, survived until 1968, when they were the last AEC trolleybuses to operate in Britain. (V. Nutton / Travel Lens Photographic)

Two of the Darlington Karrier 'W' single-deckers that Bradford acquired in 1954 were prepared for service in single-deck form, and numbered T403 and T404. Whilst the latter never saw service, and was subsequently dismantled, T403 was put on the road during the Suez crisis of 1956/7. It was popular for enthusiasts' tours and is seen here on such a duty on 6 October 1957. The location is Buttershaw terminus, to where trolleybuses were extended in 1956. Standing at the terminal stop is 'Notts and Derby' BUT 767. In 1959, T403 re-entered service as no. 785 with a new East Lancashire front-entrance double-deck body, and it ran until 1971. (J. Copland / A.D. Packer)

The eight Darlington single-deckers that came to Bradford in 1957, following the end of trolleybuses in their home town, were rebodied as double-deckers with East Lancashire front-entrance bodywork in 1959, and numbered 786 to 793. No. 788 was given an experimental Ohio Brass trolley base and springs, and trolley retrievers. It is seen in this form in Thornton Road. This equipment was subsequently removed. (V. Nutton / Travel Lens Photographic)

Bradford had several depots for its bus and trolleybus fleet, a legacy of the former tram network where depots were placed at the ends of the routes. From the mid-1930s until 1971, Duckworth Lane depot housed exclusively trolleybuses, and from the late 1960s it was the only 'all-trolleybus' depot in Britain. From 1960 onwards the majority of its allocation was the rebodied Karrier 'W' vehicles with front-entrance bodywork. On 27 March 1962, four of these vehicles are seen, from the left nos 706, 729, 728 and 705. Also in view are two 'visitors' an AEC motorbus and a 'Notts and Derby' BUT. No. 705 still retains its experimental trolley retrievers, one of six of this type so fitted in 1960. (J. Copland / A.D. Packer)

All but one of the six BUTs bought from Doncaster (which had originated with Darlington) entered service in 1962 with an updated style of East Lancashire body. These fine looking vehicles with heaters and front-entrance were some of the best appointed public transport vehicles in Britain. Numbered 831 to 835, the first of the batch is seen when newly into service at the Crossflatts terminus, between Bingley and Keighley, and the most northerly point reached by Bradford trolleybuses. Behind 831 is no. 696, one of the ten wartime 'Johannesburg' vehicles which were rebodied by East Lancashire in 1956.

The final batch of trolleybuses to enter service in Bradford were the seven former Mexborough and Swinton Sunbeam F4s, which formerly had Brush single-deck bodies. Two of these are seen in September 1964 at The Avenue Clayton, on the extension opened from the Black Bull in 1956.

# BRADFORD'S SECOND-HAND TROLLEYBUSES

Some of Bradford's second-hand trolleybuses had relatively short lives – some examples are shown here.

The oldest of the former Notts and Derby trolleybuses acquired in 1953 were seven Weymann bodied AEC 661Ts new in 1937. They were numbered 580 to 586, and used as temporary replacements for other vehicles away for rebodying, all being withdrawn by 1958. This is no. 584 at the rural terminal of the Allerton route at Prune Park Lane. (R.F. Mack)

Two BUT 9611Ts joined the fleet in 1959, these being from Brighton. Part of a batch of six, these were the only ones with English Electric motors. Numbered 802 and 803, they had a short life in Bradford and were withdrawn in 1963 and 1962 respectively. No. 802 is seen at the Halls Ings terminus of the 89 service to Thornbury. It came to grief when it overturned in June 1963.

The twelve Sunbeam Ws arriving from Hastings in 1959 entered service in their original form, although it was the intention to eventually rebuild and re-body them. A change of policy in the early 1960s meant that this never happened and consequently they had short lives in Bradford, the final three being withdrawn in October 1963. Ten had Park Royal bodies (804 to 813) the other two having Weymann bodies (814, 815). No. 812, seen here at the Union Street terminus of the Tong Cemetery service on 29 April 1961, had the shortest life of this type in Bradford, running for only 23 months during 1961 and 1962. (J. Copland / A.D. Packer)

# Huddersfield

An extensive and very popular system that ran in and around this medium sized industrial town. The fleet of six-wheelers ran in a distinctive bright red and cream livery, with many routes reaching out to the Pennine moors and hills.

In 1933, a year following the delivery of new trams, Huddersfield decided to experiment with trolleybus operation on the Almondbury route where the tramway was in need of renewal. The route opened on 4 December 1933 when six trolleybuses, of varying combinations of chassis and body to assess suitability, entered service. These included three Karrier vehicles, manufactured in the town. All were six-wheelers with high seating capacity to match that of the trams. Huddersfield never wavered from this specification, even after legislation was changed to allow longer vehicles on two-axles, and its trolleybuses became renowned for their smooth riding qualities.

The success of the initial trial led to trolleybuses replacing trams on the cross-town Waterloo to Lindley and Outlane services, where a further 24 Karrier trolleybuses entered service in November 1934. The Outlane terminus, on the very edge of the Pennine moorland, 908 feet above sea level, was the highest point reached by trolleybus in Britain, apart from Halifax's Wainstalls terminus which had been closed by that time

It was now intended to replace all the tram system by trolleybuses, and in 1936, the Newsome service was converted, followed in 1937 by that to Crosland Moor, 1938 to Birkby, Sheepridge, Bradley and Marsden, and 1939 to Lockwood, Longwood and West Vale. The Crosland Moor and Newsome services extended beyond the tram termini to Crosland Hill and Newsome South respectively. In addition, the Sheepridge route was extended to form a circular service via Woodhouse Hill, which was the steepest hill on the system at 1 in 8½. The outbreak of war delayed the final tram route conversion to Brighouse, but the last tram ran during the blackout on 29 June 1940 allowing the final part of 108 broadly similar Karrier trolleybuses (by then built in Wolverhampton following the transfer of trolleybus production) to enter service. These distinctive vehicles, with a three-window arrangement at the front upper deck, had a two-tone red livery and an attractive cream swoop on the lower front panels. The total fleet strength was 140. The only part of the tram system to be converted to motorbuses was part of the Honley route beyond Lockwood, where a low bridge prevented trolleybus operation.

A feature of the system was the legal requirement to use a coasting brake, limiting the maximum speed of the vehicle to around 15mph when descending several of the steepest hills. On some gradients, the requirement was later relaxed, but it remained on others until the end of trolleybus operations.

Fleet renewals commenced after the war, when 52 Karrier/Sunbeam vehicles with Park Royal bodies arrived between 1947 and 1949. These retained the three-window feature at the front upper deck. Among older vehicles disposed of at this time were twelve Brush bodied Karriers new in 1934, which were sold to Reading, some of these seeing further service. In March 1949, the first post-war route extensions opened, when the Sheepridge circular route was altered to run to two separate termini in council housing estates at Brackenhall and Riddings. This involved

| FACTFILE – HUDDERSFIELD | |
|---|---|
| Opened | 4 December 1933 |
| Closed | 13 July 1968 |
| Route mileage | 42 |

| FLEET PROFILE | |
|---|---|
| All six-wheel double-deck | |
| Maximum number vehicles in service | 140 |
| Rebodied vehicles | 74 |
| Second-hand vehicles | Nil |
| | |
| AEC | 1 |
| BUT | 24 |
| Karrier | 165 |
| Ransomes | 1 |
| Sunbeam | 49 |

the abandonment of the short route along Ashbrow Road.

At the end of 1949, some of the pre-war Karrier vehicles were substantially rebuilt and given new Roe bodywork. This process continued until 1953, when a total of 28 vehicles had been dealt with. Subsequently 41 of the early post-war vehicles were rebodied by Roe or East Lancashire by 1962. A final four rebuilds appeared in 1963, and unusually these comprised older bodies from vehicles previously rebuilt in the mid-1950s, the chassis of which were scrapped. New vehicles continued to be purchased, 14 Sunbeams arriving in 1951/2. Two batches of BUT vehicles arrived in 1953 and 1956 and the final new trolleybuses were 10 Sunbeams delivered in 1959, these being the last ever 6-wheel trolleybuses to be built for use in Britain.

A contraction of route mileage came in 1955, when the Brighouse route was abandoned beyond the borough boundary at Fixby. However, a short extension to the Bradley route opened in April of the following year when a branch was opened into an area of new housing at Keldregate, using some overhead materials salvaged from the Brighouse route. The final addition to the wiring came in 1957, when a turning loop was opened at Salendine Nook to cater for a schools complex. This was the only instance where a trolleybus turning facility was provided solely for schools use.

Generally the system was extensive, very well maintained and popular with the public. Only trolleybuses provided public transport along the town's main shopping streets, the corporation's motorbuses (jointly owned by British Railways), together with other company buses, operated from lesser streets or the bus station on the edge of the centre. Many of the routes were scenic, running up or along the valley sides. The long (7 miles) service on Manchester Road to Marsden ran along the Colne Valley and terminated at the very edge of the Pennines.

In the very early 1960s the decision was made to convert the other routes running outside the borough (i.e. to West Vale and Marsden) to motorbus operation. In 1962, the Corporation decided by a single vote to abandon trolleybus operation altogether, and the routes were closed in a controlled manner, generally one conversion per year until 1968. An illuminated trolleybus operated in service during the last week of operation, before carrying dignitaries on the last official journey to Outlane on Saturday 13 July.

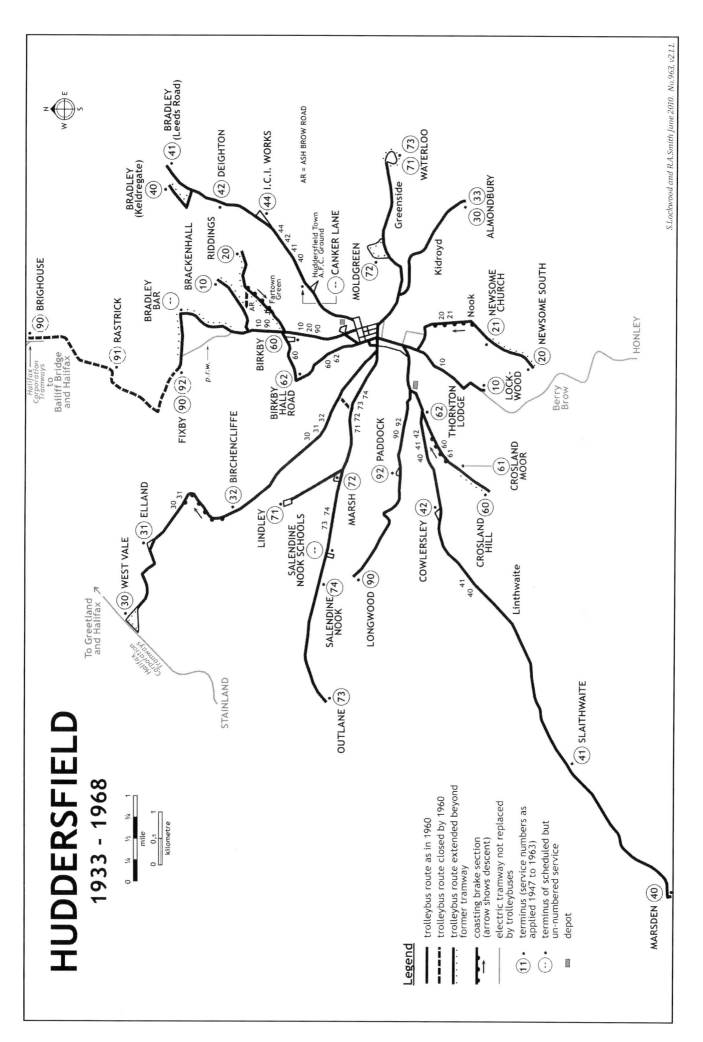

# HUDDERSFIELD
## 1933 - 1968

**Legend**

trolleybus route as in 1960
trolleybus route closed by 1960
trolleybus route extended beyond former tramway
coasting brake section (arrow shows descent)
electric tramway not replaced by trolleybuses
terminus (service numbers as applied 1947 to 1963)
terminus of scheduled but un-numbered service
depot

mile
kilometre

S.Lockwood and R.A.Smith June 2010. No.963, v2.1.1.

MARSDEN (40)

SLAITHWAITE (41)

Linthwaite

OUTLANE (73)

WEST VALE (30)
ELLAND (31)

STAINLAND

To Greetland and Halifax
Halifax Corporation Tramways

SALENDINE NOOK (74)

LONGWOOD (90)

SALENDINE NOOK SCHOOLS (--)

LINDLEY (71)

BIRCHENCLIFFE (32)

MARSH (72)

PADDOCK (92)

COWLERSLEY (42)

CROSLAND HILL (60)

CROSLAND MOOR (61)

THORNTON LODGE (62)

Berry Brow

HONLEY

LOCKWOOD (10)

NEWSOME SOUTH (20)

NEWSOME CHURCH (21)

ALMONDBURY (33)

Kidroyd

Nook

WATERLOO (73)
(71)

Greenside

MOLDGREEN (72)

CANKER LANE (--)

Huddersfield Town A.F.C. Ground

AR = ASH BROW ROAD

I.C.I. WORKS (44)

DEIGHTON (42)

BRADLEY (Leeds Road) (41)

BRADLEY (Keldregate) (40)

RIDDINGS (20)

BRACKENHALL (10)

BRADLEY BAR (--)

Fartown Green

BIRKBY (60)

BIRKBY HALL ROAD (62)

p.r.w.

FIXBY (90) (92)

RASTRICK (91)

BRIGHOUSE (90)

Halifax Corporation Tramways to Bailiff Bridge and Halifax

Huddersfield's first trolleybuses were six vehicles of differing makes. Three had Karrier E6 chassis, built in the town. This is no. 2 on test before the first route to Almondbury opened in December 1933. Note the radiator shaped outline on the front of the Park Royal bodywork – this was a common feature on trolleybuses at this time.

Over 100 of these Karrier E6s with streamlined bodywork were delivered between 1937 and 1940 to replace the majority of the trams. Several of these are seen in New Street in 1939, just prior to the street being closed to allow removal of the tram rails. During this process, overhead was erected on an alternative route to enable the service to be maintained. All the vehicles in view carry Park Royal bodywork, and the only identifiable vehicle is on the left, which is no. 128, new in early 1939. The nearest trolleybus is operating on service 81 to Birkby, a short-lived service number that was changed to 61 early in the war.

Ten of the E6s, numbered 116 to 125, carried Weymann bodies to this styling, which was more bulbous at the front than the Park Royal version. They also had electro-magnetic contactors rather than the electro-pneumatic type on the Park Royal bodied vehicles. Because of the staccato sound from these, they were nicknamed 'Messerschmitts', after the German fighter plane. This is no. 521 (formerly no. 121) in John William Street shortly before it was withdrawn in 1955. All Huddersfield's trolleybuses had 400 added to their fleet numbers in 1942. (Roy Brook / Paul Watson)

28 of the pre-war Karriers were rebodied between 1949 and 1953 with Roe bodies which included strong metal bumpers front and rear. Amongst these was no. 523, which originally had a Weymann body. It is seen at the terminal loop at Cowlersley, a regularly used short-working of the Marsden route. This was a typical 'round the houses' loop around side streets. The vehicle was withdrawn in 1962, by which time its bumpers had been removed. (J. Copland / Paul Watson)

Fourteen of these Sunbeam MS2s entered service in 1951/2. Numbered 593 to 606 in the fleet, their Roe bodies were similar, but longer, than the rebodied Karriers. No. 594 is seen negotiating road resurfacing work in Blackmoorfoot Road, on the climb to Crosland Hill. This activity is attracting much attention from children and adults alike. (Roy Brook / Paul Watson)

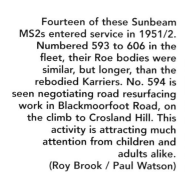

After buying, almost exclusively, Karrier or Sunbeam products, Huddersfield took delivery of twelve BUT 9641T vehicles in 1953. These were numbered 607 to 618 and had East Lancashire bodies. The first of these is seen at the Birkby terminus about 1960, after its bumpers had been removed. This was another 'round the houses' terminal loop, along Woodbine, Cobcroft and Wasp Nest Roads. The loop was originally wired just before the war to accommodate football specials to the nearby Fartown rugby ground. However, in 1945 the reversing movement for service trolleybuses at the road junction (in the far background of this view) ceased, and the service terminal was moved to this point in Woodbine Road, which was actually in the district of Fartown. (Roy Brook / Paul Watson)

More BUTs followed in 1956, a further twelve being numbered 619 to 630. The last of these is seen on the seven-miles long Marsden route. This ran along the main A62 trunk road along the Colne Valley. On 27 September 1962, no. 630 has stopped at Stubbins Road between Slaithwaite and Marsden, and the Pennine landscape across the valley can be seen. (P.J. Thompson)

All but seven of the 52 Karrier Sunbeam MS2s delivered between 1947 and 1949 (numbered between 541 and 592), had their Park Royal bodies replaced by East Lancashire or Roe bodies between 1955 and 1963. One of the first to be treated was Karrier 553, which is seen here heading this line up in the 1960s. It ran until 1965. The location is the special trolleybus terminal loop, opened in 1957, at Salendine Nook Schools on the Outlane route. (Roy Brook / Paul Watson)

One of the seven un-rebuilt vehicles mentioned in the previous caption is seen here. Karrier MS2 no. 549 was one of five of these vehicles which in the early 1960s were given the more modern style of destination indicators, completely altering their frontal appearance. It is seen here in a pleasant scene at the Bradley Keldregate terminus. This short branch off the Leeds Road route was the last route extension on the system, opened in April 1956. (C. Carter)

On the West Vale route, the outer part of the route between Elland and the terminus ran along the valley side at Long Wall, Hullen Edge. Here BUT no. 624 runs along Long Wall overlooking Elland as it approaches West Vale. (J. Copland / Paul Watson)

A well-known feature of the Huddersfield system was the terminal platform at Longwood, already featured in this book. This elevated view shows a trolleybus after it has reversed on to the platform, with the turntable plate visible. The vehicle is Sunbeam MS2 no. 589, one of five rebodied by Roe in 1959, being delivered without bumpers. (Roy Brook / Paul Watson)

| HOW THEY WENT – HUDDERSFIELD | |
|---|---|
| 5 March 1949 | Ashbrow Road |
| 9 July 1955 | Brighouse to Fixby |
| 8 November 1961 | West Vale |
| 30 January 1963 | Marsden |
| 5 February 1964 | Birkby to Crosland Hill |
| 14 July 1965 | Almondbury to Fixby |
| 13 July 1966 | Brackenhall to Lockwood |
| 13 July 1966 | Riddings to Newsome |
| 12 July 1967 | Longwood to Bradley |
| 13 July 1968 | Waterloo to Lindley and Outlane |

In January 1963, part-way through Huddersfield's trolleybus abandonment programme, some cross-town trolleybus routes were re-organised. This involved the provision of new wiring along Lord Street, to enable the Fixby and Almondbury routes to be joined. This scene shows an Almondbury trolleybus under the new wiring on Lord Street. The vehicle is a 1949 Sunbeam MS2 rebodied by Roe in 1958, seen here after having its front bumper removed. It was withdrawn in 1965.

This trolleybus is negotiating major roadworks at the junction of the Almondbury and Waterloo routes. These occurred in early 1965, and necessitated several changes of overhead layout to allow trolleybus operation as the works progressed. In this view, Roe-bodied Sunbeam MS2 no. 600 (note bumper removed) is on a journey from Almondbury to the town centre. The row of line hangers indicates the previous alternative paths through the works. The route was converted to motorbus operation in July 1965. (R.S. Ledgard)

Huddersfield's last official trolleybus was BUT no. 623, which bore extensive illuminations. This was operated in service throughout the week prior to the last civic run on Saturday July 13 1968. It is seen at Outlane terminus prior to departing for Waterloo, one evening during the final week. (Roy Brook / Paul Watson)

# HUDDERSFIELD ROUTE 90 – BRIGHOUSE

Huddersfield's first trolleybus route abandonment was the northern portion of the Brighouse route beyond the borough boundary at Fixby, closed in July 1955. Fortunately, local enthusiast and photographer Roy Brook recorded trolleybuses on this section in the early 1950s.

The terminus at Brighouse was at the junction of Bradford Road and Bonegate, on the Bradford side of the town centre. Vehicles reversed into Bonegate from the main road. This scene shows 1953 built BUT 616 arriving at the terminus. The conductor is ready to alight and supervise the reversing movement. (Roy Brook / Paul Watson)

Having passed through Brighouse town centre, the route crossed the River Calder. Karrier MS2 552 is seen on the bridge on Huddersfield Road, just prior to turning right at Brighouse station towards Rastrick. This vehicle was given a new East Lancashire body in 1955 and ran until 1963. (Roy Brook / Paul Watson)

Having passed through Rastrick, the route turned towards Fixby at the Sun Inn. Here, Sunbeam MS2 582 is coming from Huddersfield and turning right from Clough Lane towards Rastrick. No. 582 received a new East Lancashire body in 1962 and ran until 1967. (Roy Brook / Paul Watson)

# Mexborough and Swinton

This long-lived system used only single-deck vehicles, and was the first and last to be operated by a private company, the Mexborough and District Traction Company.

Trolleybus services commenced in August 1915, when two separate routes, both feeders to the tram network, opened. These were to Manvers Main colliery from Mexborough, and to Conisbrough from the tram depot at Denaby. Three Daimler Brush rear-entrance trolleybuses maintained the service. After a few months, the operation closed due to wartime conditions partly because so many of the staff had been called up, and despite efforts to maintain the Manvers Main route for the essential colliery workers traffic, services were sporadic until 1921. The Conisbrough route did not recommence until 1922. New AEC trolleybuses arrived in the 1920s, replacing the original fleet, which had been augmented in 1917 by a second-hand vehicle from Stockport.

In the late 1920s it was decided to replace the tram system, and this was done in stages until the last tram ran in March 1929. 27 centre-entrance Garrett vehicles were purchased to achieve this, and a further three entered service in 1930. The routes were extended to two termini at Conisbrough at Brook Square (Conisbrough Low) and Conanby (Conisbrough High), as well as a short branch to Kilnhurst near the depot at Rawmarsh.

The end of the trams allowed the trolleybuses to run through to Rotherham, jointly with Rotherham Corporation, whose trolleybuses now ran out to Conisbrough Low and Kilnhurst. A short branch at Mexborough along Adwick Road was opened in June 1931, and a joint service to Rotherham was introduced from this terminus. It is of interest that Mexborough vehicles displayed route letters, whilst Rotherham vehicles used route numbers for exactly the same services. In October 1934, the system achieved its maximum extent when a route from Rawmarsh, along Green Lane to the Kilnhurst Road terminus was opened.

Second-hand English Electric vehicles were purchased in 1937, these being from Notts and Derby Traction Co, followed in 1942 by a similar number of Guy trolleybuses from Hastings. These were six-wheelers, the only ones to run

## FACTFILE – MEXBOROUGH AND SWINTON

| | |
|---|---|
| Opened | 31 August 1915 |
| Closed | 27 March 1961 |
| Route mileage | 11 |

### FLEET PROFILE
**All 4-wheel single-deck**

| | |
|---|---|
| Maximum number vehicles in service | 39 |
| Rebodied vehicles | Nil |
| Second-hand vehicles | 13 |
| | |
| AEC | 3 |
| Daimler | 3 |
| English Electric | 6 |
| Garrett | 30 |
| Guy 6 –wheel | 6 |
| Sunbeam | 39 |

on the system, although not all of them entered into service.

New vehicles entered service during the war, these being six Sunbeams with utility Brush bodywork which arrived in 1943. Fleet renewal continued after the war, when a further 33 Sunbeams with Brush bodywork entered the fleet up to 1950, replacing all the pre-war stock.

The first contraction to the system occurred in September 1954 when the Rawmarsh Green Lane circular service to Rotherham was converted to motorbus operation. On 1 January 1961 motorbuses took over the Manvers Main to Mexborough part of the through route to Conisbrough High (service C), and the service from the latter terminus was re-routed to Rotherham. This arrangement lasted only three months, and on 26 March the remainder of the system was closed. The following day, a procession of trolleybuses formally closed the system, this being led by no 29, which had its roof partly removed to act as a mobile bandstand for the Rawmarsh Prize Band. The system had certainly been 'blown away' in style! Many vehicles were sold to Doncaster and Bradford, where the chassis entered service with new double-deck bodies.

Mexborough bought 30 Garrett centre-entrance single-deckers between 1928 and 1930, mainly for the joint routes to Rotherham. This 1930s commercial view shows All Saints Square and Bridgegate in Rotherham, with a Mexborough Garrett standing at the Rotherham terminus. After the war, this terminus was moved into Bridgegate, and then again to Frederick Street. In the distance is Rotherham Straker-Clough no. 47, one of four new in 1927 which were sold to Darlington in 1937.

This early post-war view shows Garrett no. 44 at the junction of the Adwick Road and Conisbrough routes. Behind the Garrett is one of the six English Electric single-deckers, numbered 64 to 69 in the fleet, bought from Notts and Derby in 1937.

The Conisbrough High terminus of service 'C' was at the Conanby housing estate. Originally, for only a short period, trolleybuses went slightly further into the estate via a one-way loop, but this was cut back to this tight turning circle. No. 4 was one of six utility bodied Sunbeam 'W' vehicles acquired in 1943. These were almost identical to those running at Darlington. All six of these vehicles were sold to Doncaster in 1954, and given double-deck Roe bodies. This one became Doncaster no. 396 and ran until 1962. (C. Carter)

The other terminus of service 'C' was at Manvers Main colliery. In highly industrialised surroundings, No. 24, the first of 16 Brush bodied Sunbeam F4s new between 1948 and 1950, turns before returning to Conisbrough High. (C. Carter)

This is the Rawmarsh terminus at Kilnhurst Road of the 'K' service, and also the 'S' service via Green Lane. A complete circle of wiring allowed trolleybuses to turn on each service. On 11 July 1954, 1947 Sunbeam 'W' no. 13 is on service 'K', with a service 'S' vehicle in the background. The latter service was withdrawn later that year, but the wires to this point on service 'K' were retained until the end of the system in 1961. (J. Copland / A.D. Packer)

The joint operation between the Mexborough Company and Rotherham Corporation is demonstrated here. This view shows Rotherham Daimler no. 6, together with Mexbrorough Sunbeam no. 35 in Adwick Road near the terminus, which was Rotherham service 8 and Mexborough service 'A'. Note the spelling of 'Mexborough' on the Rotherham vehicle. (D.A. Jones / London Trolleybus Preservation Society)

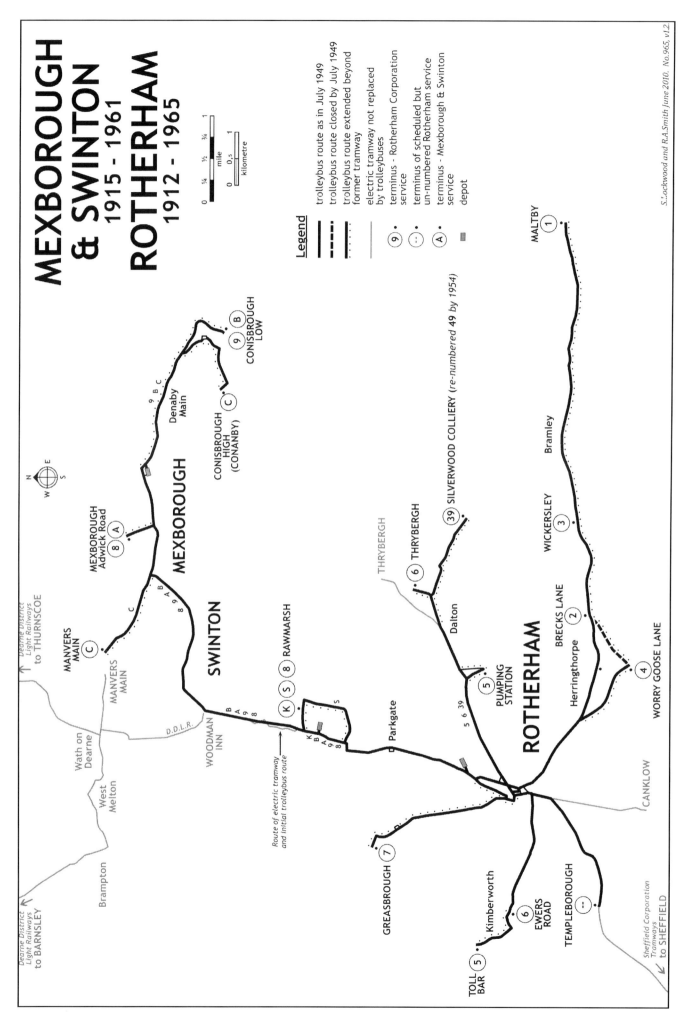

# MEXBOROUGH & SWINTON
## 1915 – 1961
# ROTHERHAM
## 1912 – 1965

### Legend

trolleybus route as in July 1949

trolleybus route closed by July 1949

trolleybus route extended beyond former tramway

electric tramway not replaced by trolleybuses

⑨ terminus - Rotherham Corporation service

⊙ terminus of scheduled but un-numbered Rotherham service

Ⓐ terminus - Mexborough & Swinton service

▓ depot

S.Lockwood and R.A.Smith June 2010. No.965, v1.2.

*Dearne District Light Railways to THURNSCOE*

*Dearne District Light Railways to BARNSLEY*

Brampton

Wath on Dearne

West Melton

MANVERS MAIN

Ⓒ MANVERS MAIN

D.D.L.R.

WOODMAN INN

*Route of electric tramway and initial trolleybus route*

MEXBOROUGH Adwick Road Ⓐ ⑧

9 B C

Denaby Main

CONISBROUGH HIGH (CONANBY) Ⓒ

⑨ Ⓑ CONISBROUGH LOW

MEXBOROUGH

C
A B
8 9

SWINTON

B
A 9
8

Ⓚ Ⓢ ⑧ RAWMARSH

K
B
A
9
8

Parkgate

GREASBROUGH ⑦

Kimberworth

EWERS ROAD ⑥

TEMPLEBOROUGH ⊙

TOLL BAR ⑤

*Sheffield Corporation Tramways to SHEFFIELD*

CANKLOW

ROTHERHAM

PUMPING STATION ⑤

5 6 39

Dalton

THRYBERGH

THRYBERGH ⑥

SILVERWOOD COLLIERY (re-numbered 49 by 1954) ㊴

BRECKS LANE ②

Herringthorpe

WICKERSLEY ③

Bramley

WORRY GOOSE LANE ④

MALTBY ①

N
W E
S

Doncaster's early trolleybus fleet consisted of 31 six-wheelers with Roe bodies. Apart from four Garretts and a Bristol (one of only two built), all were Karrier-Clough type E6 vehicles. One of the seven Karriers delivered in 1930 is seen here on test at Bennetthorpe, part of the Racecourse route.

The pre-war fleet was standardised on the Karrier E6 type with Roe bodywork. No. 32 was a 'one-off' vehicle whose chassis was chromium plated for display at the Commercial Motor Show in 1933. It is seen in post-war days as no. 332 (all Doncaster's trolleybuses had 300 added to their fleet numbers in the late 1940s). The location is the North Bridge terminus of the Bentley route. One of the 1935/6 batch of ten E6s is also in view. (C. Carter)

E6 no. 353 (formerly 53) was one of twenty E6s that entered service in 1939, these being the last six-wheelers for the fleet. It is seen at Carr House Road on the Race Course route. (C. Carter)

This commercial postcard view shows no. 377 (formerly 77), the last of nine Sunbeam Ws new in 1944/5. It is passing through the Market Place on the Wheatley Hills service. Like all these utilities, it received a new Roe body in the mid-1950s and ran until the end of the system in 1963.

MARKET PLACE, DONCASTER.

The utilities were the last new trolleybuses bought by Doncaster. In 1952, the six BUT double-deckers from Darlington were acquired, and numbered 378 to 383 in the fleet. Initially they were used mainly on the Bentley service, but following that route's closure they were seen elsewhere on the system. This is the Beckett Road terminus on 30 June 1957, where no. 380 (Darlington no. 70) is seen. This route was extended to Parkway in the following year. (J. Copland / A.D. Packer)

Nine second-hand utility Sunbeams came in 1954. The first, no. 384 had Brush bodywork, whilst nos 385 to 392 had Park Royal bodies. All ran in their original form but were rebodied by Roe between 1957 and 1959. Two, nos 389 and 385, are seen at the West Laith Gate terminus of the Balby and Hexthorpe routes. They were rebodied in 1957 and 1958 respectively. (Roy Brook / Paul Watson)

# PASSING-BY

Mothers and their children walk along the Town Moor at Newcastle beside the Great North Road. A BUT six-wheel trolleybus, built to London specification, passes-by on the Gosforth route (Mirrorpix)

A feature of the South Lancashire system was the disruption to services for the annual Whitsuntide processions in May and June. The vehicles were reversed into side streets by means of flexible insulated cables attached to bamboo poles, connecting the overhead to the trolleyheads. In May 1957, Guy no. 24 waits in the side street whilst the procession passes at Moorside, on the Farnworth route. (R.C. Jackson)

This is Almondbury, near Huddersfield, looking towards the trolleybus terminus. One of the ten Sunbeam S7 vehicles new in 1959 is standing at the turning circle in the spring of 1965, just a few weeks before the route was converted to motorbuses. Passing by is a fourth-former from the local King James' Grammar School, returning to lessons after the lunch break.

## Ramsbottom

**Lancashire's second trolleybus operation, at Ramsbottom, was unusual on two counts. It was run by an Urban District Council (UDC), and it did not connect to or replace any tramway.**

Ramsbottom is situated about two miles north of the former Tottington terminus of Bury Corporation's tram system. The local Urban District Council desired to introduce its own trams, but the costs of this were such that trolleybuses were favoured instead, a decision confirmed by a poll of the residents in 1913. Wiring was erected on a route of just over 2 miles, from Edenfield in the north, via Ramsbottom itself (including a short branch to Ramsbottom station), to Holcombe Brook in the south, connecting with the terminus of the Lancashire and Yorkshire Railway branch from Bury. This railway branch was itself the subject of experiments with electric traction, as trains on the line were powered by electricity using overhead wires from July 1913, just two weeks before the trolleybuses commenced operation on 14 August.

Initially, four rear-entrance single-deck Railless vehicles maintained the service. The Ramsbottom station branch proved not to be a success and was abandoned in October 1914, although the wiring, including the junction frogs at the Market Place was left in situ for many years afterwards. Two further Railless vehicles entered service in 1915, with metal-framed Lockwood and Clarkson bodies which proved more

| FACTFILE – RAMSBOTTOM | |
|---|---|
| Opened | 14 August 1913 |
| Closed | 31 March 1931 |
| Route mileage | 2 |
| Maximum number vehicles in service | 7 |
| Rebodied vehicles | 4 |
| Second-hand vehicles | Nil |

durable and comfortable than the previous examples. A further example with a Short Bros body came in 1922. The fleet was much rebuilt, the original cars being rebodied at least once (some sources say twice), and most had their mechanical and electrical components renewed to an extent that they had virtually replacement chassis. However, in the mid-1920s, the UDC introduced motorbuses, which gave a through service to neighbouring towns and the trolleybuses gradually faded away, latterly running only part days until the end of March 1931.

**One of the original Railless vehicles, but with replacement Lockwood and Clarkson body, is seen at Holcombe Brook terminus in the early 1920s. It bears the registration TB 8572.**

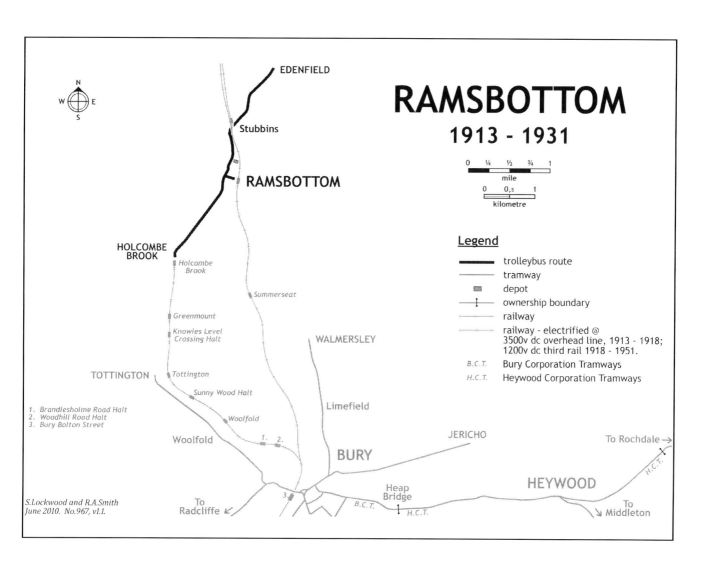

### RAMSBOTTOM
### 1913 - 1931

EDENFIELD

Stubbins

RAMSBOTTOM

HOLCOMBE BROOK

*Holcombe Brook*

*Summerseat*

*Greenmount*

*Knowles Level Crossing Halt*

WALMERSLEY

TOTTINGTON

*Tottington*

*Sunny Wood Halt*

Limefield

1. Brandlesholme Road Halt
2. Woodhill Road Halt
3. Bury Bolton Street

*Woolfold*

1. 2.

Woolfold

JERICHO

To Rochdale →

BURY

H.C.T.

*S.Lockwood and R.A.Smith June 2010. No.967, v1.1.*

To Radcliffe

3

Heap Bridge

B.C.T.     H.C.T.

HEYWOOD

To Middleton

**Legend**

| | |
|---|---|
| ▬▬ | trolleybus route |
| ── | tramway |
| ▦ | depot |
| ┤├ | ownership boundary |
| ── | railway |
| ···· | railway - electrified @ 3500v dc overhead line, 1913 - 1918; 1200v dc third rail 1918 - 1951. |
| *B.C.T.* | Bury Corporation Tramways |
| *H.C.T.* | Heywood Corporation Tramways |

Scale:
0  ¼  ½  ¾  1
mile

0  0,5  1
kilometre

**A similar vehicle is seen at the northern terminus of the route at Edenfield. (R. Marshall collection)**

# Wigan

**A trolleybus operation that ran without any statutory powers.**

Wigan Corporation Tramways was unusual in that its tram system was a mix of standard and narrow gauge (3ft 6in.) routes. In the 1920s, only two routes remained to be converted to standard gauge, and one of these was partly converted, but at great cost, the outer end being converted to motorbus operation. To save further expense, it was decided to install trolleybuses on the remaining route to Martland Hill to the north west of the town.

Four Straker-Clough trolleybuses, with single-deck Brush bodies, began operations on 7 May 1925. The route was just over 1.5 miles long, with an intermediate turning loop at Springfield.

FACTFILE – WIGAN

| | |
|---|---|
| Opened | 7 May 1925 |
| Closed | 30 September 1931 |
| Route mileage | 2 |
| Maximum number vehicles in service | 4 |
| Rebodied vehicles | Nil |
| Second-hand vehicles | Nil |

The Tramways Committee recommended that other tram routes be converted to trolleybuses, but the Corporation over-ruled this. The tram system closed in March 1931, and the trolleybuses ran until the end of the following September. Statutory powers to run trolleybuses were never obtained.

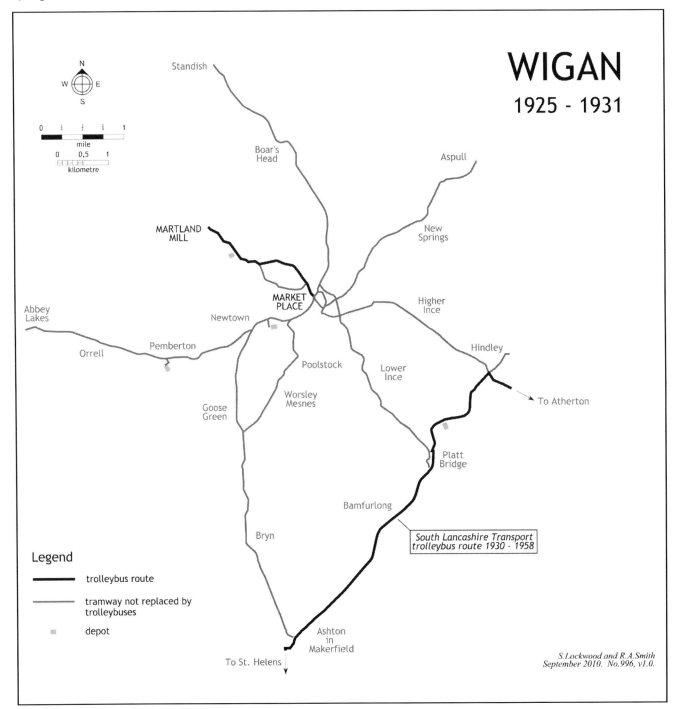

WIGAN
1925 - 1931

Legend

— trolleybus route

— tramway not replaced by trolleybuses

▪ depot

South Lancashire Transport trolleybus route 1930 - 1958

*S.Lockwood and R.A.Smith*
*September 2010. No.996, v1.0.*

154

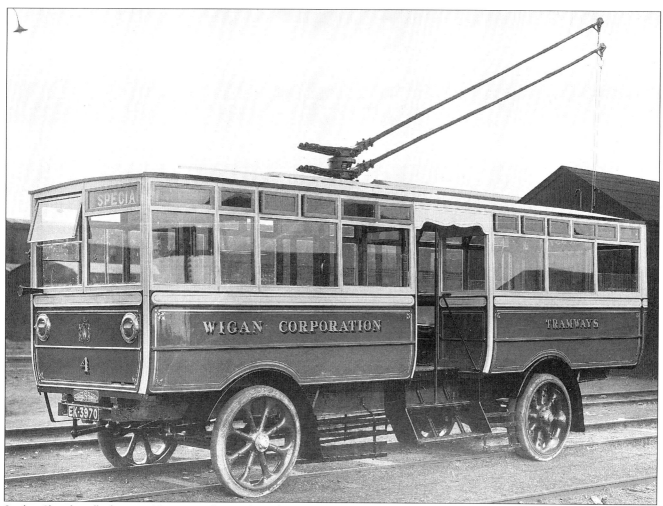

Straker-Clough trolleybus no. 4 is seen at the Brush works
before delivery to Wigan. (A.E. Old collection)

One of the Straker-Clough vehicles negotiates the intermediate
turning circle at Springfield. (Adam Gordon collection)

# St Helens

Unlike its near neighbour Liverpool, St Helens was eager to replace its trams and established a trolleybus network that included a joint route with a company operator.

An experimental trolleybus service, using four single-deck Garrett vehicles, was opened in July 1927 between Nutgrove and Prescot via Rainhill, a distance of about 2½ miles. Originally part of the municipal tramway system, this route had been operated by motorbuses since 1923. At Prescot the trolleybuses shared the terminus with Liverpool Corporation trams.

In July 1929, a route opened to Parr, at the opposite end of the town, where the trolleybuses ran a further half-mile beyond the former tram terminus. A further six single-deckers were put into service for the new route, these being of Ransomes manufacture.

A significant development came in June 1931, when the four-mile route to Haydock was opened, connecting with the South Lancashire Transport Company's trolleybus route from Atherton. A through service, jointly operated by both undertakings, was inaugurated. St Helen's share of vehicles was provided by five double-deck Ransomes six-wheelers, which were of lowbridge construction due to restrictive overbridges en-route.

Between 1934 and 1936 the remainder of the former tram routes were converted to trolleybuses, routes opening in July 1934 to Moss Bank (an extension of the Windle tram service), and along Prescot Road to Nutgrove, (allowing a through trolleybus route from Prescot to St Helens), and in May 1935 to St Helens Junction and Dentons Green. On 1 April 1936, the last trams were replaced, when the direct Prescot service via Portico was opened, allowing a circular trolleybus route to be operated to Prescot and Rainhill. For this expansion, Ransomes and Leyland four-wheel lowbridge double-deckers were put into service, most having locally built Massey bodywork.

The final development to the system came in June 1943, when a 1½-mile branch off the Dentons Green service to Acker's Lane came into use. A year previously, the fleet had been enlarged by the delivery of ten Sunbeam four-wheelers, whose chassis had been built for Johannesburg. These were eight feet wide with Massey utility lowbridge bodies. Ten conventional Sunbeams with Roe utility bodies came in 1945.

Post-war fleet renewals took place in 1950/51, when 16 eight feet wide Sunbeam and BUT trolleybuses entered service. The East Lancashire bodies were of highbridge construction, and a special arrangement had to be made to the wiring on the St Helen's Junction route to prevent one accidentally hitting a low bridge. They were almost exclusively used on the Prescot services.

However, the new vehicles did not prevent a change in policy, and most of the shorter town routes were converted to motorbuses in 1952, followed by the remainder between 1956 and 1958. All the post-war vehicles were sold for further service in South Shields (Sunbeams) or Bradford (BUTs).

*The special wiring arrangement at the Peasley Cross Road railway bridge on the St Helens Junction route is seen here. The negative wire is suspended very low, forcing the boom down to roof level. On the post-war vehicles with highbridge bodies, this would activate a power cut-out switch and stop the vehicle before the bridge was reached. Rebodied pre-war Leyland 129 is seen approaching the bridge.*

**FACTFILE – ST HELENS**

| | |
|---|---|
| Opened | 11 July 1927 |
| Closed | 30 June 1958 |
| Route mileage | 20 |

**FLEET PROFILE**

**All 4-wheel double-deck unless denoted**

| | |
|---|---|
| Maximum number vehicles in service | 66 |
| Rebodied vehicles | 21 |
| Second-hand vehicles | Nil |
| | |
| **BUT** | 8 |
| Garrett single-deck | 4 |
| Leyland | 20 |
| Ransomes | 25 |
| Ransomes single-deck | 6 |
| Ransomes 6-wheel | 5 |
| Sunbeam | 28 |

**HOW THEY WENT – ST HELENS**

| | |
|---|---|
| 2 February 1952 | Ackers Lane, Dentons Green, Moss Bank, St Helens Junction. |
| 9 November 1956 | Parr / Boardman's Lane (service at peak hours only since November 1955) |
| 11 November 1956 | Atherton |
| 30 June 1958 | Prescot / Rainhill circular |

This commercial postcard view of Church Road, Haydock, shows the rear of Atherton bound trolleybus no. 114, the last of five six-wheel Ransomes vehicles bought for the joint operation with the South Lancashire system.

St Helens' pre-war trolleybus fleet consisted mainly of low height Ransomes and Leyland four-wheelers. This is Brush bodied Ransomes no. 118, seen in the town centre when new, working on the Rainhill service. (R. Marshall collection)

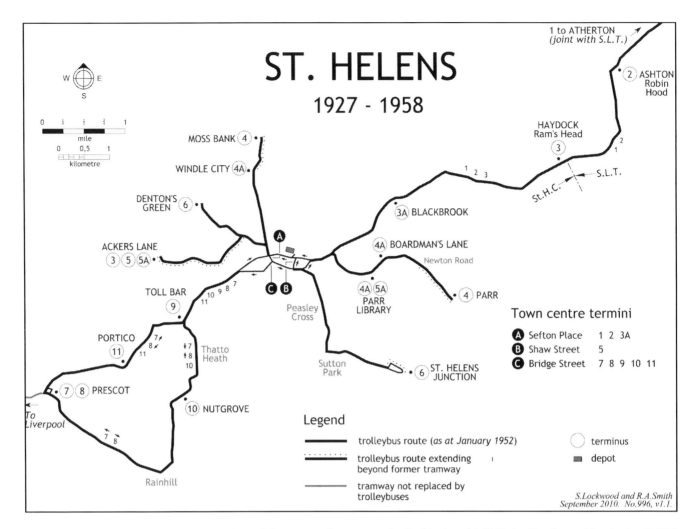

# ST. HELENS
## 1927 - 1958

1 to ATHERTON
*(joint with S.L.T.)*

(2) ASHTON
Robin
Hood

HAYDOCK
Ram's Head
(3)

St.H.C. — S.L.T.

MOSS BANK (4)

WINDLE CITY (4A)

DENTON'S
GREEN (6)

1 2 3

(3A) BLACKBROOK

(4A) BOARDMAN'S LANE

Newton Road

ACKERS LANE
(3)(5)(5A)

(A)

(C)(B)

10 9 8 7

11

Peasley
Cross

(4A)(5A)
PARR
LIBRARY

(4) PARR

TOLL BAR
(9)

PORTICO
(11)

7
8
11

Thatto
Heath

7
8
10

Sutton
Park

(6) ST. HELENS
JUNCTION

### Town centre termini

(A) Sefton Place   1   2   3A
(B) Shaw Street   5
(C) Bridge Street   7   8   9   10   11

(7)(8) PRESCOT

To
Liverpool

(10) NUTGROVE

7
8

Rainhill

### Legend

———— trolleybus route (*as at January 1952*)

·········· trolleybus route extending
beyond former tramway

———— tramway not replaced by
trolleybuses

◯ terminus

▰ depot

*S.Lockwood and R.A.Smith*
*September 2010. No.996, v1.1.*

Many of the pre-war fleet were rebodied in the mid-1940s by East Lancashire. Leyland TBD2 no. 123, new in 1934 and rebodied in 1945 is seen at Akers Lane Terminus. The post-war livery was bright red and cream, with a prominent fleetname. (H. Luff / Online Transport Archive)

158

Five 8-feet wide Sunbeam MF2s with Massey lowbridge bodies entered the fleet in 1942, these being part of an order built for Johannesburg. No. 158 is seen in Church Street in post-war days on the Boardman's Lane service, a short working of the Parr route. (D.A. Jones / London Trolleybus Preservation Society)

The only Sunbeam W trolleybuses built with low-height bodywork (ie with bench seats upstairs) were ten delivered in 1945 to St Helens. The bodies were built by Roe, and they were numbered 105 to 114 in the fleet. They were regularly used on the joint service to Atherton, as seen here in this view of no. 313 (formerly 113) approaching the Atherton terminus. All St Helens trolleybuses had 200 added to their fleet numbers in the early 1950s. (Roy Brook / Paul Watson)

A St Helens and a South Lancashire trolleybus are seen side by side at Sefton Place, the St Helens terminus of the joint route from Atherton. To the left, working on the Prescot service, is St Helens no. 382, one of the batch of sixteen trolleybuses new in 1950 which was split equally between Sunbeam F4 and BUT 9611T types. This one was the first of the BUT vehicles, and bore chassis number 001, although it was not the first of its type to enter service. Bodywork was by East Lancashire. After the closure of the St Helens system it was sold to Bradford, where it became no. 794 in that fleet. The South Lancashire vehicle is a 1930 Guy BTX with Roe bodywork. It has been modernised with a rebuilt front end. Note the London style RT type motorbuses on the left. (Roy Brook / Paul Watson)

# South Lancashire

This was a company owned interurban system, linking towns in south west Lancashire. The routes were some of the longest trolleybus routes in Britain and many of the original vehicles were running up to the very end of the system.

The South Lancashire Tramways Company decided to replace trams on its long routes centred on Atherton with trolleybuses in the late 1920s. The first section to be converted was between Atherton and Ashton in Makerfield, and operations began on 3 August 1930. This route was extended to Haydock on 21 June 1931, where it met the municipal trolleybus route from St Helens, which was opened on the same day, allowing a joint service to be provided over the whole Atherton to St Helens route, which was almost 14 miles in length. A month later, on 19 August, the route eastwards from Atherton to Swinton and Farnworth was opened. Although the two termini were less than five miles apart, the route was over 14 miles in length. The company's final trams ran on 16 December 1933, and the following day trolleybuses took over the Leigh to Bolton service via Atherton. The wiring for the three-mile section within Bolton's boundary was constructed and owned by the municipal authority, although it never operated its own trolleybuses. This completed the basic trolleybus system, which was run with a fleet of 46 Guy double-deck trolleybuses, thirty of them being six-wheelers. Owing to the number of restricted height bridges, all the vehicles were of lowbridge construction. An additional Guy 6-wheeler, (no 47), was obtained in 1935, this being a former demonstrator with full-height bodywork.

The next development was the replacement of Bolton's local tram service to Hulton Lane and Four Lane Ends with a trolleybus service operated by the company on behalf of Bolton Corporation. This commenced in December 1936 using four Leyland six-wheelers, purchased with a financial contribution from Bolton. These vehicles, numbered 48 to 51 in the fleet, became the property of Bolton after eight years when they had been fully depreciated, and they

## FACTFILE – SOUTH LANCASHIRE

| | |
|---|---|
| Opened | 3 August 1930 |
| Closed | 1 September 1958 |
| Route mileage | 32 |

### FLEET PROFILE
**All double-deck**

| | |
|---|---|
| Maximum number vehicles in service | 71 |
| Rebodied vehicles | Nil |
| Second-hand vehicles | Nil |
| | |
| Guy 4-wheel | 16 |
| Guy 6-wheel | 31 |
| Karrier 6-wheel | 6 |
| Leyland 6-wheel | 12 |
| Sunbeam utility 4-wheel | 6 |

passed to Bolton Corporation for disposal upon their withdrawal from service in 1956. Eight more Leylands arrived in the next two years. These, and all subsequent trolleybuses, were built to full height specification and were therefore never able to operate on the St Helens route.

Increased passenger traffic during the war resulted in six utility Karrier four-wheel vehicles entering service between 1943 and 1944.

The final trolleybuses to enter service were six Karrier six-wheelers in 1948. It should be noted that despite these new vehicles, none of the older trolleybuses were withdrawn from service until the 1950s.

The route network at this time was comprised of four basic services, two of which (St Helens and Farnworth) commenced from Atherton. The other two started from Leigh and ran to Bolton and Mosley Common (on the Farnworth route) respectively. Added to this was the Bolton local service to Hulton Lane which was extended to Four Lane Ends at peak hours, and another local service ran between Farnworth and Swinton. For fares purposes, the long Farnworth route was split into two overlapping sections, Atherton to Swinton, and Worsley to Farnworth.

A characteristic of the system was the multiplicity of short working turning points mostly with a triangular reverser, which were regularly used by scheduled extra journeys. There were five such points on the St Helens route alone.

By the early 1950s, the fleet had lost only one vehicle, and the 1930 Guy trolleybuses were veritable antiques, even by the standards of the day. Many of them were rebuilt to a greater or lesser extent, this often involving the provision of new front-ends to the bodywork, a process also extended to the later 1930s Leyland vehicles.

In 1955 the decision was taken to absorb the operation into the parent company, Lancashire United Transport, a large independent bus operator, and to dispense with trolleybuses. The first closure was the Bolton local service to Hulton Lane and Four Lane Ends on 26 March 1956 followed later that year by the St Helens route on 11 November.

The remaining routes lingered on until the end of August 1958, when the South Lancashire Transport Company ceased to exist. The next day, Karrier trolleybus no 71, the only one ever to be operated by Lancashire United Transport, took dignitaries, and later members of the public, on a farewell run to formally close the system.

The original South Lancashire trolleybus fleet consisted of 46 Roe bodied Guy vehicles, the first 30 of which were type BTX six-wheelers. No. 7 is seen here in original condition. In the early 1950s, this was one of two of this type which were extensively rebuilt by Manchester coachbuilder S.H. Bond.

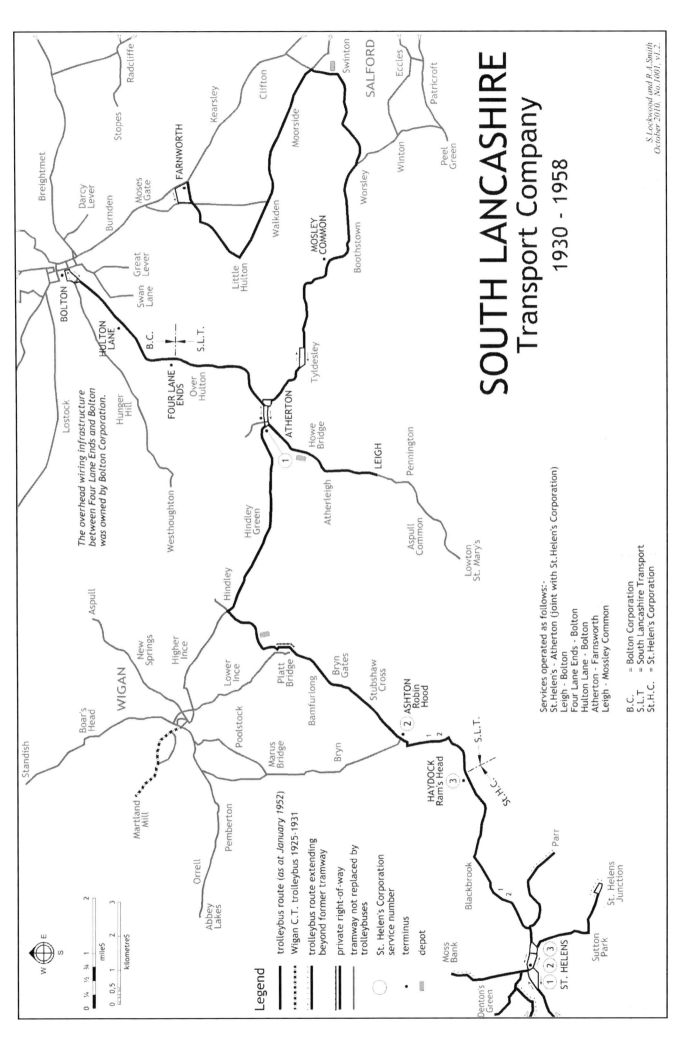

# SOUTH LANCASHIRE
## Transport Company
### 1930 - 1958

S. Lockwood and R.A. Smith
October 2010. No.1001, v1.2.

The overhead wiring infrastructure
between Four Lane Ends and Bolton
was owned by Bolton Corporation.

Services operated as follows:-
St.Helen's - Atherton (joint with St.Helen's Corporation)
Leigh - Bolton
Four Lane Ends - Bolton
Hulton Lane - Bolton
Atherton - Farnworth
Leigh - Mossley Common

B.C. = Bolton Corporation
S.L.T = South Lancashire Transport
St.H.C. = St.Helen's Corporation

## Legend

— trolleybus route (as at January 1952)

····· Wigan C.T. trolleybus 1925-1931

═ trolleybus route extending
beyond former tramway

▓ private right-of-way

═ tramway not replaced by
trolleybuses

◯ St. Helen's Corporation
service number

• terminus

▪ depot

W E
N S

miles
0  ¼  ½  ¾  1        2

kilometres
0  0,5  1      2      3

No. 40, seen here at the St Helens terminus, was one of the sixteen Guy BT four-wheelers. This post-war view shows it still in original condition. Note the Guy badge on the cab door. Behind stands a Massey bodied St Helens trolleybus. (C. Carter)

Four Leyland TTB4 six-wheelers with highbridge Roe bodies joined the fleet in 1936 to operate the local services from Bolton to Hulton Lane and Four Lane Ends. They were purchased with financial support from Bolton Corporation. Numbered 48 to 51, they were also regularly used on the full Bolton to Leigh service as seen here. On 2 May 1954, no. 49 is seen in Atherton at a point known as 'the bacca shop', en route to Bolton. A Swinton-bound Guy trolleybus is in the rear. Note that the original bulbous dash panel on no. 49 has been replaced by a plain flat type. (J. Copland / A.D. Packer)

The Leigh terminus of the routes to Bolton and Mosley Common was at the Lancashire United 'bus station' at Spinning Jenny Street. Here, no. 57, one of the six Leyland TTB4s with Roe bodywork new in 1938 waits to depart for Bolton. Beside it is 1943 Karrier W no. 61 on the Mosley Common service. Note the small headlights mounted on brackets, normal practice for South Lancashire vehicles. (C.W. Routh)

The only post-war trolleybuses in the South Lancashire fleet were six Karrier badged MS2s with Weymann bodies delivered in 1948. No. 70 is seen at the Howell Croft bus station in Bolton, with the clock tower of the Town Hall in the background. The vehicle is working on the local Hulton Lane service, which was withdrawn in 1956. (Travel Lens Photographic)

At Boothstown, between Mosley Common and Worsley on the long Farnworth route, there was provision to turn a trolleybus using detached wiring in a side street, with no frogs being used. To use this to turn, the crew needed to transfer the trolley poles three times to complete the manoeuvre. The slight gradient at this location made it easier to turn using gravity, and this view shows four-wheel Guy no. 41 in the middle of the road with poles down ready to reverse in this manner into Cooper Street. (Roy Brook / Paul Watson)

Crossing the East Lancashire Road at Swinton on a journey to Atherton is Guy six-wheeler no. 20, which has been modernised with a new front end. (Roy Brook / Paul Watson)

Swinton was the mid-point of the Atherton to Farnworth route. Four-wheel Guy no. 44 is seen here with the crew relaxing before resuming the journey to Atherton. (Roy Brook / Paul Watson)

The South Lancashire system was the nearest trolleybus system to the Leyland Motors factory, and new Leyland trolleybuses, either complete or in chassis form, were often tested on the routes. This chassis under test, with set back front axle, is possibly one built for export to Perth in Western Australia in 1933.

# Ashton under Lyne (including Oldham)

The joint route between these two towns was one of the shortest lived trolleybus operations. Ashton, however, persisted, and whilst always a small system in terms of vehicles operated, it went on to run long routes jointly with its larger neighbour, Manchester.

The need to renew tram track in Oldham Road, Ashton, prompted Ashton Corporation to introduce trolleybuses. The joint tram service to Oldham was converted also, as well as Ashton's local service which ran to the borough boundary at Hathershaw. Oldham, however, retained its local tram service to this point. Ten centre-entrance Railless vehicles worked the service, two of which were owned by Oldham. Complaints about excessive vibration and unreliability caused Oldham to swiftly re-consider this new form of traction, and the through service was switched to motorbuses in September 1926, after barely a year's operation. The local Ashton service to Hathershaw was retained, and Ashton's eight single-deckers, latterly rebuilt with pneumatic tyres and rear entrances, kept running until the equipment was worn out, the last of the type running on 19 February 1939.

However, by this time, there were other developments. Manchester City Council's desire to replace the trams on the joint service between there and Ashton with trolleybuses, resulted in Ashton introducing trolleybuses to run jointly with Manchester. These ran along the Ashton Old Road corridor to a city terminus at Piccadilly. The service was extended east of Ashton into Stalybridge, where the wiring was owned and maintained by the municipally run transport bus and tram operator, the Stalybridge, Hyde, Mossley and Dukinfield Joint Transport and Electricity Undertaking (SHMD). Operations commenced on 1 March 1938, and Ashton's last tram ran on that date.

Ashton ran its share of the service with seven double-deck trolleybuses. These comprised three Leylands purchased the previous year to replace some of the Hathershaw single-deckers, two former Crossley demonstrators, and two Crossley six-wheelers.

A further trolleybus service was opened through the town in July 1938 from Stalybridge to Manchester via Ashton New Road, but although this was regarded as a 'joint' route, it was always operated by Manchester vehicles.

In 1940, further additions to the routes in Ashton were introduced. In March a service into Manchester via Guide Bridge was inaugurated, followed in November by a route via Guide Bridge and Denton to Haughton Green. Both were run jointly with Manchester.

For this expansion, eight Crossley four-wheelers entered service. At the end of the war, six utility Sunbeams were purchased, all these entering service between 1944 and 1946. Further fleet renewals, all four-wheelers, came in 1950 (five Crossleys) and 1956 (eight BUTs).

By the 1960s Ashton was pressing Manchester to consider the abandonment of the trolleybus routes, but at that time its city neighbour was more concerned with internal matters, and in any case wished to run trolleybuses until their newest ones were free of debt. However, the Haughton Green service was converted to motorbuses in July 1960, owing to the redevelopment of the area around the terminus. Road works prompted the demise of

FACTFILE – ASHTON

| | |
|---|---|
| Opened | 26 August 1925 |
| Closed | 4 September 1926 (Oldham), 30 December 1966 (Ashton) |

Route mileage
Oldham route: 4 (Oldham 1.5, Ashton 2.5)
Manchester routes 7 (14 including joint routes to Manchester)

FLEET PROFILE
All 4-wheel double-deck unless denoted

| | |
|---|---|
| Maximum number vehicles in service | 24 |
| Rebodied vehicles | 4 |
| Second-hand vehicles | Nil |
| | |
| BUT | 8 |
| Crossley | 17 |
| Crossley 6-wheel | 3 |
| Leyland | 3 |
| Railless single-deck | 8 (plus 2 Oldham vehicles) |
| Sunbeam utility | 6 |

HOW THEY WENT – ASHTON

| | |
|---|---|
| 4 September 1926 | Oldham to Hathershaw |
| 19 February 1939 | Hathershaw |
| 3 July 1960 | Haughton Green |
| 10 October 1964 | Manchester via Guide Bridge |
| 30 December 1966 | Stalybridge to Manchester |

the Manchester via Guide Bridge service in October 1964.

The eight-mile long Stalybridge-Ashton-Manchester route ran on until the end of December 1966, when the last Ashton journey was followed into the depot by the ceremonial 'last trolleybus', no 87. Two utility Sunbeams with Roe bodies had previously been sold to Bradford (in 1960), but never entered service there.

Ten Railless trolleybuses with Short Brothers bodies were purchased for the joint Ashton to Oldham route. Two were owned by Oldham and this is their no. 2, seen before delivery. It had a short life of just over a year in service, unlike the eight Ashton vehicles, which, following the closure of the through service, ran on Ashton's local Hathershaw route until 1939. (R. Marshall collection)

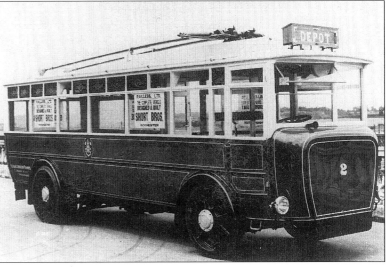

As part of its fleet for the joint trolleybus services with Manchester, Ashton bought this six-wheel demonstrator vehicle in 1938. It had been the first Crossley trolleybus built (in 1936), and, in the hope of attracting orders from there, was built to London specification. No. 58 lasted in the fleet until 1955, and is seen here at Manchester Piccadilly in company with a Manchester vehicle. (C. Carter)

Eight of these four-wheel Crossley type TDD4 vehicles entered service in 1940. No. 51 is seen turning from Aytoun Street into Portland Street at Manchester Piccadilly, showing the ornate red, white and blue livery. These vehicles were substantially similar to those entering service at Manchester. (R.F. Mack)

Following the delivery of six utility Sunbeam W vehicles, Ashton took delivery of five four-wheel Crossley 'Empire' vehicles in 1950. Again they were similar to the much larger batch of trolleybuses being placed in service in Manchester. This is no. 78, seen at Stalybridge in the early 1950s at the one-way terminal loop of the eight-mile route from Manchester. Note that tram rails are still evident. The background shows the hilly Pennine nature of the area. In the late 1950s the terminal loop was reversed in direction, and the trolleybuses were diverted into the bus station. (D.A. Thompson / London Trolleybus Preservation Society)

Ashton's final batch of trolleybuses was the eight BUT 9612Ts new in 1955/6. These had chassis assembled at the Crossley factory in Stockport, with bodies built by SH Bond of Manchester. No. 84 is seen at Stamford Park, on the boundary of Lancashire and Cheshire. From this point into Stalybridge, the wiring was maintained by the SHMD undertaking. A simplified light blue livery was applied to Ashton's vehicles from the 1950s. (D.F. Parker)

The joint operation of the Manchester and Ashton routes is demonstrated in this view of Ashton Market Place dated August 1963. Three Manchester BUTs, headed by no. 1323, are in view, as Asthon BUT no. 83 attempts to pass them on a terminating journey from Manchester via Guide Bridge. (A.D. Packer)

# ASHTON UNDER LYNE
## 1925 - 1966
# OLDHAM
## 1925 - 1926
# MANCHESTER
## 1938 - 1966

N
W E
S

0  ¼  ½  ¾  1
mile
0  0,5  1
kilometre

Waterhead

• OLDHAM

Werneth

Lees

Glodwick

Higher
Blackley

GREENGATE
211  212  •
• 211  212
GARDENERS
ARMS

BEN
BRIERLEY
211X
214  212X

Crumpsall

MOSTON
LANE

211

212
211

212

Hollinwood

• HATHERSHAW

Bardsley

Moston

p.m.
214
a.m.

212
212

214 a.m.
p.m.

212

211

Cheetham
Hill

Collyhurst

Newton
Heath

Failsworth

Limehurst

ASHTON
216X  217
218X  219

212
214

Miles
Platting

211

NORTH
ROAD
215X

EDGE
LANE
215X

THE
SNIPE
215

216  218

STALY-
BRIDGE

A

C

215  216

Audenshaw

216  218

218X

216  218

216

B

D

E

GREY MARE
LANE
219X

Open-
shaw

FAIRFIELD
ROAD

215  216

218  219

219X

217
219

217X  219X

Dukinfield

GUIDE
BRIDGE

216

218

218  219

219X

THE
TROUGH

219

210

213

Ardwick

UNIVERSITY
213X

213

BELLE
VUE
210X

210

217

DENTON
210X
217X

210

HYDE
210X

Hulme

213X

213

MOSS LANE
EAST

210

THORNLEY
PARK

210

217

GEE
CROSS
210

213  GREENHEYS

Fallowfield

217

HAUGHTON
GREEN

## Legend

━━━━  trolleybus route, as in 1955

▦▦▦▦  trolleybus route, 1925 - 1926

▬ ▬ ▬  trolleybus route, 1925 - 1939

••••••  trolleybus route extending
         beyond former tramway

▬•▬•▬  trolleybus route - no scheduled
         service

━━━━  tramway not replaced by
         trolleybuses (not all shown
         in central Manchester)

⬭  terminus - all day, every day

▢  terminus - peak hour or part day

▨  depot

## Central Manchester termini

| | | |
|---|---|---|
| A | CORPORATION STREET | 213 |
| B | CHURCH STREET | 212 214 |
| C | STEVENSON SQUARE | 211 215 216 |
| D | GEORGE STREET | 210 |
| E | PICCADILLY | 218 219 |

S.Lockwood and R.A.Smith
August 2010. No.992, v 1.0.

# Manchester

The municipal transport management did not want trolleybuses, but nevertheless ran one of the largest fleets in the country, although this was never more than a small percentage of the city's total public transport fleet.

In the 1930s, Manchester's municipal transport management, backed by its Transport Committee, considered that the tram system should be converted to motorbuses. The City Council, however, did not agree, on the grounds that trolleybuses would continue to use power generated by coal mined in Lancashire pits and accordingly it instructed the Transport Department management to replace trams on the Ashton Old Road corridor to Ashton with trolleybuses.

Despite his private reservations, the Transport Manager made steps to introduce a top class trolleybus operation, including the provision of a brand new depot for 115 vehicles at Rochdale Road.

Operations began on 1 March 1938, when the route from Piccadilly to Stalybridge via Ashton opened. This was run jointly with Ashton (as the trams to Ashton had been) and the Stalybridge undertaking (SHMD), although the latter owned the overhead in its area but no vehicles. In July, a second route opened, from Stevenson Square via Ashton New Road to meet the first route at Audenshaw and run also to Ashton and Stalybridge. Whilst regarded as a 'joint' service, it was exclusively operated with Manchester vehicles.

For these routes, 88 trolleybuses of local manufacture were purchased. Crossley and Leyland supplied the chassis, just over half of them being six-wheelers. All had similar looking Crossley bodies to a streamlined design, accentu-

| FACTFILE – MANCHESTER | |
|---|---|
| Opened | 1 March 1938 |
| Closed | 30 December 1966 |
| Route mileage | 30 (37 including joint routes) |

| FLEET PROFILE | |
|---|---|
| **All double-deck** | |
| Maximum number vehicles in service | 189 |
| Rebodied vehicles | Nil |
| Second-hand vehicles | Nil |
| | |
| BUT 4-wheel | 62 |
| Crossley 4-wheel | 106 |
| Crossley 6-wheel | 28 |
| Leyland 4-wheel | 47 |
| Leyland 6-wheel | 26 |

ated by a flamboyant livery incorporating cream swoops across the red base colour.

Further routes were opened in 1940, including a service entirely within the city, linking Rochdale Road to the University area. After the war, this route was extended, in 1946 from the University to Platt Lane Greenheys, and in 1948 from Rochdale Road to Corporation Street. Other

*Manchester's pre-war trolleybus fleet was split between Crossley and Leyland makes, and included both four- and six-wheeled vehicles. This six-wheel Leyland TTB4 no. 1070 is seen posed outside the new Rochdale Road garage during wartime. Note the flamboyant streamlined livery style and the headlamp masks and white fenders.*

routes introduced in 1940 were variations to the jointly operated Ashton route network. These were: a diversion off the Ashton Old Road service running to Ashton via Guide Bridge; and a route southwards from Guide Bridge to Denton and Haughton Green, notable because it did not run into Manchester city centre.

In the early war years, it was decided to replace motorbus routes along Rochdale Road and Oldham Road (which ran near the trolleybus depot) with trolleybuses and accordingly between the end of 1940 and 1942, trolleybuses were introduced on both these high frequency corridors to the Gardeners Arms at Moston. A further extension opened in 1943 when a short section beyond the Gardeners Arms was opened to a private bus station at the AV Roe aircraft factory at Greengate, Chadderton, which was actually just outside the city boundary.

For all these additional services, 76 four-wheel Crossley and Leyland trolleybuses entered service between 1940 and 1943, all built to peacetime standards and to the general design of the original fleet.

January 1950 saw the commencement of Manchester's final trolleybus route, this being the nine-mile service along Hyde Road to Gee Cross. The introduction of trolleybuses had been postponed by the war, and then by post-war vehicle shortages (the Hyde tram service had been replaced by motorbuses in 1947). Again the SHMD undertaking owned and maintained the portion of the wiring at Hyde and Gee Cross which was in Cheshire. 54 new Crossley trolleybuses, including 16 six-wheelers entered service for this route, these representing almost all Crossley's post-war trolleybus output.

The system, now at its peak, was impressive, running high frequency services over some lengthy routes. It was one of only three in Britain to operate night services, these running over several routes.

However, by the early 1950s the Moston vehicles and infrastructure of the Moston routes was time-expired, and the decision was taken to replace these routes with motorbuses, this occurring in two stages during 1955. Conversely, 62 new BUT vehicles were purchased for the Ashton routes, securing the immediate future of these services. Re-development in areas of the city caused the closure of the Greenheys and Haughton Green routes in 1959 and 1960 respectively. Despite Ashton pressing for the conversion of the rest of the joint trolleybus routes, Manchester decided to close the Hyde Road route in 1963, and to run the relatively new BUT vehicles until they were debt free. Impending road works meant that the Ashton via Guide Bridge route closed in October 1964. The two main Ashton / Stalybridge routes lasted until the end of December 1966, although latterly operations were run down, for instance Manchester had run motorbuses on its share of the Ashton Old Road route well before the final closure.

| HOW THEY WENT – MANCHESTER | |
| --- | --- |
| 24 April 1955 | Moston via Rochdale Road |
| 7 August 1955 | Greengate / Moston via Oldham Road |
| 31 May 1959 | Greenheys |
| 3 July 1960 | Haughton Green |
| 30 April 1963 | Hyde Road |
| 10 October 1964 | Ashton via Guide Bridge |
| 30 December 1966 | Stalybridge to Manchester |

This Leyland TB5, no. 1117, was one of 37 delivered in 1940/1 and had English Electric bodywork. It is seen nearing the city centre terminus of the Moston via Rochdale Road service at High Street, on a service 212X journey, a short working starting at Ben Brierley. From the early 1950s, Manchester's trolleybus routes were numbered between 210 and 219, and following the usual practice in this city, short working journeys were denoted by an 'X' suffix. (N.R. Knight)

The first post-war trolleybuses came in 1949. These were 38 Crossley Empire four-wheelers. Brand new no. 1204 is seen at the Piccadilly terminus of the Ashton Old Road routes in Portland Street, prior to working a 29X journey to Fairfield Road. This service would soon be renumbered to 219X. Note the pre-war six-wheeler behind, still in the streamlined livery. (The Omnibus Society)

The 4-wheel post-war Crossleys were mainly used on the nine-mile Hyde Road route to Gee Cross, opened in 1950. No. 1229 is at the Gee Cross terminus in Cheshire, under wiring maintained by the SHMD undertaking. (D.A. Jones / London Trolleybus Preservation Society)

Delivered in 1951 were 16 of these six-wheelers with Crossley 'Dominion' chassis, the only ones built. Mainly due to their heavy steering, they were unpopular with the staff, and were only used at peak hours, usually on the 210X Hyde Road service to Denton. The last of the batch, no. 1255, is seen at the Portland Street terminus of the Hyde Road route on such a working. In 1956, the terminal for this service was moved to here from George Street at the other side of Piccadilly Gardens. Then, in 1957, a one-way traffic scheme resulted in the jointly operated Ashton Old Road services moving from the opposite side of Portland Street, joining the Hyde Road services as shown by the Manchester BUT vehicle in the background. (J. Fozard)

Manchester's last trolleybuses were the 62 BUT 9612Ts with Burlingham bodies delivered in 1955/6. No. 1311 is seen at the Haughton Green terminus of the jointly operated service 217 to Ashton, which was closed in 1960. (D.F. Parker)

In the early 1960s, most of the BUTs were given a much plainer red livery. On 1 November 1966, a rather grimy no. 1306 is standing at the Audenshaw terminus of the 215 Ashton New Road service from Stevenson Square. Two months later the system would be no more. (A.D. Packer)

Manchester and Ashton's last public service trolleybuses ran on Friday 30 December 1966. The following day, two preserved trolleybuses ran on the Manchester wires only, carrying enthusiasts. One of these was a former Rotherham six-wheeler, and the other was former Manchester BUT no. 1344, which had been withdrawn and sold in 1964. It is seen during the farewell tour leaving the North Road turning loop at Clayton. Later that day it became the last trolleybus to operate in the city. (C. Isgar)

# Stockport

**The only trolleybus operation wholly based in Cheshire, this early system used a power-collection method unique in Britain.**

Stockport's only foray into running trolleybuses commenced in March 1913, when a route of just over 1½ miles long was opened. This ran from the town centre at St Peters Square, along Hall Street and Offerton Road to the borough boundary at Hempshaw Lane, Offerton. There was also a wiring link from the town terminus to the Mersey Square tram depot, including internal wiring inside the depot building itself. The Corporation ensured, very wisely, that the roads to be used by the trolleybuses were rebuilt with a smooth surface before operations commenced.

The operation was unique in Britain in that it used the German based Lloyd-Kohler system of current collection, also known as the 'Bremen' system after the German town which first introduced this method, and it used flexible cables, similar, although not identical to, the Cedes-Stoll system (see Historical account). On at least one occasion, the current collector (known as the 'monkey') became detached from the vehicle, and together with the flexible cable, returned by gravity to the depot.

Three 22-seat single-deck vehicles were supplied by Brush using a Daimler chassis, and like the Cedes-Stoll operations in Keighley and Aberdare, these proved difficult to maintain, especially during the First World War, their

FACTFILE – STOCKPORT

| | |
|---|---|
| Opened | 10 March 1913 |
| Closed | 11 September 1920 |
| Route mileage | 2 |
| Maximum number vehicles in service | 3 |
| Rebodied vehicles | Nil |
| Second-hand vehicles | Nil |

great weakness being the back axle which could not withstand the powerful torque of the traction motor. One of the vehicles was sold to the Mexborough and Swinton operation in 1916. By early 1919 operations had ceased due to both vehicles being unserviceable. Later in the year, motorbuses were obtained to run on the route, however, during 1920 one trolleybus was returned to service, due to difficulties with the new buses, and this continued until September of that year, when the operation finally came to an end. The wiring remained in position until at least 1924.

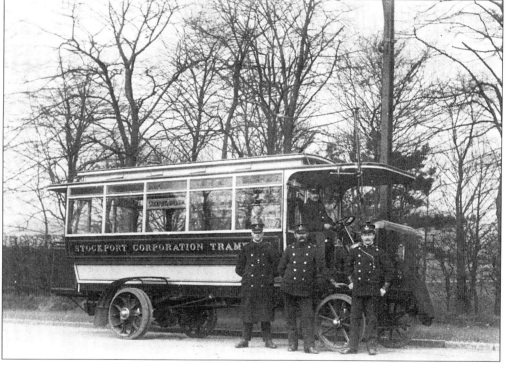

*Daimler-Brush no. 3 is seen with its crew at Offerton terminus. The current collection cable is hidden against the background of the trees.*

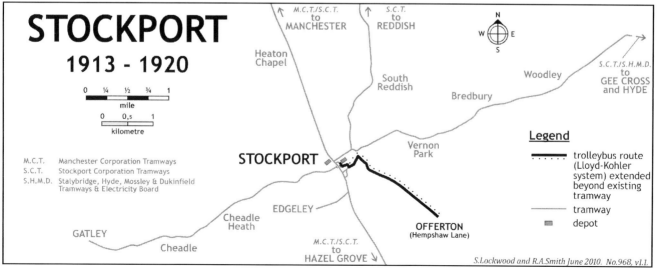

# STOCKPORT
## 1913 - 1920

0   ¼   ½   ¾   1
mile

0   0,5   1
kilometre

M.C.T.   Manchester Corporation Tramways
S.C.T.   Stockport Corporation Tramways
S.H.M.D.   Stalybridge, Hyde, Mossley & Dukinfield
Tramways & Electricity Board

M.C.T./S.C.T.
to
MANCHESTER

S.C.T.
to
REDDISH

Heaton
Chapel

South
Reddish

Bredbury

Woodley

S.C.T./S.H.M.D.
to
GEE CROSS
and HYDE

STOCKPORT

Vernon
Park

EDGELEY

GATLEY

Cheadle
Heath

Cheadle

M.C.T./S.C.T.
to
HAZEL GROVE

OFFERTON
(Hempshaw Lane)

### Legend

———— trolleybus route
(Lloyd-Kohler
system) extended
beyond existing
tramway

——— tramway

▪ depot

*S.Lockwood and R.A.Smith June 2010.   No.968, v1.1.*

# CONVERSATIONS

Chatting to the driver in Llanelly town centre. The vehicle, no. 47, is a 1946 Karrier 'W' with Park Royal 'utility' body. The chassis was sold to Bradford in 1953 and it entered service there with a new East Lancashire body in 1956 as no. 783. It ran until 1971. (R. Marshall)

This London scene, possibly on a Sunday morning, shows a smartly dressed lady chatting to a companion in Parkhurst Road, Holloway near the Nag's Head junction, which is in the background. Leyland trolleybus no. 1689, a K3 class vehicle, one of a batch of 25 that entered service in 1940, has crossed Holloway Road from Seven Sisters Road into Parkhurst Road. On the steps of the underground ladies toilets, there is a sign 'Men working on stairs – use at own risk'. (C. Carter)

This conversation is taking place in Westgate, Huddersfield in June 1965. Passing the scene is Sunbeam MS2 no. 592, which had been rebodied as late as 1963 using the 1955 East Lancashire body from no. 563, whose chassis was then scrapped. It is seen proceeding to Salendine Nook Schools to pick up schoolchildren. No. 592 was withdrawn three weeks after this photograph was taken. (J.T. Longbottom)

## Grimsby and Cleethorpes

The Lincolnshire fishing port of Grimsby and the neighbouring seaside resort of Cleethorpes operated a joint trolleybus route before both systems were unified when the public transport operations of both towns were amalgamated.

Grimsby Corporation took over the company owned tramways in its area as late as 1925. It soon made plans to replace the single-track Riby Square to Freeman Street route with trolleybuses, and extend the route along Hainton Avenue to Weelsby Road. Trolleybuses commenced operation on October 1926 with five Garrett trolleybuses, two more being obtained a year later.

It was not until November 1936 that a further route was added to the system, this being the main service from Old Market Square to the Cleethorpes boundary at Park Street, where the trolleybuses met the Cleethorpes Corporation trams (until 1936 these had been Company trams). Ten AEC centre-entrance six-wheel double-deck vehicles were purchased for this route.

The following year, on 18 July 1937, Cleethorpes converted its trams to trolleybuses, and a joint trolleybus service was instituted between Old Market Square Grimsby and Cleethorpes Bathing Pool. The Cleethorpes trolleybus fleet consisted of ten AEC four wheelers, with a further three entering service in the following year.

Reduced seaside traffic after the outbreak of war resulted in Cleethorpes selling four of its vehicles, including the three 1938 examples, to Nottingham in 1940. Grimsby, however, received its first four-wheel trolleybuses in 1944 when three utility bodied Karriers entered service. Six more Karriers with better appointed Roe bodies came in 1947, allowing the original Garrett single-deckers to be scrapped.

Cleethorpes replenished its reduced fleet in 1950 and 1951 by the purchase of four BUTs and two Crossleys (the only post-war Crossleys not to be purchased by Manchester/Ashton).

By the mid-1950s, Grimsby's original Weelsby Road

| FACTFILE – GRIMSBY AND CLEETHORPES | |
|---|---|
| Opened | 3 October 1926 (Grimsby), |
| | 18 July 1937 (Cleethorpes) |
| Closed | 4 June 1960 |
| Route mileage | 6 |

**FLEET PROFILE**
All 4-wheel double-deck unless denoted
Maximum number vehicles in service

| | |
|---|---|
| | 32 (19 Grimsby, 13 Cleethorpes) |
| Rebodied vehicles | Nil |
| Second-hand vehicles | Nil |

**GRIMSBY**

| | |
|---|---|
| Garrett single-deck | 7 |
| AEC 6-wheel | 10 |
| Karrier | 9 |

**CLEETHORPES**

| | |
|---|---|
| AEC | 13 |
| BUT | 4 |
| Crossley | 2 |

route was in need of infrastructure renewal, and the decision was taken to substitute motorbuses on the route, the last trolleybuses operating on 30 September 1955, leaving the joint Grimsby to Cleethorpes service as the only route.

On 1 January 1957, the two trolleybus systems were amalgamated under one management, a new common blue and white livery being adopted, to replace Grimsby's dark red and Cleethorpes' pearl grey and light blue colours. The decision was soon taken to abandon trolleybus operation altogether, and accordingly the trolleybuses made their last journeys between the two towns on 4 June 1960. The 1947 Karriers were sold to Bradford (never entering service), whilst the Crossleys and BUTs went to Walsall.

Seven Garrett single-deckers with centre-entrances were Grimsby's first trolleybuses. This one, no. 3, is at the Riby Square terminus of the route to Weelsby Road. (The Omnibus Society collection)

Ten of these AEC 664T vehicles with centre-entrance Roe bodies were delivered to Grimsby in 1936 for the Cleethorpes Road route. These were numbered 8 to 18, omitting no. 13. This is no. 12 turning at Weelsby Road terminus on 28 August 1955, a month before this route was converted to motorbuses. (A.D. Packer)

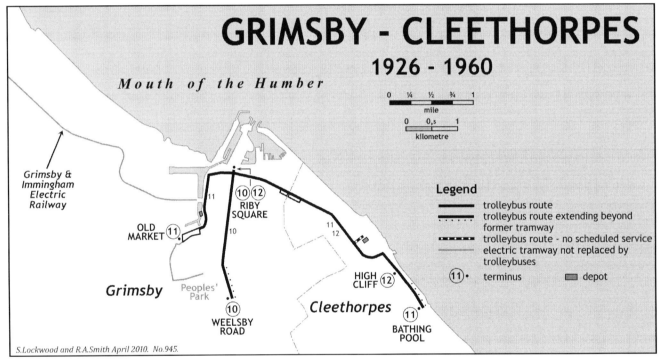

# GRIMSBY - CLEETHORPES
## 1926 - 1960

*Mouth of the Humber*

Grimsby &
Immingham
Electric
Railway

OLD MARKET (11)

(10)(12)
RIBY
SQUARE

*Grimsby*   Peoples'
Park

(10)
WEELSBY
ROAD

HIGH CLIFF (12)

*Cleethorpes* (11)

BATHING
POOL

0 ¼ ½ ¾ 1
mile

0 0,5 1
kilometre

**Legend**

——— trolleybus route
·········· trolleybus route extending beyond former tramway
▬ ▬ ▬ trolleybus route - no scheduled service
——— electric tramway not replaced by trolleybuses
(11)• terminus          ▭ depot

S.Lockwood and R.A.Smith April 2010. No.945.

Cleethorpes commenced operation in 1937 with ten Park Royal bodied AEC 661T four-wheelers, numbered 50 to 59. Two of these, including no. 57, are seen at the Bathing Pool terminus of the joint route to Grimsby. (R. Marshall)

Cleethorpes' first post-war trolleybuses were four BUT 9611Ts with Northern Coachbuilders bodywork new in 1950, numbered 59 to 62. These replaced the AEC trolleybuses bearing the same fleet numbers that had been sold to Nottingham at the start of the Second World War. No. 60 is seen having just departed from the Cleethorpes Bathing Pool terminus, showing the turning circle, and in the distance, the North Sea. (C. Carter)

Grimsby received a total of nine Karrier W vehicles, three with Park Royal utility bodies in 1944 and six with more conventional Roe bodies in 1947. This is utility no. 1, repainted in the new dark blue and cream colours of the Grimsby-Cleethorpes joint undertaking, at the Grimsby Old Market Place terminus of the Cleethorpes route. (R.F. Mack)

The last trolleybuses bought by Cleethorpes were two Crossley Empire four-wheelers with Roe bodies, new in 1951. These were the only chassis of this type to be supplied to an operator other than Ashton or Manchester. No. 64 is seen at Riby Square, picking up passengers for Cleethorpes. Note that the Grimsby-Cleethorpes dark blue was applied all over the rear of the vehicles, presumably to mask drips from the trolley heads. (R.F. Mack)

# Chesterfield

The one route operation here was never developed into a trolleybus network for the town, and it succumbed to the motorbus after a short life of not quite eleven years.

In the mid-1920s, Chesterfield decided to replace its one route tram system with trolleybuses. The route ran from Brampton in the north to Whittington Moor in the east. Trolleybuses were introduced on the Brampton to town centre section in May 1927, and the Whittington Moor section followed in July. Fourteen 30-seat single-deck Straker-Clough vehicles with centre entrances operated the service. A two-mile extension from Whittington Moor to New Whittington came into use in July 1929, this being the only development of the system. The new route included a low bridge and a railway level crossing.

In 1931, two Ransomes trolleybuses joined the fleet, these being 48 seat double-deckers, which were unable to

FACTFILE – CHESTERFIELD
| | |
|---|---|
| Opened | 23 May 1927 |
| Closed | 24 March 1938 |
| Route mileage | 5 |
| Maximum number vehicles in service | 19 |
| Rebodied vehicles | Nil |
| Second-hand vehicles | 3 |

pass under the low bridge, and were therefore not allowed to run beyond the original terminus at Whittington Moor. Three further vehicles were purchased second-hand from York in 1935, these being 32-seat Karrier single-deckers.

The Corporation resolved to develop its municipal transport system with motorbuses, and the trolleybus route was therefore closed in March 1938, when two trolleybuses with illuminated fittings formally closed the system.

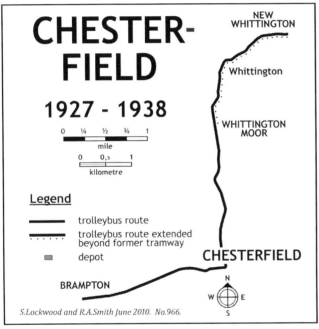

No. 6, one of the fourteen Straker-Clough trolleybuses is seen in Chesterfield town centre en route to Brampton on 5 August 1928. (S.L. Smith)

Two Ransomes D4 double-deck vehicles, nos 16 and 17, entered service in 1931. This is no. 16 seen before delivery.

# Derby

This was an extensive and busy town system with short routes on which a pattern of interworked services was operated.

Trolleybus operation in Derby began in early 1932, when the Corporation opened a route along Nottingham Road, extending beyond the tram terminus at the Cemetery, to the Creamery. Further routes opened in quick succession – in 1932 to Alvaston and Osmaston Road; in 1933 to Uttoxeter Road, Burton Road, and Ashbourne Road; and in 1934 to Normanton and Pear Tree. With the addition of a route to Browning Street in January 1935, and to Kedleston Road in the following April the basic trolleybus system was established.

Seventy double-deck trolleybuses were purchased, all but four of these being of Guy manufacture, the others being one each of Karrier, Ransomes, Sunbeam and Thornycroft types. The latter vehicle was most rare, one of only three built for use in this country.

During the middle and late 1930s extensions were made to the established route network. In November 1936, wiring along Osmaston Park Road, between Normanton and 'The Mitre' at Allenton came into use, as well as a branch off the Nottingham Road route to serve new housing at Chaddesden Park Road. The final pre-war extensions were a branch off the Kedleston Road route along Duffield Road to Darley Park in 1937, and a continuation of the Osmaston Road route from 'The Mitre' to Shelton Lock in 1938. Ten additional Guy trolleybuses were added to the fleet in 1936, followed in 1938 by six Daimler vehicles, which were the first 4-wheelers in the fleet.

An increase in passenger traffic during the war years resulted in the purchase of six single-deck Guy trolleybuses from Hastings, four of which were put into service and remained in use until the delivery of fifteen utility Sunbeams in 1944 and 1945. A wiring extension from Normanton Barracks along Sinfin Lane was opened in 1943 to serve factories engaged in war work. This service was of interest in that it was operated jointly with motorbuses.

Additions to the system continued after the war. Extensions were made to the Duffield Road route (to Kingscroft) in 1947, and the Ashbourne Road route was extended into the Mackworth Estate in two stages in the summers of 1952 and 1953, the final terminus being at Prince Charles Avenue (Morden Green). However, instead of extending the Chaddesden Park Road route further into the housing area, an improved service of motorbuses was introduced and the regular trolleybus service was withdrawn, although workmen's services operated at peak hours until 1962.

Fifty new Sunbeam trolleybuses entered service between 1948 and 1953, these being used to replace many of the elderly Guy six-wheelers.

In the mid and late 1950s, the system remained stable running with 71 vehicles. Many of the routes were linked together in a complicated cycle, so that it was some considerable time before a vehicle returned to any particular point. There were also many works and peak hour services that varied from the normal routes.

*Apart from experimental vehicles, the bulk of Derby's initial trolleybus fleet was made up of 76 six-wheel Guy BTX vehicles. Two of these are seen in snowy conditions on London Road at Alvaston. No. 115 has a Brush body and was new at the end of 1933. In the background is no. 141, new in mid-1934.*

---

**FACTFILE – DERBY**

| | |
|---|---|
| Opened | 9 January 1932 |
| Closed | 9 September 1967 |
| Route mileage | 28 |

**FLEET PROFILE**

**All double-deck unless denoted**

| | |
|---|---|
| Maximum number vehicles in service | 100 |
| Rebodied vehicles | Nil |
| Second-hand vehicles | 6 |
| | |
| Daimler 4-wheel | 6 |
| Guy 6-wheel | 76 |
| Guy 6-wheel single-deck | 6 |
| Karrier 6-wheel | 1 |
| Ransomes 6-wheel | 1 |
| Sunbeam 4-wheel | 73 |
| Sunbeam 6-wheel | 1 |
| Thornycroft 6-wheel | 1 |

---

**HOW THEY WENT – DERBY**

| | |
|---|---|
| 30 January 1960 | Browning Street |
| 10 November 1962 | Nottingham Road |
| 3 October 1964 | Burton Road to Duffield Road |
| 1 January 1966 | Sinfin Lane |
| 26 November 1966 | Uttoxeter Road via Cavendish to Midland Station |
| 11 February 1967 | Kedleston Road |
| 9 September 1967 | Morden Green, Alvaston, Osmaston Park Road, Shelton Lock |

---

The 1960s began with mixed fortunes. The portion of route between Cavendish and Browning Street was converted to motorbuses to allow the service to penetrate more of the area. However, eight new Sunbeam trolleybuses with Roe bodies, which replaced the pre-war Daimler vehicles, entered service in 1960.

1962 saw the closure of the Nottingham Road route, and the following year the Corporation announced that the trolleybus system would be closed altogether. Thus the remaining routes were closed starting in the autumn of 1964, and terminating altogether in September 1967

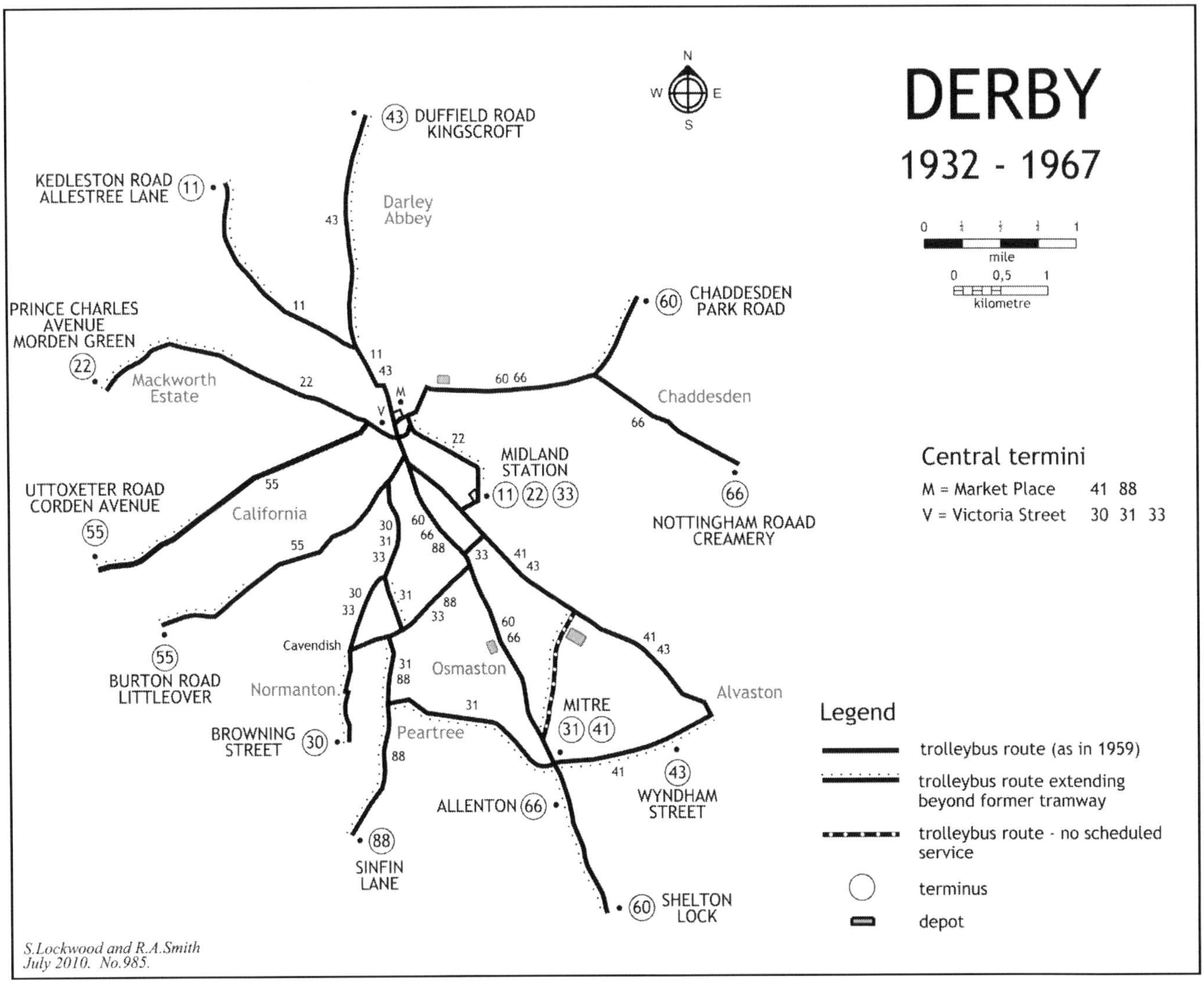
DERBY
1932 - 1967
N
W
E
S
0 ¼ ½ ¾ 1
mile
0 0,5 1
kilometre
43 DUFFIELD ROAD KINGSCROFT
KEDLESTON ROAD ALLESTREE LANE 11
Darley Abbey
PRINCE CHARLES AVENUE MORDEN GREEN 22
Mackworth Estate
60 CHADDESDEN PARK ROAD
Chaddesden
M
V
MIDLAND STATION 11 22 33
66 NOTTINGHAM ROAAD CREAMERY
UTTOXETER ROAD CORDEN AVENUE 55
California
Cavendish
55 BURTON ROAD LITTLEOVER
Normanton
Osmaston
Alvaston
BROWNING STREET 30
Peartree
MITRE 31 41
43 WYNDHAM STREET
ALLENTON 66
88 SINFIN LANE
60 SHELTON LOCK
Central termini
M = Market Place 41 88
V = Victoria Street 30 31 33
Legend
trolleybus route (as in 1959)
trolleybus route extending beyond former tramway
trolleybus route - no scheduled service
terminus
depot
S.Lockwood and R.A.Smith
July 2010. No.985.

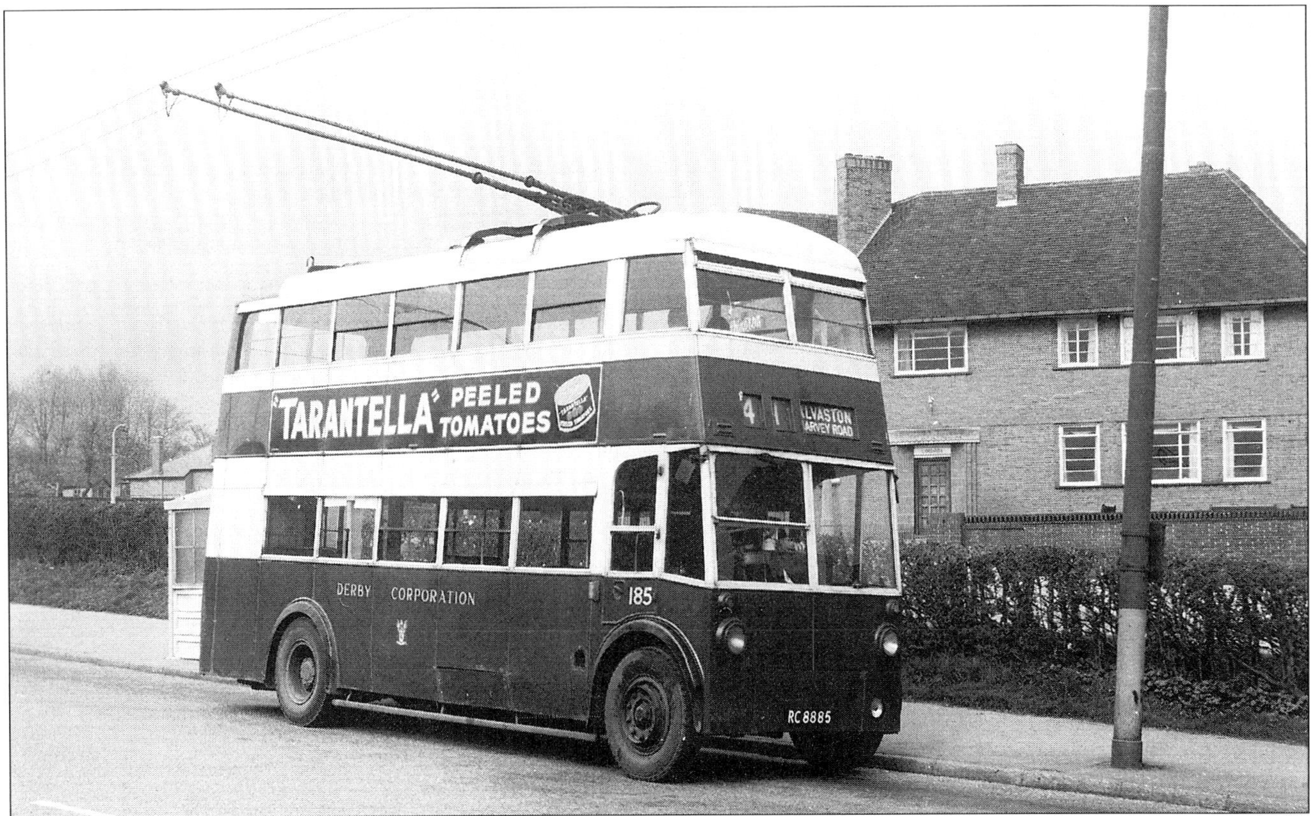
'TARANTELLA' PEELED TOMATOES
DERBY CORPORATION
185
RC 8885

Fifteen Sunbeam W utility vehicles entered the fleet between 1943 and 1946. All but the first two had Park Royal bodies. The last of the batch, no. 185, is seen at the suburban Allestree Lane terminus. Some of these vehicles had long lives, lasting in their original form into the mid-1960s. (Roy Brook / Paul Watson)

Post-war, Derby took delivery of 50 Sunbeam F4s between 1948 and 1952. The first 30 had Brush bodywork, and the remainder Willowbrook. Both types are represented here in this view of the Wyndham Street intermediate turning point on Harvey Road. On the right is 1948-built Brush-bodied no. 190, with the rear of Willowbrook bodied no. 227, new in 1952, on the left. Note the chrome plated bumpers.
(C.W. Routh)

Brush bodied Sunbeam no. 192 is seen squeezing under the railway bridge at Derby Friargate station. The small sign on the bridge (just above the roof of the vehicle), states 'Live wires, do not touch'.
(G.H.F. Atkins / courtesy and copyright John Banks collection)

Derby's main railway station, Derby Midland, is situated on the edge of the central area, and several trolleybus services terminated here. Willowbrook bodied Sunbeam no. 217 is seen here, together with one of the Brush bodied batch, no. 209,
(G.H.F. Atkins / courtesy and copyright John Banks collection)

The most southerly terminus on the system was at Shelton Lock. Seen at the turning circle here is 1952 Sunbeam no. 217 with Willowbrook body. (Roy Brook / Paul Watson)

This wiring junction was on London Road at Bateman Street. Approaching along London Road is no. 242, one of the 1960 Sunbeams on its way into the town centre on 16 September 1962. (P.J. Thompson)

In 1960, eight Roe bodied Sunbeam F4s entered the fleet, these being the only 8-feet wide vehicles. The first of the batch, no. 236, is seen at the Uttoxeter Road terminus at Corden Avenue. (R.S. Ledgard)

# Nottinghamshire and Derbyshire

A company-owned interurban system, linking towns and villages along the Derbyshire and Nottinghamshire boundary. The route into Nottingham was one of the longest trolleybus routes in the country.

The Nottinghamshire and Derbyshire Traction Company (commonly referred to as 'Notts and Derby'), was a Balfour Beatty subsidiary which operated trams on a long route between Ripley and Nottingham, as well as an entirely separate operation in Ilkeston, purchased from Ilkeston Corporation Tramways, a reversal of usual practice. These combined operations formed the basis of the trolleybus system, the first part of which opened in early 1932, on the Ilkeston section between Cotmanhay and Hallam Fields. On 1 August 1932, the three-mile gap between Ilkeston and the Ripley tram route at Heanor, never covered by trams, was opened to trolleybuses. As well as a direct Ilkeston to Heanor service, the Cotmanhay service was also extended to Heanor by means of a link from the terminus to Heanor Road

Also in August 1933, trolleybuses commenced running northwards from Heanor to Ripley, and on 4 October that year the complete 'main line', 15 miles long between Ripley, Heanor and Nottingham was opened. Three miles at the Nottingham end of the route, beyond Cinderhill, were in Nottingham Corporation territory, N & D trolleybuses running via Basford and Mansfield Road into the city centre. This was not a joint service, although Nottingham ran its own services to Valley Road, Basford (with a peak hour service extending to Cinderhill), and claimed the local revenue (less operating expenses) from the N & D operation.

Thirty two 4-wheel trolleybuses operated on the system, comprising sixteen AEC double-deckers for the main line, and sixteen single-deckers of English Electric and AEC makes, together with a solitary Guy, a former demonstrator. All the AEC vehicles had half-cabs and dummy radiators.

FACTFILE – NOTTS AND DERBY

| | |
|---|---|
| Opened | 7 January 1932 |
| Closed | 25 April 1953 |
| Route mileage 18 (21 including Nottingham wires) | |

FLEET PROFILE
All 4-wheel double-deck unless denoted

| | |
|---|---|
| Maximum number vehicles in service | 32 |
| Rebodied vehicles | Nil |
| Second-hand vehicles | Nil |
| | |
| AEC | 32 |
| AEC single-deck | 10 |
| BUT | 15 |
| English Electric single-deck | 6 |
| Guy single-deck | 1 |

The system remained stable throughout its existence. Six AEC double-deck trolleybuses entered service in 1937 to replace some of the earliest single-deckers, and ten further similar vehicles were delivered in 1941 and 1942, these entering service in wartime grey livery.

The original AEC half-cab double-deckers were replaced after the war when 15 BUT vehicles entered service in 1949. By this time the company had passed to the nationalised British Transport Commission, who had large bus interests but very little trolleybus operation. The system was closed in one go and the last trolleybus ran on 25 April 1953. Agreement having been reached for the sale of the entire fleet to Bradford City Transport, several vehicles were painted in Bradford's paler blue colours while still in N & D service. Conversely, one or two trolleybuses were despatched to Bradford before the closure, being pressed into service by their new owners still advertising 'Kimberley Ales', a brew unknown in the North!

No. 322, one of the fifteen 1932-built AEC 661T vehicles with half-cab Weymann bodies is seen in early post-war days, having just negotiated the railway bridge at Langley Mill station. (G.H.F. Atkins / courtesy and copyright John Banks collection)

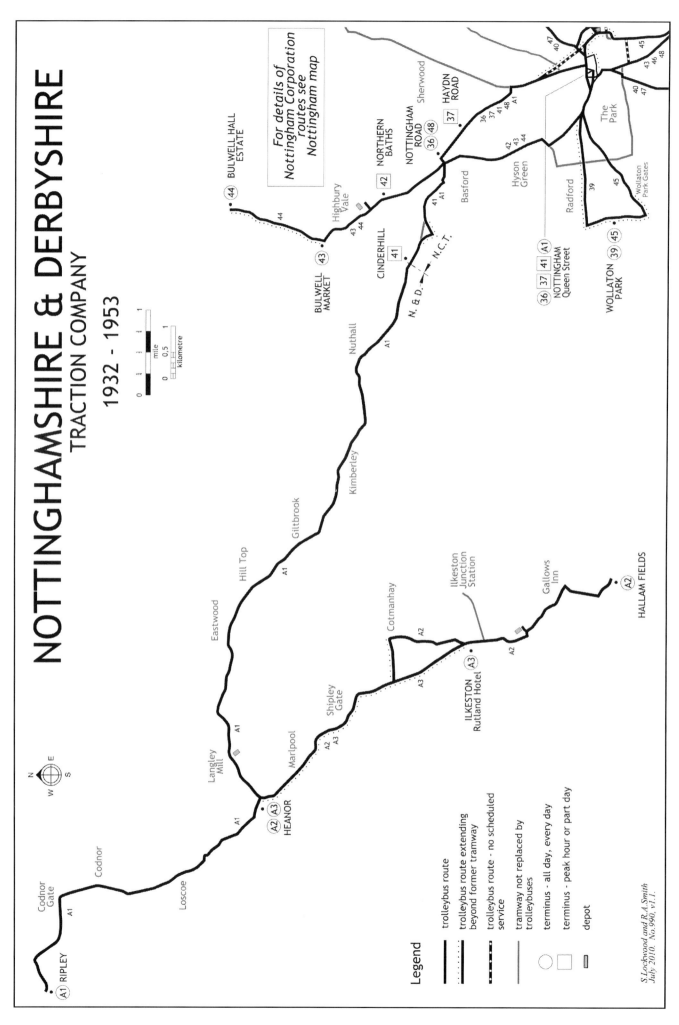

# NOTTINGHAMSHIRE & DERBYSHIRE
## TRACTION COMPANY
### 1932 - 1953

For details of Nottingham Corporation routes see Nottingham map

Legend

—— trolleybus route

········· trolleybus route extending beyond former tramway

–·–·– trolleybus route - no scheduled service

—— tramway not replaced by trolleybuses

◯ terminus - all day, every day

▢ terminus - peak hour or part day

▭ depot

RIPLEY

Codnor Gate

Codnor

Loscoe

HEANOR

Langley Mill

Eastwood

Hill Top

Giltbrook

Marlpool

Shipley Gate

Kimberley

Nuthall

Cotmanhay

Ilkeston Junction Station

ILKESTON Rutland Hotel

Gallows Inn

HALLAM FIELDS

BULWELL HALL ESTATE

BULWELL MARKET

Highbury Vale

CINDERHILL

NORTHERN BATHS

NOTTINGHAM ROAD

HAYDN ROAD

Sherwood

Basford

Hyson Green

Radford

The Park

Wollaton Park Gates

NOTTINGHAM Queen Street

WOLLATON PARK

N. & D.

N.C.T.

N
W E
S

mile
0 ¼ ½ ¾ 1
kilometre
0 0.5 1

S. Lockwood and R.A. Smith
July 2010. No.990, v1.1.

184

This is a classic portrait of 1937 Weymann bodied AEC 661T no. 301 on Nottingham
Corporation wires at the junction of Mansfield Road and Gregory Boulevard,
working on the long A1 route to Ripley. In 1953, it became Bradford no. 581 and
ran until 1958. (G.H.F. Atkins / courtesy and copyright John Banks collection)

No. 341 was one of ten Weymann AEC 661T vehicles delivered in 1941/2.
This rear end view shows it in Heanor Market Place ready to start an A2
journey via Ilkeston to Hallam Fields. As Bradford 595 it was rebodied by
East Lancashire in 1958 and ran until the mid-1960s. (R.F. Mack)

The Hallam Fields terminus of the A2 service was near the Stanton Ironworks and vehicles turned using a triangular reverser. 1941 AEC no. 335 has reversed at the terminus before departing for Ilkeston and Cotmanhay. Rebodied at Bradford (no. 589), it ran until 1968, one of the last AEC trolleybuses to run in Britain.

The fifteen Weymann bodied BUT 9611Ts entered service in 1949 and replaced the half-cab double-deckers. They were used almost exclusively on the A1 Nottingham to Ripley route. This publicity photograph shows no. 345 when new at Cross Hills near Loscoe, showing the typical nature of the route. In Bradford it was no. 762 in the fleet and lasted until 1963.

Notts and Derby trolleybuses used Nottingham Corporation wires between Cinderhill and the city centre at King Street. At the latter location, Nottingham and Notts and Derby four-wheel BUTs are seen side-by-side in April 1953, shortly before the end of the company system. Note that Nottingham 495, with Roe body, is 8-feet wide. (C.W. Routh)

# Nottingham

A busy city system whose development was suddenly curtailed in the mid-1930s. Its demise thirty years later was very swift, most of this large system disappearing in not much more than one year.

Trolleybuses were first introduced in Nottingham to replace those tramway routes that were still operated with single tracks. The first route was opened on 10 April 1927 when ten Railless double-deck trolleybuses entered service between the city centre and New Basford, via Nottingham Road. The vehicles were painted in a new green livery, contrasting with the maroon colours of the trams and motorbuses. The new colour was adopted as standard, and even today, green is the predominant colour on the city's buses and trams. The Railless trolleybuses were the last built by this concern, and eight additional vehicles needed to strengthen the service were supplied by Ransomes.

The next trolleybus service was inaugurated in February 1930, between Wilford Road and Wells Road, where the route was extended beyond the tram terminus to run to Kildare Road. Twelve further trolleybuses, equally split between English Electric and Ransomes types, were delivered to run this service.

The policy now was to convert all the tram system to trolleybuses, and in the next five years, trolleybuses were introduced on the following routes:

Wollaton Park (1931), Carlton (1932), Cinderhill (1933), Bulwell to Trent Bridge (1934), Colwick Road and Trent Bridge via London Road (1935).

This expansion resulted in a massive influx of vehicles, all these being six-wheelers of Karrier, Ransomes and latterly Leyland makes. By mid-1935 the fleet total stood at 136 vehicles. The 1934 Bulwell conversion alone brought 50 trolleybuses into the fleet.

However, this was not to last, and with a change of Transport General Manager 1934 came a change in policy.

**FACTFILE – NOTTINGHAM**

| | |
|---|---:|
| Opened | 10 April 1927 |
| Closed | 1 July 1966 |
| Route mileage | 23 |

**FLEET PROFILE**
**All double-deck unless denoted**

| | |
|---|---:|
| Maximum number vehicles in service | 157 |
| Rebodied vehicles | Nil |
| Second-hand vehicles | 12 |
| | |
| AEC 4-wheel | 4 |
| BUT 4-wheel | 13 |
| BUT 6-wheel | 102 |
| Daimler 4-wheel | 1 |
| English Electric 6-wheel | 8 |
| Guy 6-wheel single-deck | 6 |
| Karrier 4-wheel | 36 |
| Karrier 6-wheel | 49 |
| Leyland 6-wheel | 30 |
| Ransomes 4-wheel | 8 |
| Ransomes 6-wheel | 34 |
| Railless 4-wheel | 10 |
| Sunbeam utility | 5 |

Motorbuses were ordered to replace trams on their last two routes, and the trolleybus system had reached its zenith. Indeed, consideration was given in 1938 to its abandonment, but with a change of management, the idea was not pursued.

One of the original Railless vehicles, no. 8, is seen turning from Mansfield Road into Upper Parliament Street on a journey from Haydn Road, designated service 'H'. Note the 30 inch spacing of the trolleybus wiring.

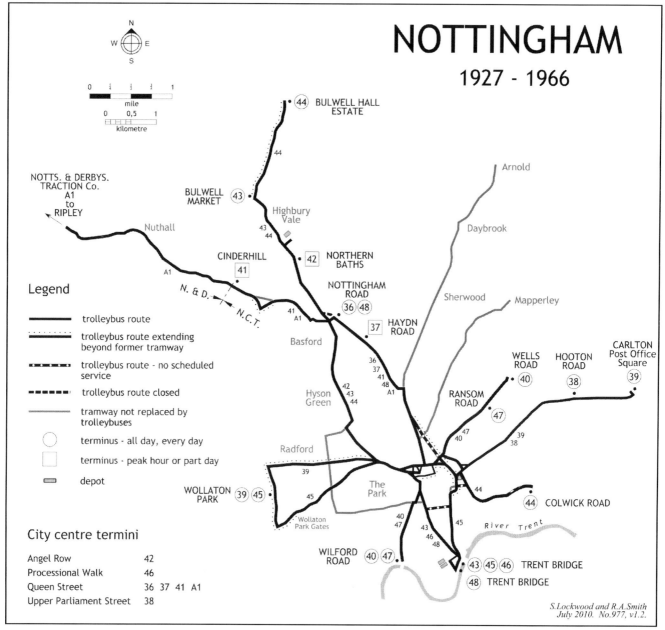

# NOTTINGHAM
## 1927 - 1966

**Legend**

——— trolleybus route

··········· trolleybus route extending beyond former tramway

▬▬▬ trolleybus route - no scheduled service

▬ ▬ ▬ trolleybus route closed

——— tramway not replaced by trolleybuses

○ terminus - all day, every day

▢ terminus - peak hour or part day

▭ depot

**City centre termini**

| | |
|---|---|
| Angel Row | 42 |
| Processional Walk | 46 |
| Queen Street | 36 37 41 A1 |
| Upper Parliament Street | 38 |

*S.Lockwood and R.A.Smith*
*July 2010. No.977, v1.2.*

The trolleybus fleet was expanded during the war to accommodate increased passenger traffic. Twelve second-hand vehicles were hastily obtained from Cleethorpes, Southend and single-deckers from Hastings. To these was added a former Daimler demonstration vehicle.

Later in the war, between 1942 and 1946, 36 utility Karrier and Sunbeam vehicles, with four different makes of bodywork arrived, the five Sunbeams being 8 feet wide and part of an un-shipped order intended for Johannesburg.

The only route development after 1935 came in 1946, when a new cross-city service 48 between Nottingham Road and Trent Bridge commenced operation. This was short lived, and ceased when the Notts and Derby operation ended their trolleybus operation into the city in April 1953.

After the war, fleet renewal commenced with the arrival of 17 Karrier and BUT four-wheelers in 1948. This was just a starter, for between 1949 and 1952, no less that 102 BUT 6-wheelers entered service, resulting in all the pre-war fleet being replaced.

The remainder of the 1950s was uneventful, and it was early in the 1960s that city centre redevelopment led to the decision to replace the trolleybuses. The first route to succumb was between Trent Bridge and Wollaton Park via London Road and Derby Road in November 1962.

It was 1965, however, when the trolleybus system was virtually annihilated. Between March and December, the whole system, apart from one route, was converted to motorbus operation.

The lone route, which was the original 1927 service to Nottingham Road, survived until 30 June 1966. A ceremonial last run took place on the morning of the following day.

| HOW THEY WENT – NOTTINGHAM | |
|---|---|
| 25 April 1953 | Trent Bridge to Nottingham Road through service |
| 3 November 1962 | Trent Bridge to Wollaton Park via London Road |
| 31 March 1965 | Trent Bridge to Bulwell Market |
| 30 April 1965 | Trent Bridge to Cinderhill |
| 31 May 1965 | Colwick Road to Bulwell Hall Estate |
| 30 September 1965 | Carlton to Wollaton Park (except Hooton Road section) |
| 9 October 1965 | Wells Road to Wilford Road |
| 31 December 1965 | Hooton Road to City |
| 30 June 1966 | Nottingham Road to City |

One of several demonstration vehicles loaned to Nottingham during the pre-war period was no. 28, a Thornycroft six-wheeler with Briush body, one of only three trolleybuses built by this manufacturer. It was used briefly in 1931 but was not successful. Its body was retained and placed on a 1933 Karrier E6A chassis, becoming no. 1 in the fleet. No. 28 is seen at the city terminus of the Nottingham Road service. (G.H.F. Atkins / courtesy and copyright John Banks collection)

This 1931 scene in Middleton Boulevard near Wollaton Park shows newly delivered Ransomes D6 trolleybus no. 39. Bodywork was by Brush.

Deliveries in the early 1930s were split between Karrier E6 and Ransomes D6 types. This is Karrier no. 352 (originally no. 52), one of a batch of ten with Metro Cammell bodies new in 1934. It is seen in post-war days at Trent Bridge. Trolleybuses had 300 added to their fleet numbers during the Second World War. (R. Marshall)

Twenty of these Metro Cammell bodied Leyland TTB4 trolleybuses entered service in 1935 for use on the Bulwell services. This is no. 132 seen before delivery.

Nottingham received 37 utility trolleybuses between 1943 and 1946, including five on 8 feet wide Sunbeam MF2 chassis diverted from a Johannesburg order. The fleet was the only one to run vehicles with each of the four makes of utility body used on the W type chassis, ie, Brush, Park Royal, Roe and Weymann. No. 442 was the first, one of four Weymann examples new in December 1943. In this view in the early 1950s, it has received a modernised front destination panel. The location is Trent Bridge, where it is arriving on a service 48 journey from Nottingham Road. (C. Carter)

Three Park Royal examples came in early 1944, numbered 452 to 454, followed in 1946 by ten more, numbered 469 to 478. No. 470 is seen at the Wollaton Park terminus of the cross-city service to Carlton. (G.H.F. Atkins / courtesy and copyright John Banks collection)

Nos 459 to 465 were Roe-bodied and new in mid-1945. Seen at the Hooton Road reversing triangle (the only one on the system) is no. 459. (G.H.F. Atkins / courtesy and copyright John Banks collection)

Brush supplied the bodies on three Karrier Ws delivered in mid-1945. These were nos 466 to 468, the last of which is seen at Wollaton Park terminus in post-war days. (G.H.F. Atkins / courtesy and copyright John Banks collection)

The first post-war vehicles, numbered 479 to 482, were four Karrier Ws with Roe bodies delivered in 1948. The first of these is seen at the Wells Road terminus. In the background can be seen no. 450, one of the five utility 8-feet wide Weymann bodied Sunbeam MF2s, numbered between 447 and 451, whose chassis were built for Johannesburg. (G.H.F. Atkins / courtesy and copyright John Banks collection)

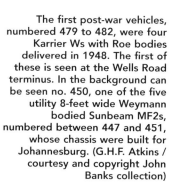

Of the 102 Brush-bodied BUT six-wheelers which entered service between 1949 and 1951, 25 were 8 feet wide vehicles numbered 500 to 524. No. 521 is seen in Upper Parliament Street at Theatre Square, passing a cinema (and queue) showing 'Sons & Lovers', based on the book written by D.H. Lawrence, a local Nottingham hero. (C.W. Routh)

Two of the much more numerous narrower versions of the six-wheel BUTs are seen here at Bulwell Hall Estate terminus on 12 July 1964. Nos 589 and 563 stand before returning through the city to Colwick Road. (D. Tate)

BUT no. 575 stands at the Old Market Square in Nottingham city centre en route to Trent Bridge. Today Nottingham's trams pass through this area. (Roy Brook/Paul Watson)

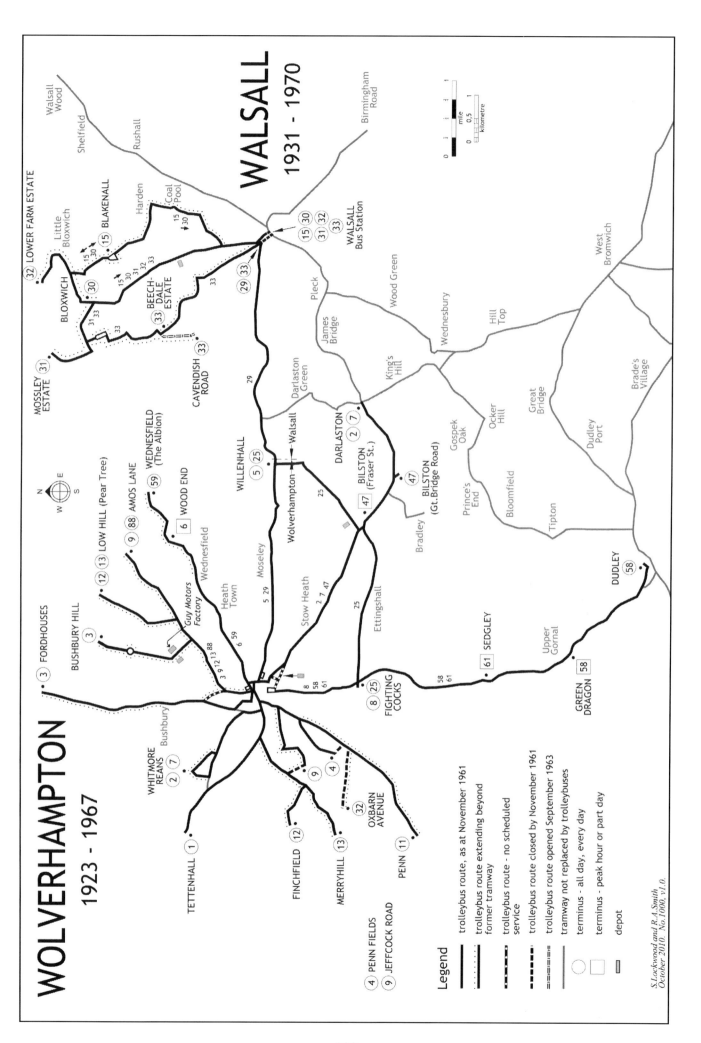

# WOLVERHAMPTON
## 1923 - 1967

# WALSALL
## 1931 - 1970

WALSALL WOOD

Shelfield

Rushall

LOWER FARM ESTATE

Little Bloxwich

BLAKENALL

Harden

Coal Pool

(32)

(15)

(30)

MOSSLEY ESTATE (31)

BLOXWICH

BEECH-DALE ESTATE (33)

CAVENDISH ROAD (33)

Birmingham Road

WALSALL Bus Station

(15) (30)
(31) (32)
(33)

(29) (33)

Pleck

James Bridge

Wood Green

Wednesbury

Hill Top

West Bromwich

King's Hill

Brade's Village

Darlaston Green

Gospek Oak

Ocker Hill

Great Bridge

Dudley Port

Tipton

Bloomfield

Prince's End

N
W — E
S

FORDHOUSES (3)

BUSHBURY HILL (3)

Bushbury

WHITMORE REANS (2) (7)

LOW HILL (Pear Tree) (12) (13)

AMOS LANE (9) (88)

WEDNESFIELD (The Albion) (59)

WOOD END (6)

WILLENHALL

DARLASTON (2) (7)

Wolverhampton — Walsall

BILSTON (Fraser St.) (47)

BILSTON (Gt. Bridge Road)

Bradley

Guy Motors Factory

Wednesfield

Heath Town

Moseley

Stow Heath

Ettingshall

5  25

5  29

25

2  7  47

25

SEDGLEY (61)

Upper Gornal

DUDLEY (58)

PENN FIELDS (4)

JEFFCOCK ROAD (9)

TETTENHALL (1)

FINCHFIELD (12)

MERRYHILL (13)

PENN (11)

OXBARN AVENUE (32)

(2) (7)

(9)

(4)

FIGHTING COCKS (8) (25)

8  58
61

58  61

GREEN DRAGON (58)

## Legend

—————— trolleybus route, as at November 1961

·············· trolleybus route extending beyond former tramway

—  —  — trolleybus route - no scheduled service

▬ ▬ ▬ ▬ trolleybus route closed by November 1961

▪ ▪ ▪ ▪ ▪ trolleybus route opened September 1963

~~~~~~ tramway not replaced by trolleybuses

◯ terminus - all day, every day

▢ terminus - peak hour or part day

▬ depot

S.Lockwood and R.A.Smith
October 2010. No.1000, v1.0.

# Wolverhampton

**This early comprehensive large town system proved that the trolleybus was ideal to provide urban mass transport.**

Wolverhampton's trolleybus system was the creation of the municipal transport General Manager, Charles Owen Silvers who was so impressed by the performance of his small fleet of Tilling Stevens petrol-electric buses, that he took the logical step of omitting the petrol engine and specified vehicles relying solely on electricity derived from overhead wires. Operations started in the conventional manner with the conversion of the single-track tram route to Wednesfield. Six Tilling Stevens centre-entrance single-deckers were used and the success of this resulted in more services being converted, those to Fordhouses and Fighting Cocks (on the Dudley Road), being introduced in 1925. This route was extended during 1927, firstly to Sedgley and then to Dudley, a distance of five miles from the town centre. Also in 1927, routes eastwards to Willenhall, and westward to Penn Fields and Tettenhall were opened.

Single-deck vehicles were needed for the initial routes because of the presence of low bridges. However, a great step forward in British trolleybus development came at the end of 1926 when the locally based Guy Motors produced their first trolleybus, a large 61 seat six-wheeler with a covered top and an open rear staircase. This was put to work on the Sedgley service. The success of this vehicle was such that between 1927 and 1931, a further 58 Guys were delivered, this time with enclosed staircases.

Meanwhile, the system was rapidly expanding year by year and the last tram ran during August 1928, allowing the Bilston route to be opened, with an extension to Darlaston the following year. 1930 saw the circular service established to Whitmore Reans, including a branch constructed specifically to serve the Courtauld's textile works. Also that year, a suburban service linking Willenhall with Fighting Cocks, which did not serve the town centre, was started. At this time, there were 70 trolleybuses in service, and the system had the distinction of being the largest in the world at that time. Towards the end of 1931, the Willenhall route was extended through to the neighbouring town of Walsall, as a joint service.

Another local motor manufacturer, the Sunbeam Motor Car Co., produced its first trolleybus in 1931, which was successfully trialled on the system, and subsequently purchased along with three others in 1932. From then onwards, all Wolverhampton's trolleybus chassis requirements were sourced from the two local manufacturers, Guy and Sunbeam. This included batches of single-deck vehicles to replace the original trolleybuses, which were required for the Wednesfield service until the headroom under the low bridge on the route was raised in 1943. From 1938 only four wheel vehicles were purchased.

The expansion of the system continued until 1935, some routes being converted from motorbus operation. From the end of 1931 and into 1932, routes to Bushbury Hill, Amos Lane, Low Hill and Penn Fields opened, followed in 1933 by those to Bradmore, Merry Hill, and Finchfield, and in 1934/5 to Penn Road and Oxbarn Avenue. After this, there were no major route developments until the 1950s, apart from the abandonment of a short stretch of route at Bradmore in 1937, where the route was terminated at a triangular reverser at Jeffcock Road.

At the outbreak of war, additional vehicles were soon required to cater for increased passenger traffic. Twelve

## FACTFILE – WOLVERHAMPTON

| | |
|---|---:|
| Opened | 29 October 1923 |
| Closed | 5 March 1967 |
| Route mileage | 49 |

## FLEET PROFILE
**All double-deck unless denoted**

| | |
|---|---:|
| Maximum number vehicles in service | 167 |
| Rebodied vehicles | 54 |
| Second-hand vehicles | Nil |
| | |
| Tilling Stevens single-deck | 32 |
| Guy 4-wheel | 73 |
| Guy 4-wheel single-deck | 4 |
| Guy 6-wheel | 72 |
| Sunbeam 4-wheel | 147 |
| Sunbeam 4-wheel single-deck | 7 |
| Sunbeam 6-wheel | 19 |

## HOW THEY WENT – WOLVERHAMPTON

| | |
|---|---|
| 24 October 1949 | Hordern Road to Courtauld's Works |
| 22 January 1961 | Oxbarn Avenue |
| 9 June 1963 | Penn Fields and Penn |
| 30 June 1963 | Tettenhall |
| 29 September 1963 | Jeffcock Road |
| 3 November 1963 | Merry Hill, Finchfield, Low Hill, Wednesfield, Amos Lane |
| 26 January 1964 | Bushbury Hill and Fordhouses |
| 25 October 1964 | Willenhall to Fighting Cocks |
| 8 August 1965 | Whitmore Reans to Darlaston |
| 31 October 1965 | Walsall |
| 5 March 1967 | Dudley |

Sunbeams from Bournemouth were obtained on long-term hire, and these remained in the town until after the end of the war, half returning in 1946 and the remainder two years later. Interestingly, these vehicles were accompanied by some Bournemouth crews. Between 1943 and 1946, 38 utility Sunbeams entered service.

Post-war trolleybus deliveries, which continued until 1950, were split between Guy and Sunbeam, the former supplying 50 chassis, and the latter 71 chassis. Most of these were 8ft wide vehicles. Some pre-war and early wartime four-wheel Sunbeams were sold to Southend and Belfast in 1950 and 1952 respectively.

Sixteen of the wartime utility trolleybuses were rebodied by Park Royal in 1952, and two routes were extended, that to Wednesfield in 1955, and the Amos Lane route in 1956.

In 1957 the future of the trolleybuses system was considered, but no untoward action was taken. A further 16 utility Sunbeams were rebodied in 1958/9, this time by Roe, and this process was completed in 1961/2 when 22 of the earliest post-war Sunbeams were similarly dealt with.

However, this investment did not ensure the future of the system and the decision was taken in 1961 to close it down. The majority of the system was converted to motorbuses between 1963 and 1965, leaving the long Dudley service to carry on, using trolleybuses with bodies only a few years old, until that too closed on 5 March 1967.

Low bridges necessitated the use of 32 single-deck Tilling Stevens vehicles for the initial Wolverhampton trolleybus fleet. No. 1 is seen at the former tram terminus at Wednesfield.

Double-deck vehicles were introduced from 1926, using locally produced Guy BTX six-wheel chassis. No. 63 was new in 1930 with a Dodson body, with the upper deck not extending over the cab. This vehicle lasted in service until late 1944, and it is seen in 'as withdrawn' condition.

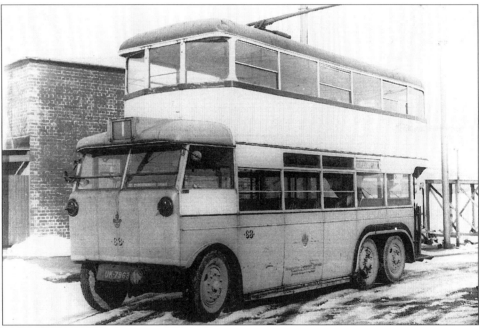

From the early 1930s, locally built Sunbeam MS2 and Guy BTX six-wheelers were bought. This 1934 Guy, no. 219, was one of eight vehicles, split equally between the two manufactures, to have this distinctive style of Beadle bodywork. It is seen in Cannock Road just after the war on a cross-town journey to Merry Hill. (S.L. Smith)

Eight Park Royal bodied single-deckers were purchased in 1934 for the Wednesfield route, where a low bridge prevented double-deck operation until 1943. Nos 206 to 209 had Sunbeam MF1 chassis, and nos 210 to 213 were Guy BTs. No. 206, seen here before entering service, was the first Sunbeam trolleybus to be fitted with single-deck bodywork. Three more single-deck Sunbeams, nos 231 to 233, came in 1936.

In the latter 1930s, there was a change of policy, and only 4-wheel vehicles were bought, but still dual sourced between Guy BT and Sunbeam MF2 types. No. 263 was the last of a batch of five Guy BTs with Roe bodies new in 1938.

The first utility vehicles in the fleet were six Sunbeam Ws with Weymann bodies which entered service in 1943. These were numbered 296 to 299, 400, 401. (Wolverhampton numbered its trolleybus and motorbus fleet in a series using alternating blocks of 100 numbers. Trolleybuses started at 1 to 99, then 200 to 299, 400 to 499 etc, with motorbuses being numbered in the other blocks). These six vehicles had relatively short lives, barely surviving ten years. No. 298 is seen at Victoria Square in the town centre. Between 1944 and 1946, a further 32 utilities were obtained, all with Park Royal bodies and numbered 402 to 433. All these were subsequently rebodied in the 1950s with Park Royal or Roe bodywork. (R. Marshall)

Service 25 was a suburban route connecting Willenhall to Fighting Cocks. About to cross Dudley Road at Fighting Cocks is Sunbeam W no. 408, with replacement body by Park Royal. The terminus was at Ward Road, to where no. 408 is heading. On the left is a post-war Sunbeam F4 proceeding towards Dudley. (J.C. Brown)

The other end of service 25 was at Willenhall, where it connected with the joint route to Walsall. Post-war Sunbeam F4 no. 478 stands at the terminus on 22 November 1959, just as an ex-Hastings Walsall trolleybus passes by in the background en-route for Wolverhampton. (C.W. Routh)

This commercial postcard view shows Spring Hill Corner, which was the terminus of the Penn trolleybus service. On the left stands no. 632, one of the final batch of Guy BT trolleybuses, numbered 482 to 607, and 631 to 654, which were delivered between 1949 and 1950.

38 Sunbeam W and F4 trolleybuses, numbered between 418 and 455 were rebodied by Roe between 1958 and 1962. No. 437, a 1947 Sunbeam W which originally had a Park Royal body, is seen in Bushbury Road, about to turn into Victoria Road (joining the wires from Amos Lane) on a return journey from Low Hill. This worked across the town to Finchfield. On the right is an unconnected wiring provision to allow trolleybuses to turn left from Bushbury Road towards Amos Lane. (C. Carter)

Passengers alight from rebodied Sunbeam F4 no. 453 at Amos Lane terminus. The vehicle will turn via the large walled roundabout beside the Pheasant Inn. (C. Carter)

# Birmingham

The first operator to commence trolleybus operations in order to replace trams and the first to use a fleet of covered-top vehicles. It went on to convert a major tram corridor to trolleybuses in the 1930s, but thereafter lost interest, and became the first modern system in a 'big city' to close.

Birmingham's redoubtable Tramways Manager, Alfred Baker, decided to experiment with trackless operation by converting the Nechells route, a short 2½-mile single-track tramway, to trolleybuses. This commenced in November 1922, when twelve Railless vehicles, with Roe double-deck bodies, entered service. This was Britain's first large scale application of double-deck trolleybus operation.

One feature of the operation was that trolleybus manufacturers, anxious to secure orders for what was potentially a very large market if Birmingham decided on the wholesale conversion of its tram system, would send their latest products for demonstration purposes. Birmingham's practice was to give these vehicles fleet numbers, even though they were never in the city's ownership. Notable amongst these was the EMB (Electro Mechanical Brake Co.) low height chassis with Roe fully enclosed body which ran between 1924 and 1926. Other makes tested were AEC, Guy and Leyland.

The fleet proper was expanded in 1926 by three Railless double-deckers with Short bodies, and an AEC with Vickers body (a demonstrator that was subsequently purchased). All these vehicles had open staircases.

By 1932 these initial vehicles were replaced by 16 new trolleybuses, comprising eleven 48 seat Leylands with half cabs and dummy radiators, as well as five larger (58 seat) AECs, with more modern looking full fronts. By this time, Birmingham was considering the replacement of its main tram routes, and it was decided to convert one route corridor to trolleybus operation. This comprised the services along Coventry Road to Yardley, running to Station Street or Albert Street in the city centre. Fifty Leylands were ordered, and the five mile route was opened on 5 January 1934. This was extended a further 2½ miles to the city boundary at

## FACTFILE – BIRMINGHAM

| | |
|---|---|
| Opened | 27 November 1922 |
| Closed | 30 June 1951 |
| Route mileage | 10 |

### FLEET PROFILE
All double-deck

| | |
|---|---|
| Maximum number vehicles in service | 90 |
| Rebodied vehicles | Nil |
| Second-hand vehicles | Nil |
| | |
| AEC 4-wheel | 1 |
| AEC 6-wheel | 5 |
| Leyland 4-wheel | 35 |
| Leyland 6-wheel | 50 |
| Railless | 15 |

Sheldon in July 1936, although additional vehicles, twelve four wheel Leylands, did not enter the fleet until September 1937. A further twelve similar vehicles arrived in early 1940.

The war years brought big changes to the operation. The isolated Nechells route was closed after operation on 30 September 1940 because of the 1½ miles that the vehicles had to run using a skate in the tram tracks to gain access to Washwood Heath depot. The sparking and arcing that this produced was not in accord with blackout regulations! On the plus side, wartime emergency powers were used to construct wiring on a 1½-mile branch from Coventry Road, along Hobbs Moat Road to the Lode Lane factory of Rover, where trolleybuses turned inside the factory grounds. This came into use on 29 October 1941.

Apart from the provision of a new turning facility at Lyndon End, east of Yardley in 1949, there were no further developments, and the trolleybus operation became included in Birmingham's tramway abandonment plans. Accordingly, the last trolleybuses ran into Arthur Street depot on 30 June 1951, ironically two years before the last tram route closed.

Railless trolleybus no. 9 negotiates roadworks on the Nechells service, at the junction of Great Lister Street and Saltley Street, On journeys to Washwood Heath depot trolleybuses used the wires on the left curving into Saltley Street, from where the vehicles trailed a skate in the tram tracks to operate to the depot.

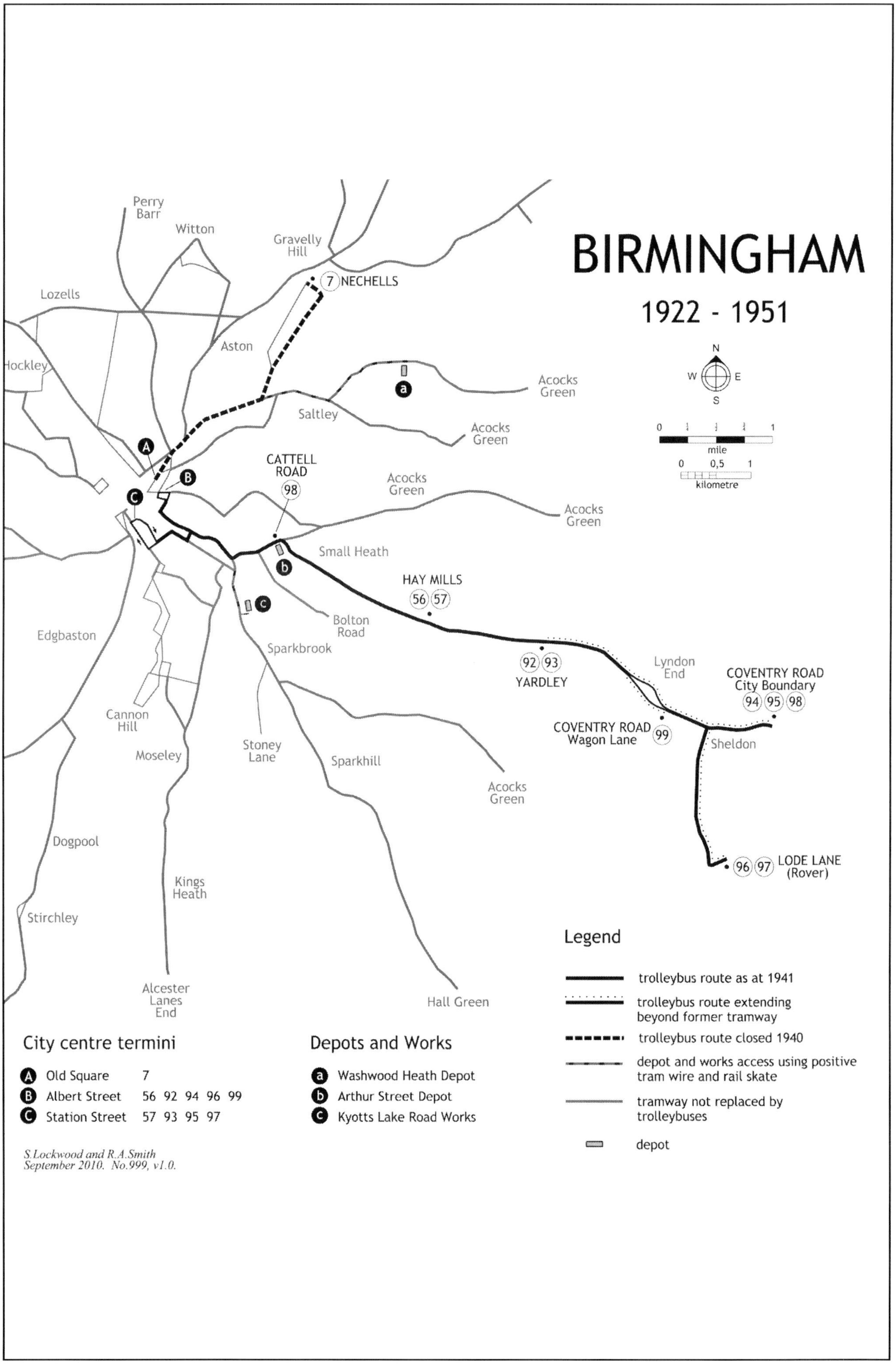
BIRMINGHAM
1922 - 1951
N
W
E
S
0
1
mile
0
0,5
1
kilometre
Perry Barr
Witton
Gravelly Hill
7 NECHELLS
Lozells
Aston
Hockley
Acocks Green
Saltley
Acocks Green
A
B
C
CATTELL ROAD
98
Acocks Green
Acocks Green
Small Heath
a
b
c
HAY MILLS
(56) (57)
Bolton Road
Edgbaston
Sparkbrook
(92) (93)
YARDLEY
Lyndon End
COVENTRY ROAD
City Boundary
(94) (95) (98)
COVENTRY ROAD
Wagon Lane
(99)
Sheldon
Cannon Hill
Moseley
Stoney Lane
Sparkhill
Acocks Green
Dogpool
(96) (97) LODE LANE
(Rover)
Kings Heath
Stirchley
Legend
trolleybus route as at 1941
trolleybus route extending beyond former tramway
trolleybus route closed 1940
depot and works access using positive tram wire and rail skate
tramway not replaced by trolleybuses
depot
Alcester Lanes End
Hall Green
City centre termini
A Old Square 7
B Albert Street 56 92 94 96 99
C Station Street 57 93 95 97
Depots and Works
a Washwood Heath Depot
b Arthur Street Depot
c Kyotts Lake Road Works
S.Lockwood and R.A.Smith
September 2010. No.999, v1.0.

This is the experimental low-height trolleybus produced by the tramway truck supplier EMB in 1924. This was never owned by Birmingham, but nevertheless was allocated fleet number 13 during its short two-year life.

Eleven Leyland TBD1 trolleybuses came in 1932 to replace the original Railless vehicles. These had dummy radiators and half-cabs. The bodies were by Short Brothers. No. 11 is seen in Old Square departing for Nechells.

The fifty Leyland six-wheelers for the Coventry Road routes were type TTBD2 and had Metro Cammell bodies. They were numbered between 17 and 66 in the fleet. On 17 June 1951, no. 20 is seen at the Wheatsheaf junction where the Lode Lane route branched off along Hobbs Moat Road. One of the later four-wheel vehicles is following. (J.H. Meredith)

The final development of the Birmingham trolleybus fleet was the purchase of 24 four-wheel Leylands. Twelve TB5s, nos 67 to 78 arrived in 1938, followed by a further twelve, type TB7, in 1940. The final vehicle, no. 90, is seen at Station Street, one of the two city centre termini of the Coventry Road services, on 17 June 1951, just two weeks before the system closed. It is operating on an enthusiasts' tour. (J.H. Meredith)

# Reading

A well-maintained and popular trolleybus operation in a medium-sized town. New vehicles and route extensions were being introduced as late as the early 1960s, before a change of policy due to outside influences forced the system's closure.

Reading's first venture into trolleybus operation involved the conversion in 1936 of the Caversham to Whitley Street tram route, whose track was in need of renewal. Six four-wheel trolleybuses of varying makes were purchased, comprising two Sunbeams (one being their first four-wheeler built and which had previously been a demonstrator), and one each of Guy, Ransomes, AEC and Leyland makes. All these had bodies of low-height construction. An unusual provision was an isolated half-mile stretch of wiring in Earleigh Road used for test and training purposes.

The success of the trolleybuses resulted in the conversion of the remaining tram route, running west to east across the town from Tilehurst to Wokingham Road. This occurred on 21 May 1939, when 24 four-wheel AEC trolleybuses with highbridge bodies entered service. At the same time a spur from Cemetery Junction on Wokingham Road, to London Road was opened.

Wartime conditions prompted the re-naming of the trolleybus termini to confuse the enemy. For instance, the Thames-side terminus at Caversham Bridge was shown as 'Promenade' and 'London Road' became 'Liverpool Road', a destination name that continued to be used after the war. A short branch off the Tilehurst service from Norcot to Kentwood was opened in July 1944, this being a wartime measure to save motorbus mileage. Meanwhile, six utility Sunbeams entered service in 1943, and unlike other systems with identical vehicles, these had a very short life, being withdrawn in 1950. However, in 1948, Reading purchased twelve elderly 1934 vintage Karrier six-wheelers from Huddersfield. Only six eventually entered service, the rest being used for spare parts.

Reading expanded rapidly in the immediate post-war years, and this prompted the need for route extensions into new housing areas. Accordingly the Whitley Street route was extended to Northumberland Avenue in June 1949, followed in August that year by a new route branching off the new Northumberland Avenue wiring at Buckland Road Junction to Whitley Wood, where a reversing triangle was provided. A branch off the Caversham Bridge route to the Reading railway stations was brought into use at the same time. Twenty BUT trolleybuses entered service for these extensions, followed in 1950 by twelve Sunbeam six-wheelers.

No further alteration to the system occurred until August 1958, when a half-mile extension to the Kentwood route was opened to Armour Hill. In 1961, the last of the pre-war AEC vehicles were replaced by twelve new Sunbeam four-wheel vehicles with front-entrance bodies, and Reading re-affirmed its faith in the trolleybus by opening a further short extension to the Northumberland Avenue route in January 1963.

Up to the mid-1960s, there had been no talk of abandoning the trolleybus system, although the portion of the Caversham Bridge route between the terminus and the Stations

## FACTFILE – READING

| | |
|---|---|
| Opened | 18 July 1936 |
| Closed | 3 November 1968 |
| Route mileage | 13 |

## FLEET PROFILE
**All double-deck**

| | |
|---|---|
| Maximum number vehicles in service | 63 |
| Rebodied vehicles | Nil |
| Second-hand vehicles | 6 |
| | |
| AEC | 26 |
| BUT | 20 |
| Guy | 1 |
| Karrier | 6 |
| Leyland | 1 |
| Ransomes | 1 |
| Sunbeam 4-wheel | 20 |
| Sunbeam 6-wheel | 12 |

## HOW THEY WENT – READING

| | |
|---|---|
| 10 July 1965 | Caversham Bridge |
| 8 January 1967 | Whitley Wood to Stations |
| 31 December 1967 | Northumberland Avenue to Stations |
| 3 March 1968 | Armour Hill to Liverpool Road |
| 3 November 1968 | Tilehurst to Wokingham Road |

had been closed in mid-1965 due to the reduction in passenger traffic and the number of other bus services that covered the same route. However, in 1966, a reluctant decision, based on the difficulty of obtaining materials to maintain the network, was taken to abandon the system. This was implemented in four stages from January 1967 and the ceremonial last trolleybus ran on the afternoon of Sunday 3 November 1968.

Five of the 1961 Sunbeams were sold to Tees-side for further service.

*Reading's first trolleybus was this Sunbeam MF1, which had been built as a demonstrator in early 1934. It had a lowbridge Park Royal body and was the first four-wheel Sunbeam. In Reading it entered service in 1936 numbered 1, and the chassis had been modernised to type MF2A specification.*

The Reading system was basically cruciform in shape, the main routes crossing in the town centre. This commercial postcard view shows the overhead wiring crossings at the junction of Broad Street and St Mary's Butts, looking west towards Oxford Road. The nearest vehicle in view is no. 104, one of the seven experimental vehicles of the initial fleet, and which had originally been no. 4. It was a Leyland TB4 type with Park Royal body.

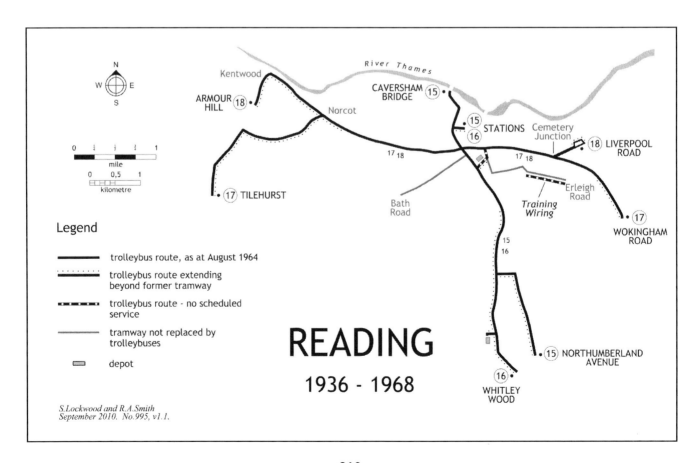

# READING
## 1936 - 1968

Legend

— trolleybus route, as at August 1964

......... trolleybus route extending beyond former tramway

▪━▪━▪ trolleybus route - no scheduled service

— tramway not replaced by trolleybuses

▭ depot

*S.Lockwood and R.A.Smith*
*September 2010. No.995, v1.1.*

The bulk of the pre-war fleet comprised of 24 AEC 661T type vehicles with Park Royal bodies, numbered 108 to 131. No. 113 is seen turning at the Wokingham Road terminus, as the conductor changes the destination blind. Upon withdrawal in 1961, this vehicle achieved fame by becoming the first trolleybus to be privately preserved, being acquired by the Reading Transport Society. It now resides, in operational condition, at the Trolleybus Museum Sandtoft. (D.A. Thompson / London Trolleybus Preservation Society)

One of the six former 1934 vintage Huddersfield Karrier E6s bought in 1948 and placed in service over the next three years, is seen at Norcot. These were numbered 158 to 163 in the fleet. This is no. 162, which was originally Huddersfield no. 12 where, on 4 October 1938, it overturned at Outlane during high winds. (C. Carter)

The first new post-war vehicles came in 1949, and comprised twenty four-wheel BUTs, of the 9611T type. These had Park Royal bodies with platform doors. No. 146 is seen reversing at the Whitley Wood terminus on 21 February 1953. Ex-Huddersfield Karrier no. 160 can be seen at the terminal stop. (J.H. Meredith)

Twelve six-wheel Sunbeam S7s were delivered in late 1950, these being numbered 170 to 181 in the fleet. No. 174 is seen at the Armour Hill turning circle, to where the trolleybus service was extended from Kentwood in August 1958. (Roy Brook / Paul Watson)

Reading's final trolleybuses were twelve Sunbeam F4s new in 1961, these being replacements for the surviving pre-war AEC vehicles. They had Burlingham front-entrance bodies and took the fleet nos 182 to 193. Seen turning from Radstock Road into Liverpool Road on the 'round the houses' turning loop at this terminus, is brand new no. 185. This vehicle was sold to Tees-side in 1968, becoming no. 10 in that fleet. (Travel Lens Photographic)

Reading introduced route numbers in the early 1960s. Sunbeam F4A no. 192, standing at the Wokingham Road terminus, displays the number for the Wokingham Road to Tilehurst route. The upper deck rear emergency door incorporated a platform to allow access to the trolley gear on the roof. (D.F. Parker)

# WEATHER

Following a heavy snowfall, this Huddersfield BUT trolleybus, no. 628, is unloading passengers in the middle of Blackmoorfoot Road on the Crosland Hill route. (Roy Brook / Paul Watson)

The 'big freeze' of early 1963 is recalled in this view of Wolverhampton Sunbeam W trolleybus no. 412 pulling away from a stop in Court Road on the Whitmore Reans route on Saturday 26 January 1963. Note the icicles hanging from the roofs of the houses on the left. (P.J. Thompson)

This press photograph was taken to show the smog which engulfed Manchester in November 1953. Crossley 'Empire' trolleybus no. 1229 is standing in the murk at the George Street (Piccadilly) terminus before departing on a midday service to Gee Cross. (Mirrorpix)

# Southend

**The compact system in this seaside town was steadily enlarged up to the end of the war, but was thereafter starved of investment.**

Two single-deck Railless vehicles commenced service in October 1925 between the town centre and Prittlewell. Unusually, these operated to augment the existing tram service. After a few months, in May 1926, the route was extended a short distance beyond the tram terminus to Priory Park, and a further vehicle, a former AEC demonstrator which had operated in Leeds, was obtained.

Expansion to the system came in August 1929, when the existing route was extended south from the town centre to the seafront at the Kursaal. Six double-deck six-wheeler Garrett trolleybuses were obtained, the first of which had an open staircase. These were followed in 1930 by a pair of English Electric six-wheelers with front exit bodywork and in 1932 by another AEC which was an ex-demonstration vehicle with a half cab and dummy radiator. This vehicle, which became Southend no. 116, is known to have operated experimentally in Bradford.

Further expansion came in 1932, when new routes previously not served by public transport were established, these being to Fairfax Drive and Eastwood Boulevard via Prittlewell, and to Hamstel Road via North Avenue. Nine four-wheel AEC trolleybuses joined the fleet at this time, these also having dummy radiators but with full fronts.

Two one-off vehicles were purchased in 1934 – a centre-entrance trolleybus, the only one ever built by the Gloucester Railway Carriage and Wagon Co, and an AEC 'Q' type trolleybus. In the same year the Kursaal route was extended westwards along the sea front to Pier Hill, near the Pier entrance, and trolleybuses operated to there in the summer months.

A further extension to the Fairfax Drive route opened in July 1935, running along Nelson Road to terminate at Chalkwell Park near to London Road and the Leigh tram

| FACTFILE – SOUTHEND | |
| --- | --- |
| Opened | 16 October 1925 |
| Closed | 28 October 1954 |
| Route mileage | 11 |

| FLEET PROFILE | |
| --- | --- |
| All 4-wheel double-deck unless denoted | |
| Maximum number vehicles in service | 34 |
| Rebodied vehicles | Nil |
| Second-hand vehicles | 14 |
| | |
| Railless single-deck | 2 |
| AEC | 17 |
| AEC single-deck | 1 |
| AEC 6-wheel | 1 |
| English Electric 6-wheel | 2 |
| Garrett six wheel | 6 |
| Gloster | 1 |
| Leyland single-deck | 5 |
| Sunbeam | 18 |

route. The final pre-war development was an eastward extension of the sea front route from the Kursaal to Thorpe Bay, opening in June 1939. Within three months the war had started and this sea front section was closed until 1945. Six four-wheel AEC trolleybuses also entered service in 1939, four of them being loaned to Bradford between 1940 and 1942. A further 36 AEC trolleybuses were ordered in 1939 to convert the tram route to Leigh and extend the Thorpe Bay service to Shoebury but these vehicles never materialised and the routes were converted to motorbuses.

The war did not prevent the growth of the network, and extensions were opened in 1942 from Chalkwell Park along London Road to the town centre and an alternative route to the Kursaal via Southchurch Road. In 1943 the wires were extended eastwards along Southchurch Road to

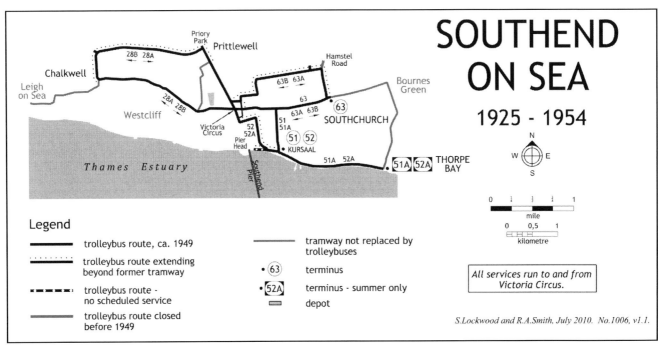

## Legend

— trolleybus route, ca. 1949

········· trolleybus route extending beyond former tramway

■ ■ ■ ■ ■ trolleybus route – no scheduled service

═══ trolleybus route closed before 1949

~~~~ tramway not replaced by trolleybuses

• ⑥③ terminus

• 52A terminus – summer only

▭ depot

**SOUTHEND ON SEA**

**1925 - 1954**

N
W ⊕ E
S

0 ¼ ½ ¾ 1
mile

0 0,5 1
kilometre

All services run to and from Victoria Circus.

*S.Lockwood and R.A.Smith, July 2010. No.1006, v1.1.*

The initial trolleybus service to Priory Park was operated by a pair of Railless single-deck vehicles originally numbered 1 and 2, but later renumbered 101, 102. The former is seen at the depot, showing the open-fronted driver's cab. (A.D. Packer)

Southchurch, and in 1944 Hamstel Road itself was wired up to provide a link between North Avenue and Southchurch. At the end of the war, nine utility Sunbeam vehicles entered service.

After the war, the system comprised the following main services: the West Circular around Chalkwell, the East Circular around Southchurch, and two routes to the Kursaal. An unadvertised summer seasonal service operated using the re-opened wiring along the seafront to Thorpe Bay.

However, there was no further development of the network, and vehicle replacements were in the form of second-hand pre-war vehicles. Five Leyland single-deck trol-leybuses new in 1936 came from Tees-side in 1946, followed in 1950 by nine Sunbeams from Wolverhampton which had been new in 1938.

By the 1950s, the Corporation was entering into agreements with the local company bus operator about the co-ordination of services, and the trolleybuses had no part in this. Accordingly, the routes all closed in 1954. The East Circular last ran on 10 February; services to the Kursaal ceased on 14 July and on 28 October a decorated AEC vehicle ran on the remaining West Circular route to formally close the system. The nine utility Sunbeams were sold to Doncaster.

In 1929, six Garrett double-deck six-wheelers entered service, numbered 104 to 109. The first of these had an open staircase. It is seen at the Kursaal sporting whitewall tyres. (A.D. Packer)

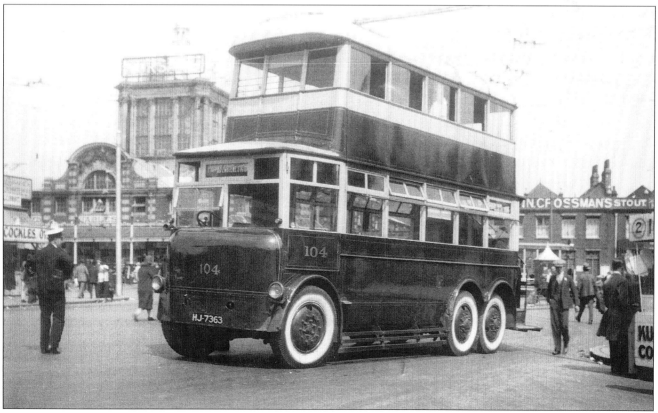

Nine AEC 661T type trolleybuses with English Electric bodies entered
service between 1932 and 1933. These had half-cabs and dummy
radiators. Nos 113 and 115 are seen operating on the Hamstel Road
service. Many of these vehicles were later rebuilt with full-fronts.

In 1939, six of these AEC type 661T vehicles entered service. Bodies were by
Strachan. No. 127 is seen in the early 1950s working on one of the suburban
circular services. This vehicle was one of those loaned to Bradford between
1940 and 1942. (D.A.Thompson / London Trolleybus Preservation Society)

Southend had nine Sunbeam W utility vehicles, numbered 130 to 138. The first had a Brush body, the remainder Park Royal. They were Southend's last trolleybuses bought new. No. 136 is seen at the Victoria Circus terminus of the West Circular services. All these vehicles were sold to Doncaster in 1954, and subsequently given new Roe bodies. This one became Doncaster no. 391. (D.F. Parker)

An unusual purchase in 1946 was a quintet of single-deck Leylands, type TB3, from Tees-side. Originally Tees-side nos 9 to 13, they became nos 139 to 143 at Southend. No. 142 is seen at work at the Kursaal, on the service to Victoria Circus. (C. Carter)

The sea-front service to Thorpe Bay was seasonal and ran as required. At Thorpe Bay terminus is one of the nine Park Royal bodied Sunbeam MF2 vehicles bought from Wolverhampton in 1948, these being numbered 144 to 152. This one, working on an enthusiasts' tour on 17 September 1950, was formally Wolverhampton no. 275, new in 1938. Behind it stands 1932 AEC trolleybus no. 113, rebuilt with a full front. It is working on the seasonal 52A service to Victoria Circus. (J.H. Meredith)

# Ipswich

**The comprehensive municipal public transport system in this medium-sized town relied entirely on the trolleybus for 27 years.**

Ipswich experimented with trolleybus operation with a short route of less than a mile in length, linking the town centre with the railway station. This was opened in September 1923 and was worked by three Railless vehicles. These were unusual in that the Short Bros bodies had an open rear veranda for smokers, and a front entrance for 'one man' operation. In July 1925, a longer route was opened to Bourne Bridge, and two further vehicles, a Ransomes and a Tilling Stevens, were obtained to assess reliability. Plans were then laid to replace the tram system in its entirety, and to introduce new trolleybus services. Orders were placed for 30 vehicles, split equally between local manufacturers Ransomes and Garrett, all with front entrances and rear exits to facilitate 'one man' operation. Accordingly, routes to Kingsway, Felixstowe Road, Lattice Barn, Derby Road Station, Whitton, Bramford Road were inaugurated during 1926, followed by the Foxhall Road route and a branch to London Road in early 1927.

Eight further Ransomes single-deckers joined the fleet between 1928 and 1930, the first five of which were to an unusual half-cab design with an open front platform. The front entrances of all these and previous vehicles with two doorways were later blanked off, 'one man' operation having ceased by the early 1930s. New routes to Nacton Road and Gainsborough Estate opened in July 1928, running via Rands Way and Kingsway to join Felixstowe Road. In 1931, wiring was opened along Landseer Road from Rands Way to Reynolds Road.

There was now a slight pause in expansion, but in 1933 the first of 40 Ransomes double-deckers entered service, these being delivered steadily up to 1938. These vehicles allowed the inauguration of further new routes – 1934 saw

FACTFILE – IPSWICH

| | |
|---|---|
| Opened | 2 September 1923 |
| Closed | 23 August 1963 |
| Route mileage | 25 |

FLEET PROFILE

**All 4-wheel and single-deck unless denoted**

| | |
|---|---|
| Maximum number vehicles in service | 70 |
| Rebodied vehicles | Nil |
| Second-hand vehicles | Nil |
| | |
| Garrett | 16 |
| Karrier double-deck | 28 |
| Railless | 3 |
| Ransomes | 26 |
| Ransomes double-deck | 41 |
| Sunbeam double-deck | 12 |
| Tilling Stevens | 1 |

**HOW THEY WENT – IPSWICH**

| | |
|---|---|
| 23 April 1939 | Rands Way / Kingsway |
| 6 September 1953 | Adair Road |
| 23 May 1954 | Bourne Bridge |
| 29 July 1956 | London Road / Hadleigh Road |
| 1 June 1958 | Foxhall Road |
| 31 May 1959 | Heath Road, Bixby Road |
| 1 October 1960 | Sidegate Lane |
| 29 April 1962 | Rushmere Heath to Whitton, Ipswich Station |
| 23 August 1963 | Gainsborough Estate, Priory Heath, Airport |

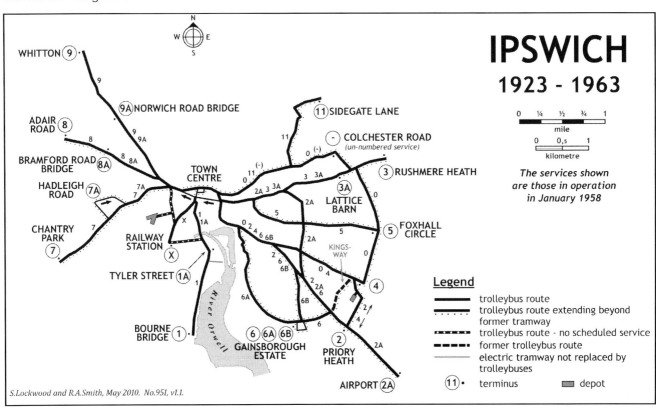

IPSWICH 1923 - 1963

*The services shown are those in operation in January 1958*

S.Lockwood and R.A.Smith, May 2010. No.951, v1.1.

Legend
— trolleybus route
······ trolleybus route extending beyond former tramway
▪▪▪▪ trolleybus route - no scheduled service
▬ ▬ ▬ former trolleybus route
~~~ electric tramway not replaced by trolleybuses
⑪• terminus
▨ depot

trolleybuses extended to Rushmere Heath from Lattice Barn, and the London Road service was extended to Chantry Park in time to serve the Royal Show held there in that year. Late 1936 saw wiring extended to Rushmere Road round to Bixby Road, whilst in 1938 a link westwards along Landseer Road to Holbrook Road, and a one way loop at Hadleigh Road on London Road were opened. The final pre-war developments were: in 1939, a link to Priory Heath along Lindbergh Road (which resulted in the discontinuance of the trolleybus service in Rands Way to Kingsway); and in early 1940 when trolleybuses started operation on the remaining western part of Landseer Road from the town centre. One further Ransomes trolleybus was acquired this year, this being reputed to be a demonstrator for export orders that could not be sent abroad due to the war.

Towards the end of the war 16 utility Karrier vehicles joined the fleet, and new wiring was opened in 1945 along Clapgate Lane. What turned out to be the final pieces of the network came about in 1947, when wiring was extended to Sidegate Lane in April and along Nacton Road from Priory Heath to the Airport in August.

The trolleybus system, now at its greatest extent, gave a comprehensive coverage of the town. Particularly to the east, there was a close network of wiring linking the various radial routes, allowing circular services to be operated. Notable amongst these was service '0', which ran around the extremity of the system in the north east and east of the town. Some 1920s Ransomes single-deckers were still in service to run on the Adair Road route, on which there was a low arch precluding the use of double-deckers. Twenty four new Karrier and Sunbeam vehicles entered service between 1948 and 1950.

By 1950 more routes were being planned to serve new housing areas, but the economics of operating trolleybuses were not now seen to be advantageous, and the Corporation ordered its first motorbuses. Some trolleybus routes were rationalised in 1951, and from 1953 trolleybus services began to be converted to motorbus operation, starting with the restrictive Adair Road route, allowing the remaining single-deck trolleybuses to be withdrawn. The last trolleybus of all to operate in August 1963 bore a prominent notice which stated 'This is DEFINITELY the last trolleybus'. Eight of the last batch of Sunbeam F4 vehicles were sold to Walsall in 1962.

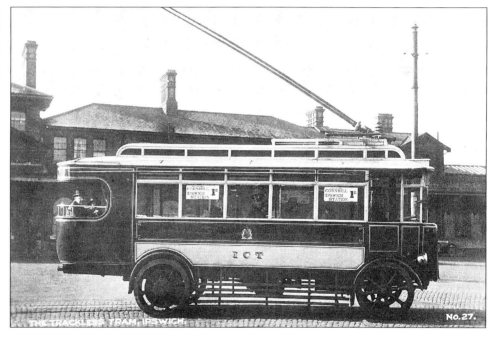

The original trio of Railless vehicles ran on a service from the town centre to the Railway Station. This commercial postcard shows one of them at the station, advertising the 1d fare. Note the open smoking area at the rear.

The Cornhill was the focus of the early trolleybus system. In this commercial postcard view, Ransomes no. 10, one of the fifteen 1926 vehicles is seen on the station service (designated 'X'). Note the electrically operated frog on the overhead in the foreground.

Five Ransomes vehicles delivered in 1928, numbered 37 to 41, had this unusual open half-cab arrangement to facilitate one-man operation. No. 38 is seen in original condition at the Lattice Barn terminus of the Woodbridge Road route, before this was extended to Rushmere Heath in 1934. These vehicles were later rebuilt with conventional front ends. (Adam Gordon collection)

Forty Ransomes D4 double-deckers entered service between 1933 and 1938. This is no. 65, one of eight delivered in 1936, and seen at Electric House in the town centre. It is having its trolley poles placed on the wires before departing on a journey to Priory Heath. Note the unpainted side-panels, a feature of this system's vehicles. The aluminium panelling both above and below the lower deck windows was buffed into an attractive-looking squared pattern. (R. Marshall)

No. 68 was the first of eighteen Massey bodied Ransomes, new in 1937, and is seen before delivery to Ipswich. (Adam Gordon collection)

220

This one-off Ransomes trolleybus joined the fleet in 1940. Bodywork was by Massey, to a streamlined design and was rumoured to have been built as a demonstrator but this has never been verified. It is seen here turning into Grove Lane on the Foxhall Road route. (Photomatic)

Ransomes single-decker no. 41 is seen in post-war days at Ipswich station. Note that the original half cab arrangement has been replaced by a more conventional full front, and that prominent advertising boards are affixed to the roof. Until conversion of the route to motorbuses in 1953, single-deck trolleybuses were required to operate on the Adair Road service due to a low bridge. (A.D. Packer)

Sixteen Karrier Ws with utility bodywork came in 1944/5, numbered 87 to 102. The first four had Weymann bodies, with Park Royal supplying the remainder. No. 100 is seen entering Cornhill, passing under the 'bridge' in Lloyd's Avenue which was wired for trolleybuses in 1949. (A.D. Packer)

Post-war trolleybus deliveries consisted of 24 Karrier/Sunbeams, all with similar-looking Park Royal bodies and numbered 103 to 126 in the fleet. Six Karrier Ws came in 1948, followed by six Karrier badged F4s in the following year (these being the only F4s to be so designated). A final batch of twelve Sunbeam F4s came in 1950. Two of this type are seen at the Landseer Road terminus of the Gainsbrough Estate services on 3 August 1961. To the right is Karrier F4 no. 110, and on the left is the rear of Sunbeam F4 no. 125. This vehicle was one of eight of this type sold to Walsall in 1962, becoming their no. 346. Note the tubular suspension of the overhead wiring. (A.D. Packer)

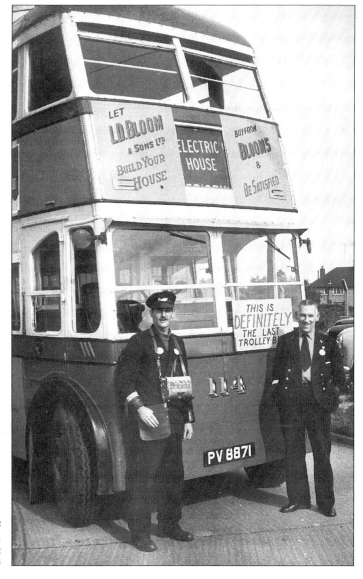

The crew of the last trolleybus is posed in front of the vehicle, Karrier F4 no. 114, after the completion of the final trolleybus journey to Priory Heath depot on 23 April 1963. (Photomatic)

222

Monument at Newcastle. Located in a prominent position in the centre of Newcastle is the Earl Grey Monument. The column, erected in 1838, is 134 feet high, topped by a statue of Earl Grey of Falloden, a noted North East politician and Prime Minister in the early 19th century, The base pedestal was high enough to be used to secure the trolleybus span wiring at this location, and the fixing bolts are still evident today. This commercial postcard view of Grainger Street, shows the Monument in the background. The trolleybus, seen proceeding towards Central Station, is no. 523, one of the 30 Sunbeams S7 six-wheelers with Northern Coachbuilders bodywork and new in 1948.

11th century castle at Mexborough. The Conisborough High route included a section traversing hilly narrow streets overshadowed by Conisborough Castle. Mexborough no. 37 is seen on the climb to the terminus with the castle keep in the background. This vehicle later became no. 845 at Bradford, being fitted with a double-deck body. (G.H.F. Atkins / courtesy and copyright John Banks collection)

Art Deco apartment block at Hastings. Marine Court is a 1930s Art Deco building which dominates the promenade at Hastings and St Leonards. It was designed to resemble the tiered decks of the 'Queen Mary' liner. Passing along the promenade is the restored Hastings open-top Guy trolleybus no. 3A, seen performing its last run under electric power on 1 June 1959, carrying civic dignitaries on the day after the Hastings system closed. (British Commercial Vehicle Museum)

# THE TROLLEYBUSES OF LONDON

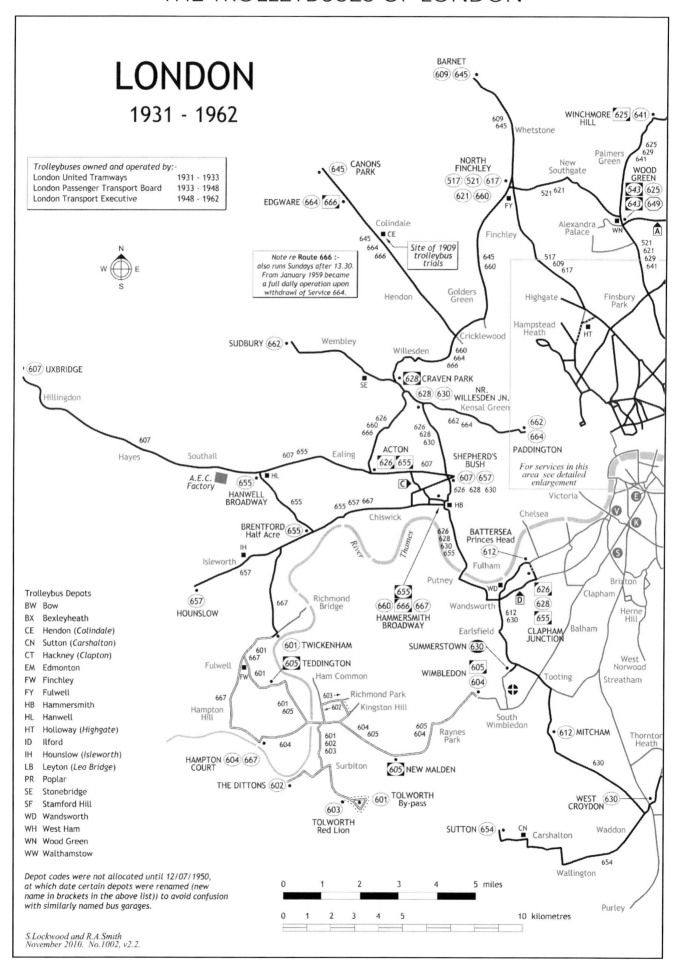

## LONDON
### 1931 - 1962

Trolleybuses owned and operated by:-
| | |
|---|---|
| London United Tramways | 1931 - 1933 |
| London Passenger Transport Board | 1933 - 1948 |
| London Transport Executive | 1948 - 1962 |

**Note re Route 666 :-**
*also runs Sundays after 13.30. From January 1959 became a full daily operation upon withdrawl of Service 664.*

Site of 1909 trolleybus trials

**Trolleybus Depots**

| | |
|---|---|
| BW | Bow |
| BX | Bexleyheath |
| CE | Hendon (*Colindale*) |
| CN | Sutton (*Carshalton*) |
| CT | Hackney (*Clapton*) |
| EM | Edmonton |
| FW | Finchley |
| FY | Fulwell |
| HB | Hammersmith |
| HL | Hanwell |
| HT | Holloway (*Highgate*) |
| ID | Ilford |
| IH | Hounslow (*Isleworth*) |
| LB | Leyton (*Lea Bridge*) |
| PR | Poplar |
| SE | Stonebridge |
| SF | Stamford Hill |
| WD | Wandsworth |
| WH | West Ham |
| WN | Wood Green |
| WW | Walthamstow |

*Depot codes were not allocated until 12/07/1950, at which date certain depots were renamed (new name in brackets in the above list)) to avoid confusion with similarly named bus garages.*

S.Lockwood and R.A.Smith
November 2010. No.1002, v2.2.

0 1 2 3 4 5 miles

0 1 2 3 4 5 10 kilometres

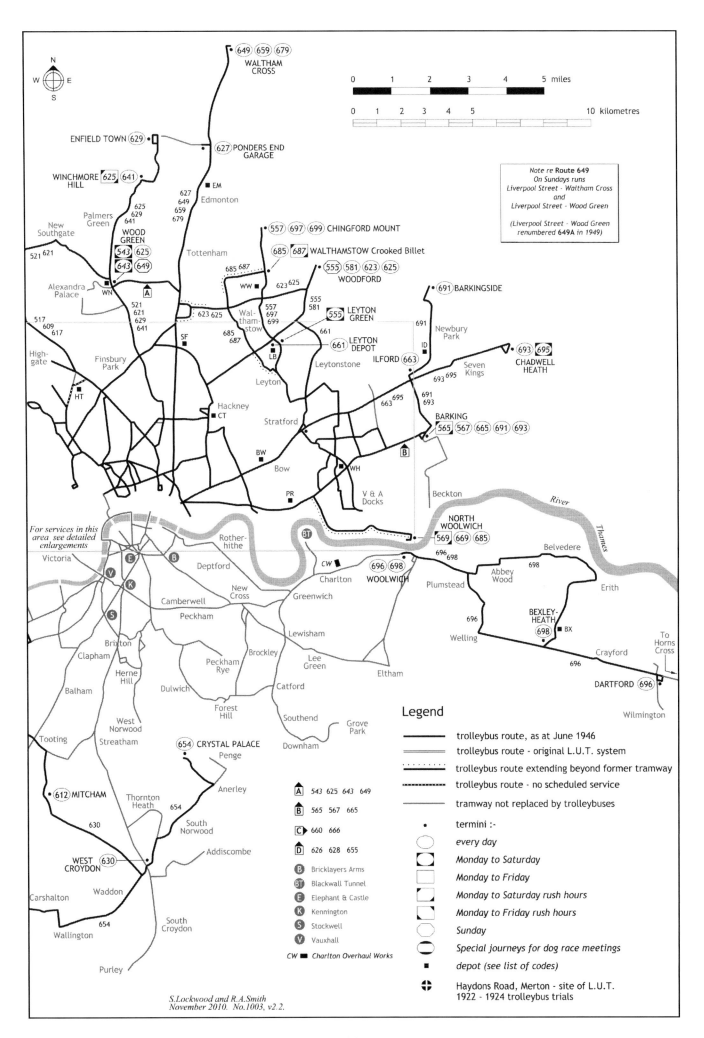

649 659 679 WALTHAM CROSS

ENFIELD TOWN 629

PONDERS END GARAGE
627

WINCHMORE HILL 625 641

EM

627
649
659
679
Edmonton

Palmers Green

New Southgate

625
629
641

WOOD GREEN

521 621

543 625

643 649

557 697 699 CHINGFORD MOUNT

685 687 WALTHAMSTOW Crooked Billet

555 581 623 625 WOODFORD

Tottenham

685 687

WW

623 625

Alexandra Palace

WN

A

521
621
629
641

517
609
617

623 625

557
697
699

555
581

LEYTON GREEN 555

691 BARKINGSIDE

Newbury Park

Highgate

Finsbury Park

SF

685
687

Wal-
tham-
stow

661

691

ID

LEYTON DEPOT 661

CHADWELL HEATH 693 695

HT

LB

Leytonstone

ILFORD 663

Seven Kings

693 695

Leyton

663 695

691
693

Hackney
CT

Stratford

BW

Bow

PR

WH

BARKING 565 567 665 691 693

B

V & A Docks

Beckton

River Thames

For services in this area see detailed enlargements

Rother-hithe

Deptford

BT

NORTH WOOLWICH 569 669 685

Belvedere

Victoria

E

B

CW

Charlton

696 698

696 698

Abbey Wood

698

Erith

V

K

New Cross

Greenwich

WOOLWICH 696 698

Plumstead

698

Camberwell

S

Peckham

Lewisham

Welling

696

BEXLEY-HEATH 698

BX

Brixton

Clapham

Brockley

Lee Green

Crayford

To Horns Cross

Herne Hill

Peckham Rye

Eltham

696

Balham

Dulwich

Catford

DARTFORD 696

Tooting

West Norwood

Forest Hill

Southend

Grove Park

Wilmington

Streatham

654 CRYSTAL PALACE

Penge

Downham

612 MITCHAM

Thornton Heath

Anerley

630

654

South Norwood

Addiscombe

WEST CROYDON 630

Carshalton

Waddon

South Croydon

654

Wallington

Purley

Note re Route 649
On Sundays runs
Liverpool Street - Waltham Cross
and
Liverpool Street - Wood Green

(Liverpool Street - Wood Green
renumbered 649A in 1949)

## Legend

—— trolleybus route, as at June 1946

—— trolleybus route - original L.U.T. system

···· trolleybus route extending beyond former tramway

-x-x- trolleybus route - no scheduled service

—— tramway not replaced by trolleybuses

• termini :-

◯ every day

◖ Monday to Saturday

▢ Monday to Friday

◣ Monday to Saturday rush hours

◪ Monday to Friday rush hours

◯ Sunday

◖ Special journeys for dog race meetings

■ depot (see list of codes)

✚ Haydons Road, Merton - site of L.U.T. 1922 - 1924 trolleybus trials

A  543 625 643 649

B  565 567 665

C  660 666

D  626 628 655

B  Bricklayers Arms

BT  Blackwall Tunnel

E  Elephant & Castle

K  Kennington

S  Stockwell

V  Vauxhall

CW ■  Charlton Overhaul Works

S.Lockwood and R.A.Smith
November 2010. No.1003, v2.2.

225

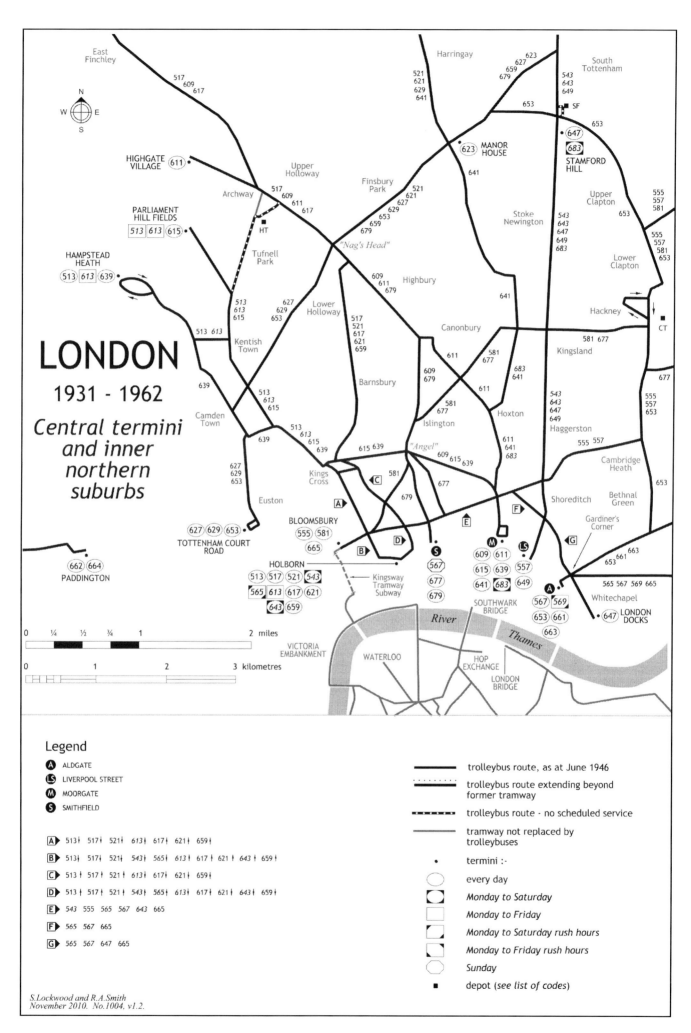

# LONDON
## 1931 - 1962
### Central termini and inner northern suburbs

**Legend**

Ⓐ ALDGATE
ⓛⓢ LIVERPOOL STREET
Ⓜ MOORGATE
Ⓢ SMITHFIELD

A▶ 513† 517† 521† 613† 617† 621† 659†
B▶ 513† 517† 521† 543† 565† 613† 617 † 621 † 643 † 659†
C▶ 513 † 517† 521 † 613† 617† 621† 659†
D▶ 513 † 517† 521† 543† 565† 613† 617† 621† 643† 659†
E▶ 543 555 565 567 643 665
F▶ 565 567 665
G▶ 565 567 647 665

——— trolleybus route, as at June 1946
·········· trolleybus route extending beyond former tramway
▬▬▬▬ trolleybus route - no scheduled service
——— tramway not replaced by trolleybuses
• termini :-
⬭ every day
◖◗ Monday to Saturday
▢ Monday to Friday
◣ Monday to Saturday rush hours
◣ Monday to Friday rush hours
⬡ Sunday
■ depot (see list of codes)

S.Lockwood and R.A.Smith
November 2010. No.1004, v1.2.

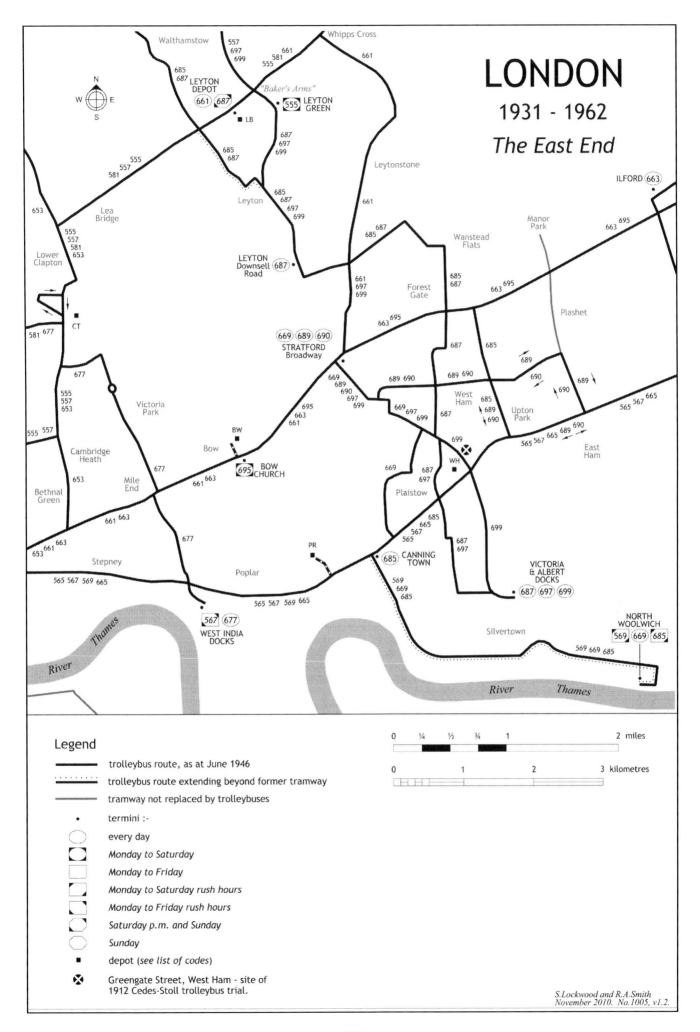

**LONDON**

**1931 - 1962**

*The East End*

Legend

— trolleybus route, as at June 1946

········· trolleybus route extending beyond former tramway

— tramway not replaced by trolleybuses

• termini :-

○ every day

◖ Monday to Saturday

▢ Monday to Friday

◪ Monday to Saturday rush hours

◪ Monday to Friday rush hours

◡ Saturday p.m. and Sunday

⬭ Sunday

■ depot (*see list of codes*)

⊗ Greengate Street, West Ham - site of 1912 Cedes-Stoll trolleybus trial.

*S.Lockwood and R.A.Smith
November 2010. No.1005, v1.2.*

# London United Tramways

The capital's first foray into trolleybus operation, and the beginnings of what was to become the world's largest trolleybus system.

The London United Tramways (LUT) operated in the west and south-west of London, and were part of the large Underground group of companies which included the vehicle chassis builder AEC. In the early 1920s, LUT was considering ways of improving loss-making tram routes including the introduction of trolleybuses. A portion of tram route in Plough Lane and Haydon's Road, Merton, was adapted for trolleybus operation by the provision of a negative trolley wire, and between 1922 and 1924 this was used to test AEC single-deck type 602 trolley vehicles, initially in chassis form only. There was no public service and no further developments took place for some years.

However, LUT was eventually faced with the renewal of its tramways in the Kingston area, both track and cars. Instead it obtained powers to convert these lines to trolleybus operation. A trial route was wired from Fulwell Depot towards Teddington during 1930, and this was used to test an AEC six-wheel trolleybus based on the 'Renown' motorbus chassis which was being introduced in London service. Other demonstration vehicles, including Karrier and Guy types were also run on this trial route, which again was not used for public service. LUT chose the AEC chassis and 60 were ordered. These had half-cabs with motor-bus style bonnets and in accordance with LUT practice, were allocated class codes A1 (nos 1 to 35) and A2 (nos 36 to 60) the difference being the type of electrical equipment fitted.

By May 1931 eight of these vehicles were ready for service, and on 16 May London's first public trolleybus service commenced, initially running between Twickenham and Teddington. When the Hampton Court to Wimbledon service was inaugurated in September 1931, the full network was opened for trolleybuses. This consisted of five routes, logically numbered 1 to 5, and was centred on

FACTFILE – LONDON UNITED
All double-deck six-wheel

| | |
|---|---|
| Opened | 16 May 1931 |
| Operation transferred to London Transport 1 July 1933 | |
| Route mileage | 17 |
| Maximum number vehicles in service | 61 |
| Rebodied vehicles | Nil |
| Second-hand vehicles | Nil |

Kingston on Thames, extending from Twickenham in the north to Tolworth and The Dittons in the south, and to Wimbledon in the west. The only other route development was an extension at Wimbledon from Worple Road to the railway station in December 1932. This resulted in the abandonment of wiring in St George's Road on the original turning loop. A further route extension was in progress from the Tolworth terminus to the Kingston by-pass, but this was not completed until after LUT ceased to exist.

One further vehicle joined the fleet in March 1933. This was an experimental trolleybus, larger than the LUT vehicles, and designed to match the seating capacity of the tramcar. Built by AEC, it was a 74-seater with a forward entrance and power doors. This very modern looking vehicle was never actually owned by LUT, being on hire from AEC. Despite this it did display LUT fleet names and legal lettering, but not a fleet number.

The entire LUT trolleybus operation passed to the newly formed London Passenger Transport Board on 1 July 1933, and its success paved the way for the mass replacement of the tram fleet inherited by LTPB.

AEC 'Diddler' trolleybus no. 42 is seen turning at Hampton Court on service 4 to Wimbledon, soon after operations started. Note that the vehicle has not yet been fitted with a central headlight. (Transport for London / London Transport Museum)

This is the experimental AEC 691T vehicle seen at the AEC factory before entering service. Although carrying 'London United' fleetnames, it was never owned by the company, and it eventually became London Transport no. 61.

Although this view dates from early London Transport days (hence the lack of fleetname on the vehicle) it does show a typical London United trolleybus crew posed in front of 'Diddler' no. 19 at Fulwell depot. Note the 'TIM' ticket machine used on the system. (Transport for London / London Transport Museum)

# London Transport

By far the biggest system, which although always extremely well maintained, was never significantly developed after the end of the war.

The London trolleybus system was the largest in the world. Its route mileage was over five times larger than the biggest provincial system, and it had over eight times the number of vehicles. This difference in these proportions reflects the extremely frequent services that were operated.

The London Passenger Transport Board, trading as London Transport (LT), inherited the LUT trolleybus system and its 60 trolleybuses, plus the experimental AEC vehicle which was subsequently brought into LT ownership and given fleet number 61. The success of this operation led to plans to replace London's trams, and to this end two trial vehicles were obtained during 1934. Both these were AECs, no. 62 having the six-wheel chassis of the previous LUT vehicles, but with a modern full front to the 73-seat body. No. 63 was a smaller 60-seat four-wheeler. The larger capacity vehicle was selected as being more suitable and bulk orders were placed with AEC and Leyland. The four-wheeler became unique in the fleet.

Tram conversion commenced in the autumn of 1935, when trolleybuses took over routes from Hampton Court to Hammersmith, and Shepherds Bush to Hounslow, the former extending the former LUT network. Two other self-contained networks replacing elderly trams were established at the end of 1935 at Croydon, linking Crystal Palace and Sutton, and at Bexleyheath, where two routes ran from Woolwich, one reaching Dartford in Kent. The unsuitability of the former municipal tram depots in this area resulted in a new trolleybus depot being provided at Bexleyheath. Trolleybus routes were numbered in the 600 series, although from 1938 some were given numbers in the 500s. The process of tram conversion continued year on year across west, north and east London as follows – 1936 – 8 routes opened; 1937-11 routes; 1938-20 routes, 1939-12 routes. The final conversions before wartime conditions halted further progress was at Poplar depot, where three tram routes became trolleybus operated in June 1940. Apart from a short extension from Woolwich Ferry to Parsons Hill opened in 1943, there were no further extensions to the trolleybus network.

Large numbers of vehicles entered service during this period, and by 1941 the fleet numbered 1721 units. All of these were either AEC or Leylands, and apart from experimental 'one-off' specimens and 68 short wheelbase Leylands delivered in 1935/6, they were to a standard specification of very similar appearance. From 1939 with the introduction of the L class vehicles, a more rounded and

*Story conitnues on page 232*

---

| FACTFILE – LONDON TRANSPORT | |
| --- | --- |
| Operation transferred from London United | 1 July 1933 |
| Closed | 8 May 1962 |
| Route mileage | 255 |

**FLEET PROFILE**
All double-deck, and 6-wheel except where denoted

| | |
| --- | --- |
| Maximum number vehicles in service | 1811 |
| Rebodied vehicles | 61 |
| Second-hand vehicles | Nil |

| | | Class code |
| --- | --- | --- |
| AEC | 695 | A, C, E, J, N, SA3, X1, X2 |
| AEC 4-wheel | 1 | X3 |
| AEC chassisless/unit construction | 202 | L, M, X5 |
| BUT | 127 | Q1 |
| English Electric/AEC chassisless | 1 | X6 |
| Leyland | 863 | B, D, F, H, K, P, SA1/2 |
| Leyland chassisless | 1 | X7 |
| London Transport/AEC chassisless | 1 | X4 |

---

### LONDON'S X TYPE EXPERIMENTAL AND OTHER PROTOTYPE TROLLEYBUSES

| Type | Fleet no. | Description | Year new |
| --- | --- | --- | --- |
| X1 | 61 | AEC 691T, London General forward entrance body | 1933 |
| X2 | 62 | AEC 663T Prototype six-wheel standard trolleybus | 1934 |
| X3 | 63 | AEC 661T Prototype 4-wheel standard trolleybus | 1934 |
| X4 | 754 | AEC / LT Prototype chassisless vehicle. Front exit | 1937 |
| M1 | 953 | AEC prototype of 'unit' construction | 1938 |
| L1 | 954 | AEC prototype of chassisless construction | 1938 |
| X5 | 1379 | Kingsway subway trolleybus with offside entrance | 1939 |
| X6 | 1670 | Prototype English Electric built chassisless trolleybus | 1940 |
| X7 | 1671 | Leyland twin steer chassisless trolleybus | 1940* |

(*former demonstrator in service from 1939, purchased by LT 1940)

## LONDON TROLLEYBUS ROUTES SHOWING THE YEAR OF INTRODUCTION

| No. | Route | Year |
|-----|-------|------|
| 513 | Hampstead-Holborn-Parliament Hill Fields | 1938 N |
| 517 | North Finchley-Highgate-Holborn | 1938 |
| 521 | North Finchley-Wood Green-Holborn | 1938 |
| 543 | Wood Green-Dalston-Holborn | 1939 N |
| 555 | Woodford-Bloomsbury | 1939 |
| 557 | Chingford Mount-Liverpool Street | 1939 |
| 565 | Barking-Holborn | 1940 |
| 567 | Barking-Smithfield | 1940 |
| 569 | North Woolwich-Aldgate | 1941 |
| 581 | Woodford-Bloomsbury | 1939 |
| 601 | Twickenham-Tolworth by-pass | 1931 |
| 601A | Tolworth-Surbiton | 1931 |
| 602 | Dittons-Kingston Hill | 1931 |
| 603 | Tolworth Red Lion-Kingston Hill | 1931 |
| 604 | Hampton Court-Wimbledon | 1931 |
| 605 | Twickenham-Wimbledon | 1931 |
| 607 | Uxbridge-Shepherds Bush | 1936 |
| 609 | Barnet-Moorgate | 1938 |
| 611 | Highgate Village-Moorgate | 1939 |
| 612 | Battersea-Mitcham | 1937 N |
| 613 | Parliament Hill Fields-Holborn-Hampstead | 1938 N |
| 615 | Parliament Hill Fields-Moorgate | 1938 |
| 617 | North Finchley-Highgate-Holborn | 1938 |
| 621 | North Finchley-Wood Green-Holborn | 1938 |
| 623 | Woodford-Manor House | 1936 |
| 625 | Woodford-Winchmore Hill | 1938 |
| 626 | Acton-Clapham Junction | 1937 |
| 627 | Waltham Cross-Tottenham Court Road | 1938 |
| 628 | Clapham Junction-Craven Park | 1937 N |
| 629 | Enfield-Tottenham Court Road | 1938 |
| 630 | Scrubs Lane-West Croydon | 1937 N |
| 639 | Hampstead-Moorgate | 1938 |
| 641 | Winchmore Hill-Moorgate | 1938 |
| 643 | Wood Green-Holborn | 1939 N |
| 645 | Barnet-Canons Park | 1936 |
| 647 | Stamford Hill-London Docks | 1939 |
| 649 | Waltham Cross-Liverpool Street | 1938 |
| 649A | Wood Green-Liverpool Street (Sundays) | 1949 |
| 651 | Barnet-Cricklewood | 1938 |
| 653 | Aldgate-Tottenham Court Road | 1939 |
| 654 | Crystal Palace-Sutton | 1935 |
| 655 | Clapham Junction-Acton Vale | 1936 |
| 657 | Hounslow-Shepherds Bush | 1935 |
| 659 | Waltham Cross –Holborn | 1938 |
| 660 | North Finchley-Hammersmith | 1936 |
| 661 | Leyton-Aldgate | 1939 |
| 662 | Sudbury-Paddington | 1936 |
| 663 | Chadwell Heath-Aldgate | 1939 |
| 664 | Edgware-Paddington | 1936 |
| 665 | Barking-Bloomsbury | 1940 N |
| 666 | Edgware-Hammersmith | 1936 |
| 667 | Hampton Court-Hammersmith | 1935 |
| 669 | North Woolwich-Stratford Broadway | 1937 |
| 677 | West India Docks-Smithfield | 1939 |
| 679 | Waltham Cross-Smithfield | 1938 |
| 683 | Stamford Hill-Moorgate | 1939 |
| 685 | North Woolwich-Walthamstow | 1937 |
| 687 | Victoria and Albert Docks-Walthamstow | 1937 |
| 689/690 | Stratford Broadway-East Ham Circular | 1937 |
| 691 | Barking-Barkingside | 1938 |
| 692 | Newbury Park-Chadwell Heath | 1938 |
| 693 | Barking-Chadwell Heath | 1938 |
| 694 | Erith-Woolwich | 1937 |
| 695 | Chadwell Heath-Bow | 1941 |
| 696 | Dartford-Woolwich | 1935 |
| 697 | Chingford Mount-Victoria and Albert Docks | 1937 |
| 698 | Bexlyheath-Woolwich | 1935 |
| 699 | Chingford Mount-Victoria and Albert Docks | 1937 |

N – denotes night service operated over whole or part of route

## HOW THEY WENT – LONDON TRANSPORT

| Date | Routes | Stage |
|------|--------|-------|
| 31 May 1938 | 651 | |
| 3 December 1938 | 692 | |
| 19 October 1943 | 601A | |
| 22 October 1944 | 694 | |
| 30 September 1950 | 612 | |
| 16 October 1956 | 565 | |
| 6 January 1959 | 664, 683, 695 | |
| 3 March 1959 | 654, 696, 698 | (Stage 1) |
| 14 April 1959 | 555, 581, 677 | (Stage 2) |
| 18 August 1959 | 661, 663, 691, 693 | (Stage 3) |
| 10 November 1959 | 567, 569, 665 | (Stage 4) |
| 2 February 1960 | 557, 669, 685, 689, 690 | (Stage 5) |
| 26 April 1960 | 623, 625, 687, 697, 699 | (Stage 6) |
| 19 July 1960 | 611, 626, 628, 630 | (Stage 7) |
| 8 November 1960 | 607, 655 | (Stage 8) |
| 31 January 1961 | 513, 517, 613, 615, 617, 639, 653 | (Stage 9) |
| 25 April 1961 | 627, 629, 659, 679 | (Stage 10) |
| 16 July 1961 | 641A | (Stage 11) |
| 18 July 1961 | 543, 643, 647, 649 | (Stage 11) |
| 7 November 1961 | 521, 609, 621, 641 | (Stage 12) |
| 2 January 1962 | 645, 660, 662, 666 | (Stage 13) |
| 8 May 1962 | 601, 602, 603, 604, 605, 657, 667 | (Stage 14) |

modern looking frontal design was adopted. The alphanumeric class designation started by LUT was continued by LT, and class letters had reached P in 1940, when the Leyland P1 trolleybuses entered service. There was never a class G, this having been reserved for a batch of single-deck trolleybuses operating on a planned route to Alexandra Palace which was never proceeded with. Unique to London, the later vehicles of AEC manufacture dispensed with the normal rigid chassis, and used a lightweight underframe to which the body was attached, thereby saving considerable cost and weight. Classes L and M were variants of this type of vehicle. Experimental vehicles were given the classification X, trolleybus 61, for instance, being designated X1.

Like the trams, trolleybuses were never allowed to penetrate the very centre of the capital, the nearest points being Hammersmith and Shepherds Bush in the west, Holborn and Tottenham Court Road in the north, and Aldgate in the east. Some routes were quite lengthy, the longest being route 655 which was 14.8 miles in length in its post-war form. It ran on a convoluted course from Acton Vale via Hanwell, Brentford, Hammersmith and Wandsworth to Clapham Junction. Another long route was the 630, which started at the Harrow Road end of Scrubs Lane (enigmatically described on destination blinds as 'Nr Willesden Junction'), running through Shepherd's Bush, Hammersmith, Wandsworth, Tooting and Mitcham to West Croydon.

Twenty-two depots served the trolleybus network, these ranging in size from West Ham and Holloway with over 150 vehicles to less than 35 at Wandsworth, Isleworth Carshalton and Lea Bridge.

There were two hills on the system steep enough to require the use of the coasting brake on the descent and run-back brake on the ascent, these being at Anerley Hill near Crystal Palace on the 654 route and Highgate Hill on the 611 route. Special batches of vehicles fitted with the brake had to be maintained for operation on these routes. All vehicles numbered 63 and above were fitted with traction batteries for off-wire manoeuvres, and a feature was the use of designated emergency turning points where battery turns were authorised. Some of these points were used frequently enough to appear on destination blinds. Although common on provincial systems, there were only three reversing triangles, these being at the foot of the aforementioned Anerley Hill, the other two being on the isolated Bexleyheath routes at Plumstead Station and Crayford.

From December 1940, 18 Sunbeam trolleybuses came on loan from Bournemouth, and they were used to bolster the services in the Ilford area. Half of them ran for a year, with the remainder running another year before departing for service in other towns. From the end of 1941, the first of 43 trolleybuses built for service in South Africa were delivered and these were all allocated to Ilford depot. The first 25 were Leylands, designated SA1 and SA2, and the remainder were AECs designated SA3. They were London's first 8 feet wide trolleybuses and had front exits, although these were blanked off for London service.

Enemy action took its toll on the vehicles and depots. Bexleyheath, Holloway and West Ham were worst hit, with the first two named suffering hits during the blitz of 1940-1941; bizarrely both were hit again during the V1/V2 rocket offensive after D Day in 1944. 17 trolleybuses were totally destroyed during this period (although two of these had been burnt out during fog), and 61 vehicles had their bodywork written off and replaced with new bodies by Weymann, East Lancs and Northern Coachbuilders.

From before the war plans were being made to replace the rest of London's trams, principally south of the river, with trolleybuses. This would have been done in ten stages and involved the purchase of a further 900 vehicles. However, it was announced in 1946 that the trams would be replaced by motorbuses.

Replacements for the trolleybus fleet were now necessary, and 77 vehicles of the new joint AEC/Leyland BUT chassis were ordered to replace the sixty ex-London United vehicles working the Kingston routes. These were delivered in 1948/9 and were designated Q1. A further 50 similar vehicles arrived in 1952/3.

The justification for the later batch was the need to replace some of the oldest 1935 vehicles, and to ensure that there would be enough modern trolleybuses to run a self-contained trolleybus network centred in Kingston should the rest of the system be converted to motorbuses.

The seemingly inevitable announcement came in 1954 that the trolleybus system would be replaced by motorbuses, with the Kingston and Hounslow routes alone surviving. Plans were laid to design a new breed of bus to replace the trolleybuses, this emerging as the Routemaster. Already one route, the 612, which ran from the Wandsworth tram depot, had been changed to the motorbus in 1950 as part of the tramway replacement programme, although only a few miles of wiring were involved. Some other routes ceased during the 1950s, but this was due to service re-organisations.

The trolleybus conversion programme started properly in March 1959 beginning with the isolated routes at Bexleyheath, and the local service at Croydon. There were 14 stages, with an approximate three-month interval between each. The plan to retain the Q1 vehicles was abandoned when LT offered some for sale whilst they were still relatively new, and was inundated by offers from Spanish trolleybus operators. All except two Q1s left London by ship in 1961. Of this pair, one (1841) with non-standard automatic acceleration equipment was scrapped and the other (1768) was preserved by LT.

It took nine years to establish London's trolleybus network and just three years to dismantle it. The last day was 8 May 1962, when the L3 vehicles operated on the Kingston routes, and K1 type Leylands ran on the 657 route between Shepherd's Bush and Hounslow. The preserved LUT trolleybus no. 1 returned to its old haunts to take an official party around the remaining routes at Kingston. Later that night, L3 trolleybus 1521 formally closed what had been the world's largest trolleybus operation when it entered Fulwell depot.

Amongst the earliest bulk deliveries of trolleybuses for London Transport were sixty-eight of these short wheelbase Leyland TTB2 type, numbered between 64 and 131. New in late 1935 / early 1936, their bodywork was split between Birmingham Railway Carriage and Wagon Co. (BRCW) and Brush. In June 1957, no. 79, with BRCW body, is seen picking up passengers at West Croydon, mid-way along its route 654 journey from Crystal Palace to Sutton. The BRCW-bodied vehicles had long lives, many lasting until March 1959, when the 654 route was converted to motorbuses in stage 1 of the conversion scheme. (C.W. Routh)

The first large batch of full-length trolleybuses was the 52-strong C1 class AEC type 664T vehicles dating from late 1935, this one having a Weymann body. No. 134 is seen passing King's Cross station on a 613 route journey to Hampstead Heath. It ran until 1955. Five of the type, but not this one, were sold for further service in Georgetown, Malaya in 1956, where they ran until 1959. (J. Fozard)

This action scene is at the Seven Stars junction, Starch Green, where the 660 and 666 routes from Hammersmith towards Acton and Cricklewood crossed Goldhawk Road, used by the 657 route between Shepherd's Bush and Hounslow. No. 291, one of the hundred-strong C3 AEC class vehicles with BRCW bodywork is crossing Goldhawk Road, as it negotiates the staggered junction from Paddenswick Road into Askew Road. It is working to Craven Park, part way along the full 660 route to North Finchley. A similar vehicle is crossing in the opposite direction and route 657 trolleybuses can be seen in the far background. Note the covers over the rear wheels of no. 291 – these were common on this class and were referred to as 'spats'.

The prototype full-length Leyland trolleybus for London was no. 384, designated type LTPB70 and it had Leyland bodywork. This entered service in April 1936 and was the only member of class D1. In July 1951, it is seen at the Uxbridge terminus of the 607 route in company with one of the 149-strong production batch designated class D2 or D3. This one is D3 no. 494 with BRCW body. No. 384 was withdrawn in 1956, and no. 494 in 1959. Note that 384, uniquely for a Leyland, was also fitted with rear-wheel 'spats'. (A.B. Cross)

There were areas where London trolleybuses ran through less urban, almost countryside, areas. One such was Mitcham Common, between West Croydon and Tooting on the long 630 route which ended up near Wembley. D2 class Leyland no. 433 with Metro-Cammell body is seen in this location on 19 September 1948. Note the final destination (at Harrow Road near Wembley) is referred to rather imprecisely as 'Nr Willesden Junction'. (London Trolleybus Preservation Society)

Like the L3 vehicles, the N class was moved westwards towards the end of its life and many ended their days at Stonebridge Park depot. No. 1667 is seen working on the 666 route between Edgware and Hammersmith, passing the complete wiring circle at North Acton Station. (C. Carter)

No. 1671 was the experimental Leyland version of the chassisless trolleybus. It was built as a demonstrator in early 1939, registered in Lancashire and originally had a 'Leyland' fleetname on the front panel. It was acquired by London later in 1939 and designated X7. Its most unusual feature was the use of a twin steer front axle, with a single rear axle. In post-war days it operated from Hanwell depot on the 607 and 655 services, and it is seen here at the Shepherd's Bush terminus before departing on a short working journey to Hayes End Road. The conventional F1 class trolleybus behind provides an almost 'mirror image' contrast to the wheel configuration.

The last conventional Leyland trolleybuses for London were 25 vehicles delivered in 1941, numbered 1697 to 1721. Class P1 had Metro-Cammell bodywork similar in appearance to the L3 class, and these were the only Leyland trolleybuses with the streamlined front end. No. 1703 is seen posed when new at Fulwell depot, fitted with local destination blinds. The P1s never operated from here. (Transport for London / London Transport Museum)

The SA3 class comprised 18 AECs with 8 feet wide Metro Cammell bodies built for Johannesburg, and delivered to London in 1942/3. No. 1759, seen at Barkingside on local Ilford route 693, displays the front doorway with folding doors which was never used. Also of note is the narrow (7ft 6in.) track of the rear axles, resulting in an overhang of the bodywork. (C. Carter)

Sixteen trolleybuses damaged early in the war received new bodies built by Weymann in 1941 and 1942. These vehicles had the prefix 'A' added to the fleet number. Leyland K1 1123 had its original body destroyed on 8 October 1940 whilst operating from Stamford Hill depot. It is seen here as no. 1123A in 1948 at Finsbury Square, Moorgate. (A.B. Cross)

East Lancashire Coachbuilders of Blackburn supplied 25 bodies between 1945 and 1948. The relevant vehicles were given a 'B' suffix to their fleet numbers. Leyland D2 407 received this body in December 1945, having been damaged at Bexleyheath depot by a flying bomb on 29 June 1944. No. 407B is at the Woolwich Parsons Hill terminus of the isolated routes to Bexleyheath and Dartford. Trolleybuses reached this point in 1943, when a short extension from the Free Ferry was opened. Standing behind is D2 no. 429 in original condition. (A.B. Cross)

Four of the short-wheelbase B2 Leyland vehicles were rebodied following wartime damage, and the opportunity was taken to lengthen the chassis to full-size specification. No. 97, also damaged in the Bexleyheath depot raid of June 1944, was one example, and it received one of the twenty replacement Northern Coachbuilders bodies built in 1946, (these vehicles being given the suffix 'C'). 97C, now re-classified type D2C, is seen at Plumstead on a 696 route working terminating at Crayford, where one of the three reversing triangles on the system was situated. (C. Carter)

The original London United class A 'Diddler' vehicles were in dire need of replacement by the end of the 1940s. A2 type no. 49 stands at Hampton Court in wintry weather on 21 February 1948. (A.B. Cross)

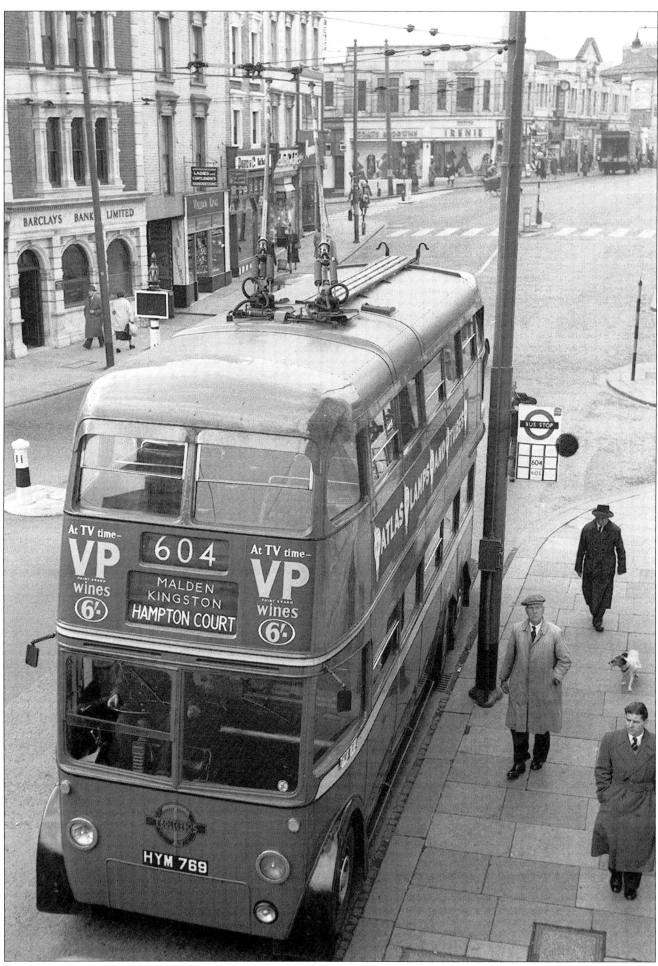

The 127 BUT vehicles new in 1948 and 1952 were attractive and popular vehicles. No. 1769, new in March 1949, is seen in this elevated view at Wimbledon terminus. In 1961 it was sold to Spain and operated on the Coruna-Carballo interurban trolleybus system, whose route was 33 kilometres long. (Mirrorpix)

# SCRAP

Much of Manchester's early trolleybus fleet was scrapped after the Moston routes were converted to motorbus operation in 1955. This selection of Crossley and Leyland vehicles await the final end in a scrapyard at Wakefield on 26 May 1956 after sale to W. North of Leeds, a prolific bus dealer and dismantler in the 1950s and 60s. (R.L. Kell)

Only six of the twelve ex-Huddersfield Karriers bought by Reading in 1948 actually entered service, the remainder being stripped for spare parts. The forlorn hulk of former Huddersfield no. 407 is seen at Mill Lane, Reading on 1 July 1951, shortly before the remains were scrapped. (J.H. Meredith)

Another famous bus scrapyard was Bird's of Stratford upon Avon. This 1956 view shows trolleybuses from three operators in the process of being dismantled, two of them being wartime vehicles originally intended for operation in South Africa. On the left is London SA1 class Leyland no. 1732, one of three withdrawn from service in 1955. In the centre background is one of the ten Massey-bodied St Helen's Sunbeam MF2s whose chassis was meant for Johannesburg. On the right is Huddersfield pre-war Karrier no. 477. The bracket still in place on the lower rear panel beside the entrance was for mounting a Royal Mail post-box, a facility common on the town's trams but not used much by the replacing trolleybuses, and which ended altogether upon the outbreak of war. (D.A. Jones / London Trolleybus Preservation Society)

## Maidstone

**A small but well-presented system which continued to develop into the 1960s.**

Apart from London's route into Dartford, the trolleybus system at Maidstone was the only one to run in the county of Kent. Operations began in May 1928, when eight six-wheel double-deck Ransomes vehicles entered service, replacing trams between Barming and the town centre. Seven more six-wheelers, these being of English Electric manufacture similar to those at Bradford, came in 1930 to allow trolleybus routes to Loose and Sutton Road to be started on 10 February of that year. These routes were worked as a through service to Barming, and involved a one way system through the narrow streets of the town centre. There was no further development to the system during the 1930s.

Due to its proximity to London and the south coast, Maidstone suffered damage from air raids during the war. In October 1940, the town centre one-way wiring was brought down, and temporary wires were erected to give two-way working in Lower Stone Street and Gabriels Hill. After repairs were made and normal working resumed, this additional wiring was retained for the remainder of the war in case history repeated itself. In addition, a wiring siding was erected at the Barming terminus to park vehicles overnight in case the depot was hit. Unusually this wiring was not over the road but allowed vehicles to park off the highway on the verge. Five utility Sunbeams were added to the fleet in 1943 and 1944, these being the first four-wheelers in the fleet.

On 22 May 1947, the Barming route was extended eastwards a distance of ⅔-mile to the Bull Inn. The original turning circle at the Fountain Inn terminus was retained and services were organised to terminate regularly at either of the Barming termini. Replacements for the original six-wheeler fleet arrived in 1946 and 1947 in the form of twelve four-wheel Sunbeams, and by early 1948 all the original vehicles had been withdrawn.

The 1950s brought a further route development when the Sutton Road service was extended from Grove Road to Nottingham Avenue on 21 June 1954. The following year two second-hand utility trolleybuses from the Llanelly system were put into service. These had been acquired in 1952, and were a visible sign of Maidstone's policy of maintaining and developing its trolleybus system by purchasing equipment

### FACTFILE – MAIDSTONE

| | |
|---|---:|
| Opened | 1 May 1928 |
| Closed | 15 April 1967 |
| Route mileage | 7 |
| Maximum number vehicles in service | 24 |

### FLEET PROFILE

| | |
|---|---:|
| All double-deck | |
| Rebodied vehicles | 5 |
| Second-hand vehicles | 9 |
| | |
| BUT 4-wheel | 2 |
| English Electric 6-wheel | 7 |
| Karrier utility | 2 |
| Ransomes 6-wheel | 8 |
| Sunbeam 4-wheel | 17 |
| Sunbeam utility | 5 |

from defunct trolleybus systems elsewhere.

A further extension to the Sutton Road route came into use on 4 May 1959, this being to the new Park Wood estate, where trolleybuses ran on a one-way circuit around the estate roads. Further purchases of second-hand trolleybuses came that year, these comprising two BUT trolleybuses from Brighton and five Sunbeams from Hastings. In addition, Maidstone's faith in the trolleybus system was confirmed when it sent the five wartime utility Sunbeams away for rebodying, and these returned in late 1960 with new Roe bodywork.

What became Maidstone's last route extension to its trolleybus system came on 19 August 1963, when the loop around Park Wood estate was extended to include Wallis Avenue East, which entailed abandoning the wiring in Brishing Lane.

Despite these developments, Maidstone could not economically sustain its trolleybus system in the conditions of the time, and it was decided to order motorbuses to replace the trolleybuses. The first batch of these entered service in late 1965, and replaced an equivalent amount of trolleybuses. Thereafter the system was operated as a joint trolleybus/motorbus service until the final trolleybus, heavily decorated and illuminated, ran for the last time on 15 April 1967.

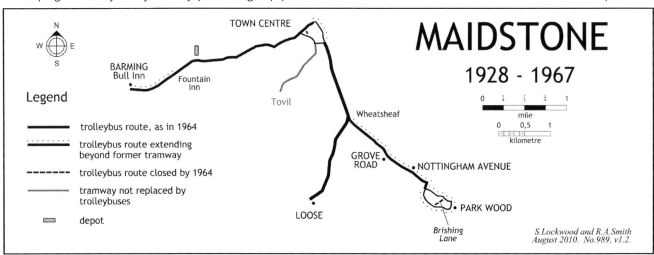

**MAIDSTONE**

**1928 - 1967**

Legend

— trolleybus route, as in 1964

········· trolleybus route extending beyond former tramway

- - - - trolleybus route closed by 1964

—— tramway not replaced by trolleybuses

▭ depot

TOWN CENTRE · BARMING Bull Inn · Fountain Inn · Tovil · Wheatsheaf · GROVE ROAD · NOTTINGHAM AVENUE · LOOSE · PARK WOOD · Brishing Lane

*S.Lockwood and R.A.Smith*
*August 2010. No.989, v1.2.*

This commercial postcard was issued to show the new bridge over the River Medway, and also the new trolleybuses which commenced operation on the Barming route in 1928. Two of the original fleet of eight Ransomes six-wheelers, nos 14 and 13, are seen on the bridge.

Expansion of the system to Loose and Sutton Road resulted in seven more vehicles being delivered in 1930. These were of English Electric type. No. 27 is seen at Loose terminus. Easy-access vehicles were not a feature of 1930s public transport! (D.A. Thompson / London Trolleybus Preservation Society)

Seventeen Sunbeam W vehicles entered the fleet in the 1940s. Five with Park Royal utility bodies came in 1943/4, and twelve with Northern Coachbuilders bodies came in 1946. Examples of both types are seen in the 1950s at Barming Fountain Inn terminus. On the left is the rear of utility no. 57, which would be rebodied by Roe later in the decade. On the right, proceeding beyond here to the Bull Inn terminus is 1946 Sunbeam W no. 72. This vehicle was the ceremonial 'last' vehicle at the closure of the system in April 1967, and it was secured for preservation now residing at the Trolleybus Museum at Sandtoft. (D.A. Thompson / London Trolleybus Preservation Society)

245

Various second-hand vehicles joined the fleet in the 1950s. The first were two Karrier Ws with utility Roe bodies which came from Llanelly in 1953. No. 84, the second of the pair, is seen at the Wheatsheaf junction of the Loose and Sutton Road routes. (D.A. Thompson / London Trolleybus Preservation Society)

The only BUT trolleybuses to operate in Maidstone were a pair of Weymann-bodied examples bought from Brighton in 1959. In their new home they retained their Brighton fleet numbers – 51 and 52. No. 51 is seen at Bishop's Way, a new road in the town centre opened in 1964, on which trolleybuses proceeding towards Barming were diverted. The left-hand set of wires allowed vehicles from Loose or Sutton Road to turn back towards the High Street. (C. Carter)

Maidstone's final purchase of trolleybuses were five 1947-built Weymann bodied Sunbeam Ws from Hastings which came in 1959. No. 87 is seen in the town centre at the Monument before departing for Loose.

# Hastings

**A seaside company operated system, with busy town services and a long route along the coast.**

The Hastings and District Electric Tramways Company sought to convert its tram system in Hastings and Bexhill to trolleybuses in the 1920s. Despite concerns from the local authority about overhead wiring along the sea front, the plans went ahead and the first route, from Hollington to the Fishmarket, opened on 1 April 1928. Over the next three years a comprehensive system was established. 1928 saw further routes opened to Silverhill via London Road, Alexandra Park, and a long route westwards to Bexhill and Cooden. The eastern part of the town was dealt with in 1929, when routes to Ore and St Helens were established, including a rural circular route linking St Helens with Silverhill via Baldslow. Also of note was the use of the very narrow High Street of the Old Town, which initially was equipped with wiring (two negative wires with a common positive) which did not allow vehicles to pass in this section. The timetables for this section were arranged so that there were periods of operation in one way only. From the 1930s this arrangement was dispensed with and two way working was allowed with care. With the addition of wiring in Elphinstone Road in 1930, and a loop to the railway station opened in early 1931, the system was virtually complete and was never substantially altered throughout its life.

The fleet consisted of 58 Guy 6-wheel vehicles, of which

FACTFILE – HASTINGS

| | |
|---|---|
| Opened | 1 April 1928 |
| Closed | 31 May1959 |
| Route mileage | 22 |

FLEET PROFILE
**All double-deck unless denoted**

| | |
|---|---|
| Maximum number vehicles in service | 58 |
| Rebodied vehicles | Nil |
| Second-hand vehicles | Nil |
| | |
| AEC 4-wheel | 20 |
| Guy 6-wheel | 8 |
| Guy 6-wheel single-deck | 50 |
| Sunbeam | 24 |

Amongst Hastings' first trolleybuses were eight Dodson bodied Guy BTX open-top double-deckers. No. 7 is seen at the Hollington terminus, where vehicles turned at a triangular reverser beside the Victoria Inn. The reverser can be seen in the background of this view.

the first eight were open-top double-deckers, the remainder being centre-entrance single-deckers. Apart from short-lived early experimental vehicles elsewhere, the open toppers were the only trolleybuses of this kind to operate in Britain in normal all year round service, and they were used mainly on the Hollington to Fishmarket route, which was the most frequent of the 12 services operated.

A significant event took place in November 1935, when the Tramways Company was purchased outright by the local bus company, Maidstone and District Motor Services, which operated the system as a subsidiary company. There was no immediate affect on operations, although there were alterations made to the trolleybus livery, which changed from brown to green and cream and the fleetname became 'Hastings Tramways Company' instead of 'Hastings and District', which appeared to be a retrograde step.

By the end of the 1930s, the fleet was in need of replacement and accordingly orders were placed for new vehicles. The war prevented the entire order being fulfilled, but 20 AEC double-deckers were delivered in 1940, allowing the open toppers and some single-deckers to be withdrawn. Eighteen of these were purchased by other operators desperate for extra capacity, and six each went to Derby, Mexborough and Nottingham. New vehicle deliveries recommenced in 1946, when ten Sunbeams arrived, followed by a further 15 in the following year, when all but four of the single-deckers were scrapped.

The only route extension to the system occurred in 1947, when the Hollington wiring was extended a few hundred yards along Battle Road to a new turning circle, eliminating the original reversing triangle at the Victoria Inn. By this time the original 12 trolleybus services had been reduced to seven, and these were further rationalised by 1950 when only four services were operated. Despite this, all the wiring, apart from the loops at Layton Road and the railway station, was in regular use until the end of the system.

The Queen's Coronation in 1953 prompted the company to renovate and place back into service the only surviving open top double-decker, which had been retained for works purposes, but latterly was derelict, and this operated a special service along the seafront. The success of this meant that this unique vehicle became a regular summer performer for many years, even after the demise of the system!

Under the terms of the legal authorisation of the trolleybus system, the local authorities at Hastings and Bexhill had powers to purchase the system at specified dates, one of which was in 1955. Hastings Council came very close to doing this, prompting the holding company, Maidstone and District Motor Services, to promote a Bill to fully amalgamate their Hastings subsidiary.

Despite local opposition, demonstrating the popularity of the local trolleybus system, the Bill was enacted and on 30 September 1957 the trolleybuses passed to Maidstone and District, their fleetname now appearing on the vehicles.

Motorbuses were ordered to replace the trolleybus fleet, and the date of 31 May 1959 was set for the final day of operation. This occurred as planned and on the following day, the open-top trolleybus, together with a 1947 Sunbeam and new Atlantean motorbus, made a special run carrying invited guests. This was the largest British trolleybus system to be closed in entirety on one day. All the post-war vehicles were sold for further service at Bradford, Maidstone and Walsall.

The remainder of the initial fleet was comprised of fifty Ransomes-bodied Guy BTX centre-entrance single-deckers. One of these is seen in this commercial postcard view of the sea front at Grand Parade, St Leonards, shortly after trolleybus services started. It is turning from Grand Parade into London Road, operating towards Silverhill.

Grand Parade, St. Leonards-on-Sea.

Fleet renewals came early in the Second World War, when 20 AEC 661T four-wheelers with Park Royal bodies entered service. No. 1 is seen at the Hollington reverser during the war, operating on cross-town service 9 to Ore. This route was discontinued after the war, when the number of services was rationalised, and latterly only four services, nos 2, 6, 8 and 11 ran, although almost all the system was covered. (W.J.Haynes)

Eighteen of the single-deckers were sold to other systems during the war, but a few remained in Hastings until the late 1940s. This damp scene shows no. 60 (formerly no. 20 and renumbered in 1940), operating along the sea front between Fishmarket and the town centre. (C. Carter)

After the war, 25 Sunbeam Ws entered service, comprising ten with Park Royal bodies in 1946, and fifteen with Weymann bodies in 1947/8. No. 21, the first of the Park Royal batch, is seen operating on the lengthy circular service 2, which ran along rural roads across the north of the town. It has just turned on to Old London Road at Baldslow, between Silverhill and St Helens. This vehicle was sold to Bradford in 1959, becoming their no. 806. (D.A. Thompson / London Trolleybus Preservation Society)

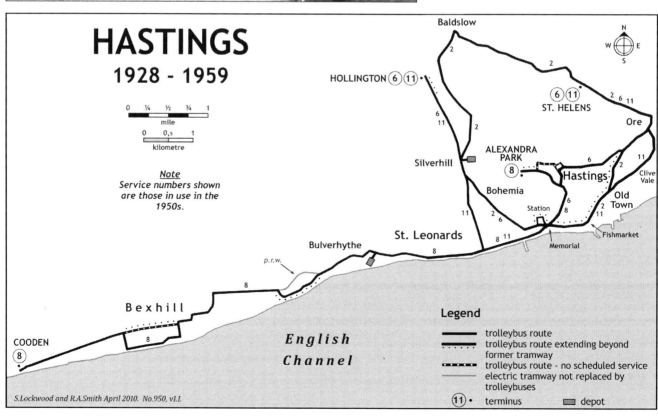

# HASTINGS
## 1928 - 1959

0  ¼  ½  ¾  1
mile

0  0,5  1
kilometre

**Note**
*Service numbers shown are those in use in the 1950s.*

Baldslow

HOLLINGTON ⑥ ⑪

⑥ ⑪
ST. HELENS

Ore

ALEXANDRA PARK

Silverhill

⑧  Hastings

Clive Vale

Bohemia

Old Town

Station

Memorial

Fishmarket

St. Leonards

Bulverhythe

*p.r.w.*

**Bexhill**

*English Channel*

COODEN
⑧

### Legend

— trolleybus route
······ trolleybus route extending beyond former tramway
▪▪▪▪▪ trolleybus route - no scheduled service
— electric tramway not replaced by trolleybuses
⑪ • terminus     ▩ depot

S.Lockwood and R.A.Smith April 2010. No.950, v1.1

250

The Weymann-bodied Sunbeam Ws were numbered 31 to 45 in the fleet. No. 32 is seen at Bexhill, crossing the railway near Bexhill station on a short working of the through service between Alexandra Park and Cooden. The small sign below the windscreen reads 'This bus passes the Bathing Pool'. After the system closed, this vehicle was sold to Maidstone where it became no. 85. (G.H.F. Atkins / courtesy and copyright John Banks collection)

The long route to Cooden via Bexhill, (latterly referred to as 'Cooden Beach' on destination blinds), terminated at a roundabout situated between the railway station and the sea. Vehicles stood at the roundabout as shown here in this rear view of no. 36. This vehicle became Walsall no. 305 in 1959. (C.W. Routh)

After the war, the Hollington route was extended a short distance to a new turning circle. AEC no. 4, in Maidstone and District livery, is seen leaving this shortly before the end of the system in 1959. (C.W. Routh)

St Helens was the terminus of routes 6 and 11, as well as a passing point on the circular route 2. There was a full circle of wiring here, which can be seen in the background to this view of AEC no. 4. The circular service continues into the distance beyond the terminus. (W.C.G. Roberts)

The open-top Guy, originally no. 3, was restored to service for the Coronation in 1953 as no. 3A. From then, it operated a summer sea front service every year between the Fishmarket and St Leonard's West Marina. This 1954 view shows the vehicle at the Fishmarket. After the abandonment of the system, it was fitted with a Commer diesel engine and is now preserved. (C. Carter)

# Brighton

This hilly system was jointly operated between the municipality and the local bus company. The vehicles of each fleet looked the same, having virtually the same livery.

Brighton's experience with electric passenger transport dates back to 1883, when the Volk's Electric Railway, still operating today, commenced running along the sea front. This was followed by Volk's remarkable, although sadly short lived, Brighton to Rottingdean Seashore Electric Railway running along the foreshore and through the sea, which ran from 1896 to 1900. A much more conventional municipal street tramway was established in the 1900s, and experiments with trolleybuses took place, both in Brighton and nearby Hove as described earlier in the Historical section.

In the mid-1930s the Corporation sought a Bill to replace trams with trolleybuses and a short length of demonstration wiring was erected at The Level in late 1935. A Portsmouth AEC trolleybus, and London's unique forward entrance vehicle no. 61, were put on display to persuade residents to support the proposals. The Bill was eventually passed, but with the proviso that services were co-ordinated with the local bus company, Brighton Hove and District (BH&D), with vehicles of both undertakings running in a common livery.

The first route was opened on 1 May 1939 between Aquarium (Old Steine) and Lewes Road, where the Corporation depot was situated. One month later, on 1 June, two more routes commenced operation to Ditchling Road (Surrenden Road), running direct via Ditchling Road, or via Preston Drove. Later that month, services commenced between Old Steine via Brighton Station to Seven Dials. The final pre-war expansion came on 1 September 1939, involving routes in the east of the town to Race Hill via Elm Grove and via Queens Park Road to Seven Dials.

All these routes were worked by Corporation vehicles, these being 44 AEC four-wheelers with well appointed Weymann bodies and locally made Allen West motors. The BH&D Company took delivery of eight almost identical vehicles just before the outbreak of war but these were put into

FACTFILE – BRIGHTON

| | |
|---|---|
| Opened | 1 May 1939 (Corporation) |
| | 1 January 1945 (BH&D) |
| Closed | 30 June 1961 (Corporation) |
| | 24 March 1959 (BH&D) |
| Route mileage | 14 |
| Maximum number vehicles in service | 63 |
| | (52 Corporation, 11 BH&D) |
| Rebodied vehicles | Nil |
| Second-hand vehicles | Nil |

storage for the time being. Four Corporation vehicles were loaned to Newcastle for a short period during 1942.

By 1944 it was realised that the company's trolleybus powers were in danger of lapsing, and therefore the BH&D trolleybuses were put into service during 1945. These vehicles had to operate from the Corporation depot until the wiring to the BH&D depot was installed in early 1946. This was located near Black Rock, and a trolleybus service was opened to that point from March 1946. Running from Black Rock to Seven Dials, it was the only trolleybus service not to run to Old Steine. It was also of interest in that it crossed the Brighton race course at Manor Hill, which on race days was closed to traffic, trolleybuses having to turn on batteries on either side of the closure.

In late 1948, the Ditchling Road route was extended to Larkfield Way, and then to Carden Hill in March 1949, to serve the Hollingbury housing scheme. August 1951 saw a further development when wires were extended from Carden Hill along Braybon Avenue and Surrenden Road to Preston Drove, creating a circular route around the Hollingbury area.

To service this route expansion, six BUT trolleybuses were purchased for the Corporation fleet in 1948, and three similar vehicles went into the BH&D fleet.

Two further BUT vehicles for the Corporation entered

S.Lockwood and R.A.Smith
September 2010. No.946, v2.0.

253

service in 1953, having previously been in storage for some years. All the post-war fleet additions closely resembled the pre-war vehicles.

The eleven company trolleybuses worked mainly on the Seven Dials to Black Rock route, plus a share of the Brighton Station and Queens Park Road circular service.

The decision to close the system was made in the mid-1950s, and this was done in two stages. All routes except those to Hollingbury and Preston Drove ceased running on 24 March 1959. This included all the routes worked by BH&D. All the post–war vehicles were sold off in this year to other British operators. 23 of the Corporation pre-war AEC trolley-buses continued running until 30 June 1961, when decorated trolleybus no. 1 formally closed the system. All the post-war BUT vehicles from both fleets were sold to other operators, Bournemouth taking seven including the three company vehicles. Maidstone and Bradford took two each, the latter opting for the pair with English Electric motors.

The mainstay of the Brighton trolleybus operation was the 44 Weymann bodied AEC 661T trolleybuses delivered in 1939, many of which ran throughout the whole life of the system. Two of these, including no. 17, are seen on a rather damp day at the main town centre terminal at Old Steine (Aquarium). Brighton's vehicles were notable for the copious amount of exterior advertising carried, and this pair was no exception, even appearing to have identical displays. (D.F. Parker)

Passengers hurry to catch AEC no. 20 at Hollingbury on service 26. From here the vehicle will climb Carden Hill on its way into the town centre via Ditchling Road. This wiring came into use in March 1949. (C.W. Routh)

The hilly nature of the Brighton system is demonstrated by this view of AEC no. 29 climbing Braybon Avenue Hollingbury, on the no. 46 service to the town centre via Surrenden Road, brought into use in 1952. (D.F. Parker)

Post-war deliveries for the Corporation fleet were eight BUT 9611T vehicles with Weymann bodies. No. 46, new in 1948 is seen at Grand Parade, approaching the town centre terminus at Old Steine. This vehicle was sold to Bournemouth in 1959, becoming their no. 289. The motorbus visible is a Southdown utility Guy Arab. (D.F. Parker)

The Brighton Hove and District (B H & D) fleet of eight AEC vehicles, similar to those of the Corporation, entered service in 1945. They were numbered 6340 to 6347 in the fleet. This is no. 6347 at the Arundel Street terminus of service 44 at Black Rock, overlooking the sea. The company vehicles did not carry the Brighton coat of arms, otherwise the livery was identical to the Corporation fleet. (R. Marshall)

Three Weymann-bodied BUTs came in 1948, numbered 6391 to 6393. These high numbers were a historical consequence of the B H & D vehicles being originally numbered together with the parent Tilling company's London fleet, and during the 1950s the leading figure '6' was dropped, this particular vehicle then becoming no. 393. The location of this view is Brighton Station on the circular service no. 42. No. 393 was also sold to Bournemouth in 1959, where it was no. 294, running until 1965. (A.B. Cross)

# Portsmouth

An intense network of trolleybus services operated in the densely populated and geographically restricted area of Portsmouth and Southsea, which is a virtual island, two miles wide and four miles long.

Portsmouth Corporation decided to replace its tram fleet with trolleybuses in the early 1930s. Fifteen trolleybuses were purchased, these being a mix of four- and six-wheel types from four manufacturers in order to assess the most suitable type. The eleven four-wheels comprised four AECs, three each of Leyland and Karrier types and one Sunbeam. The four six-wheelers were two AECs and two Sunbeams. Operations started in August 1934 on a route from Cosham railway station to South Parade Pier at Southsea. The success of the operation resulted in a further nine vehicles being purchased, these being AEC four-wheelers, and in November 1935 a service was opened from South Parade Pier, via Albert Road to Commercial Road (Portsmouth's main shopping area), then via Twyford Avenue and Northern Parade to meet the existing route at Hillsea.

A bulk order for 76 AEC four-wheel trolleybuses was now authorised to replace the remainder of the tram system, and these were delivered in 1936, allowing five more services to be introduced in October and November of that year. The last tram ran on 10 November.

The pre-war trolleybus system was now complete. The route network was complex, based around Cosham in the north, Eastney and Copnor Bridge in the east, South Parade Pier, Clarence Pier, and Floating Bridge in the south, and The Dockyard in the west. A variety of services linked each of these points, each taking alternative routes across the city. A further complication was that each service was given a different number in each direction, for instance the original trolleybus route was number 3 between Cosham and Southsea, and number 4 in the opposite direction. Subsequently there were several changes to how particular services were routed over the network, and some service numbers were re-used (eg 15/16).

Being the location of a principal naval dockyard, the outbreak of war resulted in restrictive security measures in the town which affected the trolleybus network. The services serving the sea front areas were curtailed for the duration. The quartet of six-wheel vehicles was loaned to Pontypridd between 1942 and 1945/1946.

In the years following the war there were mixed fortunes for Portsmouth's trolleybuses. New route extensions were planned, and in 1951 fifteen new BUT 4-wheel trolleybuses were purchased. However, in September of that year the first reduction to the system occurred when the Floating Bridge route was converted to motorbus operation because the low number of passengers did not justify the cost of maintaining the overhead wiring.

In January 1952, new wiring along the eastern fringe of the city allowed services running along New Road and terminating at Copnor Bridge to be extended northwards along Copnor Road to Green Lane, where trolleybuses turned by means of a reversing triangle in Madeira Road. In the following March, the 5/6 service terminating at Milton White House was extended along the full length of Milton Road and Copnor Road, beyond Green Lane to join existing routes at Hillsea, reaching its final terminus at

## FACTFILE – PORTSMOUTH

| | |
|---|---|
| Opened | 4 August 1934 |
| Closed | 27 July 1963 |
| Route mileage | 22 |

## FLEET PROFILE

**All double-deck, and 4-wheel except where denoted**

| | |
|---|---|
| Maximum number vehicles in service | 100 |
| Rebodied vehicles | Nil |
| Second-hand vehicles | Nil |
| | |
| AEC | 80 |
| AEC 6-wheel | 2 |
| BUT | 15 |
| Karrier | 3 |
| Leyland | 3 |
| Sunbeam | 1 |
| Sunbeam 6-wheel | 2 |

## HOW THEY WENT – PORTSMOUTH

(*'unique' portions of route are italicised*)

| Date | Route |
|---|---|
| 30 September 1951 | 15/16 *Floating Bridge-High Street-Cambridge Road-Copnor* |
| 26 September 1953 | 9/10 Cosham-*Kingston Crescent*-Guildhall-Victoria Road-Cosham |
| 13 September 1958 | 13/14 South Parade Pier-*Victoria Road South*-Cosham |
| 1 May 1960 | 15/16 *Alexandra Park-Gladys Avenue-Chichester Road*-Eastney |
| 1 May 1960 | 19/20 Cosham-*Northern Parade-Alexandra Park-Twyford Avenue*-Guildhall-Eastney |
| 17 September 1960 | 3/4 Cosham-North End-Fratton-South Parade Pier |
| 2 December 1961 | 7/8 Green Lane-*New Road-Fawcett Road-Waverley Road*-Clarence Pier |
| | 11/12 Green Lane-New Road-Lake Road-Dockyard |
| 22 June 1963 | 17/18 Dockyard-Guildhall-Fratton-Eastney circular |
| 27 July 1963 | 5/6 *Cosham-Copnor Road-Eastney-South Parade Pier* – Guildhall-Dockyard |

Cosham Red Lion. The final part of this expansion came on 27 September 1953, when new route 15/16 was started between Alexandra Park and Eastney, using a new wiring link between Kingston Cross and Copnor Road via Chichester Road.

Later in the 1950s the decision was taken to replace the trolleybus system with motorbuses, and this process took place between 1958 and 1963, its pace being dictated by the delivery of new motorbuses. The last trolleybus ran on 27 July 1963 without formal ceremony.

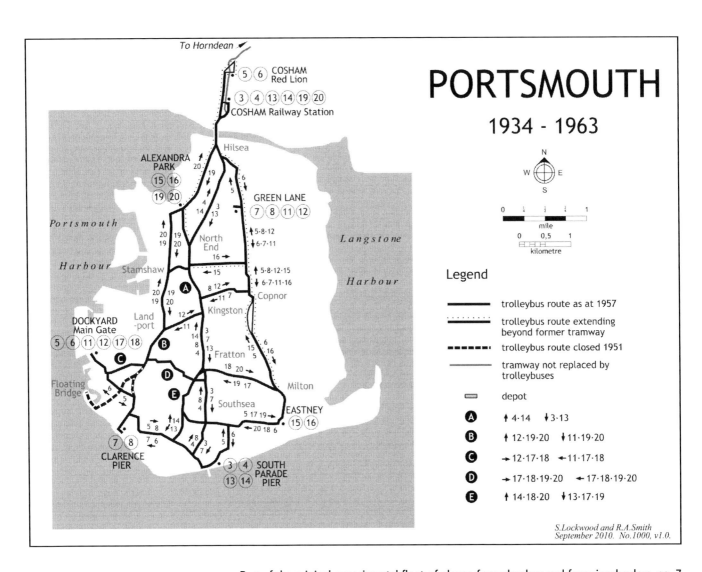

# PORTSMOUTH
## 1934 - 1963

Legend

— trolleybus route as at 1957

⋯⋯ trolleybus route extending beyond former tramway

▪▪▪ trolleybus route closed 1951

— tramway not replaced by trolleybuses

▭ depot

Ⓐ ↑4·14 ↓3·13

Ⓑ ↑12·19·20 ↓11·19·20

Ⓒ →12·17·18 ←11·17·18

Ⓓ →17·18·19·20 ←17·18·19·20

Ⓔ ↑14·18·20 ↓13·17·19

*S.Lockwood and R.A.Smith*
*September 2010. No.1000, v1.0.*

Part of the original experimental fleet of eleven four-wheelers and four six-wheelers, no. 7 was a Leyland TBD2 with English Electric bodywork. It is seen here at Bradford Junction working on the 3/4 service soon after the system opened. (R. Marshall collection)

258

Nine of these English Electric bodied AEC 661T four-wheelers entered service in 1935/6. Originally numbered 16 to 24, they had 200 added to these numbers in 1938, along with the rest of the fleet. No. 218 is seen in Gladys Avenue, outside North End depot in 1954. (D. Tate)

Like the tram, the trolleybus, with an unlimited power supply, was an ideal vehicle to use for an illuminated tableau. Portsmouth dressed up vehicles for important national events, such as the Coronation celebrations of 1937. The vehicle is AEC no. 4.

THE ILLUMINATED TROLLY-BUS, PORTSMOUTH & SOUTHSEA. 3761.

The bulk of the pre-war fleet was the 76-strong batch of AEC 661T vehicles with Cravens bodies delivered from 1936. These were numbered 25 to 100, (renumbered 225 to 300 in 1938). No. 231 is seen at the Floating Bridge terminus of services 15/16 to Copnor Bridge. In late 1951, this service was the first trolleybus route to close. (R. Marshall)

A major trolleybus terminus was at the Dockyard, close to the railway station and the ferries to Gosport and the Isle of Wight. Trolleybuses stood three deep well into the centre of the road here, as demonstrated in this view. On the left is no. 311, one of 15 BUT 9611T vehicles with distinctive Burlingham bodywork new in 1951 working the busy Eastney circular route 17 (anti-clockwise). In the centre is AEC 235 on the clockwise Eastney circle service 18. Similar vehicle 283 is on a service 12 working to Copnor Bridge. (D.A. Thompson / London Trolleybus Preservation Society)

Seen passing the depot at Eastney, where the undertaking's head office was situated, is AEC no. 235 on service 6 from Cosham to the Dockyard. On this route, the intermediate destination of 'Palmerston Road' (Southsea's main shopping area), was displayed from Cosham, and this would be turned to 'Dockyard' at Southsea. (D.A. Thompson / London Trolleybus Preservsation Society)

The northerly extent of the trolleybus system was at Cosham, and this was the only part of the system not on Portsea Island. There were two termini here, at the Railway Station and the Red Lion. Seen side-by-side at the Railway Station terminus are the last of the pre-war AECs, no. 300, and the first of the post-war BUTs, no. 301. (R. Marshall)

Portsmouth's trolleybuses served the seaside resort of Southsea, running to both the Clarence Pier and the South Parade Pier. BUT no. 310 is seen passing the latter as it runs along the sea front towards Eastney, on a service 5 journey to Cosham Red Lion. This route was established in 1953 when wiring was extended along Copnor Road to Hillsea. (Roy Brook / Paul Watson)

# Bournemouth

This system was one of Britain's trolleybus gems. A comprehensive network of routes served this seaside town, with vehicles and wiring superbly maintained and presented. Highlights were the turntable at Christchurch, and the seasonal open-top vehicles.

Operations began with an experimental route from the Square to the Hampshire/Dorset border at County Gates, a point later referred to as Westbourne. Four vehicles were hired, these being a Sunbeam six-wheeler, an AEC six-wheeler, an AEC four-wheeler and a Thornycroft single-decker. The success of the operation led to the purchase of this quartet in May 1934, and the delivery of twelve additional Sunbeam six-wheelers to replace trams on the Boscombe via Holdenhurst Road route from 22 June 1934. These vehicles had two staircases and front exits, a pattern that set the standard for all future vehicle purchases. Bulk orders were then placed for more trolleybuses of this type to replace the rest of the trams, and by early 1936 the fleet of Sunbeams had risen to 103 units, including the original experimental example which was rebuilt with front-exit in that year. The two AEC trolleybuses were converted into motorbuses.

The routes converted to trolleybus operation in 1935 were: Old Christchurch Road to Iford in March, Moordown via Winton in June, Charminster Road (Broadway Hotel) in August, and a branch off the Iford route to Fisherman's Walk in November, this being extended the following month to Southbourne. The last tram ran on 8 April 1936, when on the same day the Southbourne trolleybus route was extended to Christchurch. There were two points of note on this route. At Tuckton, trolleybuses crossed the River Stour by the narrow Tuckton Bridge, and passengers paid a supplementary fare (originally ½d) to cover the toll charge, an arrangement that lasted until the war years. At Christchurch terminus, the difficulty of turning trolleybuses in the narrow High Street was solved by the installation of a turntable in a yard adjacent to the Dolphin Hotel, where vehicles were manually turned by the crew.

From 1937, and up to the outbreak of war, further extensions to the trolleybus network were introduced. In spring 1937 these were from Moordown to Lawford Road, a branch off the Charminster Road route along Charminster Avenue to Malvern Road and an alternative route between Old Christchurch Road and The Square via Bath Road and Westover Road. The latter routing was indicated on the vehicles by a red background destination display. April 1938 saw a branch opened from Winton to Wallisdown and Columbia Road. In October of the same year wiring was brought into use in Castle Lane, linking the Charminster Road terminus at Broadway Hotel to the Moordown terminus at Lawford Road, allowing a circular service to operate. The final pre-war route addition came in April 1939, when another branch off the Moordown route was opened along Ensbury Park Road to link with the existing terminus at Columbia Road, forming another circular service.

The reduction on passenger traffic due to the war resulted in 30 trolleybuses being loaned to other operators. Commencing in October 1940 twelve vehicles (and some crews) were sent to Wolverhampton, followed by another 18 on loan to London Transport. Some of the latter subsequently saw service in Walsall, Newcastle, South Shields and Llanelly.

## FACTFILE – BOURNEMOUTH

| | |
|---|---|
| Opened | 13 May 1933 |
| Closed | 19 April 1969 (closing ceremony on 20 April 1969) |
| Route mileage | 29 |

## FLEET PROFILE
**All double-deck unless denoted**

| | |
|---|---|
| Maximum number vehicles in service | 104 |
| Rebodied vehicles | Nil |
| Second-hand vehicles | 7 |
| | |
| AEC 6-wheel | 1 |
| AEC 4-wheel | 1 |
| BUT 6-wheel | 24 |
| BUT 4-wheel | 7 |
| Sunbeam 6-wheel | 103 |
| Sunbeam 4-wheel | 39 |
| Thornycroft single-deck | 1 |

## HOW THEY WENT – BOURNEMOUTH

| | |
|---|---|
| 29 September 1963 | St Pauls Road |
| 23 August 1964 | Bournemouth Pier to Fisherman's Walk |
| 4 April 1965 | Square to Malvern Road |
| 12 September 1965 | Boscombe-Central Station-Square-Westbourne |
| 25 September 1966 | Square to: West Way, Columbia Road, Castle Lane |
| 19 April 1969 | Square to Christchurch, Tuckton, Southbourne, Jumpers |

The war did not entirely halt the development of the network, and in July 1943 the Iford route was extended along Barrack Road into Christchurch, giving a second service to this destination.

In December 1946, the intermediate service from the Square to Southbourne was extended to Tuckton Bridge. Subsequently the wiring was extended from Tuckton along Cranleigh and Beaufort Roads linking to existing wires at Fisherman's Walk, forming yet another circular service.

The final route developments occurred in the early 1950s. At Easter 1950, some seasonal trolleybus services commenced from Bournemouth Pier, using new wiring along Bath Road and Exeter Road. October 1951 saw the opening of wiring along Castle Lane, from Broadway Hotel eastwards to Iford Bridge. Again, this allowed a further circular service to be established.

New vehicles, the first since the establishment of the system in the mid-1930s, entered service in 1950/1951, these being 24 BUTs resulting in some of the 1930s Sunbeams being withdrawn. It was not until 1958 that further new vehicles appeared. These were 20 Sunbeams with a set back front axle, similar to the 'Coronation' type trolleybuses built for Hull earlier in the decade. The rear entrance/front exit was retained, with the front exit directly beside the driver. Ten more came in the following year, and a final batch of nine entered service in 1962, these becoming the last new complete trolleybuses built for service in Britain. These deliveries allowed the withdrawal of all remaining pre-war trolleybuses, except for the trio that in 1958 were converted to open top layout for operation on a summer season circular tour from Bournemouth Pier. Bournemouth took advantage of the closure of the Brighton trolleybus system to purchase seven BUT vehicles from both the Brighton operators, and these were used to operate mainly at peak hours.

In the early 1960s period the Bournemouth trolleybus system was at its peak of development. A seemingly endless procession of smart yellow trolleybuses, with white tipped booms, circled the Square before peeling-off to most parts of the town. The routes were organised in three parts, these being: the 'Main line' services along Old Christchurch Road

to Boscombe, Seabourne and Christchurch; the 'Side routes' to Moordown, Charminster Road and Castle Lane, all of which left the Square by climbing the 1 in 8 gradient of Richmond Hill; and thirdly service 25 between Boscombe and Westbourne, which was the only cross-town route.

All this was not to last and the decision was taken in 1963 to replace the trolleybuses with motorbuses. The wiring in St Pauls Road, which allowed some peak-hour journeys on the 'Side routes' to start at Lansdowne, was the first to be taken down later that year. The Main line services survived to the end, and a long procession of trolleybuses, one partly illuminated, marked the closure of the system on Sunday 20 April 1969.

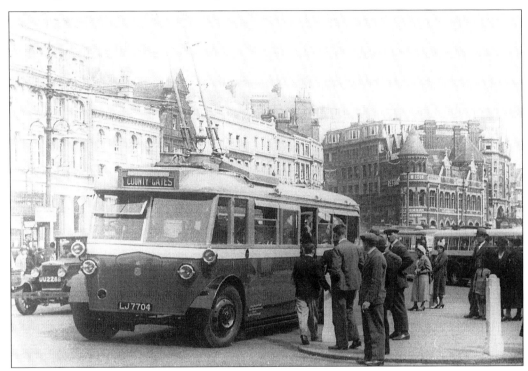

The most unconventional of the four vehicles that opened operations was the Brush bodied Thornycroft single-deck demonstrator, later purchased by the Corporation and numbered 71. It entered service painted blue, hence its nickname 'Bluebird'. Here it is seen in May 1933 loading at Bournemouth Square on the County Gates service, later known as Westbourne. This vehicle was sold to South Shields during the war. (R. Marshall collection)

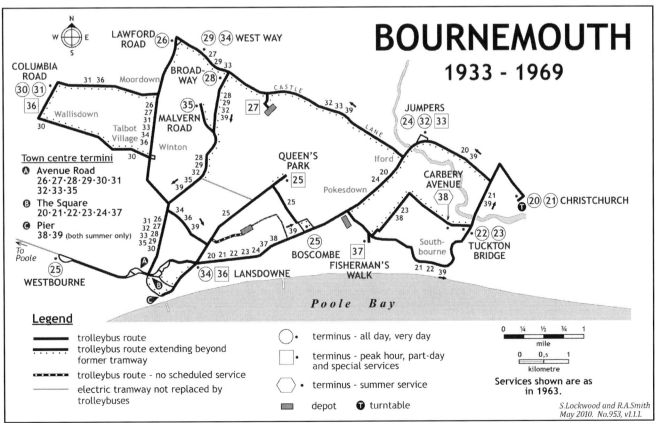

# BOURNEMOUTH
## 1933 - 1969

**Town centre termini**
- **Ⓐ** Avenue Road
  26·27·28·29·30·31
  32·33·35
- **Ⓑ** The Square
  20·21·22·23·24·37
- **Ⓒ** Pier
  38·39 (both summer only)

**Legend**
- trolleybus route
- trolleybus route extending beyond former tramway
- trolleybus route - no scheduled service
- electric tramway not replaced by trolleybuses
- ◯• terminus - all day, very day
- ☐• terminus - peak hour, part-day and special services
- ⬡• terminus - summer service
- ▭ depot  Ⓣ turntable

Services shown are as in 1963.

*S.Lockwood and R.A.Smith*
*May 2010. No.953, v1.1.1.*

The Square in the town centre was the focal point of the system where originally trolleybuses loaded at centre islands. Two Sunbeam MS2 vehicles are shown here in this commercial postcard view, looking north.

Shortly after the war, the Square was rebuilt with a central roundabout, and the loading stops were moved to adjacent roads. There are eight trolleybuses visible in this postcard view, looking east, dating from shortly after the change. In the left foreground is the rear of Sunbeam no. 123, having returned from its wartime wanderings around the country, including Newcastle, South Shields and Llanelly. It is waiting to depart to Ashley Road Boscombe on service 25A.

264

The first of the 102 strong fleet of Park Royal bodied Sunbeam MS2 vehicles delivered between 1934 and 1936 was no. 72. The rear entrance, front exit arrangement is being demonstrated in this view. Subsequently, all Bournemouth's trolleybuses bought new had this arrangement. (R. Marshall collection)

The services from Charminster Road and Wimborne Road (the 'Side routes') descended to the Square from Cemetery junction via Richmond Hill. This was steep enough for a Ministry of Transport requirement making it mandatory for the coasting brake to be used on each descent. With an Austin Atlantic car climbing in the opposite direction, Sunbeam no. 137 is at the stop near the bottom of the hill on a journey from Columbia Road. Note the lower destination indicator showing 'to and from Show' – this was a typical Bournemouth feature. (R. Marshall)

From Easter 1950 trolleybuses ran to and from Bournemouth Pier, and several services were provided during the summer period. This busy scene shows Sunbeam no. 116 at the Pier turning circle, on a journey to Charminster Road Five Ways. (R.K. Blencowe)

This is the turning circle at Kinson Road, Wallisdown, which was established in the late 1930s. Trolleybuses operated to here via Talbot Village, or via Ensbury Park Road and Columbia Road. Sunbeam no. 171 is turning into the circle having arrived from the Columbia Road direction. This was the last pre-war extension to the system. (D.A. Thompson / London Trolleybus Preservation Society)

The Boscombe terminus of service 25, a cross town route to Westbourne, consisted of a loop around streets adjacent to, and including, Old Christchurch Road. One of the post-war Weymann bodied BUT 9641T six-wheelers, no. 218, is seen in Old Christchurch Road whilst performing the terminal manoeuvre. This vehicle was renumbered to 252 in the late 1950s. In the left background operating towards the town centre along Old Christchurch Road, is Sunbeam no. 160, which in 1958 was one of three converted to open-top form, becoming no. 201. (D.A. Thompson / London Trolleybus Preservation Society)

An early 1950s scene on the 'Side routes' at Five Ways, Charminster Road, where there was a turning loop at Court Road. On the left, BUT no. 218 is proceeding towards Castle Lane, whilst Sunbeam no. 98 is operating towards the town centre on service 32, which at that time was a circular service via Boscombe, Iford, Castle Lane and Moordown. (D.A. Thompson / London Trolleybus Preservation Society)

# THE CHRISTCHURCH TURNTABLE

Perhaps the best known feature of the Bournemouth trolleybus system was the turntable at Christchurch terminus. This was the only such feature accessible to the public in Britain, apart from Huddersfield's short experience with such a device at Longwood terminus. There were other examples around the country, but these were confined to depot areas. Visitors to the historic town of Christchurch arriving by trolleybus were treated to the spectacle of turning the vehicle in a very confined space – poles hooked down – vehicle pushed round manually using muscle power – poles unhooked and replaced on the wires.

Sunbeam no. 115 is turned by its crew in this view from shortly after the Second World War. (R. Marshall collection)

A different technique is shown here - waiting passengers look on as one of the 1950s Sunbeam MF2B vehicles, no 285, is pulled round. (A.B.Cross)

Having completed the turning process and loaded passengers, Sunbeam MF2B no. 274, one of the initial batch of this type delivered in 1958, turns from the terminal yard into the High Street. The tower of Christchurch Priory can be seen in the background. (R.S. Ledgard)

Seven BUT 9611T four-wheelers were purchased from Brighton, and Brighton Hove and District in 1959. These were numbered 288 to 294. No. 290, formerly Brighton Corporation no. 47, is seen at The Lansdowne, an important trolleybus junction, on a journey along Old Christchurch Road to Cranleigh Road, Tuckton. (D.A. Jones / London Trolleybus Preservation Society)

Three of the pre-war Sunbeams, nos 157, 160 and 112, were converted to open top configuration in 1958, and renumbered 200 to 202. This work also included the removal of the front staircase and exit. The trio operated seasonal services, including a circular service around the town from Bournemouth Pier. In this view, no. 200 is at the Square en route to Fisherman's Walk at Southbourne, a regular working for these vehicles. After the demise of the Hastings system in 1959, these vehicles were the only open-top trolleybuses in Britain, if not the world.

In the early 1960s, a few of the the 24 BUT six-wheelers were rebuilt, having the front staircase and exit removed, increasing the seating capacity from 56 to 64. No. 243 (formerly no. 209) is seen in this form (identifiable by the additional window at the front of the lower deck), turning from Holdenhurst Road into Ashley Road on service 25. The wires continuing to the right proceed to Queens Park, and were used when sporting events were taking place. (A.B. Cross)

Between Christchurch and Southbourne, trolleybuses crossed the River Stour by the narrow Tuckton Bridge. No. 298, one of the final batch of nine Sunbeam MF2B vehicles delivered in 1962, is seen leaving the bridge on its way into Bournemouth. Note the prominent sign on the left regarding restrictions for trolleybuses using the bridge. (R.F. Mack)

This is an off-side view of Sunbeam MF2B no. 299, seen when newly into service. These vehicles were the last all new trolleybuses built for public use in Britain. The location is Poole Road at Westbourne and no. 299 has just started a cross-town journey to Ashley Road, Boscombe. The film 'Tiara Tahiti' being shown at the cinema was also a 1962 release, and starred James Mason, John Mills and Herbert Lom. (D.F. Parker)

# TRAINING

This scene in Derby shows a trolleybus with 'L' plates, but also being used in normal public service. This was quite legal, although it was not common practice amongst trolleybus operators nationally. The vehicle is no. 238, one of the Roe-bodied Sunbeam F4s delivered in 1960. It is approaching Normanton Barracks on a service to Sinfin Lane. (C. Carter)

This Manchester Crossley trolleybus is seen on driver training duties at the very end of its career. No. 1166, new in 1940, was the last of the pre-war fleet to survive, being withdrawn in 1960. The location is Rassbottom Street Stalybridge, outside the railway station.

Bradford invested in considerable facilities for training trolleybus drivers. In the mid-1959s it laid out a circuit of wiring in the former tramway permanent way yard at Bowling, adjacent to the Tong Cemetery trolleybus route along Wakefield Road. This was enlarged in the early 1960s and included a reversing triangle. Some trolleybuses were taken out of the normal fleet to be used exclusively for training. This is 1949 Roe-bodied BUT no. 060, formerly numbered 745 in the passenger fleet. It is operating on the Bowling training circuit shortly before the faciility was closed in 1967. Interestingly, no. 060 was restored to the passenger fleet in the following year, regaining its original fleet number, and it ran until 1970. (R.S. Ledgard)

# Cardiff

**Trolleybuses in this capital city started operations during the Second World War, the only British system to do so. It was one of only two systems to be run exclusively with six-wheel vehicles.**

Although Cardiff obtained powers to run trolleybuses over its tram network in 1934, it was not until the end of this decade that firm decisions to establish trolleybuses were made. In 1939 the City Council instructed the Transport Department (against its recommendation) to introduce trolleybuses on a route to the docks area. The outbreak of war slowed progress and it was not until 1942 that the wiring and vehicles were ready. On 1 March (St David's Day), ten new trolleybuses painted in a wartime grey livery, replaced trams on the Grangetown route. This was extended through the city centre to Llandaff Fields from that November. Initially, the trolleybuses operated on a 1d 'flat fare' system, with a static conductor supervising the platform.

No further development took place until after the war, when a bulk order for 75 vehicles was placed with BUT, these to be bodied by East Lancashire Coachbuilders to a special design incorporating two staircases and a front-exit door.

The next route to be converted was the Bute Street service to Pier Head, on which a low bridge required the use of single-deck vehicles. Accordingly, seven 1930 vintage English Electric single-deckers were acquired from Pontypridd UDC, and these veterans entered service from 17 August 1947 on the shuttle service to the Pier Head from the city centre. At the same time the original Grangetown route was extended from Clarence Road to Pier Head.

From 1948 the new BUT vehicles began to enter service, allowing more trolleybus services to be introduced. Two services to Victoria Park were inaugurated in 1948, followed by those to Roath Park in late 1949, and to Gabalfa in early 1950, when the last tram operated. In October 1950, a service opened along Newport Road, using wiring erected for access to Roath Depot, and extended to serve a housing area at Pengam.

55 of the BUT trolleybuses were now on the road, including five single-deck versions for the Bute Street route, which entered service in 1949 to replace the Pontypridd vehicles. There were still twenty of the post-war vehicle order still outstanding, and the electrical equipment for these had already been purchased. Accordingly, it was decided to convert a frequent Ely motorbus service to trolleybus operation, involving four miles of overhead beyond Victoria Park, and 13 vehicles were delivered to start the service in May 1955. One further trolleybus entered service that year, this being an additional single-decker for the Bute Street service, and this became Britain's last new six-wheel single-deck trolleybus. The balance of the 75 vehicle order (6 vehicles) was cancelled.

By the early 1960s there was a need to replace the original trolleybuses, and in October 1961 the decision was taken to abandon the system. This was achieved at a leisurely pace, commencing with the outer part of the Pengam route in late 1962. The Pier Head via Clarence Road route was closed unexpectedly due to a weak bridge at Wood Street, and the final route, to Ely, was expected to last

| FACTFILE – CARDIFF | |
|---|---:|
| Opened | 1 March 1942 |
| Closed | 11 January 1970 |
| Route mileage | 18 |
| Maximum number vehicles in service | 79 |

| FLEET PROFILE | |
|---|---:|
| All six-wheel and double-deck unless denoted | |
| Rebodied vehicles | Nil |
| Second-hand vehicles | 7 |
| | |
| AEC | 10 |
| BUT | 63 |
| BUT single-deck | 6 |
| English Electric single-deck | 7 |

| HOW THEY WENT – CARDIFF | |
|---|---|
| 24 November 1962 | Pengam to Royal Oak |
| 11 January 1964 | Pier Head via Bute Street |
| 16 December 1965 | Pier Head via Clarence Road |
| 16 April 1966 | Llandaff Fields to Gabalfa |
| 17 September 1966 | Llandaff Fields to Roath Park |
| 17 February 1968 | Royal Oak to Victoria Park |
| 27 April 1968 | Gabalfa and Roath Park |
| 3 December 1969 | Ely, Green Farm Road |

into 1970, but the normal public service was ended prematurely on 3 December 1969 due industrial action by engineering staff. However, the pre-arranged closure ceremonies went ahead in early January 1970, and some trolleybuses returned to service to run a special service to Victoria Park on 9 and 10 January. The final operation was of special private tours on Sunday 11 January, when the vehicles used had to be towed across Ely bridge to reach Ely because the wiring here had already been removed! Preserved trolleybus no 262, Britain's last six-wheel trolleybus to operate on the streets, returned to depot at 4pm to close trolleybus operation in Wales.

**Many of the original batch of Northern Counties bodied AEC vehicles ran until the mid-1960s. This is no. 204 seen on driver training duty in the city centre at Duke Street on 18 July 1963. (C.W. Routh)**

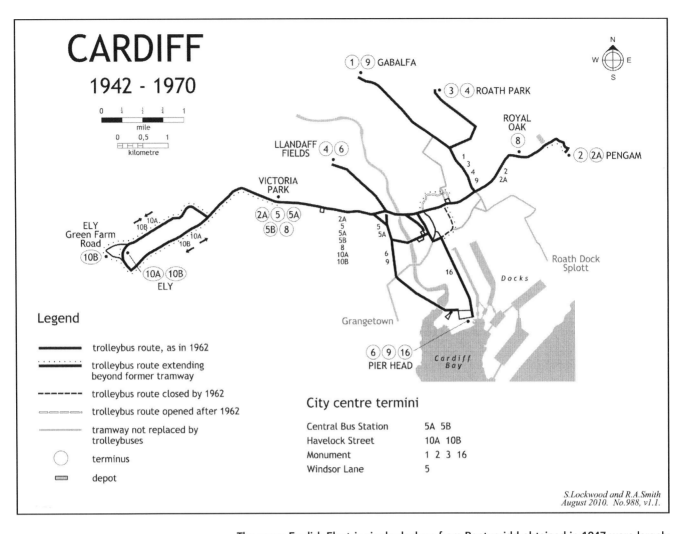

# CARDIFF
## 1942 - 1970

0  ¼  ½  ¾  1
mile

0   0,5   1
kilometre

(1)(9) GABALFA

(3)(4) ROATH PARK

ROYAL OAK
(8)

(2)(2A) PENGAM

LLANDAFF FIELDS (4)(6)

VICTORIA PARK

(2A)(5)(5A)
(5B)(8)

2A
5
5A
5B
8
10A
10B

5
5A

6
9

1
3
4
9

2
2A

16

*Docks*

Roath Dock Splott

ELY
Green Farm Road
(10B)

10A
10B

10A
10B

(10A)(10B)
ELY

Grangetown

(6)(9)(16)
PIER HEAD

*Cardiff Bay*

N
W E
S

## Legend

———— trolleybus route, as in 1962

·········· trolleybus route extending beyond former tramway

– – – – trolleybus route closed by 1962

·–·–·– trolleybus route opened after 1962

———— tramway not replaced by trolleybuses

◯ terminus

▭ depot

## City centre termini

| | |
|---|---|
| Central Bus Station | 5A 5B |
| Havelock Street | 10A 10B |
| Monument | 1 2 3 16 |
| Windsor Lane | 5 |

*S.Lockwood and R.A.Smith*
*August 2010.  No.988, v1.1.*

The seven English Electric single-deckers from Pontypridd obtained in 1947 were largely replaced by the five BUT single-deckers which arrived in 1949. However, no. 236, seen here in Bute Street, on 4 February 1950, was one of three of this type that survived until that year. It was also one of only two that ran in Cardiff livery rather than wartime grey. (J.H. Meredith)

272

The large batch of 50 BUT 9641T double-deckers started to enter service in 1948. The earliest deliveries had East Lancashire bodywork. These had two staircases and a front exit with sliding door for flat fare operation pay-as-you-enter. The rear platform incorporated a seat for the conductor. The front doors were gradually panelled over after the flat fare scheme was abandoned in the early 1950s. No. 214 is seen passing through the Clarence Bridge over the River Taff, which gave access to the Docks area. (C. Carter)

Standing at the pleasant Roath Park terminus is BUT no. 229, working on service 3 to the city centre. (Roy Brook)

25 of the BUT double-deckers to similar specification were bodied by Bruce Coachworks, a local firm based at Pengam, which had connections with East Lancashire Coachbuilders. No. 251 is seen in Wood Street on a through journey from Gabalfa to the Pier Head shortly after entering service. The front exit with sliding door is evident. In the left background is AEC no. 205, proceeding towards Llandaff Fields. (D.A. Jones / London Trolleybus Preservation Society)

The five BUT single-deckers for the Bute Street service also had East Lancashire bodies with a forward exit. No. 240, seen at the reversing triangle at the Pier Head terminus, has had this feature removed in this view dated about 1960. (Roy Brook / Paul Watson)

The 1955 route extension beyond Victoria Park took trolleybuses to Ely where a two-way loop operated in the large housing area. Here, a BUT vehicle runs along Grand Avenue on the anti-clockwise loop, designated service 10A. The central grass strip was originally intended to accommodate a reserved track tramway. (R.F. Mack / Trolleybus Museum Company)

Bruce-bodied BUT no. 253 is at the Gabalfa terminus turning circle about 1960. The following year this terminus was cut back a short distance to a new turning circle at Whitchurch Road, thus eliminating a major road crossing. The vehicle is working on a cross-city journey to Clarence Road, a short working of the Pier Head service 9. (Roy Brook / Paul Watson)

Thirteen additional BUT double-deckers entered service in 1955 for the Ely services. These had an updated style of East Lancashire body and did not include a front exit or a second staircase. No. 281 is seen leaving the less frequently used alternative terminus of the 10B service at Western Cemetery. The small, lightweight trolley heads used by Cardiff are evident on this vehicle. They were developed by the system's engineer, Felix Cunuder, and were designed to reduce wear and dewirements. (C.W. Routh)

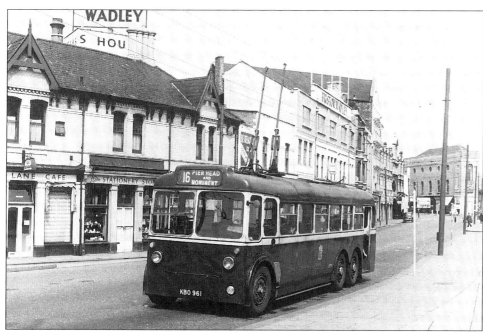

Cardiff's final new trolleybus was an additional single-decker. New in 1955 it had a modernised East Lancashire body and took the vacant fleet number 243 at the end of the previous single-deck batch. This view shows it at the Mill Lane city centre terminus of the Pier Head via Bute Street route. (Roy Brook / Paul Watson)

This view of Duke Street in the city centre on 10 May 1967 shows the wiring arrangement at the junction with High Street. Bruce bodied trolleybus no. 274, the last of the 1948-50 batch of BUTs, is seen operating on the cross-city service 8 from Royal Oak to Victoria Park. Note the set of wires turning right from Duke Street into High Street, a manoeuvre which was illegal in the latter days of the system, as a 'no right turn' arrangement existed here. On the left are the walls of Cardiff Castle. (J.C. Gillham)

# Pontypridd

Britain's smallest self-contained post-war trolleybus system was at Pontypridd, and comprised one route operated by the Urban District Council. The operation was never modernised, and it was the last system to use trolley wheels for current collection.

Pontypridd Urban District Council operated a narrow gauge (3ft 6in.) tramway over two routes, one being a 3-mile long cross town service between Treforest and Cilfynydd, and the other running westwards to the neighbouring town of Porth. This latter route was a joint service with the Rhondda Tramways Company. Towards the end of the 1920s, powers were obtained to replace the worn out tram system with trolleybuses. In the event, agreement could not be reached with the Rhondda Company to run a joint trolleybus service and this route eventually was converted to motorbus operation.

The Treforest to Cilfynydd route was converted to trolleybuses in September 1930 using seven single-deck English Electric built six-wheelers. Initially these proved inadequate to provide the service required, and the trams, and even motorbuses had to be used at peak hours. In 1931 two further vehicles were obtained, these being double-deckers and were both former demonstration vehicles. One was a Guy registered in Wolverhampton, and the other was one of the pair of Bristol trolleybuses built in 1930 and registered in Bristol. These vehicles allowed the trams to be finally retired from the route.

The trolleybus route linked highly industrial and colliery areas. The overhead wiring was very basic. At Treforest there was a reverser at John Street, whilst the Cilfynydd terminus was a turning circle beside the main road which ran along the Taff Vale. The only wiring junction was where the depot connection joined the main route at Broadway, and there were no changes to these layouts throughout the life of the system.

The outbreak of war meant that passenger traffic increased significantly, and initially four Leyland trolleybuses were loaned from Hull, the first four-wheelers to be run in

FACTFILE – PONTYPRIDD

| | |
|---|---|
| Opened | 18 September 1930 |
| Closed | 31 January 1957 |
| Route mileage | 3 |

FLEET PROFILE

**All 6-wheel and double-deck unless denoted**

| | |
|---|---|
| Maximum number vehicles in service | 13 |
| Rebodied vehicles | Nil |
| Second-hand vehicles | Nil |
| | |
| Bristol | 1 |
| English Electric single-deck | 7 |
| Guy | 1 |
| Karrier 4-wheel utility | 8 |

the town. These were replaced in 1942 by the four Portsmouth six-wheelers, comprising two Sunbeams and two AECs.

Between 1945 and 1946, eight utility Karriers were purchased, and these allowed all the existing fleet to be withdrawn, and the loaned trolleybuses to be returned. The original seven single-deckers found a ready buyer at nearby Cardiff, who required them for their Bute Street route. The eight utilities, all with wooden slatted seating, maintained the service into the 1950s.

The economics of running such a small operation, and the need to renew underground power cables as well as refurbish the hard-worked vehicles, led the council to eventually agree to replace the trolleybuses with motorbuses. The two Roe bodied vehicles were sold to Walsall in 1956, and buyers were found for the remaining six vehicles (four to South Shields and two to Doncaster) which soldiered on until 31 January 1957. Fearful of having the vehicles damaged by souvenir hunters, the council ensured that there was no publicity or ceremony to mark the passing of this interesting operation.

Trolleybus operation began with seven English Electric centre-entrance six-wheel single-deckers. An interesting feature was that the registration number sequence used only odd numbers between TG 379 and 391. No. 3 is seen soon after entering service in High Street Pontypridd. All these vehicles were sold to Cardiff in 1947, becoming their nos 231 to 237. (Vic Nutton collection / Travel Lens Photographic)

The single-deckers could not cope with the traffic requirements of the route and in 1931 this Guy BTX six-wheel double-decker was obtained. New in 1930, it was built as a demonstrator and had operated in Nottingham. Numbered 8, it is seen near the depot at Glyntaff.

No. 9 was another six-wheel double-decker bought in 1931, this being one of the only two Bristol trolleybuses built, designated type E. The other example became Doncaster no. 31. This is a builder's view of the vehicle before it was acquired by Pontypridd. (R. Marshall collection)

Post-war operations were in the hands of the eight utility Karrier Ws delivered between 1945 and 1946. This interesting commercial postcard view shows a smartly turned out no. 13, one of four with Park Royal bodies. It is passing Pontypridd Station en route to Treforest in this streetscene dating from about 1950. This vehicle was sold to South Shields in 1957, becoming no. 239.

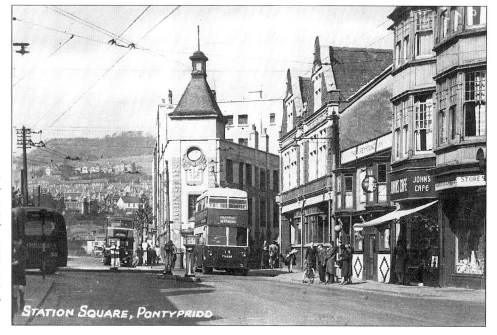

At the Treforest terminus there was a reversing triangle at John Street. Park Royal bodied no. 8, new in 1946, is seen having reversed into John Place. It became South Shields no. 236 in 1957. (C. Carter)

The Cilfynydd terminus was at a turning circle beside the road along the Taff Vale. No. 15, one of two with Roe bodywork and the highest numbered vehicle in the fleet, is seen waiting to return to Cilfynydd having turned on the circle in the background. In 1956, this vehicle was sold to Walsall, where it was no. 302. (D.A. Jones / London Trolleybus Preservation Society)

A feature of the route near the town centre was the crossing of Victoria Bridge over the River Taff. No. 13 is seen here on 18 September 1954. Note the ornate scrollwork from which the overhead is suspended, and the old bridge on the left. (J.H. Meredith)

# Rhondda

This was a trolleybus operation in a rural coal-mining district. The project failed almost as soon as it had begun, and the Rhondda trolleybus system had the shortest life of any in Britain.

The Rhondda trolleybus route was operated by the Rhondda Tramways Company, and was effectively an extension of its Williamstown tram route. It took a 'u' shaped course through mining villages, including Tonyrefail and Gilfach to Gilfach Goch. This area had collieries still in development, and it was felt that a trackless trolley system would be more suitable than a more expensive, and less flexible tram route.

The Tramways Company studied the existing trolleybus system providers, and selected a modified Brush design, specifying trolley poles instead of the Lloyd-Kohler flexible trolley collector (as used at Stockport) which was deemed undesirable. Six single-deck cars with rear platforms were ordered at the same time as the three bought by Mexborough and Swinton to start their system.

Operations began shortly before Christmas 1914, but it soon became clear that the state of the roads, together with the hilly nature of the route, were causing damage to the cars. Added to this, one of the cars crashed into a house whilst descending a hill, and by March of 1915 the service was suspended until acceptable road repairs were undertaken. This never occurred and the vehicles languished in their depot at Tonyrefail until they were sold to Clough, Smith and Co in 1920. All six reappeared at the Tees-side trolleybus operation, where the operating terrain was more favourable.

Public transport did not return to the former trackless route in the Rhondda until 1921, when a motorbus service was instituted.

Photographs of the short-lived Rhondda operation are very rare. This is no. 58, one of the six Daimler vehicles that after the demise of the system, eventually saw service at Tees-side. (R. Marshall collection)

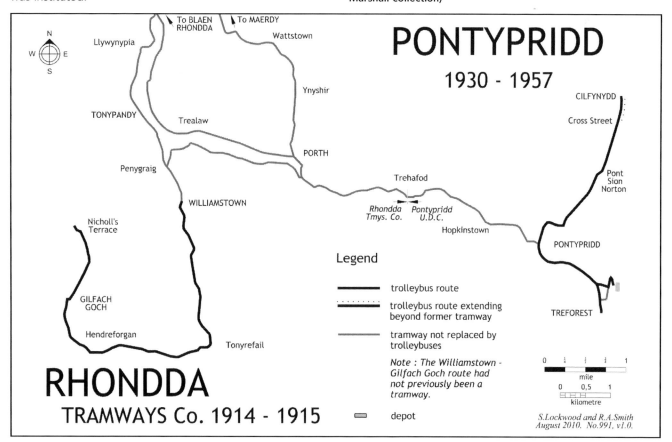

PONTYPRIDD
1930 - 1957

RHONDDA
TRAMWAYS Co. 1914 - 1915

Legend

—— trolleybus route

········· trolleybus route extending beyond former tramway

—— tramway not replaced by trolleybuses

*Note : The Williamstown - Gilfach Goch route had not previously been a tramway.*

▭ depot

*S.Lockwood and R.A.Smith August 2010. No.991, v1.0.*

279

# Aberdare

The first trolleybuses in Wales and only one of two in Britain to use the Cedes-Stoll system. Four feeder routes were introduced at the same time as the town's trams and two of these were subsequently run as tram routes.

Aberdare's trolleybus history was far from orthodox. The system was introduced by the local Urban District Council as part of what today would be described as an 'integrated transport scheme'. The new main line electric tramway through the town was complemented by four short feeder trolleybus routes, and both tram and trolleybus opened within months of each other in 1913-1914. The first trolleybus route, opened in January 1914, was from the town centre to Abernant and the vehicles had to negotiate a low bridge at Aberdare station. This was followed in early February by two routes from the southern tram terminus at Clarence Street, to Capcoch and Cwmaman respectively. Two weeks later a route from the northern terminus at Trecynon was opened to Cwmdare. The eight vehicles used the Cedes-Stoll method of current collection, the only British system other than Keighley to do so. For this reason the vehicles had to be towed by tram each day from the depot at Gladlys to each terminal point.

The system suffered the same difficulties as that at Keighley, ie unreliable hub motors and difficulty of obtaining spares during wartime. However, it was the other bane of early trolleybus operations, the poor state of the roads, that

FACTFILE – ABERDARE
| | |
|---|---|
| Opened | 15 January 1914 |
| Closed | 27 July 1925 |
| Route mileage | 3.5 |
| Maximum number vehicles in service | 8 |
| Rebodied vehicles | Nil |
| Second-hand vehicles | Nil |

**HOW THEY WENT – ABERDARE**
| | |
|---|---|
| Capcoch | 16 February 1916 |
| Cwmaman | 10 February 1919 |
| Cwmdare | 10 October 1922 |
| Abernant | 27 May 1925 |

forced the closure of the Capcoch route in 1916. The Cwmaman route closed in 1919, and the remaining serviceable vehicles struggled on into the 1920s. Consideration was given to obtaining new vehicles, the Straker type being recommended, but this came to nought. The Cwmdare route closed in 1922, leaving two vehicles to run on the Abernant service. This survived for almost a further 2½ years until the last vehicle broke down. One final twist was that the Capcoch and Cwmaman routes were incorporated into an extended tram network in the 1920s.

This is the scene at the Aberaman tram terminus, Clarence Street, shortly after the commencement of trackless services. In the foreground is the connecting trackless to Capcoch, and near the tram is the corresponding trackless car on the Cwmaman service. Note the trolley cable and the power feed point on the overhead.

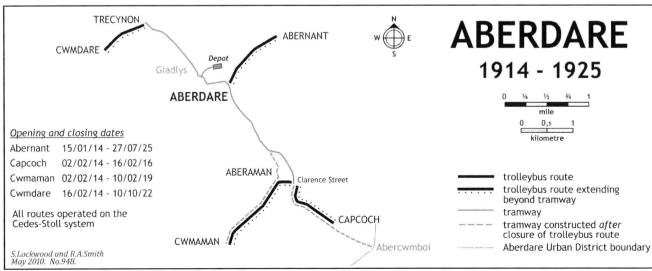

# ABERDARE
## 1914 - 1925

Opening and closing dates
| | |
|---|---|
| Abernant | 15/01/14 - 27/07/25 |
| Capcoch | 02/02/14 - 16/02/16 |
| Cwmaman | 02/02/14 - 10/02/19 |
| Cwmdare | 16/02/14 - 10/10/22 |

All routes operated on the Cedes-Stoll system

S.Lockwood and R.A.Smith
May 2010. No.948.

— trolleybus route
···· trolleybus route extending beyond tramway
— tramway
---- tramway constructed *after* closure of trolleybus route
········ Aberdare Urban District boundary

This commercial postcard view of Abernant shows, in the distance, the Abernant route trackless car stirring up the dust. The Cedes-Stoll wiring arrangement is evident.

# Llanelly

**A medium sized town network that was run by the local power supply company.**

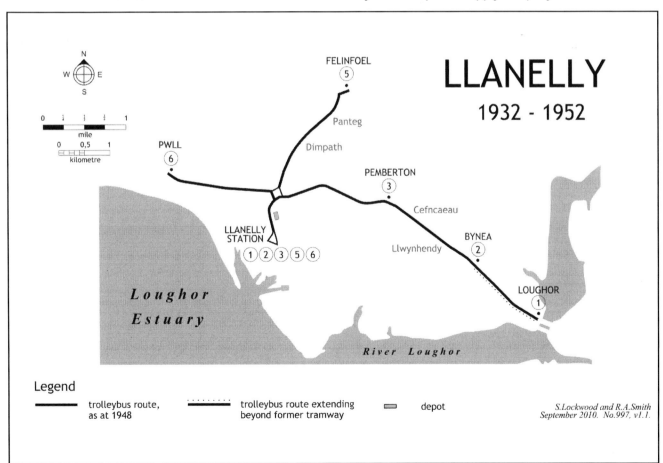

The trolleybuses in Llanelly (a town now known as 'Llanelli'), were owned by the local electricity company, the Llanelly and District Electric Supply Company, a subsidiary of Balfour Beatty (who also owned the Notts and Derby Traction Co.). The system traded as the Llanelly and District Traction Co. Operations began on Boxing Day 1932, when the tram route to Bynea in the east of the town was replaced by trolleybuses, at the same time being extended to Loughor.

Shortly afterwards, on 17 February 1933, trolleybuses were introduced on the remaining two tram routes, to Pwll and Felinfoel. The three-route system was now complete, and apart from a short extension to the Felinfoel route opened in 1943, it was never expanded throughout its lifetime.

Fourteen Leyland four-wheel trolleybuses were purchased to provide the service, but overcrowding prompted the purchase in 1934 of three Guy six-wheelers, these being vehicles held in stock by Guy, the eldest of which dated from 1931. Three more Guys appeared in 1937, which were four-wheelers with stylish Weymann bodies similar to the AEC trolleybuses being placed in service on the Notts and Derby system. A further Weymann bodied Guy, painted in a streamlined version of the Llanelly blue livery, was built at the same time for demonstration purposes, and was eventually purchased, entering service in 1940.

Increased passenger traffic during the war resulted in the loan of two Bournemouth Sunbeams between 1943 and 1945, when the first of twelve utility Karriers entered service. Initially these were painted an overall brown colour, but the final deliveries were painted green and cream, and this livery was adopted for the whole fleet.

In 1948, nationalisation of the electricity supply industry resulted in the ownership of the system passing to the newly formed South Wales Electricity Board, who sold it four years

FACTFILE – LLANELLY
Opened                          26 December 1932
Closed                           8 November 1952
Route mileage                               9

FLEET PROFILE
All double-deck and 4-wheel unless denoted
Maximum number vehicles in service         27
Rebodied vehicles                         Nil
Second-hand vehicles                      Nil

Guy                                         4
Guy 6-wheel                                 3
Karrier utility                            12
Leyland                                    14

later to the local company bus operator, The South Wales Transport Company. This heralded the demise of the system, which was badly in need of refurbishment, and the last trolleybuses ran on 8 November 1952. At the end the fleet was comprised of eight pre-war Leylands and all twelve of the utility Karriers. All the utilities were sold to other trolleybus operators, two complete vehicles going to Maidstone and the remainder, in chassis form only, to Bradford.

Three Guy BT four-wheelers, numbered 33 to 35 were acquired in 1937. These had Weymann bodies similar to those on AEC chassis for Notts and Derby. A fourth Guy was built for exhibition at the Commercial Motor Show of that year and this eventually came into the Llanlley fleet in 1940, becoming no. 36 and registered BBX 818, and not as displayed here on its rear panel. This photo of its rear end as built, shows the style of streamlined livery unique to this vehicle.

Operations began using 14 of these Leyland TB2 vehicles with Leyland's own bodywork. They were numbered 1 to 12, 14-15. No. 1 is seen here before delivery.

Twelve Karrier W utility vehicles came in 1945-6, and, together with some of the original Leylands, these formed the mainstay of the fleet in the system's later years. No. 39, one of four with Roe bodywork, is seen at the Llanelly Station terminus. The garter crest of the company is just visible on the side of the vehicle. No. 39 was one of two sold to Maidstone, where it became no. 84 in the fleet. (C. Carter)

No. 48 was a Park Royal-bodied Karrier W, the last of six delivered in 1946. It is leaving the unusual walled turning circle at Loughor terminus. Sold to Bradford (chassis only) in 1952, it received a new East Lancashire body in 1956 and as no. 784, ran until 1970. (C. Carter)

Eight of the pre-war Leylands ran until the last days of the system. No. 5 is seen at the Felinfoel terminus, adjacent to the Morris Motors factory, to where the route was extended in 1943. (D.A. Jones / London Trolleybus Preservation Society)

# DEWIREMENTS

Huddersfield's Sunbeam MS2 no. 587 has come to grief in John William Street, the main street in the town centre. Incidents such as this in the vicinity of tall buildings could cause third-party damage, as detailed in the accompanying press cutting dated 18 February 1966. (Roy Brook / Paul Watson)

## Trolley-bus arm flew through her office window

MISS GWENDA PETTRICK, 86, Crosland Road, Oakes, had a lucky escape from flying glass this afternoon when a trolley-bus arm came off the overhead lines and flew through an office window, smashing the glass and wrenching out part of the frame.

Miss Pettrick, a shorthand-typist employed by the firm of G. Tattersall, chartered accountant, John William Street, Huddersfield, was writing at her desk about 8ft. from the window at the time.... She jumped up and ran from the room.

It was the second time in about a month that one of the firm's windows had been broken in a similar way.

Road works at the awkward Delaval Road terminus at Newcastle, where trolleybuses turned on a reversing triangle, has caused Sunbeam S7 no. 501 to lose contact with the overhead wires. Two examples of 1950s Morris cars are in the foreground. No. 501 was saved for preservation and is in the care of North East open air museum at Beamish. (P.W. Price / Travel Lens Photographic)

One of the last dewirements on the streets of Britain is shown here. Bradford 846 (formerly Mexborough single-decker no. 38) has dewired outside Thornbury depot on the last weekend of trolleybus operation. (J. Fozard)

## Dundee

**This was the first trolleybus operation to open after Leeds and Bradford, and it was the first of all to close.**

Having observed developments with trolleybuses at Leeds and Bradford, Dundee Corporation decided to trial this form with a route, just over a mile long, along Clepington Road, linking at each end to tram routes at Fairmuir in the west and Maryfield in the east.

Two Railless rear-entrance single-deck vehicles were purchased, and housed at Maryfield tram depot. Turning circles were provided at each end of the route.

Despite encouraging passenger loadings, the service suffered because of the state of the roadway. The clouds of

| FACTFILE – DUNDEE | |
|---|---|
| Opened | 5 September 1912 |
| Closed | 13 May 1914 |
| Route mileage | 1 |
| Maximum number vehicles in service | 2 |
| Rebodied vehicles | Nil |
| Second-hand vehicles | Nil |

dust raised by the vehicles as they passed to and fro led to their local name – 'Stouries'. After nineteen months, the operation was closed and the vehicles were eventually sold to Halifax in 1918.

Trolleybuses were such a novelty in 1912 that commercial postcards of the vehicles were produced. One such example is this view of the 'new trackless trolley car' at Dundee. No. 68, the second of the Railless vehicles, is seen at the Maryfield terminus of the route.

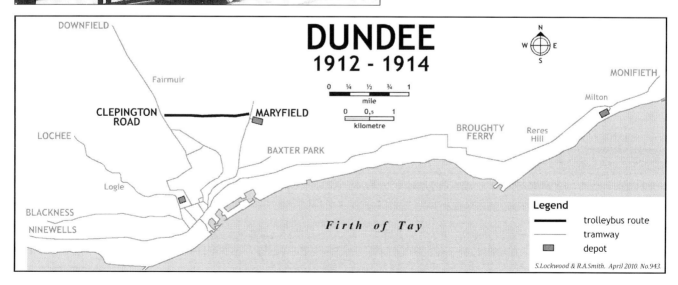

This rear view of no. 67 at the Fairmuir termiuns shows the open rear platform. (Adam Gordon collection)

# Glasgow

The Glasgow system was the only trolleybus operation to open after the Second World War and within ten years it had become one of Britain's largest, even though it never came near to matching Glasgow's vast tram and bus network.

The only 'modern' trolleybus system in Scotland was at Glasgow, and it was almost the end of the 1940s before operations began. There were two principal factors that prompted this: firstly, much of the vast fleet of trams was between 30 and 45 years old and therefore in need of replacement, and secondly, since electricity nationalisation in 1948, Glasgow was the only authority in Britain outside London still able to generate its own electricity for traction purposes. One disadvantage to trolleybus operation in the city was that the trams used bow collectors, and could not therefore share wiring with trolleybuses. Great efforts had to be made to keep tram and trolleybus routes as far apart as possible, and special provision had to be made wherever tram and trolleybus wires crossed each other.

The first public service (no 102) commenced in April 1949 between Riddrie and Polmadie, crossing the River Clyde at Albert Bridge. This was followed in November of that year by service 101, between Shawfield and Cathedral Street. In the meantime, the Polmadie route had been extended via Aikenhead Road to Hampden Park (serving the football stadium) in July 1949. These routes were re-organised in August 1950, the 101 becoming Shawfield to Royston Road (part way along the Riddrie route), and 102 became Riddrie to Polmadie with a separately numbered service 103 running between Riddrie and Hampden Park.

The vehicles purchased for these services comprised 64 six-wheelers, 34 being BUTs and the remainder being Daimlers. Originally these were intended to have a rear entrance (with doors) and a front exit. However, immediate post-war conditions did not favour the bulk production of such a specialist design, and to ensure prompt delivery,

| FACTFILE – GLASGOW | |
|---|---|
| Opened | 3 April 1949 |
| Closed | 27 May 1967 |
| Route mileage | 43 |

**FLEET PROFILE**
**All double-deck unless denoted**

| | |
|---|---|
| Maximum number vehicles in service | 194 |
| Rebodied vehicles | Nil |
| Second-hand vehicles | Nil |
| | |
| BUT 6-wheel (TB) | 34 |
| BUT 4-wheel (TB) | 90 |
| BUT 4-wheel single-deck (TBS) | 21 |
| Daimler 6-wheel (TD) | 30 |
| Sunbeam 4-wheel (TG) | 20 |

| HOW THEY WENT – GLASGOW | |
|---|---|
| 9 May 1959 | Riddrie to Hampden Park (103) |
| 26 November 1960 | George Square to Clarkston (night service 5) |
| 16 November 1964 | Linthouse and Shieldhall |
| 30 July 1965 | Summertown Road to Paisley Road Toll |
| 30 April 1966 | Riddrie, Polmadie and Rutherglen (101, 102) |
| 1 October 1966 | Millerston to Bellahouston (106) |
| 4 March 1967 | Muirend to Maitland Street via Victoria Road (107) |
| 4 March 1967 | Mount Florida to Paisley Road Toll (108) |
| 27 May 1967 | Clarkston and Muirend to Queen's Cross (105) |

BUT no. TB 14 is seen crossing the River Clyde at Albert Bridge early in the life of the system. Note the London style 'Trolleybus' logo on the front dash. London Transport had registered this as a trade mark, and possibly due to this, it was a short lived feature in Glasgow. (C. Carter)

Glasgow agreed to accept the conventional Metro-Cammell body design being produced for London's Q1 vehicles, also used by Newcastle. In early 1951, a very unconventional vehicle did appear on service 102. This was a single-deck BUT with set back front axle, allowing a rear entrance and front exit. Provision was made for a seated conductor and there were just 26 seats, with space for 40 standees. Ten further examples were delivered in 1953, with a wider exit placed behind the front axle in a more central position. From 1959, these vehicles were rebuilt with 36 or 38 seats for use with a roving conductor and the rear entrance removed.

The single-deckers were put to work on route 104 between Cathedral Street and Muirend via Cathcart Road, which had earlier commenced operation at the end of August 1952. July 1953 saw the replacement of trams between Queens Cross and Clarkston with trolleybus route 105. This brought trolleybuses into the central streets, including George Square and Glassford Street, crossing the Clyde at Victoria Bridge. Twenty four-wheel Sunbeams entered service for this route, the first five having bodywork by Alexander, the only trolleybus bodies built by this major Scottish coachbuilder.

Plans were now being laid to replace the remainder of Glasgow's trams with trolleybuses and motorbuses. Bulk orders were placed for 90 BUT 4-wheelers with 30 feet long bodies. To this was added ten 50-seat single-deck BUTs, 34 feet long and for which special dispensation was required from the Ministry of Transport.

Before these vehicles arrived, an extension to service 101 was opened in February 1956, from Shawfield to Rutherglen. Later that year, the Suez crisis prompted the introduction of trolleybuses on night bus service 5 between George Square and Clarkston, and this remained in place until well after the fuel shortages that the crisis generated.

The new vehicles started to enter service from mid-1957, and an additional route (service 107) was opened in July, running from Muirend to Maitland Street via Victoria Road.

This was followed in June 1958 by the long route (service 106) from Millerston to Bellahouston via Bridgeton Cross and crossing the Clyde at Kings Bridge. The route also included a branch at its western end to serve the heavy industrial shipyard areas at Linthouse and Shieldhall, and journeys ran to there at peak hours.

What became Glasgow's last tram to trolleybus conversion occurred on 16 November 1958, when suburban tram route 12 between Mount Florida (Hampden Park) and Paisley Road Toll became trolleybus route 108, operated by the long single-deckers. This route was entirely on the south-side of the city, and was thus the only trolleybus service not to cross the Clyde.

The system was served by three depots (referred to as 'garages'), these being at Dennistoun, Govan and Hampden, although the original fleet was housed at Larkfield motorbus garage until that at Hampden, which housed trolleybuses only, opened in 1950.

Unfortunately the tide was now turning for the city's trolleybus network. The municipal Pinkston Power Station was sold to the local electricity board in 1958, and the City Council resolved not to develop the system any further. The existing network had been established using the principle of ensuring trams and trolleybuses were kept apart as far as possible, rather than producing a co-ordinated and therefore more cost-efficient operation.

The first route withdrawal took place in May 1959, this being service 103, removing 'in service' trolleybuses between Polmadie and Hampden Park. Service 104 followed in August 1962 (just weeks before Glasgow's last tram ran), although no wiring was involved. The peak hour extension to the shipyard areas of Linthouse and Shieldhall operated by services 106 and 108 ceased in late 1964.

Conversion of the main trolleybus routes commenced in April 1966, and took place over four stages. The last trolleybuses ran in service on Saturday 27 May 1967, when unexpectedly large crowds turned out to see the last vehicle on its journey to Hampden garage.

The Daimler chassied version of the Q1 style vehicle is depicted here. TD13, one of 30 of this type, is seen at the Shawfield terminus of route 101 on 25 April 1951. The destination blinds of Glasgow's trolleybuses had a green background to the white lettering rather than the usual black. (C.W. Routh)

# GLAGOW'S SINGLE-DECK EXPERIMENT

The experimental single-decker with seated conductor was originally given the number TB 35. It had a BUT RETB1 chassis, built by Leyland and based on a design intended for export, with a Weymann 27-seat plus 40 standee body. It was exhibited at the Commercial Motor Show in London in November 1950 and entered service in the Spring of 1951.

In June 1951, TB 35 was demonstrated at the International Passenger Transport Conference in Edinburgh, and operated in George Street using the tram overhead and tracks. This view on that occasion shows the vehicle posed in George Street outside the conference venue. (The Omnibus Society)

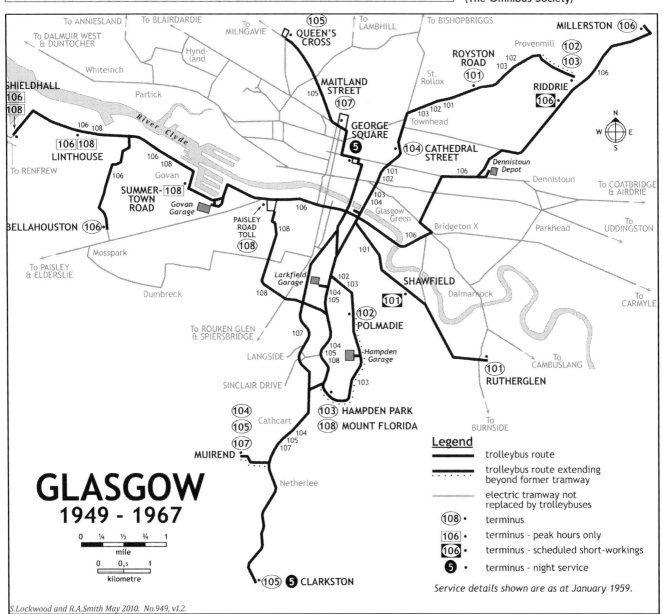

GLASGOW
1949 - 1967

Legend

—— trolleybus route

—— trolleybus route extending beyond former tramway

—— electric tramway not replaced by trolleybuses

(108)• terminus

106• terminus - peak hours only

106• terminus - scheduled short-workings

5• terminus - night service

Service details shown are as at January 1959.

S.Lockwood and R.A.Smith May 2010. No.949, v1.2.

Another view taken in George Street, Edinburgh shows the rear of the vehicle, with conference delegates in the rear standing area. Note the emergency hatch in the lower part of the rear wall, and the negative power connection to the tram tracks. On the right is part of an Edinburgh tram stop sign. (The Omnibus Society)

A production batch of ten vehicles followed in 1953. These had the same BUT chassis but with East Lancashire bodywork. The front (exit) door was positioned behind the front axle. These were numbered TBS 2 to 11, and the original vehicle was renumbered to TBS 1. No. TBS 2 was loaned to Nottingham and Walsall in early 1953, and it operated in service at both locations. It is seen here at Trent Bridge terminus Nottingham with a more conventional BUT vehicle in the background. (G.H.F. Atkins / courtesy and copyright John Banks collection)

The standee experiment was not a success and by 1959 a start was made to rebuild the vehicles to conventional format. The rear entrance was removed and the seating increased to 36, including seats on the nearside beside the driver. This is TBS 11 at the Mount Florida terminus of service 108 in September 1962. (C.W. Routh)

Twenty Sunbeam F4A four-wheelers came in 1953. The first five were bodied by Alexander, the only trolleybuses built by this Scottish concern. One of these, TG 3 (the 'G' stood for Guy), is seen at Shawfield en route for Rutherglen on 7 April 1961. The Shawfield tram terminus is in the background. (C.W. Routh)

The remaining 15 Sunbeams had Weymann bodies. TG 17 is shown at the Riddrie terminus of service 101 in September 1962, shortly after the service had been extended from Royston Road (and the 102 service cut back from here to Royston Road). By this time there was much more green in the livery, at the expense of cream. (C.W. Routh)

This is Glasgow Cross, where the High Street services from Riddrie intersected the main east west tram services. BUT six-wheeler TB 18 is seen proceeding towards Albert Bridge on a 102 journey to Polmadie. It is being followed by Alexander bodied Sunbeam no. TG 1. The BUT has had its 'via' destination screen panelled over, considerably altering the frontal profile. (Roy Brook / Paul Watson)

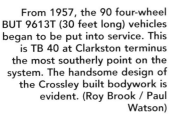

From 1957, the 90 four-wheel BUT 9613T (30 feet long) vehicles began to be put into service. This is TB 40 at Clarkston terminus the most southerly point on the system. The handsome design of the Crossley built bodywork is evident. (Roy Brook / Paul Watson)

One of the interesting aspects of the Glasgow system was the operation of a shipyard electric locomotive along Govan Road, alongside the service 106 trolleybuses where the route ran close to the shipyards of the River Clyde. The tram overhead had been removed by 1960 and a separate single line of trolleybus type overhead was used, the locomotive being fitted with twin trolleybooms instead of the tramway bow collector previously used. The Fairfield shipyard electric locomotive transferred trains of freight to and from Govan goods yard. This view shows BUT trolleybus TB51 beside the Fairfield locomotive in Govan Road on a rather wet 18 May 1962. (David Smithies)

Glasgow's final new trolleybuses were the ten single-deck BUT RETB1 type vehicles, which were 34 feet long. They were almost exclusively used on the 108 Paisley Road Toll to Mount Florida service, and in September 1962, no. TBS 15 is seen at the latter terminus, in company with a more conventional vehicle, TB30. (C.W. Routh)

Although great efforts were made to ensure that the tram and trolleybus infrastructure in Glasgow was kept as well apart as possible, there were many locations where special provision had to be made where tram and trolleybus routes intersected. One such was at the junction of Castle Street and Duke Street in the north-east of the city centre. This fine view of the junction shows Daimler six-wheeler trolleybus TD 29 proceeding south towards High Street, and round-dash Standard tram no. 495 (originally built 1903 and withdrawn 1958), approaching on Duke Street. The overhead crossing installation is described thus: 'Wide pan solid crossings for the passage of bow type collectors on the trams, and carbon insert slipper collectors on the trolleybus. Dumbell type insulator units for insulating the trolleybus negative trolley wire from the tramway positive.' (BICC)

Glasgow was the last place where trolleybuses, trams and buses from the same fleet ran together. This scene, at Bridgeton Cross shows BUT trolleybus TB56 leading a Leyland PD3 motorbus and a 'Coronation' type tram. (Roy Brook / Paul Watson)

# NEW TO BRITISH OPERATORS...

This B.U.T. single-deck trolleybus . . . for operation in Glasgow . . . has several new and advantageous features. It can carry 26 seated and 40 standing passengers at peak hours . . . almost double-deck capacity . . . but during "off-times", unprofitable dead-weight running is eliminated. Passengers enter from the rear, pay as they pass the conductor's cash desk, and leave the bus at the front end. The electrically-controlled front and rear doors prevent step accidents as the bus cannot proceed until they are closed. This new B.U.T. trolleybus will prove a great economical asset in big-city transport, where passenger loads fluctuate so greatly from hour to hour.

## ...it ends the problem of

## UNCOLLECTED FARES

## WASTEFUL DEAD-WEIGHT RUNNING COSTS

## STEP ACCIDENTS

A·E·C LEYLAND TROLLEYBUSES

*The conductor's cash desk at rear. Passengers must pass here to enter the bus.*

*Interior view showing seating arrangements and the generous standing space.*

# B.U.T. TROLLEYBUSES

**BRITISH UNITED TRACTION LTD.** HANOVER HOUSE, HANOVER SQUARE, LONDON, W.1

# INSIDES

The lower deck interior of London Transport's first trolleybus is shown here. This was no. 62, an AEC 663T six-wheeler with Metro Cammell bodywork to the general style of the subsequent mass deliveries of vehicles. Of note is the 'half-cab' arrangement, with an inward facing bench seat at the nearside front. This was a standard feature in the fleet for the first few hundred deliveries. Whilst this feature did maximise seating capacity, the lack of a full bulkhead was found to weaken the body structure, and there were issues with driver distraction and obstructed vision on the nearside. Almost all of the vehicles were subsequently rebuilt with a conventional front bulkhead and full width cab.

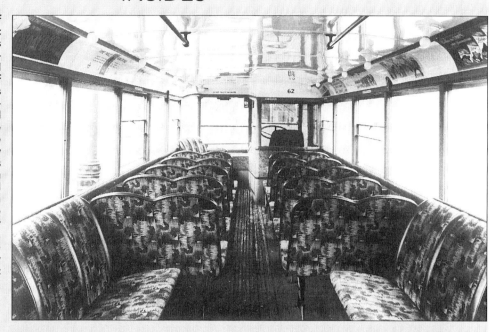

A lower saloon view of a Glasgow Daimler six-wheeler (TD 17) with 'Q1' style Metro Cammell bodywork. The long bench seats over the rear wheels, a typical feature of six-wheel trolleybuses are evident.

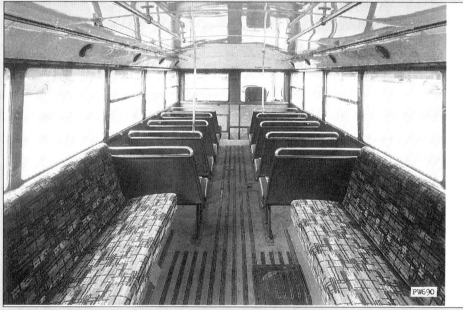

Darlington took delivery of three AEC four-wheel single deckers with Brush bodywork in 1935. This is the interior of no. 41, showing the open centre doorway, and the bench seating, including a seat directly opposite the door opening.

295

## Belfast

**Ireland's only trolleybus system, Belfast, had the largest fleet in Britain outside London.**

Belfast decided to experiment with trolleybus operation by replacing trams on the Falls Road route at the end of March 1938. Fourteen six-wheel trolleybuses were purchased, these being two each of the seven makes of trolleybus chassis that were available at the time (except for Ransomes). Eight of the bodies were provided by Harkness, a local firm that went on to supply almost all the future Belfast trolleybus bodies.

The trolleybuses were deemed a success and a bulk order for 114 AEC chassis was awarded in 1939, although the outbreak of war brought about a reduction to 88 vehicles, which were delivered in 1941/2. Routes to the east of the city were introduced in 1941 to Cregagh and Castlereagh, and in 1942 to Stormont and Dundonald. Stormont is the seat of the Northern Ireland Parliament, and the trams which had terminated at the castle gates were replaced by trolleybuses which operated into the grounds on a clockwise loop around the Parliament building itself.

A feature of these services was that journeys, with separate route numbers, were provided to run to or from the city centre via the Queens or Albert Bridges over the River Lagan.

Fourteen four-wheel utility Sunbeams joined the fleet, two arriving in 1943, and a further twelve following in 1946, allowing the Bloomfield route to open that year.

The tram conversion programme continued after the war, and 70 Guy six-wheelers entered service between 1948 and 1950. The Ormeau Road route opened in April 1948, and the long route northwards along Antrim Road to Glengormley came into use in early 1949.

The expansion continued into the early 1950s. Another long route northwards along Shore Road to Whitehouse opened in October 1950. This replaced the Greencastle tram service, and was extended beyond the city boundary to Whitehouse, in order to provide a trolleybus turning facility. This resulted in a special fare arrangement having to be applied to protect the bus service of the state-owned Ulster Transport Authority. April 1951 saw the opening of the

| FACTFILE – BELFAST | |
|---|---|
| Opened | 28 March 1938 |
| Closed | 12 May 1968 |
| Route mileage | 37 |

| FLEET PROFILE | |
|---|---|
| All double-deck and 6-wheel unless denoted | |
| Maximum number vehicles in service | 215 |
| Rebodied vehicles | Nil |
| Second-hand vehicles | 11 |
| | |
| AEC | 90 |
| BUT | 48 |
| Crossley | 2 |
| Daimler | 2 |
| Guy | 72 |
| Karrier | 2 |
| Leyland | 2 |
| Sunbeam 4-wheel | 26 |

| HOW THEY WENT – BELFAST | |
|---|---|
| 1 June 1958 | Holywood Road |
| 26 October 1958 | Ormeau Road |
| 20 May 1962 | Whitehouse branch from Shore Road |
| 20 January 1963 | Castlereagh |
| 30 March 1963 | Stormont, Dundonald |
| 14 October 1963 | Bloomfield, Cregagh, Carr's Glen |
| 5 February 1966 | Glengormley |
| 12 May 1968 | Falls Road, Glen Road, Whiterock, Whitewell |

Carr's Glen trolleybus service, replacing and extending the Cliftonville tram service. 24 BUT vehicles had entered service in 1950, supplemented by eleven second-hand Sunbeam four-wheelers dating from 1940/1, bought from Wolverhampton.

This trolleybus was numerically the last of the original experimental fleet, new in 1938. No. T14 was one of a pair of Sunbeam MS2 vehicles with Scottish-built Cowieson bodies, the only trolleybuses to be built by this firm. It is seen on a test run on Falls Road before entry into service. The 'T' prefix to the fleet number was only applied to the fourteen original vehicles, subsequent deliveries did not have this feature. The livery is blue and white.

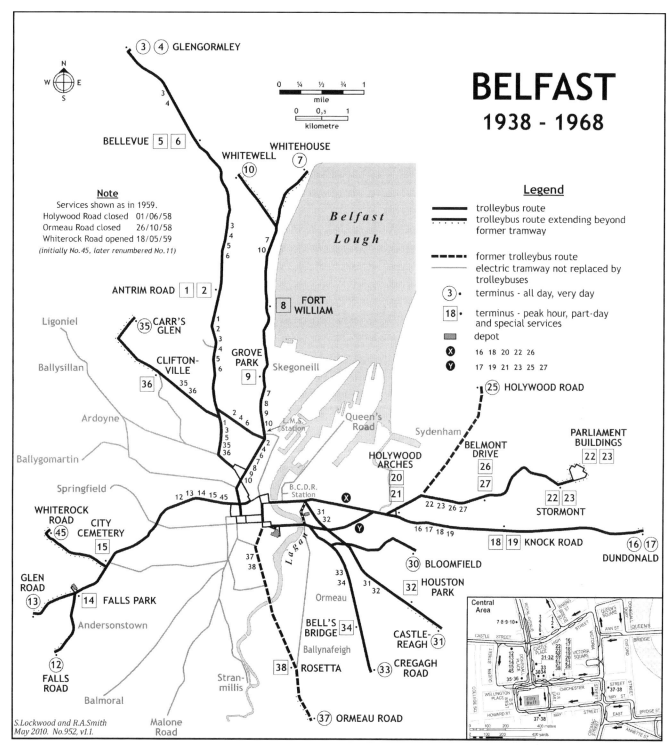

## BELFAST
### 1938 - 1968

③ ④ GLENGORMLEY

**Note**
Services shown as in 1959.
Holywood Road closed 01/06/58
Ormeau Road closed 26/10/58
Whiterock Road opened 18/05/59
*(initially No.45, later renumbered No.11)*

BELLEVUE [5] [6]

WHITEWELL
⑩
WHITEHOUSE
⑦

*Belfast Lough*

ANTRIM ROAD [1] [2]

③⑤ CARR'S GLEN

CLIFTON-VILLE
[36]

GROVE PARK
[9]

[8] FORT WILLIAM

Skegoneill

Ligoniel

Ballysillan

Ardoyne

Ballygomartin

Springfield

WHITEROCK ROAD
④⑤

CITY CEMETERY
[15]

12 13 14 15 45

GLEN ROAD
⑬

[14] FALLS PARK

Andersonstown

⑫
FALLS ROAD

Balmoral

Stran-millis
Malone Road

### Legend

——— trolleybus route
········· trolleybus route extending beyond former tramway
— — — former trolleybus route
——— electric tramway not replaced by trolleybuses
③• terminus - all day, very day
[18]• terminus - peak hour, part-day and special services
▨ depot
Ⓧ 16 18 20 22 26
Ⓨ 17 19 21 23 25 27

②⑤ HOLYWOOD ROAD

Sydenham

BELMONT DRIVE
[26]
[27]

PARLIAMENT BUILDINGS
[22] [23]

[22] [23]
STORMONT

HOLYWOOD ARCHES
[20]
[21]

Queen's Road

L.M.S. Station

B.C.D.R. Station

Ⓧ

Ⓨ

22 23 26 27

16 17 18 19

[18] [19] KNOCK ROAD

⑯⑰
DUNDONALD

31 32

③⓪ BLOOMFIELD

31 32
[32] HOUSTON PARK

33 34

31 32

Ormeau

BELL'S BRIDGE [34]

Ballynafeigh

[38] ROSETTA

CASTLE-REAGH ③①

③③ CREGAGH ROAD

③⑦ ORMEAU ROAD

37 38

*Lagan*

*S.Lockwood and R.A.Smith*
*May 2010. No.952, v1.1.*

Central Area

---

A change of manager in 1951 heralded a new policy, and the remaining tram routes were to be replaced by motorbuses, even though the Holywood Road motorbus route was converted to trolleybuses in late 1952. However, some existing trolleybus routes were extended, a branch off the Whitehouse route to Whitewell opening in April 1953. The original Falls Road service, (on which a branch to Glen Road was opened in April 1952), was extended from the Fruithill Park terminus to Casement Park in June 1954. A further batch of 24 BUTs entered service in 1953/4, their Harkness bodies having a modernised front end design.

The late 1950s brought mixed fortunes for the system. Two routes were converted to motorbuses due to impending major road works (Holywood Road) or housing development (Ormeau Road) in 1958. However, another extension to the Falls Road route, a branch from Cemetery Junction to Whiterock, opened in May 1959.

A notable event in July 1958 was the introduction of a traffic-flow system in the City Hall area, resulting in the re-modelling of the overhead. This produced a complicated layout allowing full flexibility of movement for vehicles.

One new trolleybus entered the fleet in 1958, this being a 30-foot long four-wheel Sunbeam, one of several experimental vehicles purchased to assess future fleet development. Despite this, in 1959 the decision was taken to replace all trolleybuses with motorbuses.

The routes were converted starting in 1962 with the short Whitehouse to Greencastle section and its complicated fares arrangement. The imminent construction of a new bridge over the River Lagan prompted the early demise of the eastern routes, leaving the northern and south west services to run later into the decade. The final ceremonies took place on Sunday 12 May 1968 when the last trolleybuses departed from the City Hall.

No. 12 (formerly T12), is seen in early post-war days in the city centre at Donegall Place. This was a Leyland TTB4 with Leyland bodywork. Note the beading on the nearside panelling between the two decks which formerly marked position of the pre-war streamlined 'swoop'. The vehicle is working to Stormont Parliament Buildings on service 26, which was renumbered to 23 in 1951. (W.J. Haynes)

The bulk of the initial trolleybus fleet was the 88-strong batch of AEC vehicles numbered 15 to 102, delivered in the early years of the war, between 1940 and 1942. Like all subsequent six-wheel Belfast trolleybuses, the bodywork was by the local firm of Harkness. No. 99 is seen in Donegall Square in 1951. The 'Belfast Corporation' fleetname was discontinued in the early 1950s. (A.B. Cross)

The first four-wheelers in the fleet were a pair of Park Royal-bodied utility Sunbeam W vehicles new in 1943. These were followed in 1946 by a further 12 of this type, but with Harkness bodywork. No. 135 of the latter type is seen at the city centre terminus of the Bloomfield route, soon after entering service. Both route and vehicle began operating in May 1946. Standing behind is one of the 1938 experimental vehicles still in pre-war streamlined livery. (J.F. Parke)

Trams and trolleybuses ran together in Belfast until 1954. This 1953 scene in Albert Bridge Road, looking towards the junction with Newtonards Road, shows Guy trolleybus 116, one of the seventy Guy BTX vehicles new in 1948/9, together with tram 21. Note the full rear destination display on the trolleybus, later removed, and the tubular method of overhead wire suspension. No. 116 is on a short-working journey of the Dundonald service to Knock Road. (A.D. Packer)

AEC no. 16 is seen at the Greencastle junction of the Whitewell and Whitehouse routes via Shore Road. It is working on cross-city service 12 from Whitewell to Falls Road terminus in this 1962 view. (C.W. Routh)

This is the terminus at Castlereagh, and the number of vehicles reflects the high level of service operated. On the left is the rear of AEC no. 102, the last of the batch, and on the right is Guy no. 121. (R.F. Mack)

## STORMONT

One of the best known features of the Belfast system was the terminus of service 22 and 23 at the Parliament Buildings, Stormont, seat of the Northern Ireland government. During the day, trolleybuses operated along the private road through the grounds and around the building. In the evening the gates were shut and vehicles used a turning circle just outside the gates in Massey Avenue.

Guy no. 149 is seen after having circumnavigated the impressive Parliament buildings, visible in the background. (R.F. Mack)

Emerging from the narrow passage behind the Parliament Building is AEC no. 97. (R.F. Mack)

Stormont to (The) Whitehouse. A well filled Guy, no. 119, is seen in this view at the Edward Carson Statue, and is about to leave the grounds. Its destination is set for service 7 to Whitehouse, which was not a regular working from Stormont. (R.F. Mack)

The most northerly terminus was the Antrim Road terminus of services 3 and 4 at Glengormley. Trolleybuses turned off the main road here into a narrow cul-de-sac, at the end of which was a triangular reverser. On the right at the loading point is Guy no. 103, the first of the post-war batch, and on the left is the rear of 1948 BUT no. 209 which is about to move forward to the reverser. Note the prominent 'T' on the lower panel, intended to warn following trolleybus drivers to be wary of overtaking, and the dark green/grey area around the rear dome, which disguised the greasy drips from the trolley heads. (Roy Brook / Paul Watson)

Dundonald, on the Newtonards Road, was the eastern extremity of the system. The terminus consisted of an anti-clockwise loop at the Elk Inn. Guy no. 157 has just left the terminus on a service 17 journey to the city via Albert Bridge. (C.W. Routh)

Three abreast in Donegall Place. Colin Routh captured this scene in April 1962 of trolleybuses using the extensive overhead wiring provision erected in this area in 1958. At this point these were three sets of wires in the southbound direction. From the left are; AEC no. 47, and Guys 156 and 121. Both the latter appear to be using the same innermost set of wires. (C.W. Routh)

Guy BTX 149 is seen here turning into Queen's Square from Victoria Street, where trolleybuses were allowed through the 'No Entry' signs. This was the routing for the east Belfast routes operating from the City Centre across Queen's Bridge. (C.W. Routh)

The final route extension in Belfast came as late as 1959, when a branch off the Falls Road routes was opened along Whiterock Road. This Guy trolleybus, no. 182, is seen in Whiterock Road, climbing away from the Cemetery Junction on Falls Road. (V. Nutton, Travel Lens Photographic)

Following on from the Guys, were 24 BUT 9641T vehicles delivered between 1948 and 1950. These were numbered 187 to 210 in the fleet and looked very similar to the Guys. In April 1962, no. 192 is seen in Clifton Street, climbing north out of the city centre and approaching Carlisle Circus, on a journey to Carr's Glen. In the foreground are traces of the former tram tracks. (C.W. Routh)

Another 24 BUTs came in 1953/4, these being numbered 211 to 234. They had a revised style of body with a more modern-looking frontal appearance. This is no. 212 turning from Cliftonville Road into Antrim Road during a cross-city journey from Carr's Glen to Creagagh in April 1962. (C.W. Routh)

Owing to the delays in the delivery of new vehicles, Belfast acquired eleven Sunbeam MF2 four-wheelers from Wolverhampton in 1952. These had Park Royal bodies and were new in the early years of the war. They were numbered 235 to 245 and were used at peak hours. No. 239, formerly Wolverhampton no. 289, is seen here parked out of service. When the last batch of BUTs entered service in 1954, many of these Sunbeams were withdrawn, although some, including this one, were retained until 1956. (R. Marshall collection)

Belfast's last trolleybus was an experimental vehicle new in 1958. No. 246 was a 30-foot long Sunbeam F4A four-wheeler. The vehicle remained unique and lasted in service to the end of the system. It was retained for preservation and is now part of the collection at the East Anglia Transport Museum, where it has recently been restored to full working order. The vehicle is seen here at the gates of Haymarket depot near the city centre where trolleybuses were parked in the open-air.

# LASTS

Possibly the earliest trolleybus system closure to be marked by a civic ceremony and decorated vehicles was at Chesterfield in March 1938. Two vehicles were decorated with illuminated fittings, and these are seen here at the depot. In front is one of the three Karrier vehicles acquired from York, and a Straker vehicle stands behind. (R. Marshall collection)

In contrast, some trolleybus systems faded away without any event to mark their passing. Examples were Pontypridd, Darlington and Grimsby-Cleethorpes. The last trolleybus journey on the latter system is seen here on 4 June 1960. BUT no. 160 is standing at the Cleethorpes Bathing Pool terminus before commencing the final run to Grimsby, and it is sandwiched between two motorbuses working on dance specials. (R.F. Mack)

The most imaginative trolleybus closure was probably at Mexborough in March 1961. Sunbeam F4 no. 29 had the rear section of its roof removed, and it ran at the head of the closing procession of vehicles, with a silver band playing in the open rear section. This is the scene in Rockingham Road, Swinton on 27 March 1961 as the line of vehicles passes by. Eleven years later, almost to the day, this vehicle, by then fitted with a double-deck body and no. 843 in the Bradford fleet, operated Britain's last normal public service trolleybus journey. (J. Copland / A.D. Packer)

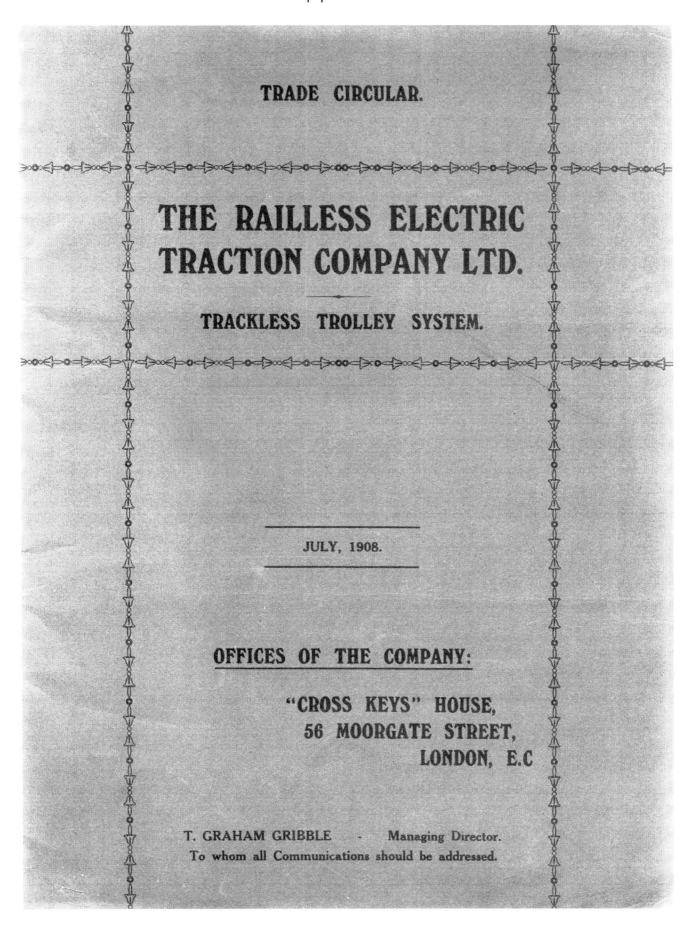

TRADE CIRCULAR.

# THE RAILLESS ELECTRIC TRACTION COMPANY LTD.

## TRACKLESS TROLLEY SYSTEM.

JULY, 1908.

### OFFICES OF THE COMPANY:

"CROSS KEYS" HOUSE,
56 MOORGATE STREET,
LONDON, E.C

T. GRAHAM GRIBBLE  -  Managing Director.
To whom all Communications should be addressed.

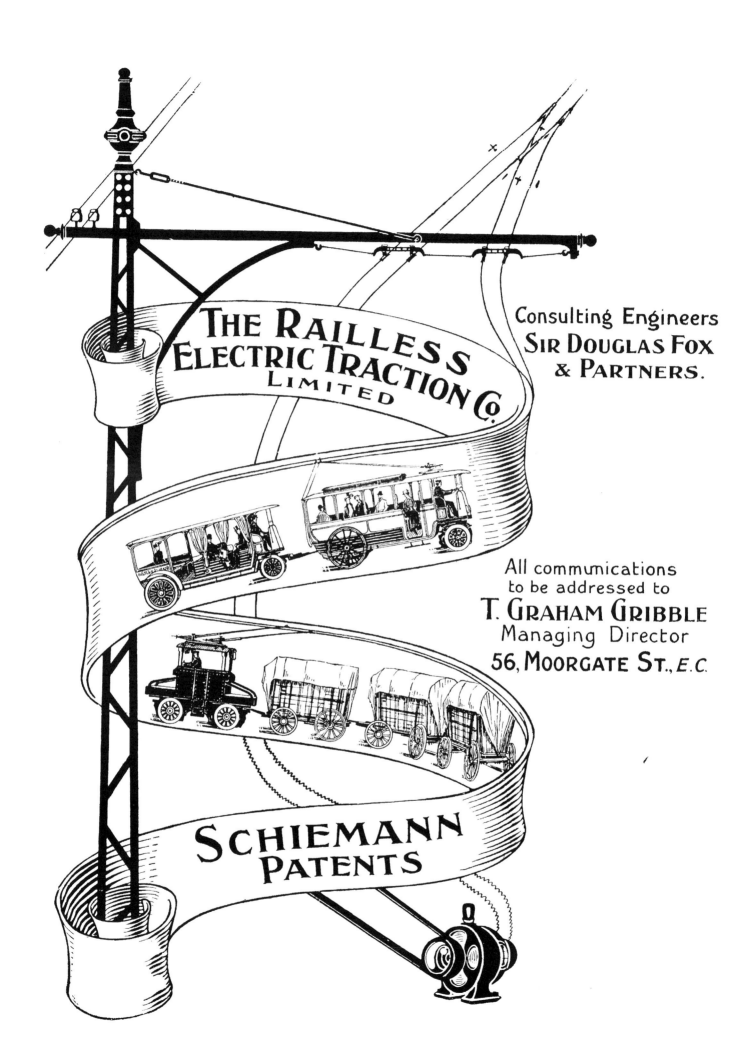

THE RAILLESS ELECTRIC TRACTION Co. LIMITED

Consulting Engineers
SIR DOUGLAS FOX
& PARTNERS.

All communications
to be addressed to
T. GRAHAM GRIBBLE
Managing Director
56, MOORGATE ST., E.C.

SCHIEMANN PATENTS

# The Railless Electric Traction Co.

## (Limited.)

Consulting Engineers - Sir DOUGLAS FOX & PARTNERS.

Managing Director - - T. GRAHAM GRIBBLE.

Secretary - - - H. O. FOSTER.

Offices - - - - "CROSS KEYS" HOUSE,
56 MOORGATE ST., LONDON, E.C.

*Communications to be addressed to the Managing Director.*

**License from Patentee**

The Railless Electric Traction Co. has acquired the patent rights of Messrs. Max Schiemann & Co. for Great Britain, India and the Colonies, as also the co-operation of that firm in the introduction of their system, the only one which has proved its efficiency and commercial success for electrically propelled road vehicles taking the current from overhead wires.

The Company have also made arrangements with the Electric Vehicle Co. of London for the supply of omnibus and other vehicles propelled by accumulators such as are described and illustrated in the following pages.

**Reports and Tests**

Reports have been prepared as the result of repeated examinations and tests of the systems described in this circular, by the Consulting Engineers, Sir Douglas Fox & Partners, and these reports may be seen by parties who wish to obtain further information at the offices of the Company, 56 Moorgate Street, London, E.C., application in the first place to be made in writing to T. Graham Gribble, Esq., Managing Director.

**Plans and Estimates**

The Railless Electric Traction Co. is prepared to furnish plans and estimates and to undertake the installation of electric traction on ordinary streets and highways for every form of transportation. It is also in a position to give professional advice upon any proposition for urban or inter-urban transportation and on all questions of engineering construction.

**Commercial Limitations of Tramways and Field for Railless Traction**

The Tramway system, immense as have been its services, is limited by its costliness to situations where the traffic is of a sufficient density to pay for it. There is, however, a great population which lacks travelling facilities, and to which a more economical construction can alone supply the need. Tramways have already been extended beyond their remunerative limit and a large amount of capital is locked up in lines which never have been profitable nor are ever likely to be.

**Various Methods of Mechanical Traction**

Mechanical traction upon the ordinary highway, without rails, has been the subject of many inventions, and all with the one object of saving the heavy cost of permanent way. The internal combustion motor, as also the steam car have been introduced in a great many forms, but the electric motor, superior by far to any of them, has in the last few years appeared as a competitor. It has now, after struggling with many difficulties, passed out of the experimental stage and is in successful operation in many places, to which reference will presently be made.

**Methods of Electrical Traction**

In the application of electricity to road traction two methods have been adopted. The first by independent motors driven by accumulators, the second by electric motors deriving their current from a pair of overhead conductors. These two systems should not be regarded as rivals but as each having their respective spheres, and in some cases supplementary one to the other. The accumulator car is more expensive to operate, but where there is sufficient traffic to pay for it, possesses the advantage of not requiring overhead wires. The trolley road-car is probably the most economical means yet devised for transportation upon the highway, and in all situations where overhead wires are permissible, furnishes the cheapest and best solution of the problem. Either of these systems can be installed for one-third of the average cost of British Tramways, or less. The Railless Electric Traction Co. is fully prepared to advise Municipalities or Companies as to the best way of dealing with any situation from thorough knowledge and experience of these and other systems of transportation.

**Advantages of Railless Electric Traction**

The principal advantages of Railless Electric Traction are as follow :

1. The cost of construction is from one-fourth to one-third of the average cost of British Tramways per mile of route. The cost of Tramway construction and equipment in so far as carried out by Municipalities which borrow money at cheaper rates than Companies, varies from £10,500 to £46,000 per mile of route, and the average of the whole is £23,500. In this average the London County Council tramways are not included because, being constructed on the Conduit system, the cost is very much higher. This great Capital Expenditure is principally due to Permanent way, but the preliminary expenses of obtaining authorisation are also heavy. Railless Electric Traction not only dispenses

facilitated by Railless Electric Traction. Tramway construction is often limited to a less route length than will properly serve the population, solely because only the denser districts will pay for it. On the other hand tramways are often extended to suburban districts to develop them, the deficits being endured by the rate payers in prospect of future return in the increased value of house property. A Railless Traction line can however develop those districts equally well and at the same time earn a profit.

5. In speed and comfort of travelling, this method can furnish all that is needed for urban transportation. The electric omnibus, popularly known as the "Electrobus" which has been now working for some nine months in London streets, operated by accumulators, has proved itself a very popular conveyance. In freedom from smell, from vibration and sudden jerks, and in powers of acceleration and control, it is certainly the best mechanically operated omnibus yet introduced. Its motor, in contrast with the internal combustion motor, is one of the simplest machines, and also one, which by long process of development upon tramways, has been perfected to the highest degree of reliability.

6. A Railless Traction line furnishes facilities which are not possessed by a tramway for the handling of a goods business over the same lines as a passenger business. On this latter, whatever goods transportation is attempted, occupies for the time being the track to the exclusion or the hindrance of the passenger car. On the Railless Traction line, there being no track, the goods car or train can draw up against the kerb, lower its contact arm, load and unload, and renew its journey in between and without incommoding a frequent passenger service. In Germany there are several of these mixed lines which are operated without any difficulty, doing a business in bulk goods by a train of cars hauled by an electric locomotive, and at the same time performing a regular passenger service with which is sometimes combined the carriage of parcels and postal matter. A description of such a line will be found on page 11.

7. In the case of crossings of railways on the level, which to tramways is often either barred or else only obtainable with much difficulty and expense, the Railless electric car, needing no interference to be made with the Railway Permanent Way, is in the same position as any other ordinary vehicle, and the Railway has no ground of objection, provided that the overhead wires are so constructed as to clear the trains and not to interfere with the telegraph and telephone wires and signals.

**Comparative Estimates**

For the purpose of illustrating the commercial advantages of Railless Electric Traction we will first take two typical cases of unremunerative British Tramways and examine their present statistics as compared with what they might reasonably be estimated to have been if the installation had been one of Railless Electric Traction. We will then give the estimates made by the Committee of the Town Council of Mulhausen upon the ground of which they decided to instal the Railless Electric line which is now in course of construction.

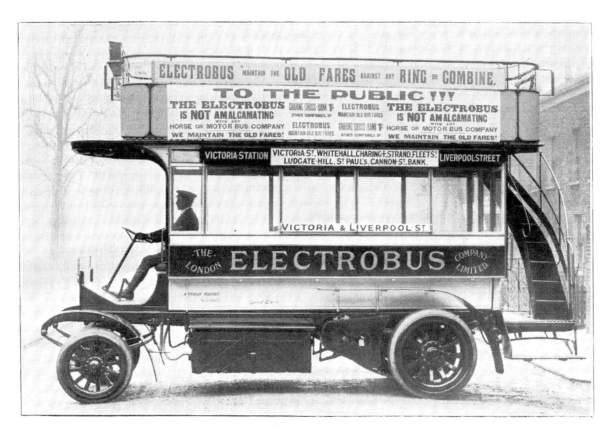

Electric omnibus with accumulators now in service on London streets.

Brewer's Dray with accumulators.

**Comparison with Wigan Tramway**

The tramway system at Wigan has the greatest route length compared with the size of the population served, of any in the United Kingdom. It is also the most unsuccessful from a commercial standpoint. It makes no provision for depreciation, and yet declares a deficit for the year of £16,392. If to this were added a depreciation fund at the rate of £400 per mile of single track, the deficit would be increased to £26,342. The average speed attained and the volume of business handled are well within the capacity of the Railless electric omnibus. In this case, adopting figures of cost and working expenses for a first class Railless Electric Line with double-decked cars and rubber tyres on all wheels, the deficit could have been replaced by a handsome surplus.

| | Tramway. Present Statistics. | Estimate for corresponding Railless Electric Traction Line. |
|---|---|---|
| Population served | 61,000 | 61,000 |
| Length of Route | 25 miles | 25 miles |
| Capital Expenditure | £515,212 | £150,000 |
| Do. per mile of route | £20,712 | £6,000 |
| No. of Cars in Stock | 67 | 67 |
| No. of Cars in use daily | 48 | 48 |
| Average speed | 8 m.p.h. | 8 m.p.h, |
| Income per car-mile | 10.09d, | 10.09d. |
| Working Expenses and Capital Charges (per car-mile) | 13.04d. | 8.45d. |
| Deficit | £16,392 | Surplus £10,000 |

**Comparison with Stalybridge Tramway**

This tramway comes next to Wigan in the annual burden on the ratepayers, which amounts to £8,199. There is in this case also no provision for depreciation, and if such were added at the rate of £400 per mile of single track, it would increase the deficit to £19,279. There is less apparent chance of ultimate rentability in the case of this tramway than that of Wigan under the present condition of traffic which only amounts to about 6½d. per car-mile. If Railless Electric Traction had been adopted, it would have been necessary to follow the plan adopted in Germany for similarly light traffic and to use single decked cars and dispense with the conductor by an automatic fare-box. Rubber tyres would also be only on the driving wheels. The very moderate average speed of 6.75 miles per hour would quite admit of this method, provided the roads were good. In this manner the working expenses and fixed charges together could be kept within the receipts and possibly some small profit might be earned. In absence, however, of experience in England, it would not be safe to assume as low working expenses as those of Germany.

|                                         | Tramway. Present Statistics. | Estimate for corresponding Railless Traction Line. |
|-----------------------------------------|:---:|:---:|
| Population served                       | 92,800 | 92,800 |
| Length of Route                         | 23.5 miles | 23.5 miles |
| Capital Expenditure                     | £258,177 | £100,000 |
| Do. per mile of route                   | £11,000 | £4,250 |
| No. of cars in Stock                    | 55 | 55 |
| No. of cars in use daily                | 41 | 41 |
| Average speed                           | 6.75 m.p.h. | 6.75 m.p.h. |
| Income per car-mile                     | 6.548d. | 6.548d. |
| Working Expenses and Capital Charges (per car-mile) | 9.44d. | 6.50d. |
| Deficit                                 | £8,199 | Surplus £330 |

This undertaking has been of late improved by the addition of Electric Lighting and Power Supply, which could of course be equally well added to a Railless Electric Traction System. The same careful economies could turn the present bad business into a good one, and in any case, there would have been a small total debt and no deficit.

**Remunerative Tramways**

Situations where tramways are remunerative might be analysed by similar comparison with an alternative Railless Traction System and when regarded purely from a commercial aspect the results would invariably be more profitable for the latter. It could be shown for instance that at Glasgow, the volume of business done in this, the greatest of our tramways, is no greater than is handled by the various kinds of omnibus in the streets of London, neither is the average speed greater than can be obtained by the electric omnibus. As a commercial undertaking the result in the case of Glasgow would be with Railless Traction to more than double the present surplus with about one-third of the Capital Expenditure. To go into such an analysis would, however, serve no useful purpose. The electric tramway is at present generally considered to be a superior means of transportation to any kind of omnibus, and wherever a tramway can be made remunerative, the ratepayer will prefer to have it, even though the rate of remuneration may be less than in the case of the electric omnibus. It is probable, however, that in the many cases of unremunerative tramways where the general public travels permanently at the part expense of the ratepayer, the community would have been better off with an economical and remunerative means of transportation. The ratepayer pays too much for the little difference he gets in class of transportation.

**Mulhausen**

The following estimates, made by the Corporation of Mulhausen, who are now engaged in constructing a Railless Traction Line, were the result of the studies of a specially appointed Commission which reported upon alternative projects for furnishing additional travelling facilities in this town. Mulhausen is a city of 100,000 inhabitants in Alsace-Germany. There is already a tramway system, but it was proposed to add to this a length of 6¾ miles of line connecting districts where the traffic would be extremely light. The committee were to report on the following alternatives:—

(1) A very cheap tramway according to the design of the Corporation engineer.

(2) A service of motor omnibuses operated by benzine engines, as per tenders of various manufacturing firms.

(3) A Railless Electric Traction Line.

The project involved a yearly service of 550,000 car-miles. The estimates of working expenses included a capital charge of 4% besides allowance for depreciation. The Committee reported as follows:—

|  | Cost of Construction. | Cost per Mile of Route. | Working Expenses per Car-mile |
|---|---|---|---|
| Tramway | £62,530 | £9,250 | 7.30d. |
| Benzine Omnibuses | £23,581 | £3,500 | 9.45d. |
| Railless Electric Traction | £25,050 | £3,710 | 5.13d. |

At the estimated income per car-mile, Railless Electric Traction alone showed prospects of commercial success and was therefore adopted.

Although the costs of construction and of operation in Germany are lower than they are in England, the experience gained proves a great comparative economy in this method over all other existing methods, and it may be safely claimed that in every situation where a tramway would pay, a Railless Electric line would pay better, and that in many situations where the tramway would not pay at all, the Railless Electric line can earn a profit.

**Rural District Lines**

Railless Electric Traction furnishes also an extremely economical method of goods transportation for rural districts. In contrast with the petrol or benzine motor which has some twelve hundred parts, and which requires a skilled driver, the electric road vehicle is one of the most simple machines, which can be driven by any intelligent villager after a few days practice.

**Monheim-Langenfeld Line**

As an illustration, the installation owned by the Rural Council of Monheim near Cologne, will serve to show the wide field which exists for similar methods. This line, 2½ miles long, connects the above village with the railway station of Langenfeld, the populations of the two villages being 500 and 2,000 respectively. The business done is first and foremost a regular passenger service by electric trolley road cars, having at special times trailers attached for workmen only. Secondly, the carriage of bulk goods, mostly farm produce, building material and manure, carried in trains of wagons, hauled by a "double-ender" electric locomotive. Thirdly, parcels and postal matter, carried on the passenger cars in space

Monheim-Langenfeld Line. Passenger car crossing goods train on same line.
The feeders for lighting and traction are shown on separate brackets on the posts.

French Bluejackets on "Electrobuses" opposite Buckingham Palace.

specially provided and under control of the Postal Authorities.  Fourthly, the supply of electric light to the cottages, the current for which is taken from the traction feeders.

The workmen are carried at an almost nominal tariff by monthly season tickets and the light is furnished at the cost of petroleum.

The traffic conditions at Monheim would have entirely precluded either a tramway or a light railway, but this line pays its way because it contains in its little measure the essential qualifications of success, namely the handling of several classes of business under one administration.

The simplest way of illustrating the commercial results is the money value of the business done per annum per head of population as compared with that of British Tramways.  This is as follows:—The population served is assumed to be the aggregate of the two villages, which is a severe assumption, because the population of the larger village use the line very little.  The receipts, thus computed are however as follows:—

| From Passenger Traffic | .... | .... | 3.56 shillings. |
| Workmens Season Tickets | .... | .... | 1.40 ,, |
| Bulk Goods | .... | .... | .... | 1.76 ,, |
| Postal Service | .... | .... | .... | 0.48 ,, |
| Total Revenue per ann. per head of population | | | 7.20 shillings. |

The Corporation-owned Tramways of Great Britain, deriving their income from passengers alone, show, as to at least one-third of them, a less revenue than the above.  There is one of them, serving a population twenty times that of the Monheim-Langenfeld district, in which the receipts are far less per head per annum.

The total cost of this little line, including all equipments, was £4,750 or at the rate of £1,900 per mile; the money was borrowed at $3\frac{3}{4}\%$ interest; $1\frac{1}{2}\%$ being set aside for amortisation.

To all those who are interested in the revival of agriculture in England and who have already learned many lessons from what has been accomplished on the Continent by agricultural co-operation, these figures must surely be of interest.  Transportation is one of the prime factors of co-operation.

At Monheim the distance of only $2\frac{1}{2}$ miles is one which is by no means beyond the competition of horsed vehicles, but electric transportation has superseded them.

At Wurzen, in Saxony, a line of the same length carrying mill produce, has also displaced horse traction.

**Small Holding Colonies**

There are, however, in England, colonies of Small Holdings established under the Act of 1892 in which the settlers transport their produce, each with his own horse and cart, for a distance of twelve miles to the market.  Where necessary, the electric train can be made up

Piano Van with Accumulators.

Railless Electric Omnibus with Overhead Wires.

Type proposed for English Traffic, with top seats, accomodating 34 people in all.

of carts which have been horsed across fields to the highway. The shafts are made removable and a special coupling is added.

**Present State of Progress of Electric Highway Traction**

The present state of progress in electric traction upon streets and highways is as follows:—

As regards traction by means of storage batteries this is as yet confined to urban transportation, but in this department much progress has been made. The "Electrobus" in London has already been alluded to, It runs between Liverpool Street and Victoria and performs 40 miles without changing batteries, and ascends Ludgate Hill without any difficulty. The control is admirable. The current consumption is no more than that of the average tramcar and the batteries are maintained on a mileage contract by Accumulator Companies. Recently a service has been started between Brighton and Hove, and the first car ran down from London to Brighton to assume its duties, without changing batteries.

In America the electric commercial vehicle with accumulators has found much favour. Hundreds of these cars for all kinds of duties are in use in New York and other great American cities. Especially for such loads as require careful transport, the electric battery car is most valuable; as for instance, pianofortes, crockery, milk, ambulance work, etc. Within its present limit of distance, which however is being rapidly extended, the electric battery car is superior in every respect to other mechanically propelled road vehicles.

**Continental Lines**

The electric trolley road car has been introduced with success on the Continent in the following places, the steady advance of the system being seen by a glance at the dates.

**Grevenbruck-Westphalia.** Short mineral line opened in 1903.
**Monheim-Langenfeld,** near Cologne. Mixed line opened in 1904.
**Veischedethal-Westphalia.** Goods line opened in 1904.
**Wurzen-Saxony.** Goods line opened in 1905.
**Grossbauchlitz-Saxony.** Mill produce opened in 1905.
**Lyons-Charbonnieres,** France. Passenger line opened in 1905.
**Neuenahr-Ahrweiler,** Germany. Passenger line opened in 1906.
**Mulhausen, Alsace,** Germany. Passenger line in partial operation
since end of 1907. To be opened in July, 1908.

**The Success of the Schiemann System**

There have been numerous attempts to attain the same objects in other ways but beyond experimental lines at Exhibitions they have not been carried any further. The Schiemann System is the only one which is in successful operation and although there is no complication in it, it has been evolved by much careful study, and lessons learned by practical experience. The modification and application of this system to the requirements of this country have also been made a special study by Sir Douglas Fox and Partners.

**General Appearance of Cars**

The general appearance of the passenger car may be, with the exception of the trolley arm, similar to that of the " Electrobus " and its smoothness of motion is the same. On the Continent, however, double-deck cars are not in vogue, but when required, a trailler is added. The double-deck car, as proposed by the Company's Engineers for this country is quite feasible. At Mulhausen the car ascends a gradient of 1 in 12 with ease and can attain a speed of 12 miles per hour on the level. The trolley-arm is constructed for a lateral deviation of 10 feet on either side of the wires, so that in a country road of 20 feet width between kerbs, it has, with the wires in the centre of the road full command of the entire width. In city streets of greater width, there are two separate pairs of trolley wires, each commanding half the width, for the "up" and "down" lines, so that altogether a width of 40 feet between kerbs is fully commanded. Even where the streets are still wider, the wires, if judiciously placed in the axis of the "up" and "down" traffic, allow the car under all ordinary circumstances sufficient deviation to cross or overhaul any other vehicle.

**Goods Trains**

The goods transportation by Railless electric locomotives has in Germany been found entirely feasible for doing a large business. The cars are arranged of a weight and with wheels of such width as to cause less injury to the road surface than the ordinary vehicles. They are also provided with a patented device for causing them to follow automatically any curve which is taken by the locomotive.

The actual cost of goods transportation per ton-mile by Railless Electric Traction is, when fairly compared, less than that by tramway. Although the current consumption is greater the capital charges reduced to ton-mile are much less. This cost per ton mile varies so greatly according to the volume of business done, that it can only be specially estimated in each particular case.

**Form of Queries**

The Railless Electric Traction Co. will have pleasure in furnishing any parties interested in this matter with a form containing queries as to the characteristics of any project, such as length of route, gradients, sharpest curves, class of pavement, density of traffic, etc., and will on receipt of the required information, give their advice as to the best way of dealing with the situation. If the occasion demands it, the Company will send their representative to examine the project on the spot. The Company is in relation with leading manufacturers and financiers interested in this class of industry, and is therefore in a position to form a rapid and sound conclusion as to the probabilities, not only of the commercial success of an enterprise, but also of its finding the support of capital.

**Tenders**

The Railless Electric Traction Co. will also when dealing with Corporations or existing Transportation Companies, submit tenders for works of this kind and enter into contracts for their complete execution.

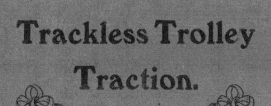

# Trackless Trolley Traction.

# THE CEDES-STOLL SYSTEM.

# Trackless Trolley Traction.

## THE CEDES-STOLL SYSTEM.

Cedes-Stoll Car Running Through Snow.

# TRACKLESS TROLLEY, LTD.,

Telephone : 8719 GERRARD.

Telegrams : " CEDESMIXTE, LONDON."

### 15-16, Cockspur Street, LONDON, S.W.

# Trackless Trolley Traction.

## THE CEDES-STOLL SYSTEM.

In our system current is taken from the overhead positive wire, and returned to the negative wire by means of flexible cables, and not by a pole or boom. Instead of an under-running wheel, or over-running shoe, the head—or actual current collector—is composed of a frame having two small grooved wheels on each side of it. One of these pair of wheels runs on the positive and the other on the negative wire, and the cable is suspended from the centre of the frame, from which point, also, is suspended a weighted pendulum, which keeps the wheels well pressed down on the wires. The wheels (or pulleys) run on ball bearings. The trolley runs quite sparklessly. The pull of the cable acting upon a very short lever arm, and the centre of gravity of the trolley being very low, no deviation of the trolley is possible, even in the case of strong transversal pulls. The conducting cable can be lengthened so as to follow the car by means of two appliances—an upper sliding knot tied to the pendulum weight and stretched by means of a spring in the latter, and a cable roller (on the left) with 10 to 12 yards of cable, which can be rolled up or let out by means of a spiral spring. Thus the car is allowed to run on the whole width of the road, to overtake other carriages, or to turn anywhere, that is to say, it accommodates itself to all kinds of traffic.

CABLE DRUM FOR SIDE-RUNNING TEN METRES.

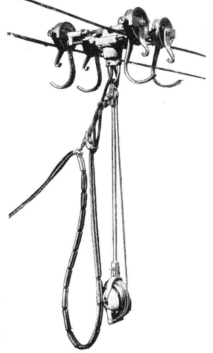

"STOLL" CURRENT COLLECTOR.

When two cars running in opposite directions meet, the drivers interchange the trolley conduits by means of detachable contact boxes. This represents an important advantage over a tram line with one track only, where the loss of time caused by waiting at passing places is sometimes considerable. The cable roller, the vertical rod-holder and the sliding rod are to be seen in one of the illustrations. The vehicle having this very flexible means of taking the current can move as much as 20 yards away from the wire, and thus has powers of adaptability in that respect which would be rarely exercised to the full extent.

The chassis of the vehicles for the transport of passengers or goods is made of pressed steel, and is supported in the axles by springs. The steering is irreversible, and the brakes act on the back wheels. The electrical part comprises a controller of the tramway pattern, resistances and two motors of 20-h.p. each, which really form an integral part of the driving wheels themselves. There are no other mechanical parts of control or transmission; it is, therefore, very simple. Hardly any lubrication is required, all the parts of the wheels and motors running on ball bearings. Further, the elasticity of the vehicle itself is considerable, as the springs only support the chassis, the body, and the passengers, but no engine,

CHASSIS, WEIGHT ABOUT 1,700 KG.

batteries or transmission gear, there being none of these mechanical complications. The suspension therefore is perfect, and notwithstanding the imperfections of the road, gives the impression of moving on rails. Vehicles carrying 3,000 kilos and over have the back wheels furnished with iron tyres.

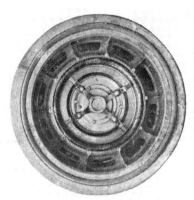

MOTOR—SIDE VIEW.

We give an illustration of the motor. The cable transmitting the current passes through the interior of the axle. The field magnets of the motor are fixed, by means of keys, on the axle itself, and so act as the nave of the wheel. The rest of the wheel is mounted as an ordinary motor on ball bearings, and is completely protected from dust. The cover serves to hermetically close the motor as well as to fix it on the axle.

Solid rubber tyres are fitted to absorb the inequalities of the road. With this device (in this vehicle where there are only two driving wheels) the braking can be done on all four wheels, two by means of an electric brake, and two by means of a mechanical brake with pedal or hand control.

It is easy to understand the smoothness in starting resulting from this arrangement, and the little wear and tear which is thereby caused not only to the motor, etc., which is an essential point, but also to the tyres. In most cases the rear wheels are driven, because that arrangement affords a more suitable distribution of the weight. As there is no transmission by chains, pinions, etc., there is consequently no mechanical loss of power at all, and the motor efficiency is over 80% in working. The design is extremely simple, and strong enough to support any shocks. The motor can be over-

EXCHANGING CURRENT COLLECTORS.

loaded for a certain time to double its output, without becoming dangerously hot. The motors of the Gmund chassis, for instance, have been running for two - years - and - nine - months without any repairs, doing 60 miles every day, whilst the cars are usually overloaded.

Our system is operating in eight towns, the running cost per car mile being only 4½d., whilst the price paid for current is 2d. per unit or over.

Bradford, Liverpool, Leeds, Sheffield, Manchester and Dundee have seen and reported most favourably on the system, the Leeds' and Bradford Corporations have obtained the sanction of Parliament to adopt it.

CARS RUNNING IN VIENNA.

CARS TURNING AT TERMINUS.

| Number of Line. | NAME OF OVERHEAD LINE, ALSO PROPRIETORS AND OPERATORS | Commencement of Operations | Capital Invested | | | Length of Line | Highest Gradient | Number of available Cars. | Accommodation | Distance covered in Car—miles | | Number estimated per year | |
|---|---|---|---|---|---|---|---|---|---|---|---|---|---|
| | | | | | | | | | | Average one Car daily | Total distance to date | | |
| | | Date | £ | s. | d. | Miles | Per Cent. | No. | Seats | Car—miles | Car—miles | Passengers | Pas |
| 1 | Gmund (N. Austria) Gmund Station—City Gmund Town Council | July 1907 | 3,125 | 0 | 0 | 2 | 4 | 2 (1 Car ordered afterwards) | 18 (With postal depart.) | 62·5 | 35,625 | 24,000 | 9( (In f only ava |
| 2 | Weidling n/r Vienna Kloskrneuburg Station, Weidling—Weidling Weidling Town Council | May 1908 | 7,083 | 6 | 8 | 2¼ | 7 | 5 (Opened with 3 Cars, 2 Cars ordered afterwards) | 22 | 75 to 119 | 81,370 | 120,000 | 23( |
| 3 | Potzleinsdorf—Salmansdorf Vienna Tramways City Tramways of Vienna | October 1908 | 7,083 | 6 | 8 | 1¼ | 9 | 4 | 24 | Summer 100 Winter 62·5 | 38,500 | — | |
| 4 | Kalksburg n/r Vienna Kalksburg—Liesing (Station) Kalksburg Town Council | July 1909 | 6,666 | 13 | 4 | 2⅜ | 1·3 | 4 (The 4th Car ordered afterwards and put into service on 10th Oct.) | 22 | 69 to 138 | 18,869 | 120,000 | In 3 6: |
| 5 | Pressburg (Hungary) Weidritztalbahn, Pressburg —Eisenbrunnl Own Company | July 1909 | 12,916 | 13 | 4 | 3⅝ | 8 | 7 (4 open, 2 closed and 1 lorry) | 24 | In Summer Sunday 10 minute service. Weekdays 15 minute service. In Winter ½ hour. | 22,051 | — | |
| 6 | Budweis (Bohemia) Artillery Barracks—Friedhof International Electricity Co. Budweis Depot | October 1909 | 1,583 | 6 | 8 | 1 | 6 | 1 | 24 | — | — | This Fried on holida carried on on 1st Nov |

### IN COURSE

| Number of Line. | NAME OF OVERHEAD LINE, ALSO PROPRIETORS AND OPERATORS | Commencement of Operations | Capital Invested | | | Length of Line | Highest Gradient | Number of available Cars. | Accommodation | | | | |
|---|---|---|---|---|---|---|---|---|---|---|---|---|---|
| 7 | Judenburg (Styria) Station—Town Robert Brand, Judenberg | November 1909 | 2,291 | 13 | 4 | 1¼ | 16 | 1 (4 Cars) | 18 (With Postal Depart) | — | — | — | |
| 8 | City Tramways of Vienna City Tramways of Vienna | December 1909 | 1,395 | 16 | 8 | 2½ | — | Motor-train i.e. | | | | | |

SUMMARY :—Electric Overhead Automobile Lines in Austria-Hungary :

| | | | | | |
|---|---|---|---|---|---|
| Capital invested | ... | ... | ... | £42,145 | 16s. 8d. |
| Car—miles covered | ... | ... | ... | ... | 196,415 |
| Number of Cars in Service | ... | ... | ... | ... | 24 |
| Total number of Passengers carried | ... | ... | ... | ... | 765,956 |

| arried | | This makes per Car-mile | Receipts. | | | Mail Service | | Staff | Fares | Fare taken per mile | Cost of Current per kilowatt—hour | Nett working costs per Car-mile | Description of Overhead Lines and Rolling Stock as per Capital invested. This was laid out for |
|---|---|---|---|---|---|---|---|---|---|---|---|---|---|
| reatest umber ried in e day ighest ings for e day | Total number carried to 10thOctober 1909 | | Total to date | | This makes per Car-mile | Indemnity per year | | | | | | | |
| sengers s. d. | Passengers | | £ s. d. | | Pence | £ s. d. | | Persons | Pence | Pence | Pence | Pence | |
| ,200 | 160,391 (In 2nd year service suspended for 2 months owing to laying of railway line) | 4½ | 950 0 0 | | 6·4 | 83 6 8 | | 2 Drivers | 2d. for Strangers 1d. & ½d. for Children & Workmen (Municipal undertaking of the town) | 1d. ½d. | 3d. | 4·8 | 2 Cars, Front Wheel drive, 2 miles Overhead Line on Wood Masts, 328 yards on Steel Masts, Garage, 656 yards Feeding Cable. *In 1st year to old Station line only 1⅜ miles long. |
| 5 0 2,800 | 338,976 | 4 | 2,757 8 10 | | 8·13 | 91 13 4 | | 1 Foreman 2 Drivers etc. | Whole Distance 3d. Intermediate 2d. 1d. | about 1d. | 2½d. Continuous Current 500 Volts | 4·48 | 5 Cars, 2¼ miles Overhead Line, with Wood and Iron Masts, Workshops, Spare Parts, Garage with Foreman's Rooms, Liveries, etc. complete. |
| ,950 | 151,000 | 4 | 1,203 15 0 | | 7·5 | No. | | 1 Mechanic 6 Drivers | 2d. Children 1d. | about 1d. | 1½d. Continuous Current 550 Volts | 4·8 | 4 Cars, Spare Parts £3,666 13s. 4d. 4 Wire-Overhead Line, Steel Masts best finish £2,166 13s. 4d. Garage, Fittings, etc. £1,250 Power Supply, Rails and Tramway Cables. |
| 0 0 2,450 | 60,289 | 3¼ | 511 17 6 (exactly three months) | | 6·52 | 25 0 0 (Only Letters) | | 1 Foreman 1 Mechanic (Converter Station) 5 Drivers and Conductors | Whole distance 3d. Intermediate distances 2d. 1½d. & 1d. | about 1d. | 2d. Continuous Current 550 Volts | 4·16 | 4 Cars, 2⅜ miles, 2 Wire Lines on Wood, Iron Masts, Garage with Workshop and Foreman's dwelling, 2 Converter Sets, 5,000 Volts of 220 Volts alternating current and 550 Volt continuous current, each 30 kilowatt capacity, Converter, Tools, Spare Parts, etc. complete. |
| 0 0 3,050 | 55,000 | 2½ | 928 3 2 | | 10·10 | No. | | 1 Manager 1 Clerk 1 Foreman 1 Inspector 10 Drivers, Mechanics and Washers, etc | Whole distance 5d. Intermediate distances 3d. 2d. | about 1¼d. | 1½d. Continuous Current 450 Volts | 5·28 | 7 Cars, 3⅝ miles Overhead-Wire Wood and Iron Masts, Garage and Office, Workshops, Staff Dwellings, large Buffer Battery 400 Ampere—hours complete with points, etc. |
| the most traffic car in service ober, 1,400 and 0 passengers. | — | | 1 Car, daily receipts to 31st October, approx. 9 10 0 1st November approx. 13 0 0 | | | No. | | 2 Drivers | 1½d. | approx. 1½d. | 2d. Continuous Current 530 Volts | — | Power Supply : Rails (— pole) and Tramway Cables (+ pole) |

## ERECTION.

| | | | | | | | | | | | | | |
|---|---|---|---|---|---|---|---|---|---|---|---|---|---|
| — | — | — | — | | — | 166 13 4 | | — | 2½d. | 2d. | 1½d. Continuous Current 550 Volts | — | Advantages of Four Wheel drive :— Ascents: All four wheels driven Descents : All four wheels with electric brakes. Steering not blocked. |

rhead Motor Cars with electric motors, in all four wheels, with trailer for
ersons (total 42 persons) for all lines with a gradient of 10 per cent.

Total amount of Fares ...        ...        ...        £6,351 4s. 6d.
Length of double-pole overhead-line erected, total 18¾ miles, of
  which 4¾ miles as 4 Wire-Line.

# Railless Electric Traction

## "THE TROLLEY BUS."

### THE "R.E.T." SYSTEM

# RAILLESS ELECTRIC TRACTION.

The R.E.T. Construction Company's System

known as

## "R.E.T."

is of

## BRITISH INVENTION AND MANUFACTURE.

Adopted by the Corporations of Leeds, Bradford, Rotherham, Dundee, etc.,

Boksburg and Bloemfontein (South Africa), Shanghai, etc.

## THE R.E.T. CONSTRUCTION COMPANY, Ltd.,

FINSBURY PAVEMENT HOUSE,

LONDON, E.C.

WORKS  -  -  -  -  -  HUNSLET, LEEDS.

TELEGRAPHIC ADDRESS: "RAILLESSLY, LONDON."　　TELEPHONE: No. 1384 LONDON WALL.
　　,,　　　　,,　　"RAILLESSLY, LEEDS."　　　　No. 4832 CENTRAL LEEDS.

DOUBLE-DECKED "R.E.T." CAR.

# AGENCIES.

*Transvaal, Cape Colony and Rhodesia :*
HERBERT AINSWORTH,
THE CORNER HOUSE, JOHANNESBURG.

*Natal and Orange River Colony :*
THOMAS BARLOW & SONS,
SMITH STREET, DURBAN.

*South America :*
THE SOUTH AMERICAN RAILLESS TRACTION CO.,
LTD.,
BUENOS AIRES, and Branches.

*Holland and Belgium :*
N. V. L. COSSOUX, C.E.,
12, PLACE ARMAND STEURS, BRUSSELS,

*Japanese Empire :*
CORNES & CO., YOKOHAMA AND KOBE.

*Dutch East Indies :*
T. GRAHAM GRIBBLE, SOERABAJA.

*Canada :*
S. A. BATHURST,
c/o C. W. STANCLIFFE & CO., LTD.,
MERCANTILE BLOCK, HOMER STREET,
VANCOUVER.

*Australia :*
KNOX, SCHLAPP & CO.,
BROKEN HILL CHAMBERS, MELBOURNE.

*India :*
THE INDIAN RAILLESS TRACTION CO., LTD.,
GLADSTONE, WYLLIE & CO.
CALCUTTA,
AND
GORDON, WOODROFFE & CO.,
MADRAS, PONDICHERRY, ETC.

*Denmark :*
A. GOUDSMIT, JR., COPENHAGEN.

*Roumania :*
A. THEODORIDI & F. P. ARCHBOLD, BRAILA.

*Portugal :*
FRANK DE M. TURNER, 11, RUA DAS TAYPAS, OPORTO.

FIGURE 6.—"R.E.T." CAR AT DUNDEE.

FIGURE 7.—RAMSBOTTOM "R.E.T." CAR, SHOWING SIMPLE FORM OF CONSTRUCTION OF TURNING LOOP OR "BALLOON END."

The railless car can be drawn up to the curb to take up or set down passengers, thus obviating the risks and inconvenience of boarding tramcars in the middle of the road. (See Figure 4).

Passenger and goods vehicles can be operated simultaneously on the same railless traction line; the goods car, or train merely lowers its contact arms when overtaken by a passenger car, and allows it to pass.

An accident to one railless car does not disorganize or delay the rest of the service.

RAPIDITY OF CONSTRUCTION.—Railless traction can be installed much more rapidly than tramways, the capital becomes remunerative at a much earlier date, and the delay and inconvenience

FIGURE 8.—" R.E.T." OVERHEAD CONSTRUCTION (BRACKET ARM TYPE).

caused by the laying and renewal of rails is entirely avoided.

COST OF OPERATION.

(1)—WORKING EXPENSES.

Close estimates of working expenses can be given only after an inspection of proposed routes has been made and a knowledge of local conditions has been acquired, but, in most districts, the working expenses of "R.E.T." cars, having

FIGURE 9.—" R.E T." STANDARD INSULATED JUNCTION.

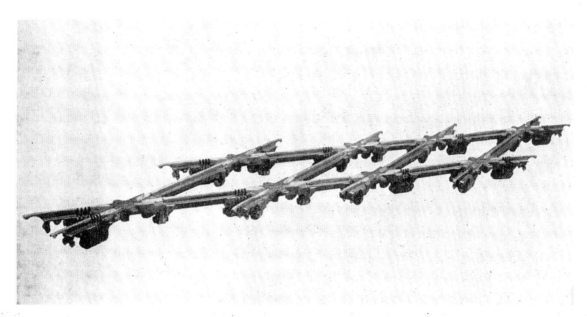

FIGURE 10.—" R.E.T." INSULATED CROSSING, MADE FOR ANY NUMBER OF WIRES (FOR RAILLESS TRACTION
LINE CROSSING ANOTHER RAILLESS TRACTION LINE).

FIGURE 10a.—" R.E.T." INSULATED CROSSING, MADE FOR ANY NUMBER OF WIRES (FOR RAILLESS TRACTION
CROSSING A TRAMWAY).

seating accommodation for 28 to 40 persons, should be from 4d. to 6d. per car mile. At Dundee the working expenses are given at 4·6d., at Leeds at 5·55d., and at Rotherham at 5·899d. per car mile.

### (2)—FIXED CHARGES.

Fixed charges may be taken as interest on capital and amortisation of loans, and are, therefore, proportional to the capital expenditure. As railless traction requires less than one-fifth of the capital needed for a tramway of the same length, the fixed charges, expressed as a charge per car-mile, will also be less than one-fifth of the fixed charges of a tramway designed for the same annual mileage over the same route.

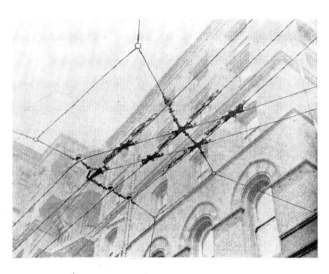

FIGURE 11.—COMBINED CROSSING AND JUNCTION.

### COMPARISON WITH OTHER MECHANICALLY OPERATED VEHICLES.

Mechanically operated vehicles may be divided into three classes, according to whether the motive power is derived from (1) Internal Combustion Engines, (2) Steam Engines, or (3) Accumulators.

(1) INTERNAL COMBUSTION ENGINES.—The internal combustion engine is essentially suitable only for working at constant load and uniform speed. It has very small overload capacity and practically no starting torque. Its adaptation to the intermittent service of passenger transportation has only been effected by the intermediary of a friction-clutch and gears of variable ratio, devices which impair its efficiency and entail excessive expenditure on repairs and renewals. The operating expenses of motor omnibuses, driven by internal combustion engines, are so high and depreciation

FIGURE 12.—JUNCTION IN TROLLEY WIRES WITH SECTION INSULATORS FITTED.

so rapid, that only in such favourable circumstances as exist in London, with its dense population and asphalted and comparatively level streets, can an equivalent revenue be hoped for.

The conditions under which motor omnibuses operate in London being unique, the returns cannot properly be used as a basis on which to estimate results in less favourable circumstances.

" R.E.T." cars, with their electric motors, ideal for intermittent traffic, depreciate only slowly, while any loss of efficiency is easily restored and the

FIGURE 13. - " R.E.T." CAR SENT TO SOUTH AMERICA.

operating expenses remain practically constant. The greater length of life of the railless car is indicated by the fact that Corporation Loans are fixed by Parliament for repayment in 10 years for railless cars and only 5 years for motor omnibuses.

Attempts have been made to improve the operation of petrol-omnibuses by adopting a petrol-electric system, but this only adds complexity while still retaining the drawbacks of the petrol engine. It is obviously more economical to generate power by large units at a central station (which in most cases cheapens its production by supplying light and power to factories, etc.) than for each vehicle to generate its own power.

(2) STEAM ENGINES.—Steam Engines are superior to internal combustion

engines for intermittent service, on account of their large overload capacity and starting torque. But in neither respect are they equal to electric motors and the difficulty of devising a satisfactory boiler prevents this type of vehicle from becoming more generally used.

(3) ACCUMULATORS.—Self-propelled vehicles using electric motors and accumulators have been adopted for certain classes of traffic, but the dead

FIGURE 14.—PACKING CASE CONTAINING "R.E.T." CAR LEAVING
THE COMPANY'S LEEDS WORKS FOR SOUTH AMERICA.

weight carried, the heavy cost of maintenance and the loss of power in the accumulators make the cost of operation much greater than that of railless traction.

**The above considerations indicate that under all ordinary conditions railless traction is more economical than tramways or any vehicles with self-contained motive power.**

# THE "R.E.T." SYSTEM.

The "R.E.T." system was designed with a view to its application in the most economical and convenient manner to the safe and rapid transport of both passengers and goods at home and abroad and to give effect to the following general considerations.

As railless traction lines are frequently used as extensions of electric tramways, the overhead line must be so constructed that the railless vehicles can cross tramway and railless routes as easily as tramcars do in similar circumstances and railless cars must also be able to operate over tramway routes if and when necessary, so that the cars can be run from outlying districts to the centre of the town and to the tramway car shed.

The overhead line must, therefore, be practically the same in the

FIGURE 15.—DOUBLE-DECKED DEMONSTRATION "R.E.T." CAR AT BRIGHTON.

tramway and railless systems, and the trolleys of the railless cars must travel on the underside of the wires.

The trolley poles of the railless car must permit it to travel on any portion of the roadway and manœuvre in and out of the traffic without diminution of speed and without risk of the trolley wheels leaving the wires. This condition cannot be satisfied by a simple combination of the trolley wheel, pole and base usually adopted on electric tramways, but only by means of the "R.E.T." patented devices.

☞ "R.E.T." IS THE ONLY SYSTEM using overhead equipment of Standard Tramway Type.

☞ "R.E.T." IS THE ONLY SYSTEM using Standard Tramway Trolley Heads.

☞ THE "R.E.T." IS THE ONLY SYSTEM in which the cars

FIGURE 16.—DOUBLE-DECKED "R.E.T." CAR.

can travel at full speed on any part of the roadway without side-pressure on the trolley wires.

☞ "R.E.T." is the only system which ensures complete freedom for crossings, junctions, and for inter-running with tramcars.

☞ "R.E.T." enables passengers and merchandise to be carried

**over tramway routes without altering the tramway wires, and obviates the necessity of passengers changing cars (See Figure 5).**

" R.E.T." enables branch lines to be constructed from main routes into factories, warehouses, docks, canal wharves, railway stations, etc., at small cost. " R.E.T." goods lorries and light road locomotives with trailer wagons can deal with large quantities of goods, agricultural produce, etc.

" R.E.T." cars are turned at the terminus of a line by means of a loop (see Figure 7) or in the straight line at any part of a road 24 feet wide.

FIGURE 17.—" R.E.T." CAR AT RAMSBOTTOM.

## " R.E.T." OVERHEAD LINE.

" R.E.T." overhead line construction, Figures 8, 9, 10 and 10*a*, is of the simplest character, Figures 11 and 12, show the most complex arrangement of fittings which could possibly be required at a crossing or junction.

Where, from considerations of expense or otherwise, cars are operated in opposite directions on a route equipped with a *single* pair of overhead wires only, one car lowers its trolley arms and allows the other to pass. The trolley arms can be lowered and replaced in about 10 seconds.

The overhead line for " R.E.T." costs only from £600 to £1,200 per mile according to local conditions, type of poles, wires and fittings employed.

## TYPES OF " R.E.T." CARS.

Double-decked " R.E.T." cars are constructed with seating capacity for 34 to 40 passengers (see Figures 15, 16 and Frontispiece), and have passed successfully through very severe tests.

Single-decked " R.E.T." cars with front or rear entry are constructed with seating capacity for 16 to 28 passengers (see Figures 17, 18, 19, 19a,

FIGURE 18.—" R.E.T." Car, Boksburg, South Africa (Front Entry Type).

20, 21 and 23), the deck to the rear platform being only 24 inches and the floor of the car being only 33 inches from the road.

A special " R.E.T." single-decked composite car to seat 24 to 32 passengers has been designed with a partition dividing the car into two sections for two classes, or to provide a smoking compartment. (See Figure 32.)

The Company has paid particular attention to vehicles for Colonial and foreign service, and has designed special single-decked cars, with seating capacity for 12 to 20 Europeans, with trailer with seating capacity for 20 to 35 Natives. These are made, where desired, on the "knock-down" plan for easy transport. (See Figures 24, 25 and 27.)

A single-decked car with seating accommodation for 28 and standing room for upwards of 20 passengers is shown in Figure 22.

FIGURE 19.—BOKSBURG FRONT ENTRY "R.E.T." CAR.

The use of trailers attached to "R.E.T." cars will cause neither danger nor inconvenience, and the sanctioning of trailers in the United Kingdom will solve the problem of dealing efficiently with rush traffic.

All the above types of cars are fitted with the Company's improved form of its patented controlled trolley, capable of the freest movements at any speed over roads at least 40 feet in width. The trolley has been much reduced in bulk and weight, while fully retaining its efficiency.

"R.E.T." cars are designed to suit all ordinary conditions of service, but special designs and quotations will be submitted to meet any specified requirements in the United Kingdom, the Colonies or foreign countries.

FIGURE 19*a*.—REAR END OF BOKSBURG FRONT ENTRY "R.E.T." CAR.

## "R.E.T." GOODS WAGONS, VANS, ETC.

The Company has made a special study of goods transport by railless traction, at home and abroad, and has designed some useful vehicles for carrying general merchandise, market and farm produce, frozen meat, etc., sewage, town refuse, coal, and other minerals, etc. Figure 26 shows a 5-ton covered wagon suitable for general merchandise, and Figure 28 a freight train with a combined capacity of 20 tons.

Road rollers and watering carts are shown in Figures 29 and 30.

The Company will be pleased to inspect and report upon routes on which it may be proposed to carry goods, etc., and to submit estimates of complete construction and equipment, working expenses, etc.

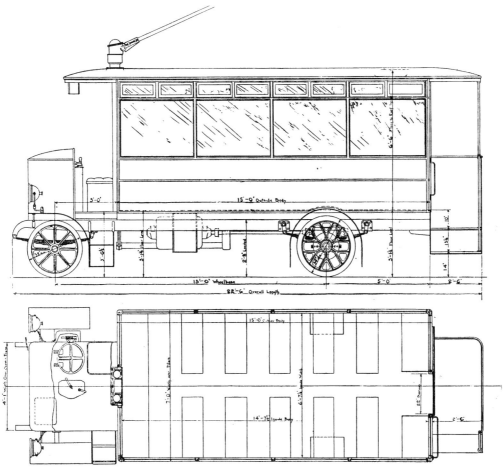

FIGURE 20.--Single-Decked "R.E.T." Car With Rear Entry.

## CONSTRUCTION, Etc., OF "R.E.T." CARS.

"R.E.T." motors are attached to the frame of the chassis and their weight is consequently entirely spring-suspended from the axle, and each of the rear wheels being independently driven by a separate motor, the necessity for differential gearing is obviated.

"R.E.T." vehicles can be fitted with either rubber or steel tyres, and with chain or chainless drive ; the materials and workmanship of the vehicles are of the highest class, and all the working parts are completely protected from dust and mud.

## RECENT IMPROVEMENTS.

The development of a special and highly efficient worm gear has enabled considerable improvements to be effected in the transmission gear, and the Company has produced some new types of Chainless Vehicles of high efficiency, reduced weight and silent working.

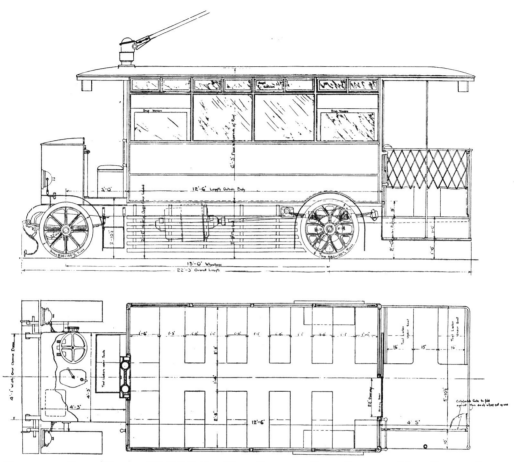

Figure 21.—Single-Decked "R.E.T." Car With Extended Rear Platform With Outside Seats.

**The many important improvements recently made in their design and construction will have the effect of still further reducing the working expenses while improving the appearance and adding to the comfort and life of the cars.**

## THE "R.E.T." PATENTED "RAIL RETURN."

Where railless lines are used as extensions of tramways it is sometimes desirable, from considerations of expense or otherwise, to house the railless cars in the tramcar shed: the "rail return," or skate, enables this to be accomplished by using the single tramway overhead

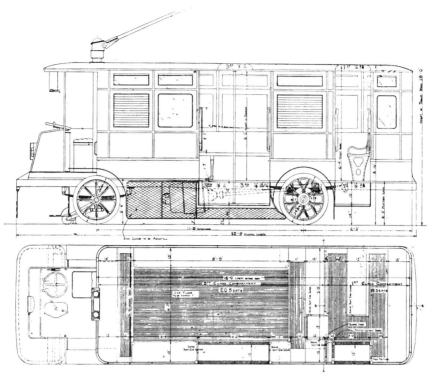

FIGURE 22.—COMPOSITE "R.E.T." CAR BUILT FOR SHANGHAI, DIVIDED INTO
TWO COMPARTMENTS.

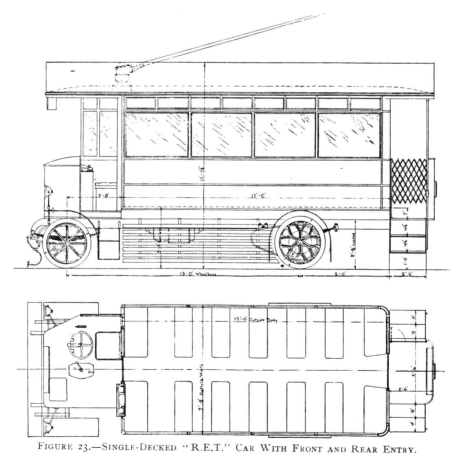

FIGURE 23.—SINGLE-DECKED "R.E.T." CAR WITH FRONT AND REAR ENTRY.

wire : one of the trolley arms of the railless car is lowered, the skate is dropped into the rail groove and the railless car can then be run in any direction over the tram lines.  (See Figure 31.)

## INSTALLATIONS.

The " R.E.T." lines in Leeds and Bradford were opened on June 20th, 1911, and have been visited by upwards of 100 deputations from British, Colonial and foreign Corporations and other authorities, all of whom have expressed themselves as very favourably impressed.

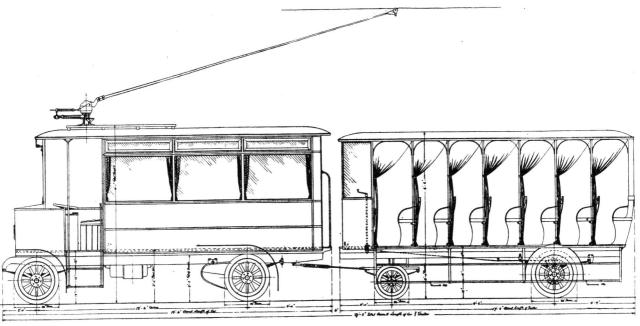

FIGURE 24.—CAR AND TRAILER FOR COLONIAL SERVICE.

" R.E.T." installations were opened for public service in Dundee in September and in Rotherham in October, 1912, and in Ramsbottom in August, 1913. These installations have successfully maintained full daily services since their inauguration. (Figures 6, 17 and 32.)

" R E.T." is being installed in Bloemfontein and Boksburg (South Africa), as well as in Shanghai, and in South America (Figures 13, 18, 22 and 34).

The Light Railway Commissioners carefully inspected the " R.E.T." system in operation at Leeds and Bradford and expressed their entire satisfaction with its working and predicted for it a wide development.

After carefully inspecting " R.E.T." in operation at Leeds and Bradford, the Colonial Premiers expressed their warmest admiration of it, one of them declaring it to be " *Just what the Colonies want.*"

There is a wide field for " R.E.T." and many important installations are projected and in course of negotiation in the United Kingdom, India, South Africa, South America and elsewhere.

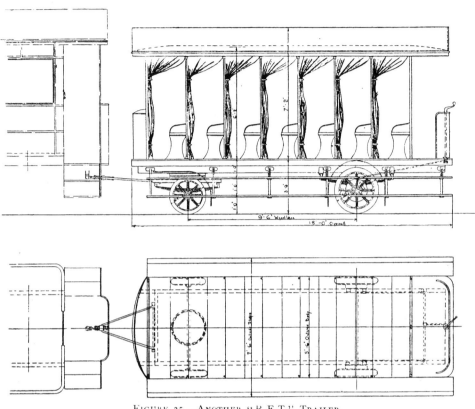

FIGURE 25 —ANOTHER " R.E.T." TRAILER.

FROM A STATEMENT MADE TO A DEPUTATION OF PRESS REPRESENTATIVES BY MR. J. B. HAMILTON (GENERAL MANAGER OF LEEDS CORPORATION TRAMWAYS) IN OCTOBER, 1911, REGARDING THE "R.E.T." SYSTEM.

It had in three months' working given every satisfaction ; the cars had not had five minutes' delay through breakdowns, and the wear and tear to the roads and to the vehicles were found to be infinitely less than with petrol motor buses. He was strongly of opinion that the new system was the best and the most perfect that modern invention had to offer.

On a question as to its suitability for narrow thoroughfares, Mr. Hamilton said on such highways it was ideal. The cars would deviate 15 feet either side of the centre of the road. The cost of working he found was about half that of motor omnibuses. He pledged his reputation as a practical operator that this was the most reliable form of traction existing. The vehicles were practically motor-omnibuses run by electricity, which

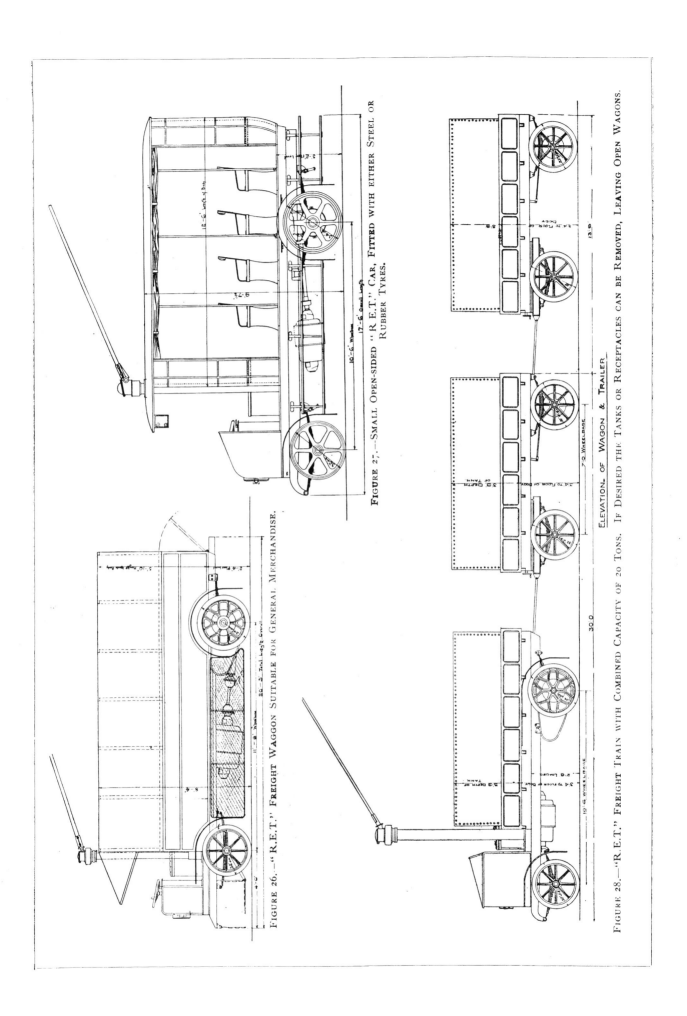

FIGURE 27.—SMALL OPEN-SIDED "R.E.T." CAR, FITTED WITH EITHER STEEL OR RUBBER TYRES.

FIGURE 26.—"R.E.T." FREIGHT WAGGON SUITABLE FOR GENERAL MERCHANDISE.

ELEVATION OF WAGON & TRAILER

FIGURE 28.—"R.E.T." FREIGHT TRAIN WITH COMBINED CAPACITY OF 20 TONS. IF DESIRED THE TANKS OR RECEPTACLES CAN BE REMOVED, LEAVING OPEN WAGGONS.

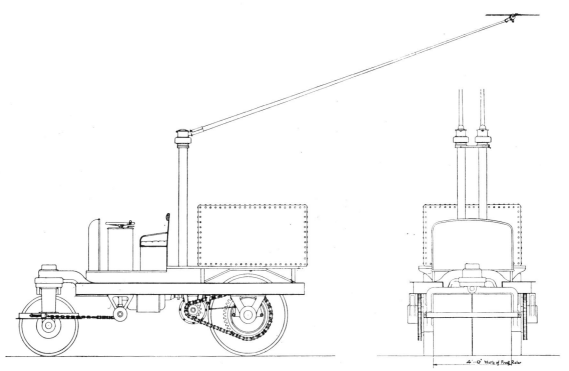

FIGURE 29.—" R.E.T." ROAD ROLLER.

meant the absence of expensive and quickly depreciating machinery, and the avoidance of vibration and noise inseparable from petrol motors. They first tried petrol motor-omnibuses, but these did not give satisfaction, owing to the wear of the roads, the expenses of repairs, and the liability to breakdowns.

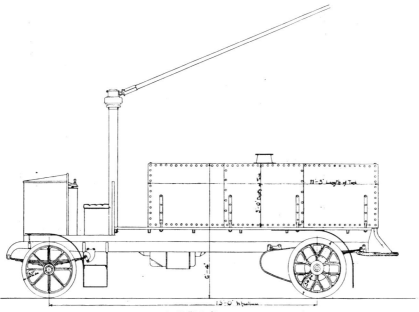

FIGURE 30 —" R.E.T." ROAD WATERING CART.

### FROM THE ADDRESS OF THE PRESIDENT OF THE MUNICIPAL TRAMWAYS ASSOCIATION AT THE NINTH ANNUAL CONFERENCE.

"The tramway construction boom stopped, not because every district that required better facilities was supplied, but because financial reasons made it impossible to proceed any further into districts unable to support a capital expenditure of £14,000 to £15,000 per mile of tramway laid. The petrol-propelled vehicle came along to meet this want, but notwithstanding its great development and general

FIGURE 31.—"R.E.T." CAR RUNNING OVER TRAM LINES AT ROTHERHAM BY MEANS OF THE "RAIL RETURN."

excellence the petrol machine with its internal combustion engine, its gear box, clutch and differential has not by any means equalled the electric motor in either first cost, simplicity, reliability or efficiency. In a word the operating costs of a petrol motor omnibus service are so high per bus mile that not much advantage, if any, is gained over the ordinary tramway including its capital charges."

"The railless system, however, comes along with a vehicle as reliable as a tramcar, and at least as cheap to operate, but with a capital expenditure on street work so low that the bugbear of heavy interest and sinking fund charges is practically non-existent."

FIGURE 32.—"R.E.T" CARS AT ROTHERHAM, AT JUNCTION WITH THE TRAMWAY. THESE CARS ARE DIVIDED INTO TWO COMPARTMENTS.

FIGURE 33.—"R.E.T." CAR ON A HEAVY GRADIENT.

# ECONOMY OF ELECTRIC POWER.

The increase in the sources of supply and its rapidly decreasing cost is expanding the uses to which electricity is applied, and recent developments point to its becoming the universal cheap power of the future. The adaptation of the electric drive in large and small works has invariably resulted in decrease in the cost of power, decrease in the cost of maintenance, and increase of production. In numerous works the output has developed by as much as 40 per cent.

FIGURE 34.—"R.E.T." IN SOUTH AMERICA.

The economy and importance of large electric power stations distributing energy at high potential over long distances has been demonstrated. The conversion of coal into electricity on a large scale will enable the energy necessary for all our estimated present needs for traction, power, lighting and heating to be supplied by 60 million tons of coal per annum, instead of the 150 million tons by the present methods, and will not only provide cheap power, but will effect a large saving in transport, and prolong the life of our coal supply. The existence of a vast supply of fuel within our own country is the principal safeguard of our commercial supremacy. Industries which obtain their power from petrol, for which we are dependent upon foreign countries, are always liable to great loss in the event of stoppage or decrease of the supply and where used as a source of power for purposes of public transport, such an event will involve the public, as well as corporations and transport companies, in incalculable loss and inconvenience.

# Appendix iv

Tramway and Railway World, May 18th 1933

# Electric Trolley Omnibuses

Informative Paper by Mr. C.J. Spencer, O.B.E., M.I.E.E.

At a joint meeting of the Institution of Electrical Engineers and the Institute of Transport, held on April 10th, Mr C.J. Spencer., general manager of the Tramways of the London Underground Group, read a paper entitled "Electric Trolley Omnibuses". After the reading of the paper some lantern slides of vehicles in service between 1908 and 1912 were shown. Mentioning the vehicles of that description inaugurated in Leeds and Bradford, in 1911, when he was tramways manager in the latter city, Mr Spencer said that they were devised in order to provide efficient transport at a relatively low capital cost and as a feeder to the tramways. Pneumatic tyres were, of course, not available, and riding qualities as contrasted with the tramways, were unsatisfactory. In 1913, Bradford Corporation placed in service a number of trolleybuses built in their shops of a much lighter and sweeter running type. The unladen weight was 3 tons 12 cwt with a capacity for 28 passengers, and a maximum speed of 17 to 18 M.P.H. Notwithstanding this advance-ment he could not pretend that this vehicle became popular. Pot holes and ruts developed in the water-bound macadam roads of the West Riding, while the stone setts were bumpy. Efforts were, however, made to improve the roads and also the vehicle until war broke out in 1914. The war stopped the development of the trolleybus but gave a fillip to the petrol omnibus.

Credit was due to Mr. R.H. Wilkinson, the Bradford Corporation transport manager, for his courage in taking up the development of the electric omnibus from the point where it had been dropped, for the vehicle was not by any means in public favour at that time. Birmingham, Wolverhampton and other undertakings followed Bradford's lead. Wolverhampton had converted the whole of its tramway system, and very recently it was decided to replace some petrol omnibus routes there with trolleybuses.

## Popular with the Public – Progressive Record

The change which had taken place during the past few years in the public view regarding to trolley-buses seemed somewhat remarkable, and he could only suggest that it was attributable to the merit of this form of traction. It must not be overlooked that in most cases the electric omnibus had replaced tramcars which were decidedly out of date, and in many cases operated over single track with passing loops. Ten years ago there were in this country 47 miles of trolley-bus routes; at the present time there were approximately 256 route miles and extensions were taking place at a rapid rate. Judging by the number of inquiries for information by post and the number of personal visits from foreign countries, particularly the colonies, there was now a worldwide interest in this form of traction. Though the system was invented in Germany or Italy, the greatest development had taken place in Great Britain, and to a lesser extent in America. It was true to say that the modern type was little more than an adapted petrol omnibus, the engine and gearbox being replaced by an electric motor with suitable electrical control gear. As a rule, the early vehicles had two adapted tramway motors. It was the practice to drive the rear wheels separately and in this way perfect differential action

was achieved. In those days mechanical differentials and back axles for heavy vehicles were by no means reliable and satisfactory, and this electrical differential was considered an achievement. Considerable trouble was experienced with the transmission gear, propeller shafts, universal joints, sprockets and worms, which were found to be too light for the heavy steering torque of the electric motor. An interesting innovation of the Mercedes-Stoll in 1909 was the placing of the motor in the hub of the wheel. This motor, which was of the rotating field type with a stationary armature which formed the axle stub, was ideal from the point of view of transmission, as universal joints, reduction gears, differential, etc., were eliminated and the drive was perfect. Unfortunately, the motor, being unsprung, was subject to all road shocks, and in the days of bad roads this was serious. With pneumatic tyres and modern roads it might be advisable to reconsider this admirable type of drive on account of its many advantages.

## Scope for Collecting-Gear Improvement

Regarding the collecting gear evolution had up to the present produced nothing better than the trolley poles. While this system allowed a liberal lateral use of the highway, giving the trolleybus almost the same flexibility of road as a self-contained vehicle, it was open to improvement, and it was mostly in the direction of a simple current collection method that further progress was desirable. If, for example, it were possible to transmit energy from the trolley wire to the vehicle by some radio transmission scheme, the collecting gear could be eliminated and the overhead wires considerably modified. The appended table gives the main dimensions etc., of the first Bradford and Leeds trolleybuses compared with the latest type of trolley-bus now in service on the Wimbledon-Hampton Court route of the London United Tramways:

|  | Bradford and Leeds trolleybus 1911 | AEC – English Electric trolleybus 1933 |
|---|---|---|
| Type of vehicle | Single-deck | Double-deck |
| Passenger seating capacity | 28 | 74 (plus 5 standing) |
| Length overall | 20 ft. 3in. | 30 ft. |
| Width | 7 ft. | 7 ft. 6 in. |
| Unladen weight | 3 tons 12 cwt. | 7 tons 18 cwt. 1 qr. |
| Laden weight | 5 tons 7 cwt. | 12 tons 12 cwt 3 qrs. |
| Unladen weight per seated passenger | 2.5 cwt. | 2.1 cwt. |
| Equipment | 2 motors of 20 h.p. | 1 motor of 80 h.p. |

The driving control gear to-day was very different from pre-war days, the hand controller having been displaced by foot control, thus allowing the driver to have both hands free for the steering wheel. The adoption of one motor instead of two had considerably improved the control apparatus, as the driver merely pressed a pedal with his foot in the same way as a motorist used the accelerator pedal. The controller itself operated the contactors simply by a small relay current, with the result that there was no breaking of heavy currents at the controller contacts, these currents being broken by contactors in a strong magnetic field. The maintenance of such apparatus was negligible on account of its extreme simplicity.

## Motor Progress – Regenerative Economy

"The modern traction motor," said Mr Spencer, "developed largely for tramways and railways, is an infinitely better piece of machinery than its prototype. The weight in pre-war days was about 70 lb. per H.P., whereas the latest type of motor used for trolleybus operation is only 12 lb. per H.P. By the introduction of commutation poles and heat resisting insulation it is possible to abuse this machine to almost any extent without harm, and while it is normally rated at 80 H.P., it is capable of giving for short periods 100 H.P. Field shunting is done to a much greater extent than with the early motors and it is of interest to note that the shunting is now done, not entirely with a view to more speed, but in the interests of economical working. What has wrongly been termed 'super saturation of fields' is now becoming common practice. A motor has been designed which, with a full field, gives little more than about half the maximum speed of the omnibus, the rest of the speed being obtained by shunting, which has the effect of cutting down the resistance waste very considerably.

"The experience on the London United Tramways with a motor of this type shows that a saving in current consumption of about 18 per cent. has been achieved and the maximum current required for starting has been reduced by 30 per cent. This development, which is of very recent origin, has had a beneficial effect upon the cost of operation in that while electric current is perhaps cheap, it represents a considerable portion of the total cost of operation.

"Another development which has taken place almost on parallel lines, and for the same purpose, is the use of the regenerative possibilities of electric motors. Compound motors are used and when decelerating or descending a gradient, current is generated by the motor acting as a dynamo and returned to the trolley wire and distributing system. The energy is therefore utilised for the operation of other vehicles which otherwise would be wasted in friction. It is obvious that with this system there should be a considerable saving in energy, which is claimed to be about 20 to 25 per cent on hilly routes, in addition to the saving in wear of the lining of brake shoes, drums etc."

## Conditions that Affect Conversions

In dealing with the conditions that make tramway conversion advisable or inadvisable, the author remarked that the trolleybus-system was not suitable for all traffic circumstances. Before replacing a tramway system consideration must be given to the obligations, statutory or otherwise, of the tramways. Workmen's traffic, and the difference between the peak and slack traffic had to be considered. Notwithstanding that for the L.U.T. experiment routes were selected where the difference between the peak and slack traffic was not so great as elsewhere, it has been necessary to run 25 per cent. more car miles with the trolleybus than was necessary with the tramcar. Fortunately, the traffic has increased in a like ratio, with the result that the change had not been disadvantageous.

The following were the relevant figures for the first complete year of operation:-

### L.U.T. Electric Trolley Omnibuses
### Year 1932

| | Amount £ | P.C.M. d. |
|---|---|---|
| Traffic Receipts | 153,811 | 15.07 |
| Operating expenses | 124,598 | 12.21 |
| Operating balance | 29,213 | 2.86 |

(Note. – No provision is made in the above figures for depreciation.)

| | |
|---|---|
| Route miles | 17 |
| Vehicle Miles run | 2,449,017 |
| Passengers carried | 26,887,817 |

The problem with which the company was faced was to spend £550,000 in modernising the tramway system, or scrap the tramcars and replace them with either trolleybuses or petrol omnibuses at a much lesser cost. To have used petrol omnibuses would have necessitated the scrapping of the whole of the electrical equipment in the area; further, it was estimated that, as the cost of the operation per car mile of the petrol omnibus would be more than that of the trolleybus, it was not so advantageous.

The capital cost, namely £235,000, or £13,800 per route mile, might seem somewhat excessive, but it included a sum of £66,000 to clear the company's liability for the reinstatement of roadways.

It was estimated that the revenue would be 16.0d per car mile, and the cost of operation 12d. The actual revenue for a full year was 15.07d, and the operating cost 12.21d. Two reasons might be given for the actual revenue per car mile not being as good as anticipated. One was that 1932 was a year of depressed traffic; the second was that it was necessary to run 25 per cent. more car miles than was run by the tramcars. The revenue from the increased car miles run offset the lower earnings per car mile. The operating cost per car mile was less than that of a petrol omnibus of a similar capacity doing similar work, but he hesitated to make exact comparisons. If the cost of operation was the same for both vehicles, the chief advantage of the trolleybus was its extremely sweet and silent operation and its odourlessness, plus its acceleration and, compared to a tramcar, its flexibility.

From the foregoing it would be seen that if the trolleybus was to replace the tramcar on busy routes, the great need was for a vehicle of larger capacity. Evolution in design was tending in that direction. A vehicle was now in operation on the Wimbledon – Hampton Court route, designed to give greater carrying capacity, as the direct outcome of the work of a committee representing the builders and the Underground railway, omnibus and tramway group. It was licensed to carry 74 seated passengers and five standing. It embodied many novel features, including an entrance towards the front, pneumatically controlled and operated by the driver, in order to relieve the conductor of some of his platform duties, thus leaving him more time to deal with fares, tickets, etc. If this experimental vehicle succeeded he could foresee the possibility of a further invasion of tramway territory. Without it, or something like it, he could not visualise any rival to the tramcar, except an underground railway, for the carriage of large masses of people in a reasonably short time."

# Appendix v
# Huddersfield Corporation Transport.

MINISTRY OF TRANSPORT,
Metropole Buildings,
Northumberland Avenue,
London, W.C.2.
15th December 1938.

Sir,

I have the honour to report, for the information of the Minister of Transport, in accordance with the order dated 3rd November, 1938, the results of my Inquiry into the circumstances of the Trolley Vehicle accident which occurred about 8 a.m. on 4th October at Leech's Hill, Outlane, on the Huddersfield Corporation system.

Trolley Vehicle No. 12, a double deck 6 wheeler, was descending this hill at moderate speed in a storm of wind and rain of exceptional violence when, emerging from the shelter of houses, the front was struck by the wind and diverted across the road; the driver lost control and the vehicle struck the kerb on the off side of the road, ran up a low bank and overturned, falling on its left side in the roadway.

There were only two passengers, one in the upper saloon and one in the lower saloon; the former received a slight cut, while the latter and the conductor escaped uninjured, the driver suffering severely from shock. Apart from surface damage to panels and much broken glass the main timber structure of the body and the basis suffered surprisingly little damage.

## Locality of Accident

The route on which No. 12 Trolley Vehicle was working was between Waterloo, about 2 miles east of the Town Centre, (Kirkgate) and Outlane, about 4 miles west. It is, on the whole, a long rising gradient from Kirkgate along Trinity Street and New Hey Road to the top of Leech's Hill, where the New Hey Road is joined on its north side by another main road from the east, Lindley Moor Road.

At this junction, pole 181, which is a fare stage and an "All Cars Stop", the road to the Outlane terminus, some ½ mile further on, falls for about 180 yards at 1 in 14.7, at the same time curving slightly to the left. Road width is 31 to 32 ft. between the kerb of the footpath on the left (south) and a kerb, low bank, and low wall of loose rubble, on the north side. Road surface is stone setts, well worn and probably rather slippery when wet.

There are a number of houses along the south side of the road, the last of which is just beyond Pole 181, and thereafter there is a gap of about 200 ft. to the next house. The slope of the ground is falling sideways to a valley on the south, and it is easy to imagine that a south-westerly gale might cause gusts of exceptional force across the road at this point.

All wheel tracks across the road were effaced by the heavy rain, but the point at which the front wheels first struck the right

The scene of the incident as shown in the local press. No 12 survived its ordeal and was sold after the Second World War to Reading, where it ran as no 162. (see page 211).

hand kerb was 90 yards beyond Pole 181; from this point the right hand front wheel track could be followed for about 8 yards till it reached a distance of about 5 ft. 6 ins. beyond the kerb, by which time it had mounted the bank to a height of about 2 ft. 9 ins.

The final tilting angle of the bus before overturning on its left side would be approximately 25 degrees, which is the angle which a new bus has to attain under the regulation static tilting test; under conditions of impact and violent rocking the bus might well have overturned at a much smaller angle.

## Description of Vehicle.

The trolley vehicle in question, No. 12, is a double deck 6 wheeler seating 64 passengers, with chassis by Karrier Motors, composite body by the Brush Electrical Engineering Company, and Electrical Equipment by Metropolitan Vickers Ltd. It weighs 8 tons 12 cwts. empty, was supplied in November 1934, and has run about 165,000 miles to date.

The control arrangements are, left foot-power control pedal, right foot-air brake pedal, and left hand-lever of hand brake (pull on). The vehicle has a compound wound motor with regenerative control and rheostatic braking, both of which are operative at certain points of the return movement of the control (left foot) pedal.

Movement of the power control pedal operates a series of electric contactors. It has a range of 10 notches, of which the first four gradually cut out the starting resistance, and the fifth gives no starting resistance but full field; the sixth to ninth notches gradually weaken the shunt field, and the final notch shuts out the shunt field. To obtain regeneration or rheostatic braking, it is necessary to have gone beyond the fifth notch of power, and to have attained a speed of 12 to 15 m.p.h., before the pedal can be allowed to come back to the regenerative or rheostatic notch positions, the latter of which is marked by a small projection close to the pedal which can be detected by the foot.

All electrical power and braking circuits were tested and examined after the accident and found to be in good condition.

The air brake equipment, by Messrs. G.D. Peters, consists of brake cylinders for each wheel, an air reservoir of 1.15 cubic feet capacity and an electrically driven compressor mounted on the right hand side of the chassis; also a compressor governor mounted on the floor of the cab, brake pressure gauges indicating pressure in system and pressure of application, and an application valve operated by the driver's right foot pedal. The compressor governor is set to cut in at 75 lbs. pressure and to cut out at 100 lbs.

There is an air strainer on the suction and a drain cock on the lower side of the reservoir, the handle of which is closed when in the vertical down position.

The electric power supply for the compressor is taken from the terminals of a double pole switch which also switches the traction control circuit, through a pair of Zed type fuses to the compressor motor, a similar pair of fuses being provided for the control circuit.

The hand brake operates on the rear wheels of the vehicle only.

This vehicle had had a "B" overhaul a fortnight previously; this includes, among other items, removal of brake drums and examination of brake shoes, some of which were renewed. When I inspected it all drums and shoes were clean and in good working condition; the brake rigging also had been examined and adjusted during this overhaul.

Driver Roebuck, who was driving Trolley Vehicle no. 12, is 37 years of age and had been employed as a tramcar conductor in the Corporation Transport Department since 1924, having previously done a little driving as second man on a lorry; he had been under instruction as a trolley vehicle driver since November 1937, passed as such on 29th March, 1938, mainly on the Waterloo-Outlane Route.

He stated that he had taken out No. 12 that morning from the shed, had tested the hand and air brakes and had run to Waterloo, thence to Outlane and thence back to Waterloo without any trouble. He had made a large number of service stops (probably 50 to 60 on the double journey) and had used his air brake continuously, but he could not recollect whether he had actually noticed the compressor working, and he had not looked at his pressure gauge at all.

Returning from Waterloo and approaching a stop in Southgate near the City centre, he found that an application of the air brake had no effect and he looked at his reservoir gauge and saw that he had less than 25 lbs. pressure. He succeeded in stopping in Southgate and then after looking at his gauge he got out of his cab and opened the drain cock of the air reservoir; there was a faint hiss of air escaping and he shut it again while it was still hissing. He got into the cab again and told Conductor Sherwood that he would have to have another vehicle as the air brake had failed. He then drove forward slowly to the next stop in Kirkgate, where Inspector Cudworth was on duty and Roebuck got out and called to him. Cudworth came over while Roebuck was trying the air reservoir drain cock again; he then opened the main switch, looked at the fuses which appeared to be in order, but decided to change them for another pair of fuses of which Cudworth brought one from the Inspector's Office, the other being one of the spare fuses carried on the vehicle. After changing them Roebuck reclosed the main switch, but the compressor still did not start and the air gauge showed a negligible pressure.

Both men are quite certain that the drain cock was closed, and it will be noted from the description above that the control circuits are on the same switch as the compressor, so it is certain that that switch must have been closed before the vehicle could move.

There were a number of passengers waiting and, as noted above, the weather was very bad.

Up to this point the evidence of both Cudworth and Roebuck is substantially unanimous and it is supported by that of Conductor Sherwood, but thereafter there is some conflict between their statements.

Cudworth said that he pointed out that it was an awkward situation with the number of passengers waiting, as he had not got another vehicle available, one spare vehicle having just been taken for another casualty; that Roebuck then said that he thought he could manage this trip but that he would be back late as he would have to run very carefully, and that he (Cudworth) then told Roebuck to go very carefully and not to trouble about being late back as a relief vehicle would be provided for his next trip.

Roebuck said that the Inspector told him that he had not another vehicle available and that he must do the trip to Outlane, going very carefully; he agreed that Cudworth told him not to worry about being back late. Sherwood generally supported his driver's account.

Roebuck started away and travelled without incident or difficulty as far as the top of Leech's Hill; he was quite definite that the compressor did not start up again after leaving Kirkgate as he was naturally looking out for this, and at one intermediate stop he again dismounted and opened and closed his drain cock which again gave a very faint hiss.

He did not come to a stand at Pole 181 at the top of Leech's Hill but slowed to walking pace and then proceeded at about 10 to 12 miles per hour. Both the passengers and Sherwood confirmed that they came almost to a stand and then proceeded at a very moderate pace down the hill.

Roebuck stated that as he passed the end of the houses he felt the front of the vehicle caught by a very violent gust of wind which threw him off his balance; his hand brake was not applied at the time, but he caught hold of it as soon as he recovered, at the same time applying the air brake in the hope that this might have some effect. He found, however, that he could not stop the vehicle with the hand brake nor could he straighten it with only one hand on the steering wheel and he shouted to warn his conductor. He said that it was possible that his left foot might have slipped when he lost his balance and thus applied power.

The vehicle ran across the road to the right hand kerb and up the low bank, rocking violently once or twice before it overturned on its left side in the roadway, throwing Roebuck into the lower corner of the cab.

After the accident the trolley booms were removed to facilitate lifting and the vehicle was then towed back to the car sheds; a driver who took it back stated that the hand brake was in good adjustment, and that testing it on the way he had found that on the level he could, by application of this brake, compel the powerful towing vehicle to change gear down.

On arrival a temporary electrical feed was taken to the terminals of the control and compressor main switch, the trolley books leads having been disconnected, and on closing this switch the compressor immediately started up, ran up to full pressure and cut out correctly; Pressure was then released by repeated brake applications and the compressor again started up automatically when pressure had fallen to 75 lbs. Subsequent examination revealed no defect in the electrical or mechanical portions of the brake equipment; the compressor governor is a substantially built piece of apparatus with a rubber diaphragm working under a plunger which in turn operates a linkage to switch contacts of heavy construction and in satisfactory condition. The air pipes leading to the governor were dismantled but no obstruction could be found. The main electrical braking and other circuits were also tested and examined and found to be in order.

## Conclusion.

Consideration of the circumstances of this accident may be divided under three heads (a) the initial failure of the air brake, (b) the action of Driver Roebuck in continuing to work the vehicle in service, and of Inspector Cudworth in permitting this, after it had been discovered that the air brake was defective and (c) the actual accident.

## (a) Failure of the air brake.

It seems almost certain that the compressor was working properly when the vehicle was taken from the shed that morning, as the use of the air brake at the majority of the stops which were made on the first double trip would certainly have exhausted the capacity of the reservoir earlier. The capacity is adequate for about 20 to 25 average applications and there must have been 50 to 60 stops apart from the descent of a number of gradients. Conductor Sherwood was tolerably certain that he had heard the exhaust on release of the air brakes on several occasions during the first trip. It is also clear that the compressor was not cutting in properly for some short time prior to the stop in Southgate and thereafter until the accident.

On the other hand, when the vehicle had been towed back to the shed after the accident, the compressor cut in and worked properly as soon as the electric supply was connected.

It would appear therefore that there must have been an intermittent failure of some kind and it seems probable that this failure may have rectified itself by the shock of overturning. Such failure might be (i) in the air system or (ii) in the electrical system.

As regard (i) the air system, it will be noted that evidence which seems reliable limits the possible cause of accident to a very small portion of the system, viz., the compressor governor itself and the air pipe immediately adjacent thereto. If the latter had become completely blocked so that the governor diaphragm remained under full pressure while the rest of the systems became exhausted, or if the plunger or linkage of the governor jammed in the "switch open" position, or if the contacts failed to close the circuit owing to dirt or foreign matter, the compressor would have failed to cut in; with these exceptions, however, it is difficult to imagine a fault elsewhere on the system which would have produced the results which occurred. I think that a pipe blockage which would form itself and remains tight under road vibration for a substantial time against 70 lbs. air pressure or more, and would then be released by the blow of overturning without leaving any trace, is most improbable; close examination failed to find any visible cause of failure in the compressor governor itself when dismantled.

Of the electrical system (ii) the only portion which comes under suspicion is the circuit on the compressor side of the main control and compressor switch; this switch itself and the supply to it may be eliminated, as a fault would have affected the normal power control circuits of the bus. The apparatus on this circuit consists of a pair of Zed fuses, the compressor motor, the compressor governor, and the connecting leads and terminals. All of these were examined, and the compressor governor itself was dismantled in my presence, but no defects or loose terminal or contact could be found. The compressor motor commutator was in good condition and the brushes were not badly worn; they were moving freely in the brush holders and the springs were good. There are two brushes on each brush holder arm.

There remains the question of the Zed type fuses in the compressor circuit. These screw into contact and a very small degree of slackness is sufficient to break the contact. It is possible that they were loosened by vibration thus causing the first failures, and that when replaced by Driver Roebuck in Kirkgate they were not screwed fully home. Failures of this nature do occur; I was informed by the Electrical Foreman at Huddersfield that this was the first thing he would look at in a sudden failure on the road, and I had similar information from other undertakings, both as to loosening by vibration, and failure to screw tight home.

The Bakelite surface of one of the fuse bases was marked by a groove which indicated that the porcelain fuse carrier had to be screwed very tightly home to ensure contact being made by both ends of the fuse cartridge, and I noted that contact was broken by turning the carrier backwards through a very small arc. Trying this carrier with a spare fuse cartridge, it was possible to screw the carrier quite reasonably tight while the fuse cartridge was still loose and not making good contact. There were also distinct marks of burning on two of the contacts, suggesting a loose contact and arcing at some time.

When discussing this matter with the manufacturers of the fuses, I ascertained that, for locations subject to vibration, their present practice was to provide a rubber ring on the shoulder of the fuse carrier, the compression of which acts as a locking ring; the fitting of this ring necessitates an additional washer or packing of the base contact to ensure that the fuse cartridge makes good contact at both top and bottom. In the fuses on No.12 these additional washers or packing had not been provided, and it would appear, therefore, that these rubber rings also had not been fitted; in any case they were not in place on the fuse carriers at the time.

The maintenance of good contact under the vibration of the vehicle was, therefore, dependent entirely on the tightness with which the fuse carriers were screwed into their bases.

In these circumstances, I think it is quite possible that one of these fuse carriers worked loose under vibration, thus leading to the original failure, and that on replacement by Driver Roebuck, one of them was not screwed home hard enough to make contact; on the other hand, it does seem improbable, though not impossible, that the shock of overturning caused it to make contact. There is, however, another possibility which must not be overlooked, that one of the staff casually felt the fuse holders to see that they were screwed up tight, between the time that the bus overturned and the time when the compressor circuit was tested and found good after return to the depot; in this connection it must be noted that the Corporation staff were not aware at first that there had been an air brake failure, and in such circumstances a man might have taken such action automatically without realising that it had any bearing on the cause of the accident, and he might thereafter have failed to recollect having done so.

In view of all the circumstances, I think that the cause of the failure must have been in the electrical circuit of the compressor, either one of the fuses not being screwed fully home, or some dirt or foreign matter having lodged between the contacts or in the linkage of the compressor governor, later becoming dislodged by the shock of overturning and not traceable during dismantling. I think the former is distinctly more probable.

## (b)      Continuing in service with defective air brake.

Evidence as to the primary responsibility for this is conflicting. Inspector Cudworth said that the initial suggestion came from Driver Roebuck, to the effect that he could take the vehicle to Outlane and back, but would probably be late owing to having to run cautiously. Roebuck, on the other hand, alleged that Cudworth told him that he had not another vehicle available, and that Roebuck would have to do the trip to Outlane and back, after which another vehicle would be available for the next trip. Conductor Sherwood in general supported Roebuck's version, but did not hear the whole conversation.

It is impossible, and indeed unnecessary, to determine the precise truth of the two versions of this discussion. Inspector Cudworth had no business to permit (much less to suggest if he did so) the operation of a heavy double decked vehicle, with its principal brake out of action, on the severely graded routes which are characteristic of this system; he was aware moreover, that Roebuck had comparatively little experience as a driver, and should have realised that any offer he may have made was probably attributable to the "Valour of Ignorance".

Roebuck suggested that he was afraid he would get into trouble if he refused to take this vehicle on the Inspector's orders. I do not accept this excuse as having any real foundation and I cannot imagine that the Manager of any responsible transport undertaking would do otherwise than support the action of a driver in such circumstances.

I recognise that both men, particularly Cudworth, were influenced by their anxiety to avoid inconvenience to the travelling public at peak hour under very bad weather conditions, the next vehicle being probably 10 minutes later, but this should not have been allowed to weigh against the serious risks of operation on a severe hilly route with such a grave defect in the control equipment. Assuming both the spare vehicles normally available near the town centre for emergency use had already been put into service, another could have been obtained from the depot in about 10 minutes.

Indeed, in my opinion, the long falling gradients which would have to be traversed on the return journey from Outlane, probably with a full load of passengers, and leading into the denser traffic of the town centre, would have involved much more serious risks than those of the accident which actually occurred.

Certain defects of a minor nature may occur in service which might he accepted temporarily if otherwise grave discomfort or inconvenience would be caused to a considerable number of passengers; the circumstances in this case however, admit of no doubt.

I consider, therefore, that both Inspector Cudworth and Driver Roebuck are gravely to blame, and the greater share of blame must certainly he attributed to the former, the man in authority whose duty it was to prohibit operation, even if Roebuck had initially offered to take the vehicle, which I rather doubt, although I do not think he made serious protest.

Inspector Cudworth is 63 years of age and has been with the Corporation for 37 years, having been an Inspector for 14 years; he has a good record.

Driver Roebuck's service is given above; his driving experience is too short for comment on his record.

## (c) The accident itself.

In my opinion, what probably happened was that Roebuck started to descend the hill at a speed which would normally have been quite moderate and reasonable, but was distinctly too high for the conditions of extreme caution necessitated by his very limited brake power. As he emerged from the shelter of the houses, the front of the vehicle received a violent buffet from a gust of wind which threw him off his balance to his own left, making it difficult for him to apply the hand brake (left hand) with much force and, at the same time, forcing the front of the vehicle to the right more than he could control by the pushing movement of his right hand alone on the steering wheel.

I think it is very likely that when he was thrown off his balance his left foot involuntarily pressed down the control pedal, thus applying power, but it is also possible that he did this intentionally with some idea of obtaining the use of the rheostatic brake; under such conditions it is not unnatural that he failed to do so, and the vehicle rapidly gathered speed beyond his power to control by the hand brake while at the same time, he could not straighten its path with only one hand on the steering wheel.

From actual demonstration, I am satisfied that it would have been possible to have descended this hill in safety, even under the abnormal weather conditions prevailing, by the use of either hand brake alone or rheostatic brake alone, but to do this it would have been necessary to exercise extreme caution and to have kept the vehicle down to a speed no greater than walking pace from the brow of the hill onwards. An experienced driver could have done this with the rheostatic brake, while an inexperienced driver could have equally well done it with the hand brake alone. I have no doubt that when he found the vehicle gathering speed across the road Roebuck lost his head.

## Recommendations and Remarks.

I think that the Corporation should draw the attention of their staff to the circumstances which led to this accident and make it clear that neither the inspector nor the driver was justified in permitting the operation of a trolley vehicle on the hilly routes of this system with such an important part of the equipment defective.

Inspector Cudworth suggested at one time that he was under the impression that No. 12 had an electric coasting brake. This is a special brake or rather "control" which is fitted to certain vehicles on this and other systems for the descent of certain particularly severe gradients; it entails a stop at the top of the gradient for switching on, after which the power control, regeneration and rheostatic brakes are all out of action, and the vehicle can coast down at a speed of about 10 m.p.h. being held by a rheostatic braking effect through a special fixed resistance. This control will hold the vehicle at this slow speed, but will not bring it to a stand so that the hand and/or air brake is required in addition. The fact that it requires a dead stop at both top and bottom of the gradient for switching in and switching out, and other considerations, limit the application of this control to places where it is specially required, and it would not have been a practicable substitute for the air brake. In any case it was not fitted to No. 12.

I think that the circumstances indicate the necessity for Inspectors being thoroughly familiar with the control and handling of vehicles whose operation they have to supervise. Cudworth had been a tram driver until 14 years ago when he was appointed inspector; he had a course of tuition in driving trolley vehicles; and had qualified as a driver when they were introduced at Huddersfield about 4 years ago, but had not driven in service since that date. I think that if he had had more practical experience of handling these vehicles over the route concerned, he would not have permitted Roebuck to keep the vehicle in service with a defective air brake. There are obvious difficulties about ensuring that the senior members of the traffic staff have such practical knowledge, when a system is changed over from tramway to trolley vehicles, but methods should be found to overcome these difficulties. Similarly there are difficulties which must be overcome in the selection and training of drivers for trolley vehicles from among a staff who have been employed on a tramway system and are accustomed to a non-steerable vehicle.

The original 30 trolley vehicles purchased by Huddersfield Corporation have the controls arranged as described above, with the left pedal operating power, regeneration and rheostatic braking, and the right pedal operating air brake only. The 95 later vehicles have the rheostatic brake operated by the initial movement of the right pedal, which on further depression operates the air brake. I think the latter arrangement is much to be preferred, as with it there is no question of having to apply power and come back to a specified position in order to obtain rheostatic braking. An additional advantage is that the first depression of the right pedal cuts off the power circuit, so that an accidental depression of the left pedal, as probably occurred in this case, would have had no adverse results.

Although general standardisation of controls has for long been a Requirement of the Ministry in respect of all Trolley Vehicles owned by any one undertaking, this minor difference had been accepted when all the more recent Huddersfield vehicles were approved, as it was recognised as an improvement in design and the rheostatic brake was formerly regarded as a supplementary feature only. The circumstances of this accident however indicate that the operation of the rheostatic brake by the first movement of the air brake pedal may be of substantially greater value as compared with operation on the return stroke of the power control pedal.

It is necessary to appreciate clearly the difference between regenerative "control" and rheostatic "braking". The former is a luxury, convenient and advantageous in many conditions of operation but providing a moderate retardation only, and not capable of bringing the vehicle to a stand or even to a speed lower than about 10 to 12 m.p.h.

Rheostatic braking on the other hand is a powerful and efficient brake which will bring the vehicle down to a very low speed, such that it is within the power of the hand brake alone to stop it.

The operation of regenerative control by the return movement of the power pedal, and rheostatic braking by the first movement of the air brake pedal is therefore a considerable simplification of control, and I recommend that the Corporation should investigate the practicability of modifying the equipment of their original 30 vehicles to embody this arrangement, thus making them identical with the later vehicles of their fleet.

The fitting of a coasting brake as described above for specified routes involving exceptionally severe gradients, is an additional complication which is of value in special conditions only. I do not see any necessity for fitting this to all vehicles in a fleet, provided enough vehicles are so fitted to operate all services on the specified hilly routes, and reliable arrangement are made to ensure that only vehicles so fitted are allowed to work these routes.

The Zed type of fuse is commonly regarded as suitable for the general conditions of use on Trolley Vehicle subsidiary circuits with 500 volts working pressure. I think that it would be desirable to draw the attention of the staff generally to the importance of correct insertion of these fuses and of screwing them well home.

Reference has been made above to the improvement devised by the manufacturers to avoid loosening by vibration. I understand that steps are already being taken by the Corporation to ensure that the rubber locking rings are fitted to the fuse carriers on all their trolley vehicles, the requisite alterations being made to raise the lower contact in the fuse base. I understand also that the fuse manufacturers are already taking steps to investigate the position in other trolley vehicle undertakings who are using this type of fuse, with a view to suggesting any necessary improvement on these lines.

A larger and improved type of this fuse has recently been placed on the market specially for trolley vehicle work, with a Bakelite locking ring which, when properly tightened, should avoid any risk of loosening through vibration, in a manner even more positive than the rubber ring referred to above.

This accident also draws attention to the value of a visible and/or audible low air pressure alarm, such as is fitted by London Transport and some other undertakings on their latest equipments.

In the circumstances the overturning of this vehicle is no reflection on the inherent stability of the design.

I have the honour etc. A.C. Trench

# TROLLEY BUSES
## Single Deck and Double Deck

# 1 OF 40

## *"English Electric" Trolley Buses for Bradford Corporation.*

The Electric Trolley Buses supplied to Bradford Corporation by The English Electric Company have given such satisfaction in service that a further order has been placed with this Company for eleven Single-deck four-wheel and twelve Double-deck six-wheel vehicles—**and now DAR-LINGTON, MAIDSTONE and NOTTINGHAM Corporations have ordered respectively six Single-deck four-wheel, seven Double-deck six-wheel and six Double-deck six-wheel vehicles.**

*There's a reason ; may we tell you ?*

# BIBLIOGRAPHY

## General

*The Electric Trolley Bus*, Bishop, Pitman 1931
*Trolleybus Trails*, Joyce, Ian Allan 1963
*British Trolleybuses*, Symons and Cresswell, Ian Allan 1966
*History of the British Trolleybus*, Owen, David and Charles, 1974
*British Trolleybus Systems* Joyce, King & Newman, Ian Allan 1986
*Guy, Karrier & Sunbeam Trolleybus Chassis List*, PSV Circle 1990
*British Trolleybuses 1911 to 1972*, Lumb, Ian Allan, 1995
*World Trolleybus Encyclopaedia*, Murray, Trolleybooks *2001*
*The Trolleybus Museum at Sandtoft – Guide and Handbook*, Venture Publications 2010

## System by system

*The Trolleybuses of Newcastle upon Tyne*, Hanson and Canneaux, Trolleybooks 1974 and 1986
*Newcastle Trolleybuses* (Trolleybus Classics no. 19), Lockwood, Middleton Press 2006
*The Trolleybuses of South Shields*, Burrows, Trolleybooks 1976
*South Shields Trolleybuses* (Trolleybus Classics no. 22), Lockwood, Middleton Press 2007
*British trolleybus systems – The Hartlepools*, King and Watson, Buses February 1970
*British trolleybus systems – Darlington*, King, Buses July 1968
*Darlington Trolleybuses including the tramways* (Trolleybus Classics no. 12), Lockwood, Middleton Press 2004
*Tees-side Trolleybuses – an industrial system* (Trolleybus Classics no. 14), Lockwood, Middleton Press 2005
*York City Buses*, Jenkinson, Autobus Review Publications 1984
*York Trams and Trolleybuses*, Marsden, Middleton Press 2007

*Kingston upon Hull Trolleybuses*, Wells, Trolleybooks 1997
*Hull Trolleybuses* (Trolleybus Classics no. 11), Morfitt and Wells, Middleton Press 2004

*Keighley Corporation Transport*, King, Advertiser Press, 1964
*Keighley Tramways and Trolleybuses*, Marsden, Middleton Press 2006

*Halifax Corporation Tramways*, Thornton and King, Light Rail Transit Association 2005
*Halifax Passenger Transport 1897 to 1963* – Hilditch, Oakwood Press 2006

*Leeds Transport volume 2 (1902 to 1931)*, Soper, Leeds Historical Transport Society, 1996

*Bradford Corporation Trolleybuses*, Venture Publications, 1993
*Bradford Trolleybuses* (Trolleybus Classics no. 10), Lockwood, Middleton Press, 2003

*The Trolleybuses of Huddersfield*, Brook, Manchester Transport Museum Society 1976
*Huddersfield Trolleybuses* (Trolleybus Classics no. 9), Lockwood, Middleton Press, 2002

*Mexborough and Swinton Trolleybuses* (Trolleybus Classics no. 24), Barker, Middleton Press 2008
*Rotherham's Trolleybus Service*, Simpson, National Trolleybus Association (article in Trolleybus Magazine no. 107, 1979)

*Trams and Trolleybuses in Doncaster*, Buckley, Wharncliffe Books 2003
*Doncaster Trolleybuses* (Trolleybus Classics no. 26), Barker, Middleton Press 2011

*Around Ramsbottom*, Ramsbottom Heritage Society, Chalford Publishing, 1995

*Trolleybuses to Wigan Pier*, Stretch, National Trolleybus Association (article in Trolleybus Magazine, May 1969)

*Trolleybuses in St Helens*, Stretch, National Trolleybus Association (article in Trolleybus Magazine no. 71, 1973)
*St Helens Trolleybuses*, Sandford, Regent Transport Publications 2004

*South Lancashire Tramways*, Stretch, Manchester Transport Museum Society 1972
*A Trolleybus to the Punch Bowl*, Thompson, Triangle Publishing 2003

*Passenger Transport in Ashton under Lyne*, Hyde, Manchester Transport Museum Society 1985
*The Manchester Trolleybus*, Heaps and Eyre, Ian Allan 2008
*Manchester and Ashton under Lyne Trolleybuses*, (Trolleybus Classics no. 25), Lockwood, Middleton Press 2010

*Stockport Corporation Tramways*, Marshall, Manchester Transport Museum Society 1975
*The Stockport 'Bremen' Trolleybuses*, Bett, National Trolleybus Association (Article in Trolleybus Magazine no. 156, 1971)

*Grimsby and Cleethorpes Trolleybuses* (Trolleybus Classics no. 21), Barker, Middleton Press, 2006

*Chesterfield Trolleybuses* (Trolleybus Classics no. 13), Marsden, Middleton Press 2005

*Derby Trams and Buses*, Derby Museums, 1980
*Derby Trolleybuses* (Trolleybus Classics no. 8), Barker, Middleton Press 2001)

*Nottinghamshire and Derbyshire Trolleybuses* (Trolleybus Classics no. 17),
Marsden, Middleton Press 2005

*A History of Nottingham City Transport*, Marshall, Nottingham City Transport 1960

*Nottingham City Transport*, Groves, Transport Publishing Company 1980
*Nottingham Trolleybuses*, Bowler, Trolleybooks 2008

*Trolleys at Walsall*, Smith, Ian Allan (Article in 'Buses Annual' 1970)

*Walsall Trolleybuses 1931-1970*, Harvey, Amberley Publishing 2009

*A History of Wolverhampton Transport – 1833-1929*, Webb and Addenbrooke, Birmingham Transport Historical Group 1987

*A History of Wolverhampton Transport – 1929-1979*, Addenbrooke, Birmingham Transport Historical Group 1995

*Wolverhampton Trolleybuses 1961-67 (Trolleybus Classics no. 20)*, Sidwell *2006*

*A Nostalgic Look at Birmingham Trolleybuses 1922-1951*, Harvey, Silver Link Publishing, 1997

*Birmingham Trolleybuses (Trolleybus Classics no. 23)*, Harvey, Middleton Press 2007

*Reading Trolleybuses*, Hall, Trolleybooks 1991

*Reading Trolleybuses (Trolleybus Classics no. 5)*, Hall, 1997 Middleton Press

*Southend on Sea Corporation Light Railways* (The Tramway Review no. 40), Anderson, Light Railway Transport League, 1964

*Southend Corporation Transport*, Delahoy, 1986 Yarnacott Publications, 1986

*Ipswich Buses – an illustrated history*, Cobb, Ipswich Buses Ltd 1990

*Ipswich Trolleybuses (Trolleybus Classics no. 15)*, Barker, Middleton Press 2005

*The London United in the Kingston area* (Tramway Review no. 104, 1980), Tustin

*The London Trolleybus vol. 1*, Blacker, Capital Transport 2002

*The London Trolleybus vol. 2*, Blacker, Capital Transport 2004

*London Trolleybus Routes* Taylor, Capital Transport 1994

*London's Trolleybuses a fleet history*, PSV Circle and Omnibus Society 1969

*The Maidstone Trolleybus*, Scotney, National Trolleybus Association 1972

*Maidstone Trolleybuses (Trolleybus Classics no. 4)*, Harley, Middleton Press 1997

*Hastings Trolleybuses (Trolleybus Classics no. 3)*, Rowe, Middleton Press 1996

*Brighton Trolleybuses (Trolleybus Classics no. 18)*, Henbest, Middleton Press 2005

*Fares Please – A History of Passenger Transport in Portsmouth*, Watts, Admiral Publishing 1987

*Portsmouth Trolleybuses (Trolleybus Classics no. 7)*, Cox, Middleton Press 2001

*Silent Service – The story of Bournemouth's trolleybuses*, Chalk, Omnibus Society 1962

*Bournemouth Trolleybuses Official Souvenir Brochure 1933-1969*, Chalk, Bournemouth Corporation Transport 1969

*Bournemouth Trolleybuses (Trolleybus Classics no. 6)*, Pearce, Middleton Press 1996

*Bournemouth Trolleybuses*, Bowler, Trolleybooks 2004

*The Cardiff Trolleybus*, Bowen and Callow, National Trolleybus Association

*Cardiff Trolleybuses (Trolleybus Classics no. 16)*, Lockwood, Middleton Press 2005

*Passenger Tramways of Pontypridd*, Large, Oakwood Press 1977

*British Trolleybus Systems: Pontypridd*, Newman, Buses, February 1978

*British Trolleybus Systems: Rhondda*, Newman and Taylor, Buses April 1982

*The Tramways of Aberdare* (Tramway Review nos 139-141, 1980), Wiseman, Light Railway Transport League 1980

*Llanelly Trolleybuses*, Griffiths, Trolleybooks 1992

*British Trolleybus systems – Dundee*, Newman, Buses February 1969

*Glasgow Trolleybuses*, Deans, Scottish Tramway Museum Society 1966

*Glasgow Trolleybuses Supplement*, Deans, Scottish Tramway Museum Society 1967

*A Nostalgic Look at Belfast Trolleybuses*, Maybin, Silver Link Publishing 1993

*Belfast Trolleybuses*, Harvey, Amberley Publishing 2010

A drab post-war scene at Forster Square, Bradford, showing utility Karrier W trolleybus 704 with Roe body. This rather battered-looking vehicle stands on the setted roadway before departing to Frizinghall, a short-working turning point on the Saltaire via Manningham Lane route. (W.J.Haynes / Paul Watson)

This is the unique centre-entrance trolleybus built by the Gloucester Railway Carriage and Wagon Co in 1933, and marketed as the 'Gloster TDD'. The low centre entrance was achieved by placing the traction motor at the rear of the chassis, behind the rear axle. After being exhibited at the 1933 Commercial Motor Show, it operated at Southend, being purchased by that undertaking in 1934, and numbered 122 in the fleet. (R. Marshall collection)

One of the pioneering 30 feet long Walsall Sunbeam F4A trolleybuses was operated at Portsmouth in 1955 during a municipal transport conference. No 864 is seen at the Dockyard terminus, in company with one of Portsmouth's pre-war AEC vehicles. (D. A.Jones / London Trolleybus Preservation Society)

The last single-deck trolleybuses bought by Ipswich were a trio of Ransomes vehicles new in 1930. No. 42 is seen here when new. Sister vehicle 44 was saved by the British Transport Commission after withdrawal in 1953, and is currently in the care of the Science Museum.

IPSWICH CORPORATION SINGLE-DECK TROLLEYBUS OF 1930.
BUILT BY RANSOMES SIMS & JEFFERIES LTD. IPSWICH.

Grimsby's first post-war trolleybuses were six Karrier Ws with Roe bodies new in 1947. No. 19, the first of the batch, is seen at the Weelsby Road terminus in August 1955.
(A.B. Cross)

London Transport's prototype six-wheel trolleybus was AEC 663T type no 62, new in 1934 and designated type X2. It set the standard for hundreds of similar looking vehicles which formed the bulk of the pre-war fleet. The location is the AEC works.

One of the wartime AEC trolleybuses, intended for Johannesburg, is seen in wartime guise with headlamp masks and white markings. No. 1751 is working on an Ilford local route where these vehicles spent their entire lives.
(S.L. Poole / A.B. Cross)

Rebodied Bradford Karrier W no 732 climbs Whetley Hill on the high frequency Duckworth Lane route, on which these vehicles operated for over twelve years.
(J. Copland / A.D. Packer)

A busy scene at Ashton Market Place shows Manchester BUT no. 1304 loading passengers for Stalybridge. In the background is one of Ashton's post-war Crossley trolleybuses.
(Roy Brook / Paul Watson)

Two Birmingham Leyland six-wheelers, nos 19 and 38, are seen at the Hay Mills short working turning circle. No. 38 on the right is on driver training duty on 28 March 1951, just three months before the closure of the system. (A.D. Packer)

Passengers queue to board trolleybus no. 200 at Bournemouth Pier for an open top trip around the town via circular route no. 39. (Travel Lens Photographic)

# THE FINAL ACT – BRADFORD 1972

Thursday February 10: All trolleybuses withdrawn from service.
Friday March 24: The final public trolleybus services operate.

Tuesday March 7: Eleven trolleybuses return to service
Saturday March 25: Special pre-booked tours operate

Sunday March 26: Special tours followed by the final civic trolleybus journey.

Normal public service journeys ended on the late evening of 24 March. The final runs were the 10.52pm City to Duckworth Lane on service 8 (worked by no. 706) and the 10.57pm City to Thornton on service 7 (worked by no. 843). Karrier W no. 706 is seen prior to its final public trip in Sunbridge Road, waiting to move onto the queuestand to pick up passengers. No duplicate vehicles were provided on either of the last journeys, other than motorbuses. (Robert Anderson)

Members of the public had one last opportunity to ride on a trolleybus on Britain's streets on the following Saturday and Sunday, when pre-booked tours operated. The last one of these took place on the Sunday morning of the final day, 26 March. All tours ran to the same pre-set route. The final vehicle on the last tour was ex-Mexborough vehicle no. 845, and it is seen here at Thornbury terminus turning from Hawthorn Street into Leeds Road. (Robert Anderson)

The last trolleybus journey of all was the civic run carrying invited guests only. This was operated by ex-Mexborough no. 844, and commenced from the City Hall at 3pm, running via Thornton, Duckworth Lane and City to Thornbury depot. This is the scene at the latter point as the vehicle turns off Leeds Road to run down the depot yard into the Works. (Robert Anderson)

A classic scene from the closing days of the British trolleybus. Coming around Town Hall Square at Bradford in 1971 is no. 843, a vehicle with a rich history, during a journey to the outlying village of Thornton. The City Hall, with its clock tower, is prominent in the background. (Robert Anderson)

# Adam Gordon Books

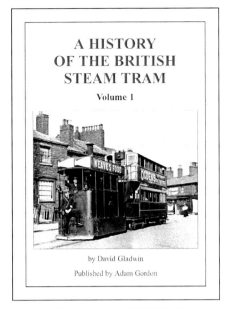

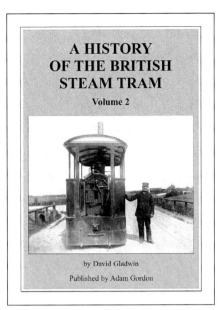

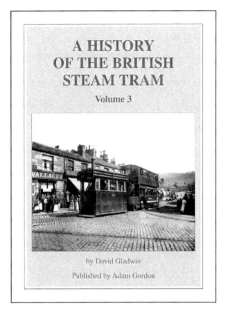

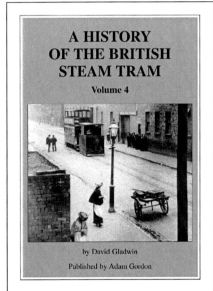

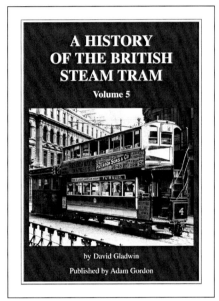

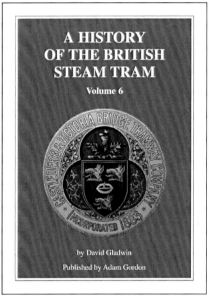

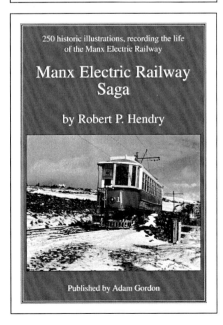

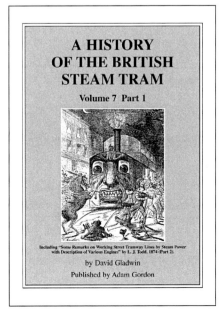

# Adam Gordon Books

**Bibliography of British & Irish Tramways.** David Croft & Adam Gordon, A4, softback, 486pp, £35

**British Tramcar Manufacturers: British Westinghouse and Metropolitan-Vickers.** David Voice, B5, softback, 110pp, £16

**British Tramway Accidents.** F. Wilson, edited by G. Claydon, laminated hardback, 228pp, £35

**The Life of Isambard Kingdom Brunel.** By his son, reprint of the 1870 edition, softback, 604pp, £20

**Treatise upon Cable or Rope Traction.** J.Bucknall Smith plus some other literature on that subject, 434pp., all reprints, card covers, limited print run of 125, £45

**The Definitive Guide to Trams (including Funiculars) in the British Isles, 3rd edition.** D. Voice, softback, A5, 248pp, £20

**The Development of the Modern Tram.** Brian Patton, hardbacked, 208pp, profusely illustrated in colour, £40

**Double-Deck Trams of the World, Beyond the British Isles.** B. Patton, A4 softback, 180pp, £18

**Double-Deck Trolleybuses of the World, Beyond the British Isles.** B. Patton, A4, softback, 96pp, £16

**The Douglas Horse Tramway.** K. Pearson, softback, 96pp, £14.50

**Edinburgh Street Tramways Co. Rules & Regulations.** Reprint of 1883 publication, softback, 56pp, £8

**Edinburgh's Transport, Vol. 2, The Corporation Years, 1919-1975.** D. Hunter, 192pp, softback, £20

**Electric Railway Dictionary, definitions and illustrations of the parts and equipment of electric railway cars and trucks.** Reprint of 1911 publication by R. Hitt, huge number of figures including numerous very detailed scale drawings, 350pp; hardbacked in buckram, limited print run of 125, £45

**Electric Tramway Traction.** A. Greatorex (Borough Engineer and Surveyor, West Bromwich), reprint of 1900 original, 92pp, hardbacked in buckram, limited print run of 125, £25

**Fell Mountain Railways.** Keith Pearson, A4, hardback, 362pp. £45

**The Feltham Car of the Metropolitan Electric and London United Tramways.** Reprint of 1931 publication, softback, 18pp, £5

**Freight on Street Tramways in the British Isles.** David Voice, B5, softback, 66pp, £12

**The Age of the Horse Tram.** David Voice. A4, laminated hardback, 208pp, £40

**Hospital Tramways and Railways, third edition.** D. Voice, softback, 108pp, £25

**How to Go Tram and Tramway Modelling, third edition.** D. Voice, B4, 152pp, completely rewritten, softback, £20

**London County Council Tramways, map and guide to car services, February 1915.** Reprint, 12" x 17", folding out into 12 sections, £8

**Manx Electric Railway Saga.** Robert P. Hendry. A4. Full colour. 144 pp, hardback. £38.80.

**Metropolitan Electric, London United and South Metropolitan Electric Tramways routes map and guide, summer 1925.** Reprint, c.14" x 17", folding out into 15 sections, £8

**Modern Tramway, reprint of volumes 1 & 2, 1938-1939.** A4 cloth hardback, £38

**Monorails of the World.** D. Voice, A4 softback, 96pp, colour, £25

**My 50 Years in Transport.** A.G. Grundy, 54pp, softback, 1997, £10

**Next Stop Seaton! – 55 Years of Modern Electric Tramways Ltd.** Second revised and enlarged edition, D. Jay & D. Voice, B5 softback, 142pp, coloured covers, £20

**Omnibuses & Cabs, Their Origin and History.** H.C. Moore, hardback reprint with d/w, 282pp, £25

**The Overhaul of Tramcars, reprint of LT publication of 1935.** 26pp, softback, £6

**The History and Development of Steam Locomotion on Common Roads.** W. Fletcher, reprint of 1891 edition, softback, 332pp, £18

**The History of the Steam Tram.** H. Whitcombe, hardback, over 60pp, £12

**A History of the British Steam Tram, Volume 1.** D. Gladwin, hardback, coloured covers, 176pp, 312 x 237mm, profusely illustrated, £40

**A History of the British Steam Tram, Volume 2.** D. Gladwin, hardback, size as above, coloured covers, 256pp, £40

**A History of the British Steam Tram, Volume 3.** D. Gladwin, hardback, size as above, coloured covers, 240pp, £45

**A History of the British Steam Tram, Volume 4.** D. Gladwin, hardback, size as above, coloured covers, 256pp, £45

**A History of the British Steam Tram, Volume 5.** D. Gladwin, hardback, size as above, coloured covers, 256pp, £45

**A History of the British Steam Tram, Volume 6.** D. Gladwin, hardback, size as above, coloured covers, 256pp, £45

**A History of the British Steam Tram, Volume 7.** D. Gladwin, Includes a complete reprint of Some Remarks on Working Street Tramway Lines by Steam Power with Description of Various Engines. By Leonard J. Todd, May 1874. 1008pp in 2 parts, hardbacked, limited print run of 400, £95

**Street Railways, their construction, operation and maintenance.** C.B. Fairchild, reprint of 1892 publication, 496pp, hardback, profusely illustrated, £40

**Toy and Model Trams of the World – Volume 1: Toys, die casts and souvenirs.** G. Kuře and D. Voice, A4 softback, all colour, 128pp, £25

**Toy and Model Trams of the World – Volume 2: Plastic, white metal and brass models and kits.** G. Kuře and D. Voice, A4 softback, all colour, 188pp, £30

**George Francis Train's Banquet, report of 1860 on the opening of the Birkenhead tramway.** Reprint, softback, 118pp, £10

**My Life in Many States and in Foreign Lands.** G.F. Train, reprint of his autobiography, softback, over 350pp, £12

**Tram and Bus Tokens of the British Isles.** David Voice, B5, colour, softback, 66pp, £20

**Trams Across the Wear: Remembering Sunderland's Electric Trams.** Stephen Lockwood. A4, laminated hardback, 160pp, £35

**Trams, Trolleybuses and Buses and the Law before De-regulation.** M. Yelton, B4, softback, 108pp, £15

**The Tram Driver.** by David Tudor, hardbacked, 72pp, £20

**Tramway Review, reprint of issues 1-16, 1950-1954.** A5 cloth hardback, £23

**Tramways and Electric Railways in the Nineteenth Century, reprint of Electric Railway Number of Cassier's Magazine, 1899.** Cloth hardback, over 250pp, £23

**Tramways – Their Construction & Working.** D. Kinnear Clark, reprint of the 1894 edition, softback, 812pp, £28

**Life of Richard Trevithick.** two volumes in one, reprint of 1872 edition, softback, 830pp, £25

**The Twilight Years of the Trams in Aberdeen & Dundee.** All colour, A4 softback, introduction and captions by A. Brotchie, 120pp, £25

**The Twilight Years of the Edinburgh Tram.** A4 softback, includes 152 coloured pics, 112pp, £25

**The Twilight Years of the Glasgow Tram.** Over 250 coloured views, A4, softback, 144 pp, £25

**The Wantage Tramway.** S.H. Pearce Higgins, with Introduction by John Betjeman, hardback reprint with d/w, over 158pp, £28

**The Wearing of the Green, being reminiscences of the Glasgow trams.** W. Tollan, softback, 96pp, £12

**Works Tramcars of the British Isles.** David Voice, B5, softback, 238pp, £25

## TERMS OF SALE

RETAIL UK – for post and packing please add 10% of the value of the order. Orders £100 and over post and packing free. I regret that I am not yet equipped to deal with credit/debit cards.

RETAIL OVERSEAS – postage will be charged at printed paper rate via surface mail, unless otherwise requested. Payment please by sterling cash or cheque, UK sterling postage stamps, or direct bank to bank by arrangement.

SOCIETIES, CHARITIES etc. relating to tramways, buses and railways – a special 50% discount for any quantity of purchases for resale is given provided my postal charges are paid.

WHOLESALE (TRADE) DISCOUNTS FOR MULTIPLE COPIES OF THE SAME TITLE post free – details are available from Adam Gordon.

**ADAM GORDON**
**Kintradwell Farmhouse, Brora, Sutherland KW9 6LU**
**Tel: 01408 622660  E-mail: adam@ahg-books.com  Website: www.ahg-books.com**

Ashton under Lyne Crossley trolleybus no. 53 stands at
Stalybridge terminus in the mid-1950s. (R.F. Mack,
colour added by Malcolm Fraser)

London C2 type AEC trolleybus no.194 is
seen at the Hammersmith terminus of
route 660 to North Finchley. (Roy Hubble)

Belfast Guy trolleybuses nos 145 and 149 are seen entering the grounds of Stormont Castle.

Trolleybus fans gather at Longwood terminus, Huddersfield on Sunday 9 July 1967, during a special trip to commemorate the end of trolleybus operation on the route three days later. The vehicle, no.548, had a 1947 Karrier MS2 chassis and a 1961 East Lancashire body. It was Britain's last operational six-wheeled trolleybus to bear the Karrier name. (Roy Brook)